HOMER'S
TRADITIONAL ART

JOHN MILES FOLEY

HOMER'S
TRADITIONAL ART

THE PENNSYLVANIA STATE UNIVERSITY PRESS
UNIVERSITY PARK, PENNSYLVANIA

Library of Congress Cataloging-in-Publication Data

Foley, John Miles, 1947–
  Homer's traditional art / John Miles Foley.
       p.   cm.
  Includes bibliographical references and index.
  ISBN 0-271-01870-4 (alk. paper)
    1. Homer—Technique.   2. Epic poetry, Greek—History and
  criticism.   3. Oral-formulaic analysis.   4. Oral tradition—Greece.
  5. Rhetoric, Ancient.   I. Title.
  PA4175.F65   1999
  883'.01—dc21   98-51850
                                                               CIP

Published by The Pennsylvania State University Press,
University Park, PA 16802-1003

It is the policy of The Pennsylvania State University Press to use acid-free paper
for the first printing of all clothbound books. Publications on uncoated stock sat-
isfy the minimum requirements of American National Standard for Information
Sciences—Permanence of Paper for Printed Library Materials, ANSI Z39.48-1992.

To the memory of
Hannah Frances Foley Kelly

For all my days remaining

"To Homer"
John Keats

Standing aloof in giant ignorance,
Of thee I hear and of the Cyclades,
As one who sits ashore and longs perchance
To visit dolphin-coral in deep seas.
So thou wast blind;—but then the veil was rent,
For Jove uncurtain'd heaven to let thee live,
And Neptune made for thee a spumy tent,
And Pan made sing for thee his forest-hive;
Aye on the shores of darkness there is light,
And precipices show untrodden green,
There is a budding morrow in midnight,
There is a triple sight in blindness keen;
Such seeing hadst thou, as it once befel
To Dian, Queen of Earth, and Heaven, and Hell.

CONTENTS

PRONUNCIATION KEY

To make the experience of South Slavic epic more realistic, I offer the following brief pronunciation key, intended for the nonspecialist. The reader may use it to approximate the sound of singers' and characters' names, for example, or of various traditional phrases in the original language; these occur chiefly in Chapters 2–5. All instances of South Slavic language in this book are set in the Latin alphabet, with the customary diacritics, rather than in the Cyrillic alphabet, regardless of which system was used for initial publication (if any). Both of these alphabets, regularized by the great collector and linguist Vuk Karadžić in the mid-nineteenth century, are entirely phonetic. For more specific information, see Magner 1972.

Consonants pronounced approximately like their English counterparts:

b, d, f, g (hard, as in "get"), k, l, m, n, p, s, t, v, z

Consonants without direct English counterparts:

c	[ts], as in rats
ć	[tch], ch pronounced at the front of the mouth
č	[ch], ch pronounced further back in the mouth, as in chair
j	[y], as in toy or yes
dj	[dy], as in the phrase and you
lj	[ly], as in million
nj	[ny], as in the phrase on your
h	similar to English, but rougher, more aspirated (like German ch)
š	[sh], as in show
ž	[zh], as in azure
dž	[j], as in judge
r	trilled or rolled sound, as in three in some British dialects; often in Spanish

Vowels

    a   [a], as in m**a**ntra
    e   [ɛ], as in s**e**t
    i   [ee], as in tr**ee**
    o   [o], as in f**o**r
    u   [oo], as in m**oo**n
    r   trilled or rolled vocalic sound

Vowels can be temporally long or short; vowel quality does not vary with duration. For present purposes, I omit all tonal and accentual qualities because tone and accent are well beyond the scope of analysis in this volume. On the role of these features in the structure of the South Slavic decasyllabic line, see Foley 1990: ch. 5.

PREFACE

This volume attempts a straightforward answer to a difficult and engaging question: *What difference does oral tradition make to our understanding of the* Iliad *and* Odyssey? Although it can be posed simply enough, this has always been an extremely demanding question. Even before the research undertaken by Milman Parry and Albert Lord had highlighted the pretextual origins of Homer's poems, classical scholars had long been trying to assess the importance of oral tradition for the documents that have reached us.[1] Since Parry's and Lord's initial textual analysis and fieldwork in the 1920s and 1930s, the mass of evidence for an oral epic tradition in ancient Greece has grown enormously, thanks in no small way to Lord's own widening of the perspective from Homer to worldwide oral traditions in general. But even with the existence of an archaic Greek oral tradition demonstrated to most scholars' satisfaction, and with thousands of books and articles trained on its linguistic, structural, and historical aspects, we still struggle with the hardest challenge: "So what?" If Homer connects with oral tradition in some way, what importance does that connection have for our experience of the artifacts? What impact does that lineage have for twenty-first-century readers of these cornerstones of Western literature and art?

Let me offer a telegraphically brief answer—saving the "long" answer for the book itself—by taking a moment to explain the title. *Homer's Traditional Art* addresses the three crucially interlocked areas identified by those three words. First, *Homer* is here understood only secondarily as "an author," presumably the latest and finest practitioner of ancient Greek epic. While it is indisputable that an individual (or individuals) personally and idiosyncratically molded the *Iliad* and *Odyssey* that survive to us, I will be maintaining that "Homer" most essentially designates the poetic tradition as a long-term, ongoing phenomenon that comprises many individuals. Evidence from ancient Greek, South Slavic, Mongolian, and Anglo-Saxon will be presented in support of the argument that "Homer" names the tradition, that his is an anthropomorphic and legendary formulation, a "sign" or *sêma* for the best of singers, the source of all the best songs. Such a figure lives beyond the limitations of everyday reality, in a liminal world of legend that does not translate to conventional biographical format without apparent contradictions and exaggerations. Understanding Homer in this way removes many of the uncertainties inherent in the so-called Homeric Question and fosters a clearer view of "his" peculiar hold on the ancient imagination as well as the true nature of "his" poetic genius.

The second element in the title, *traditional*, is of equal importance. This concept has suffered from much misunderstanding in the past, so let me be as specific as possible about its intended usage in this book. In alluding to "tradition" I do not refer to the kind of abstraction that we glimpse in terms like "literary tradition," in which much of the network of continuity is constructed by critics organizing individual texts from an outsider's perspective, often with the help of historical context, documentary evidence of influence or intertextuality, and the like. Nor do I point toward a monolithic mass, a basically inert inheritance that one generation transmits to the next without much, if any, modification; this notion of tradition as a keepsake or antique has been much criticized, and with justification. Neither abstraction nor monolith, the poetic tradition under examination in this volume is first and foremost a *language*—a specialized and highly idiomatic language to be sure, with a focused purpose and a particular content and context, but nonetheless a language. As such, a tradition is always evolving within certain rules or boundaries, always proving a somewhat different "thing" from one performance to another and from one practitioner to another, always remaining a process larger and richer than any of its products. Varying within limits, the Homeric epic tradition proves dynamic rather than static, explosively connotative rather than restricted in focus, bristling with idiomatic implication rather than claustrophobically clichéd. As a homemade proverb cited throughout the book puts it, "oral tradition works like language, only more so."

If it is a language, then who spoke it? Like any language, the Homeric register is far too complex and evocative an instrument to be the creation or property of any one person, no matter how gifted, or even of any small group of people. It is, after all, traditional. But fluency is well within the reach of any single person, and creative management of its expressive power and implications lies within the reach of any poet who commands this special medium, subject of course to the limitations of talent and experience. The wide spectrum of South Slavic oral epic poets—a few superb, a few barely mediocre, and most of them somewhere in between—illustrates the basic principle: tradition provides the language, but it is the speaker who breaks the silence, whether eloquently or otherwise. Remove the language and all connection to the traditional context is lost, but remove the performing poet and the silence resumes. As with any medium, while an artistic heritage is always theoretically in the public domain, artistic brilliance is the achievement of relatively few. The tradition and the individual both matter.

Before moving on to the third term in the title, we might pause a moment over a word that does not appear in the title and phrase *Homer's Traditional Art*—the vexed designation "oral." In the wake of myriad discussions of this term and especially of fieldwork reports from around the globe, it now seems appropriate to reverse the original priority of terms in the expression "oral tradition." That is, "oral" moves into the background while "traditional" assumes a more prominent role in the foreground. The reasons for this reversal of priorities are many and are discussed at length later in the chapters that follow. As a stopgap, however, we may be content with a few key observations, namely (1) that scholars and fieldworkers generally concur that the supposed "Great Divide" of orality versus literacy does not exist; and (2) that it is becoming more evident that "traditional" is dependably diagnostic of the verbal art under examination, while "oral" is not. To the contemporary imagination, fueled not simply by texts but now also by electronic codification and transmission, the abstraction of orality—of the Other—may initially seem the more fundamental distinction between literature and what we customarily call "oral tradition." We wonder how such marvels as the *Iliad* and *Odyssey* could be fashioned without our culturally dominant technology of text-making and -exchange, how such a miracle of creation could even be feasible. But then comes the challenge of distinguishing among orally composed poetry, oral performances of written materials, and the myriad different forms that originate in (some kind of) orality but reach us only as textual records. "Traditional" speaks to both the origins and the ongoingness of all of these varieties, to their differences as well as their similarities, and offers a context for their present-day interpretation that is at least partially recoverable. Indeed, one of the major burdens of *Homer's Traditional Art* will be the demonstration, both in theory and by example, of how we can recover that context.

With the third word in the title we approach the single issue that burns most brightly in studies in oral tradition, but which has so far received the least attention. What about Homer's *art*? Do we need a special poetics, an approach uniquely tailored to works that emerge from oral tradition? Succinctly put, this book will respond with a carefully measured yes. It will argue that there are ways in which we certainly must understand Homer differently, but also that these roots just as certainly do not require a wholesale abandonment of present critical practices. On the one hand, we need to recognize the special idiomatic meaning encoded in the poetic language of the epics. We need to be aware, for example, that "green fear" (*chlôron deos*) is code for supernaturally inspired terror; that Andromache addresses Hektor during their meeting in *Iliad* 6 via the traditional form of lament, as if he had already been killed and she were even now singing his death dirge; that as a Return Song our *Odyssey* implies a much larger and more pivotal role for Penelope than has been assumed. Without a traditional poetics these aspects of Homer's poetry are invisible or inaudible, and the experience of his art is diminished. I call such idiomatic features "signs," and maintain that we must learn to read behind them.

On the other hand, an approach that recognizes the traditional fabric of Homer's poems will also overlap generously with the various literary approaches we already use with great efficacy. Dichotomies, whether between orality and literacy or between diverse interpretive approaches, will never provide sustainable perspectives; they always end up reducing rather than amplifying our appreciation of Homer's art. For one thing, traditional poetics and the various literary approaches often mark separate paths to the same set of insights. In the second example given above, we already know how much Andromache fears Hektor's return to the battlefield; considerations from social status, gender roles, implied mythology, thematic patterns, and the like contribute to a poignant portrait of her tragic helplessness. In this instance the lament form simply adds idiomatic force to her words, making her plea even more intense and heartrending by telescoping this moment and the time when, mourning the actual demise of her husband and Troy's champion toward the end of the *Iliad*, she will intone the ritual for real. In this way the perspective from what I call *traditional referentiality*—the resonance between the singular moment and the traditional context—regularly proves complementary and enriching, rather than at odds with other perspectives.

Then too, we should expect that many traditional strategies for expression will have engendered related textual strategies, so that there will always be a degree of continuity between the two (never entirely disparate) modes. In this regard, it is only fair to admit our lack of knowledge about the precise position of these Homeric poems vis-à-vis oral tradition. While there can be no doubt that an oral tradition was the genesis of ancient Greek epic as we have it, there are just too many unknowns about recording and transmission to specify with absolute confidence and certainty the relationship between the two. Scholars on both sides of the critical fence have quite often assumed too much, from one extreme arguing for direct transmission of oral performance to surviving text and from the other extreme insisting that Homer's poems as we have them are too polished, too monumental to be anything except literate and textual. Both viewpoints obscure the real complexity of the situation by forcing a reductive "solution" that ignores some of the evidence and some of the logical interpretations of that evidence. Because in my opinion it is crucially important to avoid either extreme, *Homer's Traditional Art* will proceed under what I take to be the minimal defensible assumption—that the *Iliad* and *Odyssey* are *oral-connected* works of verbal art, that they employ the idiom of oral tradition and assume an audience fluent in that idiom.

Mimicking an exercise to be practiced throughout the book, then, I ask the reader to combine the three words in the title—*Homer, Tradition*, and

Art—into a single unit of expression, a composite utterance or unitary "word." Let *Homer's Traditional Art* stand for an approach that seeks to read the poems in their traditional context, as the product of a process embodied in the name "Homer" and, most important, as verbal art. If this discussion succeeds in opening up some fresh perpectives on ancient Greek epic, whether unprecedented or (just as important) complementary to perspectives gained from other approaches, then it will have earned its composite title. To put it another way, if this contribution to Homeric scholarship and studies in oral tradition can reach beyond the structural and mechanistic level to deepen our understanding of Homer's excellence, then it will have fully justified its existence.

Because *Homer's Traditional Art* aims at a wide spectrum of readers, from the advanced undergraduate to the professional scholar, its presentation follows a carefully designed, two-level scheme of text and apparatus. The most basic arguments of the book are made in very plain language and backed up by examples drawn from the *Iliad* and *Odyssey* and, where appropriate, from the South Slavic and Anglo-Saxon poetic traditions. The text thus serves as the bedrock of the overall exposition, and is intended as a freestanding, readable resource that can be apprehended and discussed on its own merits without further qualification. The second part of the presentation is the apparatus, contained entirely in the endnotes and appendices. Intended primarily for the professional scholar, the apparatus provides textual citations, relevant Homeric scholarship, and additional comparative materials to ballast the arguments made in the text. The student and comparatist will, I hope, occasionally find food for thought in the more specialized apparatus, just as the professional scholar will expect the evidential support given therein. But if I have succeeded, the text can also be read by itself, without necessary reference to that support.

I owe the impulse to write *Homer's Traditional Art* to many sources, which it is a pleasure to acknowledge here. Proceeding from the general to the particular, let me start by mentioning the gradually increasing emphasis I have tried to place on enlarging the audience for studies in oral tradition. In concert with Lord's comparative stimulus and the developing research and scholarship in scores of different fields, it seems more and more important to open what has been chiefly a specialist discourse to all who wish to participate and would profit by doing so. This was the goal in establishing the journal *Oral Tradition* in 1986, as well as its two companion series of books, the Lord Studies in Oral Tradition and Voices in Performance and Text. More recently, the assembling of a chapter titled "Oral Literature Today" for the *HarperCollins World Reader* (1994a) and especially the formulation of the pedagogical handbook *Teaching Oral Traditions* (1998a) represent efforts to bring the fruits of scholarly inquiry to a larger, more diverse audience. It is my hope and intention that the present volume might trace the same trajectory.

In that connection I should also stipulate that this is a book focused on Homeric epic. I am interested most essentially in reading the *Iliad* and *Odyssey*. Although it is not primarily a comparative study, as are most of my earlier writings, it still draws heavily on the South Slavic oral epic tradition and makes frequent reference to other traditions, especially Anglo-Saxon. In that spirit I hope that the book proves useful not only to classicists and their students but also to specialists and nonspecialists in Slavic studies, the medieval European literatures, folklore, anthropology, and any of the scores of other areas where oral traditions present themselves as forces to be reckoned with.

Among the women and men whose midwifery brought *Homer's Traditional Art* to this point, Jenny Strauss Clay deserves special thanks for her urging of a book that "takes things from the beginning," that sketches the implications of oral tradition for Homeric poetry in terms that nonspecialists can follow. I also owe a particular word of thanks to Barry Powell, Burton Raffel, and the anonymous readers of the manuscript for Pennsylvania State University Press; as well as to Philip Winsor, whose editorial expertise and singular devotion to crafting books (for all of the right reasons) have faithfully guided me throughout the process of turning inchoate ideas into tangible reality.

Colleagues and friends whose advice, published scholarship, or both have been especially important for this enterprise include Ronelle Alexander, Mark Amodio, Flemming Andersen, Pertti Anttonen, Egbert Bakker, Michael Barnes, Richard Bauman, Vibeke Boerdahl, Nancy Mason Bradbury, John Buteau, Robert Cochran, Mary Crane, Robert Payson Creed, Anastasios Daskalopoulos, Sioned Davies, George Dimock (*in memoriam*), Thomas DuBois, Mark Edwards, Ruth Finnegan, Donald Freeman, Donald Fry, Scott Garner, Chao Gejin, Bryan Hainsworth, Barbara Kerewsky-Halpern, Joel Halpern, Joseph Harris, Lauri Harvilahti, Molly Herbert, Carolyn Higbie, Lauri Honko, Daniel Hooley, Dell Hymes, Bonnie Irwin, Martin Jaffee, Minna Skafte Jensen, Ahuvia Kahane, Werner Kelber, Yuri Kleiner, Svetozar Koljević, Anne Lebeck (*in memoriam*), Françoise Létoublon, Albert Lord (*in memoriam*), William Lossone (*in memoriam*), John McDowell, Anne Mackay, Richard Martin, Nada Milošević-Djordjević, John Moore (*in memoriam*), Michael Nagler, Gregory Nagy, Joseph Nagy, Susan Niditch, Wulf Oesterreicher, Walter J. Ong, Ward Parks, Lori Peterson, Boris Putilov (*in memoriam*), Kurt Raaflaub, Steve Reece, Alain Renoir, Joseph Russo, Merritt Sale, Sampulnorbu, Ursula Schaefer, David Schenker, Anna-Leena Siikala, Denise Stodola, Lotte Tarkka, Aaron Tate, Barre Toelken, Barbara Wallach, and Zhalgaa.

As with individuals, so with institutions. The Department of Classical Studies at the University of Missouri–Columbia has been a nurturing environment for this project, as has been the Center for Studies in Oral Tradition on the other side of the same campus. I am grateful to all the colleagues, students, and staff at these two *oikoi*, as well as to the College of Arts and Sciences, in particular Deans Larry Clark and Theodore Tarkow, who have done so much to support research and scholarship in these fields. Let me also acknowledge the university's support in the form of the W. H. Byler Professorship in the Humanities and the Curators' Professorship in Classical Studies and English. Many thanks are owed as well to the Milman Parry Collection of Oral Literature at Harvard University, especially for permission to use and quote from the unpublished South Slavic epic performances recorded acoustically and in writing by Milman Parry and Albert Lord. The curator of the Parry Collection, Stephen Mitchell, generously provided ready access to these materials, and Thomas Butler, who oversees the organization and usage of the South Slavic texts, has also been a tremendous help and a good friend to this project.

For support of my research and for providing otherwise unencumbered time to put the results into the present format, I am particularly grateful to institutions that granted fellowship aid. These include the American Council of Learned Societies, whose 1976–77 fellowship funded a year's residence at the Parry Collection and thus enabled me to make preeditions of numerous South Slavic epics from the Stolac region; and whose subsequent 1995–96 fellowship supported the major part of the writing of *Homer's Traditional Art*. Inside this Homeric ring, a 1980–81 Fellowship from the John Simon Guggenheim Foundation and a 1990–91 research leave from the University of Missouri–Columbia fostered the development of much of the analytical methodology used in this book. I would be remiss not to mention as well the seventy-two participants in the six Seminars for College Teachers titled "The Oral Tradition in Literature," funded by the National Endowment for the Humanities, who spent many summer months on our campus. They were the first audience for many of the ideas in this volume, and I therefore owe them a special debt.

As with any project that took shape over an extended period of time, I have also had the benefit of colleagues' reactions at conferences and lectures in this country and abroad. Among those I want particularly to remember here are the annual conventions of the American Philological Association, American Folklore Society, and Modern Language Association; as well as special gatherings at Odense University, the University of Copenhagen, the Centre des études homériques (Grenoble), the University of Helsinki, Turku University, the University of Natal-Durban, the Sonderforschungsbereich at the Universität Freiburg, the second Albert Bates Lord Conference (St. Petersburg, Russia), the University of Cardiff, the Mysore Institute of Folklore and the University of Shantinikatan (India), and the Chinese Academy of Social Sciences (Beijing). The two Folklore Fellows Summer Schools in 1995 and 1997, at Mekrijaervi and Lammi, Finland, respectively, offered ideal venues for lengthy presentation and extensive discussion of many of the issues raised herein in a truly international context. I am very grateful to colleagues from often underrepresented areas in Asia and Africa for the many provocative reactions and sound suggestions made during the Finnish seminars.

Published sources for citations and original-language quotations in this volume are as follows: for the Homeric epics, the Oxford standard editions (Monro and Allen 1969); for the Homeric Hymns, Allen 1946; for the South Slavic narratives, the *Serbo-Croatian Heroic Songs* series (*SCHS* 1953–) and Karadžić 1841–62; for "Deor," Malone 1966; and for other Old English poetry, the *Anglo-Saxon Poetic Records* (Krapp and Dobbie 1931–53). Quotations from unpublished South Slavic epics are made from my trial editions of the acoustic records and dictated texts from the Milman Parry Collection; these narratives are cited according to that archive's usual system (see Kay 1995 and the *SCHS* series), with italic numbers designating acoustically recorded songs (either sung or recited) and roman numbers designating performances taken down in writing through dictation. Translations from the Homeric poems are based on Lattimore 1951 (*Iliad*) and 1965 (*Odyssey*), with occasional modifications; those from South Slavic and Anglo-Saxon are entirely my own.

Versions of some of the arguments made in this book have been tested in published form as well. Parts of Chapter 1 appeared in Egbert Bakker and Ahuvia Kahane, eds., *Written Voices, Spoken Signs* (Cambridge: Harvard University Press, 1997), 56–82. Likewise, selections from the latter part of Chapter 2 appeared in *Arethusa* 31 (1998): 149–78. Finally, selections from the first part of Chapter 3 were published in *Transactions of the American Philological Association* 126 (1996): 11–41. I gratefully acknowledge the work of the editors and reviewers who helped to clarify and strengthen these links in the chain.

Finally, I take this opportunity to thank those closest to the hearth and the actual making of this book: Anne-Marie, intrepid long-distance reader; Elizabeth, *discipula multarum linguarum*; Isaac, master of merriment; Joshua, *cuisinier nonpareil*; John Miles, Jr., *moj dečak na srcu*; and Hannah Frances Foley, *moja majka na mjestu*. They all have a share in *Homer's Traditional Art*.

INTRODUCTION

Reading Bellerophon's Tablet

Let us begin with a riddle. If Homer's epics derive from an oral tradition, as most scholars agree, then what do we make of the episode of Bellerophon's tablet, an undeniable instance of written communication memorialized in Book 6 of the *Iliad*?[1] This celebrated episode, often cited as the single unambiguous reference to writing in Homer, starts with Proitos' wife taking rancorous revenge against the virtuous and unsuspecting Bellerophon. Miffed by his lack of interest in her extramarital overtures, she seeks to have him murdered by inverting reality—by claiming to her husband that Bellerophon was the aggressor, that he had in fact tried to seduce her. Here then is the result (6.166–80, with the Greek word *sêma* intentionally left untranslated):

So she spoke, and anger took hold of the king at her story.
[Proitos] shrank from killing [Bellerophon], since his heart was awed by such action,

but sent him away to Lykia, and handed him murderous *sêmata*,
which he inscribed in a folding tablet, enough to destroy life,
and told him to show it to his wife's father, so that he might perish.   170
Bellerophon went to Lykia in the blameless convoy
of the gods; when he came to the running stream of Xanthos, and Lykia,
the lord of wide Lykia tendered him full-hearted honor.
Nine days he entertained him with sacrifice of nine oxen,
but afterwards when the rose fingers of the tenth dawn showed, then   175
he began to question him, and asked to be shown the *sêma*,
whatever he might be carrying from his son-in-law, Proitos.
Then after he had been given his son-in-law's wicked *sêma*
first he sent him away with orders to kill the Chimaira.

Bellerophon's subsequent defeat of the fearsome Chimaira wins him only
further life-threatening challenges, as the Lykian king attempts anew to
carry out the encrypted death sentence vicariously by sending the ac-
complished young warrior against the Solymoi, the Amazons, and an un-
specified troop of local champions, all of whom he likewise dispatches one
after the next. Suspecting a divine connection, the king then reconsiders
his position and offers Bellerophon his daughter and half of all he owns.
The message mandating execution, once so pressing, is now apparently
forgotten.

But how was it communicated in the first place? Homer mentions in-
scription and a folding tablet, but does not describe the process of en-
coding and decoding Proitos' command. Is he merely making passing
reference to a technology of communication he does not himself under-
stand, perhaps a method of transferring information that came to his at-
tention via a folktale from another culture? If on the other hand we believe
that Homer does understand and perhaps even use the technology of tex-
tual surfaces and inscriptions, just what sort of graphic signs (*sêmata*) are
these—alphabetic, ideographic, or semasiographic? Could this passage
perhaps be taken as incontrovertible proof that writing and reading had
gained ascendancy by the time of the *Iliad* and *Odyssey*, and that the per-
spective from oral tradition must be abandoned? Or does some other
explanation exist for how Bellerophon's death warrant—the deadly but
covert message to "kill the bearer"—was delivered? These questions de-
serve answers.

First, there is no reason why Homer and his tradition could not have ap-
propriated this brief tale from another culture, but even such a likely hy-
pothesis does not explain his conception of the message as "signs."[2] Sec-
ond, critical opinion varies on what these signs actually were;[3] since we
lack an explicit account, inflexible advocacy of any single possibility must
prove fruitless. It also misses the point, because none of the three hy-
potheses—alphabetic, ideographic, or semasiographic—gets to the core

of what Homer means by "signs." Third, scholarship over the past twenty years, especially field research on living oral traditions, has taught us to distrust the false dichotomy of "oral versus written" and to expect complex inventories and interactions of oral and literate in the same culture and even in the very same individual.[4] Given these realities, it is safe to assume that the approach from oral tradition will continue to produce valuable insights even if we someday manage to put a stylus in Homer's hand. What matters is the nature and persistence of the traditional language as an expressive medium. For all of these reasons, then, the story of Bellerophon's tablet certainly gives us no cause to abandon the perspective from oral tradition.[5]

What it does give us is an insight into how Homer thinks about what the tablet "says," and how the silent surface conveys its dire secret. To name the letters (or ideographs or other symbols) the poet employs the term *sêma*, "sign," a word that we will examine in some detail over the course of this book. But even at such an early stage we cannot afford to be unaware of its specialized Homeric sense. To translate *sêma* as merely the tablet or whatever is scratched on it is not merely inadequate; worse yet, such a view obscures an ancient technology of representation by converting it into our own dominant technology for communication. As we shall see, *sêmata* in the *Iliad*, *Odyssey*, and Hymns are first and foremost tangible symbols that point toward larger concerns or ideas that would otherwise remain hidden or secret, windows that open onto emergent realities knowable in no other way. Such signs include Zeus' omens, funerary markers for heroes, the scar on Odysseus' thigh, even the olive-tree bed itself. When Homer construes the "kill the bearer" message on Bellerophon's tablet as a group of *sêmata*, then, he is not designating an alphabet, a collection of ideographs, or any other real-world writing system. Rather he is identifying a technology he does not possess—writing and texts—as a species of the sign-language that he does possess—traditional, idiomatic representation. The written codification, he is explaining, must be a kind of *sêma*, analogous in its function to the tangible signs that betoken divine intervention, a fallen hero's glory, Odysseus' identity, or the long-delayed reunion of Penelope and Odysseus. Signs project reality, index knowledge, cue expectable because traditional meanings. The markings on Bellerophon's tablet do the same; therefore they are *sêmata*.[6]

So much for Homer's and his tradition's concept of signs. As this volume proceeds, we will be expanding that sense of *sêma* to name all of the traditional strategies in his poetic repertoire, all of the signs by means of which he brings the *Iliad* and *Odyssey* out of tradition and into performance or text. That is, we will be concerned with a great deal more than the fifty-eight occurrences of the word *sêma* in the *Iliad*, *Odyssey*, and Hymns. Our redefinition of the term as a critical tool will cut a much larger swath, taking in every recurrent pattern at every level of organization throughout those works. Under this expansion Homer's traditional signs will thus include the myriad formulaic expressions for which he is renowned, the typical scenes or themes that recur throughout the poetry, and even the largest-scale "sign" of all, the Odyssean story-pattern often called the Return Song. For our purposes, then, "swift-footed Achilleus" qualifies as a *sêma*, as does "rose-fingered dawn"; the same is true of the multiform scenes of feasting, lament, assembly, arming for battle, and so on. Although Homer himself does not call these features of his specialized language *sêmata*, we should note that they do qualify as such: they function as idiomatic markers to index "secret" meanings knowable in no other way. In short, they bear implications beyond their literal sense. They project *traditional referentiality*.

Construed in this way, the *sêma* thus offers us a way out of the unsustainable dichotomies that have hindered the study of oral tradition as a creative force behind the Homeric poems. Instead of setting up oppositions like structure versus aesthetics, orality versus literacy, oral tradition versus text, individual artistry versus traditional inheritance, and so forth, Homer's traditional signs illustrate the necessary linkage between composition and reception. That is, the signs are more than just conveniently shaped building materials; they support fluent realization of the architect's dream. They are more than metrical and narrative stopgaps to keep the story going under the pressure of performance; they constitute a language rich in idiomatic implication. They do not inhibit a bard's imagination or diminish his freedom of expression; rather they provide a unique way of speaking that engages the resources of the poetic tradition with inimitable efficiency and grace. Even when *sêmata* came to be inscribed on the real-life equivalent of Bellerophon's tablet, they did not automatically lose all expressive power. Rather they continued to deliver their secrets as long as there was an audience or readership who knew the code, someone who could read the signs on their own terms and in their own context.[7]

In this book I strive to read Homer's traditional *sêmata* in just this way — *as a coherent language* — to the extent permitted by our twenty-five centuries' distance from the epic tradition and by the handicap imposed by its limited extant remains. In doing so I will make no special claim about the precise relationship between our texts of the Homeric poems and their oral traditional background, in part because I believe that the evidence is insufficient to support a confident final pronouncement and in part because our goal is not to establish the exact place of these poems in the cultural history of Greek literacy. As noted above, fieldwork from all over the world has shown time and again that cultures and even individuals make use of both "oral" and "written" channels or media on an everyday basis. Indeed, today the notion of a culture entirely unexposed to the written word seems to be largely a romantic fiction, and, correspondingly, even the most text-dependent of modern Western cultures support healthy oral traditions as part of their expressive repertoires. As I have argued elsewhere,[8] the crucial measure must not be crude abstractions like "orality" or "literacy" that mask more than they reveal, but rather the actual, dynamic language or register employed for a given species of verbal art. For our purposes here, the crucial measure must be the Homeric way of speaking (and hearing and reading). What are the assumptions inherent in this unusual medium? What implications are encoded in the recurrent phrases, in the multiform scenes, in the story of the returning hero that has so many cognates in other Indo-European traditions? What advantage does fluency in the Homeric register offer for composition and especially for reception? These are some of the particular questions this book addresses as part of its overall agenda, an ambitious agenda that can be distilled into a single framing question: What difference do their roots in oral tradition make to our understanding of the Homeric poems as verbal art?

Proverbs and Signs

Proverbs and *sêmata* work similarly. Both represent highly efficient strategies for economically communicating traditional meanings. Modest in extent and superficial sense though they may be, these "bytes" of language act as touchstones, providing ready access to implied cultural or mythic knowledge and serving as guides through a thicket of individual instances by foregrounding what those instances share. In this sense proverbs and *sêmata* are not unlike Odysseus' bow-shot through the axeheads; their trajectory graphically reveals the basic unity and alignment of separate events or situations.

In what follows I take advantage of this similarlity between aphorisms and signs by presenting a series of six homemade proverbs that preview some of the fundamental issues examined in this book. If these recently fabricated "old saws" function correctly, clothing theoretical principles in the garb of folk wisdom, their messages should prove both memorable in themselves and easily applicable to a variety of situations. As the opportunity arises, I will echo these proverbs throughout the chapters that follow, seeking to remind the reader not only of the core ideas that underpin these studies, but also of some elusive distinctions that the dominant contemporary technologies of communication have obscured. Like refrains— and indeed like *sêmata*—these facsimile proverbs will serve as indexes or keys to understanding Homer's traditional art.

For the moment I will explain each proverb only telegraphically, preferring to let its full meaning emerge in the context of usage and discussion throughout subsequent chapters. Nonetheless, the six proverbs and the brief gloss appended to each will provide a rough map for some of the most prominent points on our analytical journey, as well as a ready reference for reviewing the basic tenets of the theoretical argument after the fact. With these perspectives in mind, then, consider the following nuggets of "folk wisdom":

I. *Oral tradition works like language, only more so.*

Oral traditions—and by extension the texts that derive from oral traditions—are not collections of items but elegant expressive instruments dedicated to specific purposes. They are not warehouses or inventories of things but rather *languages* that offer enormous communicative potential for fluent speakers and hearers (and, potentially, for writers and readers). We understand oral traditions best not when we worry over their superficial narrowness or limitations, but when we seek to discover their enhanced signification and rich coding. Because oral traditions tend to employ focused varieties of language (or registers), they customarily sacrifice the broad applicability of general-purpose language in order to do fewer things well. In this respect they are usually more densely idiomatic and resonant than everyday registers.

II. *Performance is the enabling event, tradition the enabling referent.*

In the case of a living oral tradition, the very act of performance bears special meaning. When a singer bows the *gusle*, strums the *tambura*, sings a prelude, joins hands with a co-singer, or in some other way indicates that the performance has begun, he or she prescribes a preselected channel for communication. It is that channel to which the audience must also tune in order to establish and maintain a coherent exchange. In the case of an oral-derived, textualized tradition, performance can be keyed rhetorically, using some of the same signals but now transposed to a written libretto that guides readers to the correct channel. In either situation the event of performance, real or rhetorical, enables the exchange. The second part of the proverb teaches that signs point toward traditional referentiality, toward a set of idiomatic implications, whether in performance or text. Traditional referentiality enables an extremely economical transaction of meaning, with the modest, concrete part standing for a larger and more complex whole.

III. *Composition and reception are two sides of the same coin.*

For many years studies in oral tradition privileged composition over reception, seeking to explain the apparent miracle of the preliterate singer's performance of long epic. This focus on tectonics downplayed the role and responsibility of the audience or reader and shifted emphasis away from what the performance or text actually meant—or, more precisely, *how* it could mean. But traditional language offers a referential as well as a compositional advantage, provided that the audience or reader is fluent in that specialized tongue. When the referential advantage diminishes (not necessarily immediately upon the advent of writing and texts), the traditional language may be cast aside and a more useful expressive instrument may take its place. Thus reception and composition are indissolubly linked.

IV. Artis causa, not metri causa.

"For the sake of art, not for the sake of meter" speaks most directly to the formulaic diction so typical of Homeric epic, which appears to be shaped primarily according to the demands of the hexameter—*metri causa* is the usual term. If this is so, some have asked, then how can we ascribe poetic excellence to Homer? Could he exercise any choice in naming people and gods in his epics, for example, or was he simply a prisoner of his inherited diction, forced into compliance by the tyranny of a prefabricated language? This proverb contends that meaning and art come first, that stock expressions like the recurrent names for people and gods have resonance not as original creations or situation-specific usages but as traditional signs. The signs themselves may be metrically governed, but their implications are not.

V. Read both behind and between the signs.

To read *behind* Homer's signs is to tap into their idiomatic and traditional implications, to take into account the otherwise hidden associations for which they stand *pars pro toto*, the part for the whole. Since it has so far been comparatively neglected, such traditional referentiality will be our primary concern. But that focus in itself is not enough. We must also be aware of what lies *between* the signs: the local, immediate, and individual details that are full partners in the negotiation of Homeric art. The best perspective is a balanced and stereoscopic view that neglects neither side of the process.

VI. Instance meshes with implication.

Such a balanced, stereoscopic perspective recognizes the inseparability of the instance and its implications. The art of the *Iliad* and *Odyssey* stems neither solely from the uniqueness of the instance nor solely from its traditional meaning, but rather from their interaction. We cannot afford to neglect either between-the-signs singularity or behind-the-signs resonance.[9]

A Chapter-by-Chapter Itinerary

As already observed, *Homer's Traditional Art* concentrates on a single question: What difference do their roots in oral tradition make to our understanding of the Homeric poems as verbal art? In attempting an answer that does justice to the complexity and importance of that question, I have organized the book into four parts, with a total of eight chapters plus an afterword. The opening part consists of Chapter 1, "Homeric Signs and Traditional Referentiality," and focuses on the nature and dynamics of *sêmata*, or signs, in Homer. This discussion sets the agenda for the volume as a

whole, illustrating how Homer employs what he calls *sêmata* to index tra-
ditional implications, and how that strategy also applies to trademark pat-
terns of language and narrative structure in the epics. Part II comprises
Chapters 2–4 and treats the much-cited but understudied comparison of
Homer with South Slavic epic, juxtaposing a living oral tradition to the
manuscript texts of the *Iliad*, *Odyssey*, and Hymns. In the first of these
chapters I consider the advantages and the limitations of the analogy, with
particular attention to the anthropomorphized figure of the legendary
singer (called Hasan Ćoso, Isak, Ćor Huso, and by other names) whose "life
history" much resembles what can be recovered of Homer's biography.
The middle chapter in this section treats the specialized epic languages of
archaic Greek and South Slavic, urging a carefully drawn comparison and
contrast rather than a simplistic superimposition or outright disjunction.
As a prelude to later discussion, Chapter 4 illustrates how the specialized
South Slavic language encodes traditional referentiality, how its various
features tap into networks of implied meaning for the fluent audience or
reader.

The third part of the book, Chapters 5–7, applies the theory developed
in the opening chapter and the comparative principles illustrated in Chap-
ters 2–4 directly to the art of the Homeric poems. Here the goal is to dem-
onstrate exactly what difference a background in oral tradition makes, col-
lating multiple instances of traditional signs and deriving the implications
they bear. In doing so we proceed from larger to smaller signs. Thus Chap-
ter 5 treats the *sêma* of the Return Song story-pattern, the Indo-European
tale-type that underlies the *Odyssey*, making reference to the wealth of par-
allel songs in other traditions (especially South Slavic) and reconsidering
such fundamental issues as the overall unity of the poem, Penelope's char-
acteristic ambiguity, and the end of the *Odyssey*. Chapter 6 then inves-
tigates the next smaller level of *sêma*, the typical scene or theme, concen-
trating on two multiple occurring sequences: the feast in the *Odyssey* and
the lament in the *Iliad*. Chapter 7 rounds out this part with an analysis of
the traditional referentiality of Homer's phraseology, from ubiquitous
noun-epithet formulas like "swift-footed Achilleus" and "wine-dark sea"
through rhetorical markers that forecast speech strategies and on to the
implications of the recurrent diction associated with sleep. As the core of
the whole presentation, Chapters 5–7 attempt to show how the specialized
language and structure of oral tradition really make a difference, how they
actively enrich Homer's art. The register or "way of speaking" thus pro-
vides not a barrier or handicap to be overcome, but an evocative medium
for the realization of epic poetry that draws from the best of both worlds—
the individual, local, and unique on the one hand and the recurrent, tradi-
tional, and idiomatic on the other.

Since the proof is in the pudding (to cite a real rather than another home-
made proverb), I devote the fourth part and final chapter to a rereading of

an extended passage from Book 23 of the *Odyssey* according to the theory and examples worked out over the first three parts. Thus I examine the role of the Return story-pattern as Eurykleia confronts Penelope with the news for which they have been waiting so long, as Penelope at first refuses to believe that Odysseus is back, and as the story reaches its *telos* (fulfillment) with the final recognition and the olive-tree bed. Since this sequence of events involves the typical scene of Bath or Anointment, I also take the opportunity to read behind that sign, bringing its traditional referentiality into play alongside the unprecedented and unparalleled actions that happen between the signs. Nor is the level of phraseology neglected in this rereading. Looking at selected *sêmata* over the course of lines 69–103, I make explicit the implications of both the phraseology as a whole and certain signs in particular. A traditionally glossed text and an *apparatus fabulosus* (story-based apparatus) support this demonstration. In all dimensions the goal of the final chapter is twofold: to read both behind and between the signs, to give both the tradition and the poet their due, and to acknowledge the network of implication that meshes with the uniqueness of each situation. The volume closes with a brief afterword introducing a third witness to the referential and artistic importance of traditional oral sign-language: the Anglo-Saxon lyric poem "Deor."

PART I

HOMER'S
SIGN-LANGUAGE

1

HOMERIC SIGNS
AND TRADITIONAL
REFERENTIALITY

houtô toi tode sêma piphauskomai
Thus I expound to you this *sêma*
—*Odyssey* 23.202

This volume focuses on the roots of Homeric epic in an ancient Greek oral tradition, exploring Homeric art not as a literary triumph over that heritage but as the direct product of its unique, empowering agency. That is, it considers how the bard and his tradition employed a dedicated medium for expression to achieve a more than literary art.[1] Our exordium in this chapter and in the study as a whole is the unassuming noun *sêma*—not as in the contemporary linguistic and literary approach called "semiotics," but as a trope and a term in the native poetics of ancient Greek epic poetry. To indicate where we are headed, I take *sêma* as a sign that points not so much to a specific situation, text, or performance as toward the ambient tradition, which serves as the key to an emergent reality. *Sêma* both names and is the tangible, concrete part that stands by contractual agreement for a larger, immanent whole, and as such it mimics a central expressive strategy of Homeric poetry: traditional referentiality.[2] Within the marked idiomatic language of the *epos*, and of other traditional oral works as well, many

such signs or units—whether actually labeled as *sêmata* or not—are spe-
cially licensed to bear more than their individual, unmarked lexical or se-
mantic burdens. Enriched within the augmented discourse, these "bytes"
of phraseology and narrative pattern serve to index traditional ideas, char-
acters, and situations, standing by prior negotiation for much more than
a literary reading alone can decode.[3] As suggested above, oral traditions
work like languages, only more so.

Background: Opportunities and Limitations

In order to come to terms with what I take as a current and demanding ver-
sion of the Homeric Question, in which we are asked to move from com-
position to reception and from structure to meaning, we first need some
understanding of a few important moments in the history of studies in oral
tradition. The following remarks briefly summarize some turning points
in the evolution of this approach, with emphasis not so much on the well-
known sequence of events as on the entrenched perspectives these events
engendered. As we shall see, it has in fact been the rediscovery of ancient
Greek oral tradition that has, paradoxically, both enhanced and dimin-
ished our capacity to hear what Homer was saying.[4]

When Milman Parry began his epochal research with his master's (1925)
and doctoral theses (1928a, b), he was seeking to demonstrate the *tradi-
tional* character of Homeric style. Thus his elaborate analyses of noun-
epithet formulas such as "swift-footed Achilleus" (*podas ôkus Achilleus*) or
"grey-eyed Athena" (*glaukôpis Athênê*) were intended to establish that the
Iliad and *Odyssey*, far from being the creation of a single person or the com-
posite result of a massive editing project, had roots sunk deep in a poetic
tradition, an inherited craft of which Homer was presumably the latest
and finest practitioner. For Parry everything derived from utility, and the
traditional poet was one who dextrously manipulated a ready-made lan-
guage, the bequest of generations of bards who had gradually evolved and
polished it to the highest degree.

The hypothesis of *orality*, it should be stressed, came only later, after
Parry was exposed to accounts of oral traditions from various lands, es-
pecially to Matija Murko's writings on the South Slavic epic and V. V.
Radlov's reports on central Asian epic.[5] Eventually, in the company of
Albert Lord, he would undertake a full-scale collecting expedition to then-
Yugoslavia, recording thousands of performances chiefly from nonliterate
guslari (epic singers) either acoustically or by dictation. On the basis of
this analogy, he and Lord seemed to confirm an oral as well as traditional
Homer, a poet who composed under the continuous pressure of perfor-

mance, a poet for whom a ready-made, useful idiom was thus of the greatest practical importance.

Upon this foundation Lord built a comparative edifice of imposing proportions, a construction project eventually involving many hands that is still very much under way.[6] The initial level of language examined was the *formula*, or phraseological "word," defined by Parry as "an expression regularly used, under the same metrical conditions, to express an essential idea" (1928a: 13). At the start, noun-epithet combinations like "prudent Telemachos" and "white-armed Hera" were the sole object of his analyses, but later he and Lord turned their attention to other dimensions of Homer's and the *guslar's* poetic language in an effort to understand the formulaic structure of the poetry as a whole. The next tier of what they described as ready-made compositional units was that of *themes*—"words" at the level of recurrent, typical scenes—defined by Lord as "the groups of ideas regularly used in telling a tale in the formulaic style of traditional song" (1960: 68). Events such as feast, assembly, arming the hero, and the like were shown to be tectonic staples of the singer's repertoire, varying as necessary to suit the particular situation but in their general outline and verbal content quite stable and recognizable from one instance to the next. The third level of structure, and the largest of the traditional units, was the less-studied *story-pattern* or tale-type, a compositional "word" coextensive with the entire epic narrative. For the *Odyssey* this is the Return Song pattern, which in its tale of an absent hero who comes back in disguise to test his wife, defeat his rivals, and reclaim his place and possessions underlies literally thousands of epic songs from the South Slavic, Albanian, Russian, and other traditions.[7] This critical program, drawn up from the reasonably close fit between Homeric Greek and Moslem South Slavic epic, was then applied to both living and manuscript-based traditions in a multitude of genres across the board, and the Parry-Lord theory of traditional oral composition gained widespread currency.[8]

But these first few steps not only blazed an exciting new path in Homeric studies; they also set the agenda for subsequent discussion, foregrounding certain concerns while necessarily deemphasizing or even submerging others. First and foremost, the early theory privileged composition over reception, placing almost exclusive emphasis on explaining how the oral poet managed the apparent miracle of composition in performance. The audience was credited as a shaping force, to be sure, but the stress was placed on the ways in which they influenced the composer and not on their role in completing the circuit of communication. Another hidden problem, and one closely linked to the privileging of composition, lay in the very nature of the evidence brought forward on Homer's style. Parry began his demonstration by isolating formulaic diction, at first only noun-epithet phrases but later less rigid phraseology, characterizing it initially as a traditional and later as an oral inheritance. But the most telling feature of his witnesses to the existence of an ancient Greek *oral* tradition is that they were in fact *seen*; that is, they were visually culled out as discrete items according to their *textual* identity. Although Lord also described a living grammar of formulaic composition in *The Singer of Tales*, he and most other scholars spoke more often of self-contained, separable items or elements in lieu of the language they constituted, of isolated integers rather than a composite mathematics of expression.[9] The hypothesis of oral tradition in Homer was based on literate concepts and explicated via a textual mindset.

This contradiction in terms—a textually conceived and defined orality—exposes a third shortcoming of the early Parry-Lord theory, or "strong thesis." At the heart of this approach from the beginning had lain the untested assumption that "oral" could always and everywhere be distinguished from "written," that the two modes were typologically opposite, mutually exclusive. Given this assumption, the scholarly task simply amounted to sorting ancient and medieval texts, which of course could be known only via the manuscripts that survive, into one of the two available categories.[10] The hypothesis of a transitional text, situated midway between the two perceived poles, was therefore unacceptable: if there were no real difference in kind between and among documents, then the hard-won explanations of composition-in-performance and of the role of constituent building blocks would founder.[11] Assimilation to the conventional literary model would be only too ready, especially given the pressure applied by scholars who felt that the Oral Theory sacrificed Homer's art on the altar of tectonics and mechanism.

There have been a number of liberating responses to the "strong thesis." First, the impulse to unearth archetypal similarities has been balanced in succeeding years by the need to distinguish among different traditions, genres, and media. Reports from the field have fractured universalist assumptions, revealing the palette of worldwide oral traditions to be at least as various as the wonderfully heterogeneous (but finally much smaller and narrower) collection of verbal art we call "literature." Put simply, different traditions—with their diverse performers, languages, expressive units, and social contexts—work differently, as do the various genres within them. There can be no better example of this need to distinguish as well as compare than the fact that the original and still primary analogy for Homeric and other oral traditions is the Moslem South Slavic epic—a single subgenre of epic from a single tradition that matches the *Iliad* and *Odyssey* in several important dimensions.[12] But the same subgenre proves less congruent with texts and performances from many other traditions, and the definitions and concepts based on Moslem epic deserve to be pluralized—a goal quite possible of achievement even elsewhere within the same oral tradition.[13] Likewise, the media through which we come to know traditional oral forms—from an actual performance through audio and video facsimiles and on to textual transcriptions—have an enormous impact on just how we "read."[14] Making and becoming fully aware of these distinctions can only improve our grasp of verbal art in and from oral tradition.

Second is the matter of *language*. Whatever the tradition, genre, or medium, we must view its "words" not as detachable, isolatable items but as elements that collectively make up a coherent, idiomatic "way of speaking."[15] Instead of seizing upon formulas as playing cards to be shuffled and reshuffled, we need to understand their emergence as the result of a process governed by grammatical and syntactic rules that define a particular variety or register of language. Rules for the structure and texture of phraseology will of course vary from one tradition and genre to the next, and even within a single genre there will be room for individual (idiolectal) and regional (dialectal) species of the poetic language. But the point is that the poet composes not so much by manipulation of ready-made building blocks as through fluent command of an idiom dedicated to a single purpose.[16] The situation is similar for those larger "words" not so immediately dependent on linguistic principles, that is, for the typical scenes and story-patterns that inform many narrative works.[17] They too are part of the specialized, dedicated idiom through which poet and audience communicate in a highly focused transaction, as are any other linguistic, paralinguistic, or nonlinguistic features licensed for usage within the given tradition and genre.

A third major development in recent years has to do with the exposure of the Great Divide of orality versus literacy as a false dichotomy, and with its replacement by a more realistic model. Just as evidence has accumulated on the variety of oral traditional performances that can still be attended in our time, so numerous witnesses from ancient, medieval, and modern traditions have stepped forward to testify against this once unquestioned typology.[18] To put the matter positively, these witnesses have together described a *spectrum of expressive forms*, all the way from living oral traditions experienced in the field to highly textual works that nonetheless betray roots in oral tradition. And, instead of muddying the waters, thereby destroying our ability to discriminate meaningfully among categories, this spectrum has in fact pointed the way toward understanding how and why traditional forms can so stubbornly survive the advent of writing and texts, at least for a time.[19] Since these forms constitute a real and singularly expressive language, rather than a standard kit of handy compositional tools, there is no reason why they should immediately cede place to an entirely new, unrelated mode of expression. To an important extent language and poetics persist, and *sêmata* will continue to function as *sêmata*, at least for a while and with certain qualifications, whether spoken as "winged words" or scratched on a tablet. An airtight typology of oral versus written now seems an unsupportable imposition on the complexity of cultural activity. Just so, an overnight abandonment of mother tongue in favor of foreign language is much too tidy an explanation for the many voices of traditional verbal art.

The Riddle of Referentiality: *How* Does Homer Mean?

How then are we to read behind Homer's traditional signs? An effective response to this formidable challenge depends on recognizing that composition and reception are two sides of the same coin, and that in turn entails focusing on the special dynamics of Homer's (and his tradition's) language or way of speaking. In pursuing this goal we should be under no illusion that we can simply assume the role of the original audience for these and other traditional poems, and indeed such a goal may not even be desirable as we seek to read Homeric poetry in and for our own time as well as on its own terms. But some attention to reception of the *epos* within its native idiom will solve cruces generated by the double myopia of privileging composition and assuming congruency with literary, post-traditional poetics. By recovering something of what the *sêmata* imply, our reading experience will be uniquely enriched.

The core of our inquiry thus depends on the nature of referentiality in traditional oral works in general, and in the Homeric texts in particular. As demonstrated elsewhere across numerous works and different areas, the art of traditional poetry is an immanent art, a process of composition and reception in which a simple, concrete part stands for a complex, intangible reality. *Pars pro toto*, the part standing for the whole, as it were.[20] "Grey-eyed Athena" and "wise Penelope" are thus neither brilliant attributions in unrelated situations nor mindless metrical fillers of last resort. Rather they index the characters they name, in all their complexity, not merely in one given situation or even poem but against an enormously larger traditional backdrop. Likewise, singular instances of feasting scenes, guest-host encounters, or Return songs naturally engage plural contexts, with their implied wholes brought into play under the agreed-upon code and dynamics of Homeric idiom. Referentiality is traditional, and the *sêmata* serve to "slot" the variety of individual instances in a familiar, identifiable context.

An unassuming line from South Slavic epic offers a simple example of how traditional meaning can be encoded, and of how it must be figured into the reception of such works.[21] Ubiquitous throughout the Moslem songs, "San usnila, pa se prepanula" ("You've dreamed a dream, so you're frightened") regularly occurs as a response to a report of a battle about to begin or some other dire event on the near horizon, and is customarily spoken by someone apparently in charge to the supposedly less qualified reporter. Its proverbial nature marks a gently chiding, somewhat patronizing attitude on the part of the person who seeks to dismiss the threat as merely a dream and therefore not to be taken seriously. The proverbial meaning of this South Slavic *sêma*, however, mandates something that cannot be predicted without the immanent contribution of the poetic tradition: to wit, the "dream" will very soon become a reality, and ignoring its warning will cost many lives. Clearly, the brutal irony of the unfolding drama depends crucially upon apprehending the formula in its traditional context, on being aware of the prolepsis onto which the sign institutionally opens.

Viewed plainly, this property of traditional referentiality amounts to nothing more than a special case of a fundamental linguistic principle: the essentially arbitrary relationship between sign and meaning. A brief parable will illustrate the point. We know that ultimately there is nothing innate in the morphemes "ship," *bateau*, or *nêus* that conveys the idea of a vehicle particularly well suited for travel on water. These English, French, or Greek words—or ultimately their Indo-European precursors—come to signify as they do on the basis of continued usage in social context. Additionally, any such item can take on more than lexical significance in certain cases, as for example when a landlubber unschooled in nautical jargon divulges his or her amateur status by calling an elegant seagoing craft not a "ship" but a "boat." Like their apparently more basic etymologies, all such idiomatic changes rung on the semantics of standard meanings are absolutely arbitrary impositions on the morphemes that bear them. They can lay no claim to inherent signification, but serve their institutionalized expressive functions under the continuing social contract of language.[22]

Traditional referentiality is no different. The special valences assigned to certain phrases or other units within the Homeric register emerge not from some primeval license but from the continuing demands of fluent, economical communcation in a traditional context. Far from constraining poetic expression, these recurrent signals provide a dedicated avenue to traditional meaning above and beyond the usual literary repertoire of communicative channels, collectively yielding more than the sum of their parts and uniquely enabling both composition and reception. Thus noun-epithet phrases like "grey-eyed Athena" or "purple-cheeked ships" refer not just—or even principally—to the goddess' eyes or the ships' hue, but rather use those characteristic yet nominal details to project holistic traditional concepts via synecdoche. The part stands for the whole, *pars pro toto*. This strategy extends the fundamental arbitrariness of language at the same time that it extends its significative "reach," with the phrase indexing a character, object, or event in its extrasituational, extratextual wholeness. While there is certainly nothing literal in the grey eyes or purple cheeks that lexically projects such complexity, these phrases engage their referents institutionally through a process of slotting. By traditional usage the simple part projects a complex and immanent richness. Oral traditions work like languages, only more so; using such a language means reading behind as well as between the signs.

Other kinds of phrases, as well as the "larger words" of narrative, are part of the same process. The nominal meaning of "intimate word" (*pukinon epos*) implies the idea of "a message or communication of great importance, one that if properly delivered and received would change the present course of events profoundly."[23] As James Holoka has pointed out, the simple phrase *hupodra idôn* ("looking darkly") also bears an idiomatic implication; it "conveys anger on the part of a speaker who takes umbrage at what he judges to be rude or inconsiderate words spoken by the addressee" (1983: 4). In these and so many other brief phrases, examples of which are treated in Chapter 7 of this volume, the extra layer of meaning is not the singular creation of a particular event or context, but a traditional harmonic that adds resonance to each of its occurrences.

If we move to the larger unit of typical scene, we note the same phenomenon. When a woman enters upon a formal lament in the *Iliad*, she will regularly observe a three-part structure that consists of (1) a statement that "you have fallen," (2) a summary of personal history and the dire consequences for those left behind, and (3) a final intimacy.[24] This matrix is not a constraint or handicap under which the poet labors, but the traditional form that drives reception. At the most expansive level of all, the *nostos* pattern—the well-worn path of the returning hero blazed in numerous Indo-European traditions[25]—informs the *Odyssey* narrative by indexing its contents according to familiar, evocative actions. In each of these cases and at each of these levels, the referent for the concrete signs in the performance or text lies outside the immediate performance or text. Instance meshes with implication. Referentiality is immanent and traditional.

Of course, not all phrases, scenes, or story-patterns function with identical force, any more than all traditions, genres, or media obey precisely the same expressive rules. Certain formulas or narrative patterns resound more deeply than others, and it would be a mistake to assume an absolute congruency of signification, of what I have elsewhere called "word-power."[26] At any level, whether in an unmarked standard variety or in a highly dedicated traditional dialect, language cannot and does not work in so lockstep a fashion. We will do better to conceive of the value-added meaning of the Homeric and other traditional idioms as a quality that manifests itself in different ways and to different extents: some phrases and scenes serve a chiefly workaday function, some are imbued with rich and complex associative meanings, and most fall somewhere in between those extremes.

Since we are describing a language that functions idiomatically rather than a kit of ready-made items, we should not fail to note the less obvious cues alerting us to the fact that this kind of specialized communication is taking place. The mere invocation of the hexameter rhythm and diction, in addition to whatever particular phrases or scenes command more specific attention, opens a channel for reception of the performance text. One aspect of the diction is its recognizable otherness: characterized by archaisms and dialect forms, this "way of speaking" is dedicated to one purpose only—the composition and reception of Homeric poetry. As we shall see in Chapters 3 and 4 on the comparison between Homeric language and the South Slavic epic register, the simple choice of the marked epic language as the medium of discourse speaks volumes. The very act of designating such a specialized idiom brings the world of heroic epic within the significative reach of poet and audience with great efficiency. The most important *sêma* is the register as a whole.

With this background in mind, we can explain the workings of traditional referentiality by invoking the model of a network of instances or nodes that extends far beyond the present performance or text.[27] In effect, the immediate context, always an artificially limited horizon for the play of this kind of verbal art, opens onto the more realistic "text" of the ambient tradition. Individual occurrences of *sêmata* or "words"—whether phrases, scenes, or larger patterns—and the idiomatic language in general contribute to what will always be an only partially textualized network, but one that is nonetheless always present to each of its components. We can thus observe that the singular instance derives its meaning not only from tapping the usual lexical and semantic resources, but also by participating in the grander design of traditional referentiality. These signs defer primarily neither to contiguous "echoes" nor to particular instances in other performances or texts, but to the immanent implication that each instance is licensed to bear by fiat.[28] *Sêmata* signal the ambient tradition.

In this respect we can see how the impasse of mechanism versus aesthetics arose. If one perceives such signs as merely useful and repetitive rather than resonant and constitutive, there are indeed only two choices one can make: either to impute to every recurrence a catchall generic meaning or to struggle to discover something genuinely unique about each iteration. By sensing how "words" and a language project a different kind of referentiality, however, we can aspire to the best from both worlds. Alongside the natural fecundity of traditional expression stands the differentiating or diversifying context of the individual situation. Reading behind Homer's signs also means reading between them, discounting neither traditional nor situation-specific meaning. The essential and liberating point is that even the most singular action or event is naturally suspended within a network of implication.

Empowered Speech: The Role of Register

In exploring this network of implication, let us concentrate for the moment on one aspect of traditional referentiality: the nature of the special language in which the artistic transaction takes place. As noted above, the history of studies in oral tradition shows time and again that the "words"—the cognitive units of traditional expression[29]—resist universal definition; phraseology and narrative structure must be ascertained on their own terms from one tradition, genre, and medium to the next. One needs, in short, to learn each language, or each variety of language; to attempt a uniform definition of "words" across this remarkable diversity of forms is to resort to reductionism.

What rationalizes such natural heterogeneity, however, is the expressive strategy we have identified as traditional referentiality. Moreover, since this core principle stands as an enabling feature of *composition*, it should figure just as prominently in the decoding process of *reception*. At both ends of the circuit, arbitrary yet institutionalized meanings are keyed by performance (whether real or rhetorical) and evoked by reference to tradition. As we put it aphoristically above, performance is the enabling event and tradition is the enabling referent.[30]

This proverb moves reception into the foreground, along with composition, and erases what has always been a false boundary between living oral traditions and texts that derive from oral tradition. Instead of categorizing works by what are, finally, impertinent criteria, the proverb directs our attention to two factors of primary importance. First is the matter of *performance*, which, as the anthropologist Richard Bauman observes, "represents a transformation of the basic referential . . . uses of language," and "which says to the auditor, 'interpret what I say in some special sense; do not take it to mean what the words alone, taken literally, would convey'" (1977: 9).[31] When performance is keyed, the audience is signaled to receive via a designated channel and according to specific assumptions and rules. Even when performance must be rhetorically invoked in a text meant for readers, the keying strategies and their expectable responses will still be available to any author and reader who share a working knowledge of the idiom. The empowering aspect of performance, real or rhetorical, is its identity as an event, which mandates a particular kind of communicative exchange. Put another way, the very phenomenon of performance offers a context for the utterance and its reception. Likewise with *tradition*, which constitutes the field of reference to which performance adverts. As we shall see, value-added phrases, scenes, and other patterns resonate in a network of signification, with the singular instance dwarfed—but implicitly informed—by the whole. All that is required for the transaction to succeed is a measure of fluency at both ends of the transmission.

Such fluency depends on three aspects of traditional verbal art: performance arena, register, and communicative economy.[32] *Performance arena* designates the "place" that performer/author and audience go to compose and receive the work. In living traditions, this amounts to a series or collection of actual physical sites, at which the oral narrators and their audiences accomplish the exchange. It is the many Ottoman courts and later the village coffeehouses of Moslem South Slavic epic, or the less well defined but equally numerous special occasions (weddings, family gatherings, evening assemblies) of its Christian epic counterpart. But even when we can stipulate an actual geographical location, it is fundamentally the event that defines the physical place (and not vice versa), that indexes it along with all other such actual sites as the particular "virtual" space associated with a special kind of communication. Thus there is no wholesale dislocation when the performance arena changes from a "real" site to a rhetorically induced forum in a text. The performer-audience relationship is no longer face-to-face, but it rhetorically recalls the same arena because it mirrors the same event. It may do so with varying degrees of success, of course, depending above all on the fluency shared by composer and audience. But whatever the case, entering the performance arena means opening a specific, dedicated channel for communication and participating in a focused kind of exchange. Whether face-to-face or at one textual remove, this much is prescribed simply by the "locus" where the performance takes place.

When poets and audiences enter the arena, they must converse in the local vernacular. Anthropological linguists refer to such speech varieties, selected by "recurrent types of situations" (Hymes 1989: 440), as *registers*. It is characteristic of these specialized idioms, as noted above, that they consist of a somewhat unusual version of the contemporary language, perhaps maintaining archaisms and different dialect forms alongside more current, streamlined speech, as in the case of the Homeric register.[33] Thus, for instance, Homer maintains two equivalent endings for the genitive singular ending of second-declension nouns: *-ou* alongside uncontracted *-oio*. The two-syllable form proved metrically useful and was therefore selectively preserved as an alternative to the (more modern) monosyllabic inflection. And there is good reason to believe that the *Iliad* and *Odyssey* retain vocabulary items from Mycenaean formulaic phrases, among them *depas* ("cup"), *temenos* ("private enclosed property"), and *phasganon* ("sword"). In both cases the unusual, out-of-date form or word marks the idiom as somehow special. In other words, the retention of forms and vocabulary that would be archaic in the contemporary language indicates that the criteria for linguistic maintenance or updating are different in the traditional register. The same rule of thumb applies to the incorporation of alternate dialect forms in the Homeric *koinê*, which like the *-ou/-oio* ending cited above offer metrical pliability and, once admitted to a formulaic phrase, resist change.[34]

These specific features are typical of the Homeric epic register, but the principle applies much more widely, with the particular shape of the register deriving from the linguistic and prosodic traits of the given language and genre. For example, living genres may exhibit important constitutive dimensions of loudness, pitch, gesture, or other performative characteristics, as in the case of South Slavic magical charms.[35] These audible or visible features may be just as significant in keying the poetic performance as the lexical or morphological signals that have survived the process of manuscript-making in ancient and medieval texts. But specific tradition-dependent and genre-dependent features are much less important for our purposes than the given register's more general identity as a dedicated, unified language exclusively devoted to communication in the performance arena. Neither Homer nor the epic *guslari* turn to their curious forms of ancient Greek and South Slavic in an attempt at antiquarianism, but rather because over time these poetic registers have come to serve as finely tuned instruments for the expression of their target narratives. By definition, no other medium could do as well. Furthermore, the very efficacy of the register is the best reason for continuing its use into the early stages of textuality. The method and medium are wholly dedicated to a specific goal, marked for the accomplishment of this purpose to the exclusion of all other purposes. Why, then, would the poet and audience immediately forsake such a unique expressive strategy when textuality is just entering the world of discourse, an infant technology merely taking its first few steps? Why suddenly introduce an unintelligible language into the performance arena when all parties involved are already fluent in a language so well suited to the purpose?[36]

The answer is obvious and simple: a highly developed, mutually intelligible language is far preferable to the alternative, especially in the early stages of the new medium. To reroute the exchange from the dedicated idiom to any other tongue is to short-circuit the remarkable *communicative economy* of the traditional oral register. To avoid confusion, let me stipulate immediately that this quality of economy in composition and reception is not at all the same phenomenon as the "thrift" studied by Parry and Lord, which as far as I can tell is a tradition-dependent property of ancient Greek *epos* that does not translate well, if at all, to either South Slavic or Anglo-Saxon traditional verse.[37] I speak here not of the thrifty surface of the phraseology, the integers themselves, but rather of the economy of expression, the mathematics of the process. If a short phrase such as *pukinon epos* or *hypodra idôn* can index a complicated traditional idea, then it offers evidence of significative economy in that idiom. A simple part projects a complex whole.

This scenario has important implications for referentiality and art. Poets using the traditional register are not constrained at the level of diction because their phraseology naturally reaches beyond the present moment or situation to the immanent network of traditional implication. In fact, this unique echoic function engages an automatic context that is available only via the dedicated register. To simulate this context outside the register— to speak at the same level of implication but unidiomatically—would be an extremely awkward undertaking at best. For one thing, it would require an enormous commitment of supplementary information to close the idiomatic gap, and even then the experience of the work of verbal art would be very different. But the poetics we have been describing supplements the most immediate performance or text extremely economically by automatic referral to a place, the performance arena, and to a register, the language native to that place. Homer's stock-in-trade is not the *apparatus criticus* of nineteenth-century and later editions, but the *apparatus fabulosus* (story-based apparatus) of the poetic tradition.[38] Instead of employing introductions, appendices, footnotes, and other textual prostheses, Homer depends upon traditional signs.

Sêmata and the Poetics of Recognition

Let us now turn directly to these traditional signs, or *sêmata*, with the aim of understanding them as both instances of and a name for traditional referentiality. First a bare minimum of statistical background. The word and term *sêma* occurs a total of fifty-eight times in Homer: thirty-three in the *Iliad*, twenty in the *Odyssey*, and five in the Hymns.[39] It will perhaps surprise no one that in the martial context of the *Iliad* the greater number of instances apply to burial mounds, but in the adjacent cosmos of the *Odyssey* only three of twenty mark the last tangible sign of heroic enterprise, and the Hymns have no such usages. Leaving aside the mortuary *sêmata*, which nonetheless exhibit a distinct kinship of meaning,[40] let us recall a few of the other occurrences.

Although their particular application ranges widely—from Zeus' relatively frequent omens, the identifying marks on Aias' lot and Dolon's spoils, and Orion's Dog (the brightest of all stars that also forebodes evil) to signs measuring achievement in athletic contests, Teiresias' prophecy of the oar and winnowing shovel,[41] and especially the famous scar that projects Odysseus' identity—these thirty-six other *sêmata* all share a common thrust: they signal an emergent reality. As keys to otherwise hidden events or information, each of them marks a prolepsis, a connection from what is present and explicit to what is immanent and implied. Indeed, each of them is uniquely effective because it charts a unique revelatory pathway. For example, Zeus' portents often provide a predictive basis for action or conclusion, as when Nestor urges the Achaeans not to depart in *Iliad* 2 or when, seven books later, Odysseus tells the withdrawn Achilleus of Zeus' propitious signs for the Trojans. The marks on Aias' lot and Dolon's spoils determine priority and action, and the comparison to the traditionally resonant *sêma* of Orion's Dog makes Achilleus' advance toward Hektor that much more ominous. Even when the sign indicates only the length of a *solos-* or a discus-throw, it portends the direction of the narrative, whether of Aias' victory in the Funeral Games or the disguised Odysseus' distinguishing himself in the Phaeacian competition.

Of all Homeric *sêmata*, however, I choose to concentrate here on the sign-language employed by Penelope and Odysseus in the self-fashioning that constitutes their final recognition. In considering the implications of this remarkable series in particular and of other cues as well, we naturally must be willing to admit our less than optimal preparation for entry into the performance arena and our less than perfect fluency in the Homeric register. We are not and can never become Homer's and his tradition's contemporary audience. But we should also resist the temptation to "throw out the baby with the bathwater." Not being able to hear with the clarity and responsiveness of an ancient Greek audience does not necessarily amount to mishearing. Some of the resonance of language and narrative structure can be recovered, and with patience the traditional referentiality of these masterworks can be at least partially reconstructed.

Such is the case, for example, with Laura Slatkin's persuasive rebuilding of Thetis from a bit player in the Iliadic drama to a goddess whose covert power is sufficient to shake Olympian foundations. Not that Homer explicitly "inscribes" her larger mythic character in any episode constituting our *Iliad*; quite the contrary. But Slatkin is able to recover Thetis because she understands the special nature of spoken and unspoken in Homeric epic. As she puts it:

> The mythological corpus on which the poet draws, taken together, constitutes an internally logical and coherent system, accessible as such to the audience. The poet inherits as his repertory a system, extensive and flexible, whose components are familiar, in their manifold variant forms, to his listeners. For an

audience that knows the mythological range of each character, divine or human—not only through this epic song but through other songs epic and nonepic—the poet does not spell out the myth in its entirety but locates a character within through allusion or oblique reference.[42]

This is a principle that operates in traditional oral art around the world, frustrating outside researchers at the same time that it enables a highly economical discourse among insiders who "speak the register." The more highly coded the particular idiom, the further removed it must be from the contemporary unmarked standard—whether at the level of phraseology or of mythic pattern.[43] Indeed, even Slatkin's terminology of "allusion" and "oblique reference," to which we as textually trained scholars are driven, bespeaks our lack of acquaintance with the mode of signifying via traditional signs. As I will argue below, whether they are specifically labeled as *sêmata* or not, we need to read all of Homer's "words"—the formulas, narrative patterns, and other units of utterance—not as textual ciphers but as signals potentially rife with implication, as keys to an emergent reality. These signs are by nature proleptic—expandable in some way during the process of reception—and we must give ourselves a chance to understand how and what they mean.

It is just such a chance that Penelope provides Odysseus during the final stages of their rapprochement. Consider first the succession of signs that punctuate Books 19–24. First, Penelope recognizes the *sêmata* that the stranger has offered (19.250), the mill woman speaks a portent before Odysseus that the suitors should feast their last (20.111), and the returning hero reveals his telltale scar to Eumaios and Philoitios (21.231). Portending the slaughter, Zeus then thunders *sêmata* as Odysseus strings the bow (21.413); afterward, Eurykleia chastises her mistress for refusing to believe her report of the longed-for revenge, citing the *sêma* of the scar as proof (23.73).[44] Then we reach the heart of the sequence, as Penelope responds to Telemachos' complaint about her obstinacy that she and Odysseus share *sêmata* that are "hidden" (*kekrummena*) to others, known only to themselves (23.110). The ruse involving the olive-tree bed follows, with Penelope suggesting that the immovable bed be transplanted outside her chamber, and Odysseus announcing that there is a great *sêma* built into the bed (23.188) and that he will now expound it (23.202)—a signal that effectively restores his identity as no other signal could, mimicking the strategy of traditional referentiality at the same time that it undeniably establishes the completion of his *nostos*, or return. Notice that the relationship between bed and identity, between sign and meaning, is essentially arbitrary: the bed need not signify Odysseus' return, but tradition certifies that it does.[45] What is more, like all *sêmata* the olive-tree bed provides a unique pathway to knowledge outside the immediate moment. Penelope says as much when, having recognized the *sêmata* (23.206), she stipulates their necessary *tradi-*

tional meaning (23.225): she is persuaded that Odysseus is home, and the *nostos* has reached its climax. Odysseus then tells her of Teiresias' prophetic *sêma* (23.273) before the scar and its recognition by Laertes (24.329, 346) bring to a close this dense, reverberative sequence of signs.

In order to gain a sense of the more immediate narrative progression as against its punctuation by recurrent signals, let us now narrow the focus to the skein of *sêmata* between lines 69 and 230 of Book 23. There are in fact six clustered instances in the space of about 160 lines, far the highest concentration anywhere in Homer, and they reveal much about the deepest concerns of the poem as the *Odyssey* draws toward what the ancient critics called its *telos*, or "fulfillment." [46]

First, we encounter Eurykleia chastising her mistress Penelope for refusing to believe her report of the slaughter and Odysseus' homecoming (70–79):

"τέκνον ἐμόν, ποῖόν σε ἔπος φύγεν ἕρκος ὀδόντων,   70
ἣ πόσιν ἔνδον ἐόντα παρ' ἐσχάρῃ οὔ ποτ' ἔφησθα
οἴκαδ' ἐλεύσεσθαι· θυμὸς δέ τοι αἰὲν ἄπιστος.
ἀλλ' ἄγε τοι καὶ σῆμα ἀριφραδὲς ἄλλο τι εἴπω·
οὐλήν, τήν ποτέ μιν σῦς ἤλασε λευκῷ ὀδόντι,
τὴν ἀπονίζουσα φρασάμην, ἔθελον δὲ σοὶ αὐτῇ   75
εἰπέμεν· ἀλλά με κεῖνος ἑλὼν ἐπὶ μάστακα χερσὶν
οὐκ ἔα εἰπέμεναι πολυκερδείῃσι νόοιο.
ἀλλ' ἕπευ· αὐτὰρ ἐγὼν ἐμέθεν περιδώσομαι αὐτῆς,
αἴ κέν σ' ἐξαπάφω, κτεῖναί μ' οἰκτίστῳ ὀλέθρῳ."

"My child, what sort of word escaped your teeth's barrier?   70
Though your husband were here beside the hearth, you would never
say he would come home. Your heart was always mistrustful.
But here is another *sêma* that is very clear. I will tell you.
That scar, which once the boar with his white teeth inflicted,
I recognized it while I was washing his feet, and I wanted   75
to tell you about it, but he stopped my mouth with his hands, would not
let me speak, for his mind sought every advantage. Come then,
follow me, and I will hazard my life upon it.
Kill me by the most pitiful death, if I am deceiving you."

Eurykleia's traditional rhetoric lies mostly below the textual surface in this rejoinder to Penelope's intransigence. She opens the speech with a highly resonant question: namely, "What sort of word escaped your teeth's barrier?" This query appears six times in the *Odyssey*, indexing a situation in which an older, wiser, or otherwise more authoritative person chastises another for not knowing better, for not trusting him or her. Additionally, the phrase imputes a rashness on the part of the person addressed, suggesting that something needs to be set right.[47] It is the same signal with which Zeus begins his promise to help the wanderer by chastising Odysseus' champion Athena (1.64; doubled at 5.22); Athena as pseudo-Mentor scolds Telemachos for distrusting the gods' power to intervene (3.230); Eurykleia chides her still disguised master himself for thinking she would not be strong enough to conceal his identity (19.492); and Antinoos derides the minor suitor Leodes for suggesting they stop their attempts to string the bow (21.168).[48] These quite separate moments are slotted by the "teeth's barrier" exclamation, which provides an implicit traditional context in which to place a variety of different moments. Like other reverberative phrases in the Homeric register, it furnishes a guide for negotiation of the narrative landscape. Reading behind this sign helps us to read between the signs.

Another cue—this one marked by actually calling it a *sêma*—is in fact the famous scar (*oulê*) that unambiguously identifies Odysseus. Like other such signs, it reaches beyond the present, immediate situation to an event that precedes the period covered by our *Odyssey*; that is, its meaning lies not in the mere fact of the scar but in its unique testimony, as verified by implicit referral to the prior episode of the young Odysseus' wounding by the boar. The sign thus keys an emergent reality—namely, that this is indeed the returned hero—and it is a reality that cannot be gainsaid.[49] The bridge between the *oulê* and the man is as strong and durable as the relation between any *sêma* and its traditional referent. We may observe that in warning Penelope as she does, Eurykleia is both employing and citing an absolutely fundamental trope of Homeric representation. She pinpoints the scar, which has an obvious traditional referent; and she terms it a *sêma*, to the traditional force and meaning of which there can be no appeal. Together with the "teeth's barrier" phrase, this second key lends enormous power and authority to what the old nurse says, all of the power and authority that conventionally reside in the only partially textualized network of tradition.

A short while after this episode Penelope must face another rebuke of her trademark obstinacy, this time from her son Telemachos, who complains of her "heart harder than stone" (103). She responds that she is much at a loss to determine what to do, and perhaps we cannot blame her for that confusion, but she closes her speech to Telemachos by assuring him that she and Odysseus have *sêmata* (110) hidden from others, known only to the two of them. In avowing the existence of these signs, Penelope is of course pointing toward the olive-tree bed, but she also provides a working definition of a *sêma* in the process. To all others, the bed will be simply a bed: its nominal identity as a functional human artifact, nothing more and nothing less, will exhaust its meaning. But to those "in the know," it also harbors an institutionalized signification as the uniquely fashioned union of nature and culture to which only Penelope, Odysseus, and a single serving-maid are privy. These three alone can expand the tangible item to an intangible reality; they alone can project traditional referentiality from the concreteness of the *sêma*. They alone are the competent audience versed in the special implications of the bed, and therefore able to "read" it. It is with some confidence, then, that Penelope assures her son that she has the means to identify her husband quite unequivocally, for, with the sole exception of the serving-maid (and of course the audience or readership fluent in Homeric "sign-language"), she and Odysseus are in effect the only fit audience for this particular *sêma*.[50]

The test of the bed thus becomes a test of the poetic efficacy of the traditional register, as Penelope begins the gambit with an intentional and provocative *mis*reading: she asks the old nurse to make up Odysseus' own bed outside their chamber. When Odysseus objects, it is with the fervor of one who possesses disqualifying evidence, that is, one who calls into question Penelope's abrogation of traditional referentiality. Only if the bed has been torn from its living trunk, he complains, could it be moved from its rooted place—and, we may add, from its rooted signification. In explaining how he created the bed, and thereby making evident its implied meaning, he begins by announcing that there is a great *sêma* built into the bed (188) that will have prevented any man from dislocating it. Just like all of Homer's traditional signs, the permanence of its referentiality cannot be compromised except by the most radical of misconstruals—severing the link between sign and signification.

Via the familiar Homeric strategy of ring composition, Odysseus frames his account of the bed's making with the phrase that stands as the epigraph to this chapter: "Thus I expound to you this *sêma*" ("*houtô toi tode sêma piphauskomai*," 23.202). In both of these framing instances, the sign points away from the immediacy of the here and now and toward a time and set of actions outside the scope of our *Odyssey*. It recalls an origin, a source of meaning that lies far beyond the reach of explicit textual signification. This same sign also serves as the key that unlocks an emergent event, the climactic and unifying event of Odysseus' long-awaited apotheosis toward which the epic has been working for more than twenty-two books. *Sêma* marks this particular moment, placing it against the backdrop of an implied reality, so that the audience is set, as Slatkin puts it, "the apparently paradoxical task of listening for what is unspoken" (1991: xvi). In short, Odysseus here refutes the literal in favor of the immanent, affirming both his own emergent identity and the overall strategy of traditional referentiality.[51] Penelope, it turns out, was absolutely right: by a *sêma* she shall know him.

And so she does. The poet tells us that this final stage in her process of recognition, marked as well by an indexical formulaic description ("and the knees and the heart within her went slack"), stems directly and unambiguously from Odysseus' explication of the *sêmata* (23.205–6). As before with the "teeth's barrier" phrase, a key signal meshes harmoniously with a *sêma* to enrich our sense of the unfolding drama. Surveying the eight additional occurrences of knees and hearts being loosed provides a map for reading all of the different situations in a single general context: abject and sudden helplessness in the face of an inexorable power or event.[52] As a result, we come to realize, once again by implication and inimitable expressive economy, how deeply Penelope is affected, how her stubborn, self-preserving refusal to believe in Odysseus' return has finally melted away. Her recognition, we are told, and told traditionally, is both disabling and enabling—the slackness phrase indicates by convention its overwhelming and irresistible force, while the *sêma* citation effectively re-creates Odysseus before her. She goes on to ask him not to be angry with her, explaining that she was guarding against any possible deception and invoking the example of Helen, whom she likewise exculpates through drawing a parallel to her own situation. All that remains, then, is her stipulation, again via the marked idiom, that he has convinced her by "reading" the bed sign, something no other mortal man could have done (23.225–30):

"νῦν δ', ἐπεὶ ἤδη σήματ' ἀριφραδέα κατέλεξας 225
εὐνῆς ἡμετέρης, τὴν οὐ βροτὸς ἄλλος ὀπώπει,
ἀλλ' οἶοι σύ τ' ἐγώ τε καὶ ἀμφίπολος μία μούνη,
Ἀκτορίς, ἥν μοι δῶκε πατὴρ ἔτι δεῦρο κιούσῃ,
ἢ νῶϊν εἴρυτο θύρας πυκινοῦ θαλάμοιο,
πείθεις δή μευ θυμόν, ἀπηνέα περ μάλ' ἐόντα." 230

"But now, since you have recounted clear *sêmata* 225
of our bed, which no other mortal has ever seen,
but only you and I, and there is one serving-woman,
Aktor's daughter, whom my father gave me when I came here,
who used to guard the doors for us in our well-built chamber;
so you persuade my heart, though it has been very stubborn." 230

Of *Sêmata* and Speech-Acts

Citing *sêmata* has persuaded other hearts as well. Zeus' portents, Odysseus' scar, Orion's Dog, the prophecy of the oar-become-winnowing-shovel—all of these and more constitute signs that mimic a fundamental strategy for representation throughout Homeric epic and in many other oral and oral-derived traditions: a concrete signal pointing institutionally toward a traditional network of associations. Those phenomena and objects actually named as *sêmata* have explicit definition; in these fifty-eight cases traditional referentiality is effectively stipulated with what I take as a term in the native Homeric poetics. Via the very speech-act of calling something a *sêma*, Homer and his tradition mark it as an item or event that serves as the key to an emergent reality.[53] This is why the most important quality of the inscribed signs on Bellerophon's tablet is not their written-ness but their characterization as *sêmata*.[54] As noted earlier, that death warrant bears meaning not because of its mysterious technology of alphabetic letters or ideographs or other visual ciphers (so comfortably but misleadingly parallel to our own primary communications technology), but because it engages the same technology and expressive force as do all of the other Homeric *sêmata*. Moreover, and not incidentally, all of those other Homeric signs have nothing whatsoever to do with writing, tablets, or textual representation. From our modern point of view, the fact of inscription may seem to be the crucial quality, but from Homer's perspective it is the act of identifying the inscription as traditional signs—and thus slotting it along with Zeus' omens, the olive-tree bed, and more—that makes it so powerful and insistent. Instead of trying to read the tablet's message as written encoding, then, we should be focusing on its unique "semantics." *Sêma* as speech-act serves to align divergent items and events along the unifying axis of traditional referentiality.

This same linchpin effect is also an enabling characteristic of the Homeric register at large. At every level, from mere adoption of the specialized language through the specific "words" of phraseology and narrative pattern, the signs provide much more than a way to get the compositional job done. Like the *sêmata* on Bellerophon's tablet, they are linked by traditional usage to a resonant background of implied meaning. Once textualized, Homeric speech-acts can only too easily lose their directive force, and what were once evocative signals can become clichés disparaged by critics from the ancient world to the present day. We worry over why the sea is "wine-dark" in a particular episode, or why Homer featured Hera's white arms on a given occasion, or why Achilleus is so enraged when Priam initially refuses to be seated in *Iliad* 24. But if we understand these commonplaces as the kinetic signals that they are, then we know that description and characterization are economically managed via linchpin formulaic phrases, and that Achilleus' rage stems quite logically from Priam's threat to disrupt the idiomatic progression from mourning through anointment to feast and finally to the mediation they both seek.[55] This is the kind of representational power inherent in Homer's traditional signs. Far from being an obstacle to be overcome, they collectively offer an irreplaceable expressive instrument, constituting not a dilution but an enhancement of the referential power of language. Once again, oral traditions work like languages, only more so.[56]

Indeed, one could say with justice that the Homeric register consists not of building blocks but of speech-acts that foster highly focused expression of all kinds. Intone the formulas, instance the typical scenes, and, as long as the audience or reader is reasonably fluent in the register, you accomplish far more than a superficially coherent narrative or metrically acceptable lines. Singular moments are implicitly framed as familiar situations, as when sixteen quite different passages in the *Iliad* and *Odyssey* are all subtly contextualized by the "silently to silence" line.[57] By virtue of its connection to the larger traditional paradigm, the Ithakan feast in *Odyssey* 1 plays off the embarrassment of the host Telemachos and the rude, intemperate behavior of the suitors against the ideal of feasting with its usual expectations of enhanced social harmony. In each of these instances, and myriad more, traditional referentiality constitutes a stage or background for the individual and unique. Homeric poetics thus offers the best of both worlds, placing the unparalleled action or event within an implicit context, shortchanging neither the "literary" individuality of Homer nor the traditional resonance of the epic register. Our reception of the poems, and of all verbal art that employs a similar poetics, must therefore be attentive to both dimensions. We must read both behind and between the signs.

Conclusion

In positing a centuries-old oral tradition as his answer to the Homeric Question, Milman Parry's strongest argument was also his simplest point: the formulaic language he analyzed was so developed and complex, so systemic, that no single individual could ever have invented it. Much of this chapter builds on that argument. I suggest that Homer's signs—both the explicitly labeled *sêmata* and the entire Homeric register—are so richly endowed with traditional referentiality that they could not be the creation of any single poet, no matter how gifted. No one person invents an entire language; no one person individually conceives a way of speaking, an idiom of speech-acts, from nothing. Poets must always use the traditional language and speech-acts in an idiosyncratic fashion, to be sure, inevitably putting a personal stamp on their performances or texts, but the register must remain the joint property of all singers in the tradition (with audiences and readers as co-owners) or lose its function as an expressive medium. Indeed, as we shall see by reference to South Slavic oral epic over the following three chapters, the strength and persistence of a living oral traditional register derive precisely from its being shared, over time and place, among many poets and many audiences as a functional, dedicated

language. Its value as a communicative medium stems not from its whole-
sale originality but from its ability to serve as a precise, malleable, and ele-
gant vehicle for a variety of poems, poets, and performances. Homer's un-
deniable creativity is rooted in traditional referentiality; they cannot be
separated.[58]

In the end, I would certainly agree with Parry and many of his follow-
ers that the Homeric register is extraordinarily useful, but not solely or
even principally for the reasons he gave. Whereas many have described
the utility of ready-made diction and narrative machinery, restricting their
attention to *compositional* values, I emphasize the inimitable usefulness of
the signs as speech-acts, as signals that point toward emergent realities, as
keys that unlock the word-hoard of traditional associations. This is the
perspective from *reception*, a perspective that pays equal attention to what
lies behind and between Homer's signs. In the end, it is the virtually
proverbial power of *sêmata* that makes them so valuable to both the com-
posing poet and the receiving audience or reader. Homer's "words" work
not *metri causa* but *artis causa*.

In the three chapters that follow we will be turning our attention to a
comparative study of the South Slavic Moslem epic singers, or *guslari*, the
oral poets who have often been summoned as a parallel to Homer. Our
concern will be to examine four fundamental issues. After considering the
viability of the analogy between the two traditions and the *guslaris'* own
views on themselves and their craft (Chapter 2), we will compare the spe-
cialized registers of the two epic poetries (Chapter 3) and explore the
traditional referentiality of the South Slavic singers' "way of speaking"
(Chapter 4). Throughout the exposition we will be seeking a fair, straight-
forward evaluation that highlights important similarities between Homer
and the *guslar* but also gives due attention to their inevitable differences.

PART II

HOMERIC AND SOUTH SLAVIC EPIC

2

HOMER AND THE
SOUTH SLAVIC *GUSLAR*
The Analogy and the Singers

On je pjevač bio što ga nije bilo u Hercegovini.
He was a singer like no other in Hercegovina.
—Ibro Bašić on Isak

ἐξ ἀρχῆς καθ' Ὅμηρον ἐπεὶ μεμαθήκασι πάντες,
Since from the beginning all have learned according to Homer,
—Xenophanes of Colophon on Homer

For us Homer lives only in manuscripts and fragments of papyrus. We cannot record his songs, interview his colleagues or pupils, or even "page through" a sound archive of his or peer poets' disembodied performances. Thus, however much scholars may be able to derive analytically about the oral tradition in which those textual remnants are rooted, there has long been a need to consult a living witness, one who can testify firsthand about the real-life workings of this unfamiliar technology of communication. It was for this reason that Milman Parry and Albert Lord first journeyed to the former Yugoslavia, in an attempt to test Parry's *textual* theories about Homeric oral tradition in the living laboratory of South Slavic *oral* epic, to learn about the *aoidos* through direct study of the *guslar*.[1] From that pioneering effort has emerged a comparative field of vast proportions, affecting scores of cultures all over the world and throughout history, and shedding new light on long-standing problems of genesis, transmission, structure, and interpretation.[2] At the same time, there have also been rea-

sonable objections raised—most fundamentally to the very applicability
of the "Yugoslav analogy" itself, and therefore to all that stems from it.[3]

Here and in the following two chapters we seek to embrace not just one
but both sides of the argument by carefully considering what the analogy
can—and also what it cannot—tell us about Homer's and his tradition's
epics. To put the matter as directly as possible, we shall be asking: *Is South
Slavic epic a useful, apposite comparison for Homer?* And, perhaps not sur-
prisingly, the answer will necessarily be mixed: in some ways the compar-
ison is fruitful; in some ways it is less helpful. In other words, the major
goal of these three chapters is to move past the oversimplification of yes or
no, right or wrong, all or nothing, to the kind of reasonable calibration and
balanced explanation that will support the weight of a serious inquiry into
Homer's traditional art.

Toward that end let us proceed in two steps in the present chapter. The
first section, "Proposals and Challenges," will briefly review the salient
history of the South Slavic analogy to this point, focusing on a range of of-
ten unexamined assumptions, both those that inform the comparative vi-
sion and those that underlie the major objections to the method. On close
scrutiny certain of these assumptions will prove defensible and produc-
tive, others questionable or even misleading. The second section, "What
the *Guslari* Say," will begin making the case for a balanced, suitably cali-
brated comparison by addressing some of the most obvious and pressing
issues from an "inside" perspective. We will examine what the singers
themselves have to say about their art of traditional verse-making, both
within the poems and in conversations they had with Parry and Lord's na-
tive assistant Nikola Vujnović, himself also a *guslar*. This discussion will
include treatment of the "legendary singer," variously called Hasan Ćoso,
Isak, Ćor Huso, and by other names, who in many respects offers a sug-
gestive comparison for Homer.

In the following two chapters we will move from the singers to their
songs and the traditional register in which they are performed. Chapter 3
will test the real linguistic and structural similarities between the Homeric
and South Slavic "ways of speaking" in terms of formulaic structure, en-
jambement, metrical irregularities, dialect, and archaism. It will also in-
quire whether the compositional units of typical scene and story-pattern
translate well from one tradition to the other. Chapter 4 will address what
is finally the most important challenge for both immediate and compara-
tive purposes—traditional referentiality. We will be posing the "So what?"
question: namely, what bearing do these compositional facts have on the
reception of South Slavic epic, on the *guslar*'s traditional art?

An important caveat must precede our deliberations. Overgeneraliza-
tion is ever a danger in any analytical exposition, especially a comparative
analysis, but perhaps nowhere does it loom more threateningly than in a

study of the verbal arts of the former Yugoslavia. Even before the present hostilities further fragmented linguistic and cultural groups, the tangled history of the region over many centuries had translated to a forbidding complexity of ethnicities, languages, and therefore oral traditions. I will thus limit my remarks to two bodies of collected oral tradition from the South Slavic region: chiefly the Moslem epic songs recorded by Milman Parry and Albert Lord in the 1930s, by far the largest available collection of epic performances from the former Yugoslavia; and, in a supporting role, the Christian epic narratives taken down through dictation by Vuk Stefanović Karadžić and his co-workers during the first half of the nineteenth century. Since it is exclusively on the Moslem epic songs that the comparison with Homer has been based, this focus seems heuristically sound. Additionally, since research has revealed that within the larger epic dialect both regional and individual varieties exist,[4] I will further restrict the sample to songs recorded in the region of Stolac in central Hercegovina.[5] In this way we can be assured of basing our investigation on a reasonably homogeneous sample.

Proposals and Challenges

Parry and Lord were certainly not the first to suggest or even to actively explore a possible analogy between Homer and South Slavic oral epic.[6] Just as some aspects of their so-called Oral Theory were anticipated as early as the first-century Jewish apologist Flavius Josephus,[7] so numerous other scholars from the nineteenth century onward had already noticed similarities of various kinds between the ancient Greek *aoidos* and contemporary South Slavic *guslar*. Of those who truly influenced (and not just anticipated) Parry and Lord's work, two of the more important were Arnold van Gennep, whose 1909 book *La Question d'Homère* characterized the *guslar* as shuffling formulaic phrases like playing cards; and Gerhard Gesemann (1926), whose idea of a "composition-schema" was very close to the Oral Theory's notion of theme or typical scene. Most significant, however, was Matija Murko, the Slovenian philologist who actually conducted extensive fieldwork among oral epic singers in the former Yugoslavia and reported his chiefly descriptive findings in a series of publications often cited by Parry.[8] All three of these scholars explicitly connected the living oral poetry of the South Slavs with the manuscript texts of Homer; Murko went so far as to study the phenomenon of oral tradition *in situ*.

But where the Parry-Lord theory represented a clear advance over any previous comparative research was in its formulation as a thesis, with one foot firmly planted in the time-honored texts of Homer and the other just as firmly fixed in the little-known but still living epic tradition of the South Slavs. The thesis was both simple and radical: the traditional structures that Parry had so thoroughly analyzed in the *Iliad* and *Odyssey* must necessarily be linked to oral composition in performance. The proof was analogical: because Homeric diction, known only in texts, was mirrored in the unambiguously oral performances of the *guslari*, Homer must also have been an oral bard. With its double perspective of philological inquiry and anthropological fieldwork, the Oral Theory seemed to many to offer a promising explanation for numerous knotty problems in Homeric studies and, eventually, a fresh perspective on myriad other works in ancient, medieval, and modern tongues.

Such a "strong thesis" was necessary to fracture the contemporary sinecure of literary criticism, to begin to alert classicists and others to the textcentrism that they had unwittingly been practicing.[9] Only a wholesale rethinking of how such poetry was made, performed, transmitted, and appreciated—with concomitant revisions of canonical concepts like "work," "author," and "audience"—could overcome the cognitive inertia that post-Gutenberg societies have always felt in conceiving of unwritten media. Parry and Lord's proposal had the singular merit of forcing a top-to-bottom reconsideration of possibilities that scholarship had long ago foreclosed upon: Can verbal art also exist before the advent of texts? Could Homer's clichés and recurrent scenes have some purpose or meaning beyond the "anvil chorus" of their steady, predictable deployment? In retrospect, perhaps the most significant contribution made by the strong thesis—and by the rediscovery of oral tradition behind Homer—was less to answer such questions than merely to make it possible to pose them.

But the all-or-nothing approach exacted a high price as well. Forging a necessary link between expressive style and the event of oral composition in performance meant subscribing to a typology of opposites. Orality did battle against literacy across the Great Divide; texts were "proven" to be the product of oral or literate composition by tests for style. If an ancient or medieval text passed the test, it was admitted to the cadre of bardic works; if not, it was consigned to the literary canon.[10] The criteria for such analyses rested on the unproven assumption that all oral traditions—no matter the language, no matter the genre—employed the same compositional and discursive units: formulas (recurrent phrases), themes (typical scenes), and story-patterns. Of course, that assumption was originally generated on the basis of Homeric and South Slavic epic alone, more precisely on the juxtaposition of Homer and one single subgenre: the South Slavic Moslem epic. As we shall see below, this particular subgenre happened to be an excellent choice for the comparison, being in many ways parallel to (though certainly not wholly congruent with) the *Iliad* and

Odyssey. But the point remains that the Oral Theory's view of worldwide oral traditions was in effect balanced on the head of a pin.

This, then, was the inescapable irony of the strong thesis. Its claims—an orality entirely distinct and distinguishable from literacy, with universal features and archetypal expressive units—were radical enough to force a much-needed review of many of our most cherished presumptions about verbal art in general, and the *Iliad* and *Odyssey* in particular. At the same time, as a first approximation it also ran roughshod over differences that were to emerge in stark relief as the comparison moved beyond the relatively close kin of Homer and Moslem epic to the extended international family of oral traditions. By positing an alternate kind of verbal art with universal characteristics, Oral Theory both unlocked a door and left it dangerously ajar: if further research unearthed either written works with these same features or oral traditions lacking them, the entire thesis would be called into question. And that was precisely what was to happen.[11]

To some degree, this sequence of developments mimes the natural life cycle of any theory that proposes to overturn the consensus on a broad cultural issue. General, even simplistic statements must precede more finely crafted, in-depth accounts; negative reactions to initial proposals are a part of the overall process, whatever the particular field of inquiry. Nonetheless, it must also be acknowledged that many of the most immediate objections to the Oral Theory arose in specific response to the yoking together of Homeric and South Slavic epic.

Critics objected most strenuously on two grounds, leading to what we may call the "general-quality argument" and the "length and complexity argument," species of which still persist today.[12] The former position holds that the South Slavic epics cannot compare to the *Iliad* and *Odyssey* in terms of what is perceived as quality—their overall organization, fullness of expression, characterization, and so forth. Unfortunately, virtually all scholars who have rendered this rather vague but summary judgment have consulted the South Slavic works only in translation, with little or no experience of the original-language text, never mind of the performances from which those texts derive. Although they would rightly insist on a knowledge of ancient Greek as the merest prerequisite to professional academic study of Homer, these scholars do not extend the same requirement to study of the *epske pjesme* (epic songs). In my mind this fundamental shortcoming simply disqualifies vague abstractions about "general quality," which can at most refer only to the clarity or literary appeal of the English rendering.[13] And this is to say nothing of the tautology entailed in prescribing "quality" as equivalent to what one perceives as the (literary) merit of the Homeric poems. Such a parochial concept simply leaves no room for other kinds of excellence, just as it unnaturally restricts the possible range of Homer's own excellence.

The argument from length and complexity involves a multitude of related criteria. First is the more straightforward matter of sheer size: since most of the South Slavic epics, even most of the longer performances from the Moslem tradition, fall far short of the *Iliad*'s sixteen thousand or the *Odyssey*'s twelve thousand lines, can the two poetries really be responsibly compared? Could an oral tradition truly manage to produce poems of Homeric size, or were compositions of such magnitude reserved for the literate poet? Leaving aside the matter of whether the two Panhellenic epitomes that have reached us were really representative of ancient Greek epic in general,[14] we may pose parallel questions directly to the *guslar*. Two performances in 1935 by Avdo Medjedović—of *The Wedding of Smailagić Meho*, at 12,311 verses, from 5–12 July and of *Osmanbeg Delibegović and Pavičević Luka*, at 13,326 verses, from 17–20 July[15]—offer one answer, proving that songs of Homeric length could indeed be found in an unambiguously oral tradition, specifically in the South Slavic tradition.

Other answers have come from further afield—from the oral epics recorded in various parts of India and those found along the Silk Roads throughout central Asia and on into China, for example, all of which can far exceed the Homeric poems in length, exposing mere size as a hopelessly arbitrary criterion of oral or literate composition.[16] Can works of Iliadic and Odyssean proportions be fashioned by oral bards? Comparative investigations have proven beyond doubt that such enormous poems can, and indeed have been, produced orally by singers.[17] Then there is the related matter of "immanent" or "notional" epic. Performances from various regions in India and Africa, for example, illustrate how singers in certain traditions never even consider singing the "whole" epic in one sitting. Their practice is rather to perform a representative section or episode that implies the unsung entirety of the poetic tradition, a concrete part that stands for the always immanent whole. On those special occasions when an outside influence has provided an occasion for making explicit what is customarily implicit, a work of great length has sometimes resulted.[18] Can we be sure that the *Iliad* and *Odyssey* were not products of such a process?

Complexity is a much slipperier measure, a highly subjective and at heart a textual notion that privileges the individual performance-text over its tradition, the sign over its signification. Is *The Wedding of Smailagić Meho* as "complex" as the *Odyssey*? Medjedović's poem can certainly boast some memorable moments centered around timeless human quandaries: the young man Meho on the brink of adulthood and chafing at the tether of his father's intransigence; the Peisistratean comradeship between Meho and his standard-bearer Osman; the initial encounter between Meho and his eventual bride Fatima during a heroic rescue; a grand battle and resolution replete with valorous acts deserving South Slavic *kleos*; and so forth. This magisterial performance even features a long series of invitations and a muster list that rival the Catalogue of Ships and Men in Book 2 of the *Il-*

iad.[19] As for large-scale organization, Medjedović's *Smailagić Meho* follows a track well known to its most immediate audience (if not to readers from outside the culture)—namely, the Wedding Song, which by narrative recipe customarily features a boy's coming of age, rescue of a threatened young woman, and defeat of a formidable enemy force.[20] The difference is that this particular performance of the song and song-type is a tour de force. Exploring thoroughly mapped familiar territory with an even-handed combination of the singer's individual initiative and the rich implications inherent in the poetic tradition,[21] Medjedovic´ paints a well-known picture in a familiar style, but does so on his own grand tableau.

But whatever this version's merits, is it a priori fair to expect such a work, recorded as recently as 1935 from a butcher in Bijelo Polje and published only in 1973, to compete in every respect with poems that have stood as cornerstones of Western civilization for nearly three millennia? By virtue of their unique place in Western art, Homer's epics enjoy a deeply cultural complexity to which no other work can ever aspire, by definition. All of those centuries, from ancient and Byzantine times through European literature from the Renaissance to the present day, have celebrated Homer as the first poet and his poetry as the wellspring of verbal art. Even from the most committed multicultural perspective, no other work can rival the Homeric epics in what we understand as complexity and depth, simply because no other work can match their historical preeminence in Western culture.[22] Would it not be better and fairer to ask whether songs like Medjedović's *Smailagić Meho* succeed first on their own terms, within their own poetic universe, and then on a comparative level? When we do invoke this more realistic frame of reference, which unlike the extant remains of ancient Greek epic includes examples of talented, average, and lesser singers and songs, Medjedović's poem stands out as a genuinely complex and articulate expression of South Slavic heroic mythos, and an intriguing new voice in the international colloquy.[23]

One last point needs attention before leaving the arguments from "general quality" and from "length and complexity." Even if we are able to consult the *epske pjesme* in the original language, on their own terms, and against at least a modest background of other performances and *guslari*, one troubling question will always remain for the outsider. To what extent can a reader (or even a listener) from outside the culture hope to grasp what any given song *implies*? Whereas Western culture has long made Greek mythology a part of the educational fabric from childhood, and Western literature is everywhere heavy with allusions to what we take as a common heritage, the implied "superstory" behind South Slavic epics has no such resonance for most of us. Beginning at an early age, many North American and Western European readers acquire a detailed knowledge of the personality traits of Odysseus, Athena, Achilleus, and Zeus, learned through stories from the epics and elsewhere, and we enrich our every reading of the *Iliad* and *Odyssey*—and their literary descendants—by reference to that common cultural store. But we normally come equipped with no parallel experience of, for example, Djerdjelez Alija, Velagić Selim, Tale of Orašac, and their many fascinating adventures across the face of Bosnia and eastern Europe. Lacking such a resource, we are severely handicapped in the ongoing challenge of construing their personalities and exploits, and our understanding of the *epske pjesme* must suffer as a consequence. If for example we do not know that Tale of Orašac is the trickster par excellence, and yet the indispensable champion in any major battle,[24] we may take him simply as a boorish bumpkin begging alms. The South Slavic tradition may seem to lack complexity. The *guslar* may seem to nod.

This already thorny problem is exacerbated by the very medium of oral tradition. As we have seen in Chapter 1, it is in the nature of traditional oral works to signify idiomatically, to depend upon an indexed, proverbial kind of meaning that places a substantial responsibility on the audience or reader. It is not enough simply to be able to translate the *guslar*'s phrases and typical scenes literally and textually; we must be able to see beyond their surfaces to what they stand for, *pars pro toto*.[25] Beyond even a grasp of the language and culture, then, lies the challenge of learning the traditional idiom—in this case, not just the South Slavic language available in current grammars and dictionaries but the special, marked epic diction that the poet uses to such expressive advantage. Like Homer, the *guslar* has access to a special assortment of verbal signs, some of which resonate with substantial "extra" associations. If we read these signs only textually, imprisoning the singer within our lexicon, we will miss an important aspect of his artistry. Indeed, we run the risk of wholly misconstruing his poem, in which case it will be the audience and not the *guslar* who is "nodding."[26] In reference to all verbal art, but especially to oral tradition, quality and complexity are properties not simply of *composition* (the work or text as object) but equally of its *reception* (what the audience or reader is able to make of the object or experience). We must be able to read behind as well as between the signs.

To review briefly, then, the history of the South Slavic analogy began with Parry's and Lord's strong thesis, a comparative method that broke important new ground, making possible the discovery or rediscovery of oral traditions in dozens of areas as well as the very conception of another kind of verbal art.[27] In order to accomplish these worthy goals in a climate that knew only literature and texts, the thesis had to be generalized, forceful, and largely unqualified. Thus Parry and Lord linked expressive style directly to "orality," that "other" condition of human communication, basing their universalist hypothesis on empirical data from the Homeric poems and a single subgenre of South Slavic epic.

With further evidence from folklore and anthropology, and with the natural maturing of the strong thesis, the time now seems right for a "second growth." We know from firsthand observation and report that oral traditions do not always show the Oral Theory's "universal features." We know from firsthand observation and report that living oral traditions do not always segregate written and oral operations: even the very same person may engage in both.[28] Perhaps most tellingly, we know from firsthand observation and report that the "ways of speaking"—the expressive styles—linked with oral traditions can persist into texts, serving as communicative idioms in a new medium.[29] Clearly, unless we choose to ignore these realities, what is necessary is a retooling of the strong thesis, along with a reshaping of the model from a dichotomy to a spectrum wide and deep enough to contain the remarkable variety of witnesses that scholars have brought to light. Enough has already emerged to illustrate that oral traditions and their kin are vastly more heterogeneous than the literary, textual works that our histories and theoretical categories struggle to contain. Given this sobering truth, it is yet more imperative that we pursue a double aim: to fashion a model that can accommodate the formidable diversity of traditional oral forms at the same time that it promotes the study of each on its own terms. The challenge will be to accommodate both the poetics of the one and the poetics of the many. Let us begin by consulting the singers themselves.

What the *Guslari* Say

Information about South Slavic singers and oral epic performances can be divided into two types: internal or poetic evidence, from within the poems; and external or ethnographic evidence, from conversations recorded during fieldwork. It is Albert Lord's estimable legacy that we have a great deal of the applicable information already in hand. We know about the Moslem singers' nonprofessional status in modern times,[30] the content and extent of their repertoires, the learning process they typically underwent, the physical and social circumstances of their performances, and so forth. Lord's descriptions, together with the continuing work of Stephen Erdely and others, have helped to conceptualize the *guslar* as both an individual teller of tales and a member of a centuries-long, then-living epic tradition, and by analogy have aided us in imagining how Homer and his tradition could have managed to compose and transmit epics like the *Iliad* and *Odyssey* over generations without the aid of writing.[31]

The present discussion will concentrate on two points of comparison, one internal and one external. Within the South Slavic poems I will consider the idealized images of the *guslar* and his performance that emerge from a brief survey of selected songs, chiefly from the region of Stolac. These passages do not constitute ethnographically reliable observations, of course, but they do illustrate ways of thinking about oral epic that are "inscribed" in the ongoing "volume" of tradition, available to and consulted by all of the singers in one form or another. Outside the poems I will examine the Stolac singers' conversations in order to shed light on the "legendary *guslar*," a bard of remarkable achievement who is best understood not as the real-life individual his descendants claim he is, but as an anthropomorphization of the epic tradition. In so doing I will suggest that this larger-than-life figure may provide a parallel for Homer, with both figures effectively serving as *sêmata* for their implied traditions.

Internal Evidence: The Proems

The Stolac songs contain no extended portraits of composing bards to match those in *Odyssey* 1 and 8. There is no Phemios, no Demodokos, to be found in these glorious tales from the days of the Ottoman Empire. The major internal evidence about singers, performance, and audience stems rather from proems, or *pripjevi*, much like the prologues to the Homeric epics but with two important differences.[32] The attested *pripjevi* are naturally much more numerous than the two prologues that survive from ancient Greek epic tradition, and they also generally prove denser with clues about the general assumptions behind the performance to come. By highlighting some recurrent features in these proems, we can gain considerable insight into the dynamics of epic performance from an insider's perspective, and in the process provide a suggestive comparison for Homer.

For example, in virtually all cases the Stolac *guslari*—and singers from other regions as well—speak of the activity of song-making as something undertaken not by "I" but rather by "we." Although the performer may appear to be solely responsible, his introduction to the performance explicitly recognizes its collective, traditional nature in a series of first person plural verbs. Here is an example from one of Ibro Bašić's sung versions of *Alagić Alija and Velagić Selim* (6597. 5–9 [start #2]):[33]

A po tome, djeco moja draga,	Then in turn, my dear children,
Ako *mogli* i ako *umjeli*,	If *we can* and if *we know how*,
Da *rečemo* pa junačku pjesmu	Let *us tell* then a heroic song
Od staroga vakta i zemana;	From that olden period and time;
Davno bilo, sad se spominjalo.	Long ago it was, now it is being remembered.

Construing the process traditionally, Bašić conceives of the song as something *we* tell to the best of *our* ability.[34] He emphasizes the group nature of

.rformance with the vocative phrase *djeco moja draga* ("my dear chil-
‿   ), one of many such formulaic cues singers employ to address their
audiences, real or implied. We may compare this collective notion with the
last line of Homer's address to the Muse in the *Odyssey* (1.10): "Of such
things, from somewhere, O goddess daughter of Zeus, speak also *to us*"
(τῶν ἁμόθεν γε, θεά, θύγατερ Διός, εἰπὲ καὶ ἡμῖν). Like the *guslar*, the *aoidos*
asks that the stories he has just briefly sketched be spoken "also to us," that
is, to the poet and his audience. And where, or better when, do South
Slavic songs or their events originate? Bašić and other *guslari* consistently
project the songs and their events into the deep past, making their present
performance a kind of reenactment or reincarnation.[35] "Long ago it was,"
says Bašić here, echoing many of his peers in a favorite formula, and "now
it is being remembered."

The performance arena, always at its core a virtual site, moves both geo-
graphically and chronologically. Just as the present performance is per-
ceived as only the latest in a long and continuing series of enactments
through historical time, so the singers also envisage it as only one among
many such present-day events in different places. Alongside the vertical,
diachronic pluralism, in other words, they assume a horizontal, synchronic
pluralism. This and other features characterize a *pripjev* sung by Salih
Ugljanin from the Novi Pazar district (*SCHS*, vol. 2, no. 1: lines 6–10):

Sad po tome, moja braćo draga,	Now in turn, my dear brothers,
Pa velimo da pesmu brojimo.	So we wish to count out a song.
Ej! Davno nekad u zemanu bilo,	Eh! Once long ago it was in time,
Davno bilo, sada pominjemo	Long ago it was, now we are remembering
Na ovome mestu i svakome.	In this place and in every other.

In addition to the singer and his most immediate audience, the "we" who
are remembering the song has here become all of the audiences who, to-
gether with an entire tradition of *guslari*, have participated in making and
remaking the song. The traditional act thus unites generations of singers
and audiences, placing the emergent event—what is occurring here and
now—against an expansive and resonant background. In a sense, then,
any one performance stands *pars pro toto* for the tradition as a whole, with
the *pripjev* serving as the first step in invoking that referential context. In
terms of our discussion in the opening chapter, any one performance
stands as a *sêma* for the epic tradition.

Even within that broad context, Ugljanin's use of the verb *brojiti* ("to
count, enumerate") for the act of epic singing may at first seem curious, but
it is actually quite revelatory of the insider's point of view. Generations of
scholars have commented on the additive, paratactic nature of the Ho-
meric and the South Slavic poems, usually focusing on the poet's diction:

colon by colon, line by line, scene by scene, the singer of tales has been characterized as making his verse incrementally.[36] Now we have a clue from inside the tradition that the poetry is indeed being composed "by the numbers," as the *guslar* describes the expressive strategy of "counting out" a song. This embedded notion of increments, whether at the level of phraseology, narrative scenes, or story-patterns, will be important for our consideration of the South Slavic singer's special poetic dialect in the following chapter.

The proems also testify that the act of remembering or enactment is a central and natural part of human culture and society, and they do so by juxtaposing proverbial, quotidian truths to the act of epic song-making. In the *pripjev* to the same performance of *Alagić Alija and Velagić Selim* examined above, the Stolac singer Bašić prefaces his exhortation to his "dear children" in this way (*6597.1–4* [start #2]):

Aj! Teško junaku ne pijući piva,	Ay! It's hard for a hero not to have a drink,
Mladu momku ne ljubeć' djevojku,	For a young man not to kiss a maiden,
A i nožu u nejakoj ruci,	And for a knife in a weak hand,
A i pušci u strašivoj ruci.	And for a rifle in a timid hand.

On the basis of the momentum generated by appealing to such obvious cultural verities, many of them recurrently illustrated in the very heroic songs introduced by these stylized *pripjevi*, the *guslar* stresses the integral role of epic singing against the backdrop of social traffic as a whole. Epic performance is hardly construed as an unusual or singular event: like the collective "we" and the historical and geographical ubiquity of the songs, these proverbs urge the pluralism and ongoingness of performance, portraying it as a creative act shared by many people over different times and places in a continuing series of realizations.

A final *pripjev*, this one by the Stolac *guslar* Salko Morić from a sung version of *Hrnjičić Omer Rescues His Father and Uncle* (*892.1–12*), will illustrate a few additional dimensions of the singer's perspective on his art. In this passage Morić addresses not Homer's inspiring, all-knowledgeable Muse but rather the South Slavic bard's most immediate partner in performance, the *gusle* he is playing.[37] Then, in an interesting parallel to the invocation to the Catalogue of Ships and Men in *Iliad* 2,[38] he questions whether he has the vocal stamina to undertake successfully the physically demanding feat of epic performance:

Oj! Tanke gusle, moja davorijo,	Oj! O slender *gusle*, O my harmony,
Jesam li ja vama govorijo?	Did I speak to you?
Vi guslite, ja ću zapjevati,	You do the playing, I'll begin singing,
Ako mog'o i ako umijo	If I can and if I know how
I ako me grlo poslužilo;	And if my throat serves me; 5
Čini mi se poslužit' me neće,	But it appears it will not serve me,

Jer je moje grlo zagorilo—	Because my throat is on fire—
Pijuć' vino, kunijuć' se krivo,	Drinking wine, swearing falsely,
Hakajući, konje dekajući.	Yelling "ho!" and "git!" at horses.[39]
Vid' po tome da pjesmu reknemo,	Look, in turn let's tell a song, 10
Što je prije bilo u zemanu,	What happened before in time,
Šta su stari radili junaci.	What the ancient heroes did.

Just as Homer describes the enormity of his task by asserting that not even ten tongues, ten mouths, an unbreakable voice, and a heart of brass will suffice unless he has the Muses' help (2.488–92), so Morić seems to doubt his throat's capacity to hold up for the duration of the song.[40] The *guslar's* worry is of course proverbial and traditional, a *sêma* that helps to set the stage for his narrative, and suggests that some similar motivation may have been at the root of Homer's rhetorical induction to the Iliadic Catalogue.

These proverbial moments from the Stolac *pripjevi* provide an insider's perspective on one of the knottiest problems in Homeric studies, namely, the relationship between the poet and his tradition. From the insistence on "we" and "us" to the retrojection of the songs and their events into a deep and common cultural past, the singers conventionally describe the creative act of epic verse-making as a joint enterprise that is replicated again and again across a broad expanse of different times and places. Like other *guslari* each will perform the song, and like other audiences this particular group will listen and participate. Note that such a symbiotic relationship exclusively privileges neither the individual nor the tradition. In fact, these recurrent signals in the proems do just the opposite: they mandate a cooperative dynamic, a situation very much in line with the interactive model of individual poet and traditional referentiality introduced in Chapter 1. Additionally, for the Stolac singers it appears that remembering and enactment are the same process, a composite act integral enough to social life to deserve comparison with courtship and expectable feats of bravery. What is more, that performance can be idiomatically keyed—the communicative channel opened—by emphasizing the difficulty of the undertaking.[41] Just as the *pripjev* is itself a signal that a certain kind of event is about to take place, fulfilling its function as the first recognizable feature on a map for the South Slavic *oimê* or "pathway" that the singer and audience will be treading together, so each of these smaller *sêmata* play a contributory role in that overall generic function. And all of them point toward the same basic principle: that tradition and individual cannot be separated, that they function as partners in the making and remaking of South Slavic epic.

External Evidence: The Legendary Singer

Conversations with the Stolac singers, conducted by Parry and Lord's native assistant Nikola Vujnović, offer another perspective on the interplay of individual and tradition by illuminating a proverbial figure who embodies that tension. On the South Slavic side this figure, known by many different names, amounts to a celebrated master *guslar*, a singer so hyperbolically accomplished and revered that he can only be the stuff of legend. Nonetheless, even though they usually denied ever having encountered this paragon themselves (he was too old, or he lived somewhere else, or he was always traveling), the real-life singers who described his exploits absolutely insisted that he was a real person. Furthermore, he was universally cited as without doubt or qualification the most prominent forebear in their personal bardic lineages. In fact, since they had no information whatsoever about the singers preceding him, this figure assumed the role of "first ancestor," in effect the father of the ongoing genealogy of epic singers that led to them.

In what follows I interpret this legendary singer as an anthropomorphization of what we name by the abstraction "tradition," as a representational strategy that allowed *guslari* to talk about what they and their peers jointly inherited and continued to practice. For such a purpose the apparent conflict between reality and legend actually proves functional, in that it images the dyad of individual and tradition by portraying the collective inheritance as an ancestral master bard whom in most cases they never met. This strategy places the legendary singer just beyond the reach of historical and geographical fact, in a liminal area comfortably unconstrained by the limits that reality places on each actual *guslar* and his activities. Just as every performance draws meaning from the larger poetic tradition that it necessarily implies, so each individual singer defines himself by claiming professional descent from the great bard. Both performance and singer become instances of tradition; they become *sêmata*.

I also suggest that the circumstantial facts of the Homeric case point toward a similar conclusion, that is, that "Homer" may be more an eponym than a name, that it may designate the tradition of ancient Greek epic poetry by construing it as a single, supremely gifted individual.[42] This perspective resolves the otherwise frustrating discrepancies of "fact" among even the earliest of ancient testimonies on Homer by explaining contradictory biographical details and attributions as the natural outgrowth of a figure who lives on the cusp of real-life bardic practice and the alternate reality of legend. For how can the legendary singer serve his various constituencies, all of whom claim him as a famous and legitimizing forebear, except through his multiformity and ubiquity? If this is the case, one can easily see how the imposition of a modern model of authorship—with all of its built-in assumptions about author, work, audience, and the individual's relationship to a solely textual tradition—has impeded our understanding not simply of who Homer was, but also of the fundamental nature of his art.

South Slavic Epic

As they worked their way through the former Yugoslavia recording what was eventually to amount to a "half-ton of epic,"[43] Milman Parry and Albert Lord sought to provide realistic background for the South Slavic oral performances they were engaged in studying. An important dimension of their efforts at contextualization, rare among fieldworkers during the first third of this century, consisted of carefully planned and wide-ranging conversations conducted by their assistant Nikola Vujnović with most of the *guslari*. As a singer himself, Vujnović commanded an authority and offered a kind of credibility no scholar could match. Moreover, because his questions were designed and monitored by Parry, they had the added advantage of sustained pertinence to the task at hand—understanding the art of the *guslar* and its possible relationship to the Homeric poems.

In the region of Stolac in central Hercegovina, historically the first of the six districts in which they made extensive field recordings, Parry and Lord collected epic songs from twenty-seven different singers. Of these, three emerged as especially prominent because of the substantial size and relative quality of their repertoires of Moslem songs—Ibro Bašić, Halil Bajgorić, and Mujo Kukuruzović.[44] All three of them participated in lengthy conversations with Vujnović, covering such matters as personal data (home village, occupation, family and individual history), the process of learning to compose epic, repertoires with sources for each song, the nature of the "word" as a compositional and expressive unit in epic poetry, and numerous specific questions about the sung and recited performances and dictated texts that Parry and Lord had already recorded.[45]

Prominent among the skein of topics they covered was a striking and memorable figure: a bard of great achievement and consummate reputation, a *guslar* whom each man valued far above any other singer. Ibro Bašić called him Isak, as did Mujo Kukuruzović; Halil Bajgorić referred to him as Hasan Ćoso. But whatever name was assigned to this figure—let us call him the *Guslar*—he was clearly recognizable by his highly unusual, even unique actions and attributes, many of them legendary in character, and by his dual identity as palpable fiction and historical fact.

Most obvious among the *Guslar's* telltale characteristics were his extremely advanced age and his chronological placement at the origin of the singer's own bardic lineage. He was not merely venerable; he was customarily quite ancient, having lived as many as 120 years or more. Kukuruzović was the most forthcoming about the details of Isak's superficial decrepitude, noting that in his final years the toothless singer was unable even to direct his own horse. Nor at that point could he play or for that matter hear the one-stringed, lutelike *gusle* that was his conventional accompaniment in earlier days. But these crippling handicaps were, it turns out, only apparent, since Kukuruzović's Isak was beloved enough to merit a companion to lead his horse for him, and resourceful enough to learn to perform without the instrument—an unheard-of practice in the Moslem tradition before outsiders began to encourage oral dictation.[46] Along with emphasizing the *Guslar*'s sheer age, customarily in terms that defy ordinary human biology, all three Stolac singers thrust him at least two generations back in history, well beyond their fathers' time and out of the reach of their personal experience, to the very beginning of their genealogies as singers. Thus they were never actually able to meet Isak or Hasan Ćoso, they explain, and could report on his remarkable accomplishments only at second hand.[47]

Unlike all other singers in their experience, whose breadwinning occupations of farmer, butcher, blacksmith, and the like required most of their attention and energy, the *Guslar* earned his modest living entirely through the performance of epic. As Bašić tersely put it, "To je njegov zanat bijo" ("[Singing] was his profession"). Indeed, all three bards testify, this master singer's unparalleled excellence qualified him to perform in the courts of Ottoman beys and pashas, an anachronistic privilege and honor granted to no one else.[48] Paid more often in kind than with negotiable currency, the *Guslar* lived without much in the way of material goods, essentially as a pauper. In pursuit of his craft and in response to invitations from far and wide, Hasan Ćoso traveled "everywhere throughout the world," says Bajgorić; "he never dug or plowed, never rode a horse, but always carried a rifle and a few staples on a pack-animal. Traveling lightly, he enjoyed his playing," and was very seldom to be found in his home village, which each singer located at an entirely different actual site.

Nor was Hasan Ćoso or Isak the least bit ordinary in his capacity for epic singing. The *Guslar* conventionally boasted an enormous repertoire, fifty songs and up, and, more significantly, his songs were regarded by the Stolac *guslari* as the finest that had come down to them. That is, while each of the three also cited "real" bards—most often fathers and uncles—as teachers or most immediate sources for specific tales, they were unanimous in crediting the *Guslar* as the ultimate source for the best songs they knew. Additionally, Hasan Ćoso and Isak were understood as extraordinarily seminal in their influence, transmitting the choicest of epic tales not just to the teachers of these three Stolac singers and their regional colleagues but, against all apparent practice, to poets in other, often far-flung districts as well.[49] In range as well as depth of influence the *Guslar* was absolutely unique.

But what stamps this seminal figure as unmistakably a creature of legend rather than history, to be sought in tradition rather than field ethnography, is the performance of one or more extraordinary feats during what each singer carefully portrays as a "real" lifetime. For Bajgorić this was Hasan Ćoso's miraculous ability to leap twelve paces at the advanced age of 101, an Olympian accomplishment that he situates within the "so they say" (*kako pričaju*) frame used throughout the conversations to appeal to an unidentified authority and thus avoid the claim of eyewitness reportage. Like so many other aspects of his characterization, this duality of extreme age and remarkable agility represents the *Guslar* as a contradiction in terms, an icon who embodies contrary roles or designs. Professional singer welcome at the courts of beys and pashas, and yet the simplest of paupers with barely enough means to support his itinerant existence, this oxymoronic figure lives outside the quotidian world inhabited by his bardic progeny.

Indeed, his singing skills are powerful enough that he can override the usual physical limitations to which *guslari* are subject, and on occasion even shift the prevailing axis of cultural and religious practice. Kukuruzović's Isak, for example, once sang for six straight hours without putting down the *gusle*,[50] a superhuman feat when measured against reality: in actual practice, South Slavic epic performance is so vocally demanding that singers seldom go much more than thirty minutes without a break for rest and refreshment.[51] More impressive even than this incredible bardic stamina, however, was the paradigm shift he caused at the bey of Posavina's wedding. While the *Guslar* characteristically distinguished himself by supervening ethnic and religious boundaries and performing by special invitation at wedding celebrations of all denominations, Isak, as Kukuruzović tells the story, went a sizable step further. His performance in honor of the bey proved so compelling that the sheet of fabric segregating the male and female segments of the audience was removed, and the Moslem statute requiring the separation of men and women at a wedding was temporarily suspended. It perhaps goes without saying that this amounts to an impossible, unprecedented relaxation of a religious law that also bears supreme cultural authority; precisely because it is so unlikely, it constitutes a defining action, a kind of credential that identifies this singer as the legendary *Guslar*. How powerful is the poetic tradition? Kukuruzović's Isak gives us one set of answers: powerful enough to transcend ordinary physical limitations and to "rewrite" Qu'ranic law.

Another kind of answer, and a third kind of legendary feat, is furnished by Bašić's tale of Isak and his challenge by an upstart *guslar* named Gačanin. As the story opens, Gačanin hears of the great bard Isak and is determined to seek him out in order to see who is the better singer. Traveling to Rotimlja, where Bašić (but neither Kukuruzović nor Bajgorić) situates the *Guslar*'s home, he stops at a roadside inn for coffee. There he takes the opportunity to ask directions and advice from the *kahvedžija* (coffeehouse attendant), who, though Gačanin does not suspect it, is Isak himself.[52] The attendant confirms that Isak lives in the nearby town of Rotimlja and is famed for his prowess in epic performance, and even points in the direction of the great man's residence. At this juncture Gačanin confides that he himself is also a singer of some talent, and that he has come from afar to challenge Isak to a contest. Eager to help, the attendant offers to make the introductions by bringing his customer to his own home later on to meet the celebrated bard, whom he promises in the meantime to summon personally.

Now the *kahvedžija* happens to spot Gačanin's *gusle* protruding from his pouch and innocently asks to try it out. Gačanin generously accedes, and the attendant strikes up a version of *The Wedding of Smailagić Meho*.[53] All those in the coffeehouse are immediately entranced, and refuse to allow him to stop; he thus goes on to sing not just one but an unspecified number of epic songs to an enthusiastic response. Mightily impressed, Gačanin then orders another cup of coffee and inquires from whom the attendant-turned-*guslar* might have learned the songs he has just so brilliantly performed. Upon being told "from Isak," Gačanin blanches, and has second thoughts about accompanying his host to Rotimlja and measuring himself against the paragon responsible for these remarkable songs. "I'm not going, not on your life," he tells the *kahvedžija*, "not if you heard those songs from him. I used to think there was no one better than I am, but you're better." Gačanin then beats a hasty retreat homeward, still unaware of his host's true identity but thoroughly educated about what we might from our perspective describe as the difference between a *guslar* and the *Guslar*.

So what does the legendary singer represent for Bajgorić, Bašić, and Kukuruzović? Besides furnishing an idealized source for their best songs, what function does this figure perform? For a start, consider the contradictions among the biographies ascribed to the *Guslar*. First is the variance in name and place of origin. Hasan Ćoso comes from Bajgorić's home village of Dabrica, and is said to have been born not far from Bajgorić's father's house, while according to Bašić (a native of Vranjevići in the Mostar region) Isak hails from Rotimlja, where he can still occasionally be found. Kukuruzović, on the other hand, mentions neither a birthplace nor a residence, insisting that Isak was always itinerant, and in fact the *Guslar*'s general life-pattern bears him out: for all three singers, the core of the master singer's identity is his very rootlessness or, more precisely for present purposes, his ubiquitousness. As a figure whose only true "home" is the performance arena—a place defined by the recurrent activity of singing epic rather than by conventional geography[54]—his most basic "regional" allegiance is to the site of his next performance, which shifts only on a superficial level. Small wonder, then, that he is so often remembered in terms of those performances and other memorable feats that can be retold and re-experienced as legend.

Linked to biographical diversity in name, birthplace, residence, and so forth is the *Guslar*'s unparalleled, virtually mythic stature. He was the only singer who was always paid to perform, invited to weddings of all denominations, and summoned before beys and pashas, the only one for whom singing was a true profession and sole means of support. In single-minded pursuit of his craft, undistracted by the everyday economic and ethnic concerns that affected all real-life *guslari* known to Bašić, Bajgorić, and Kukuruzović, he can be meaningfully compared to mythic luminaries like Mustajbey of the Lika, Djerdjelez Alija, Tale of Orašac, and other leading citizens of South Slavic heroic epic. Like those timeless and immortal heroes, the *Guslar* operates in a world that suspends the usual rules. Like them, he exists outside the customary social matrix of getting a living and sharing a family and community, and likewise outside any bona fide historical context that would constrain as well as define his character and accomplishments. In a sense, Hasan Ćoso / Isak lives alongside the heroes whom his descendants celebrate in epic performance, earning his own measure of South Slavic *kleos* as the "best of singers."

From this mythic ancestor stem not only the finest of songs but also the unassailable authority of a bardic primogenitor. The fact that each Stolac singer ascribes different actual songs to the *Guslar*—or even that the same singer may cite him as the source of different songs from one conversation to the next—does not discredit such attributions. For one thing, even the actual singers interviewed by Parry and Lord regularly modified their accounts of where they learned their songs, a manifestation of the impertinence of our concept of "authorship" and the primacy of the poetic tradition rather than evidence of faulty memory or sloppiness.[55] In the case of the *Guslar*, as with all aspects of traditional oral epic from phraseology through story-pattern, specific details are important only insofar as they foster the general traditional dynamic of variation within limits. The legendary figure can persist only in his multiformity—living here or there, named this or that, responsible for one set of "finest songs" or another. Unfixed by history, texts, and the feedback loop of information that they support, his Protean lack of definition serves his bardic constituency well: descendants can fashion the *Guslar*'s image differently, shaping his biography to mesh with their own life histories and experiences of epic singing.

Likewise, filtering the song-inheritance through one or more intervening generations, and thus conveniently removing the process from merely historical or ethnographic assessment, provides each *guslar*'s songs with the unmistakable sanction of legend. When a real-life *guslar* performs them, he appropriates the *Guslar* as a direct ancestor and makes himself the present-day embodiment of the greatest of all bards. In the process, individual and tradition coalesce, the tangible instance standing *pars pro toto* for the larger, intangible whole of the poetic tradition. Such a melding is possible only if each *guslar* can conceive of the master singer as a legendary figure with two distinct but complementary dimensions: he must be a named, situated, and superficially realistic individual who nonetheless has accomplished "epic" feats in singing. He must be a *guslar* with an acceptably focused, believable biography whose deeds as *Guslar* far outstrip anything one might expect of a real-life singer. He must assume the double identity of finite instance and ongoing tradition. He must, in short, serve as a *sêma*.[56]

Archaic Greek Epic

Like Hasan Ćoso and Isak, the multiform figure whom generations have called Homer seems to have occupied a liminal niche midway between the quotidian world of actual singers and performances on the one hand and the legendary sphere of epic events and the "famous deeds of men" (*klea andrôn*) on the other. The plain facts of the matter as represented in ancient sources are much discussed elsewhere,[57] so let us summarize the situation by juxtaposing two observations made by J. A. Davison on the vexed issue of the Homeric Question in antiquity. Combining both the references in which the name "Homer" is used and those in which his identity must be inferred, Davison comes to "a strong impression that for the Greeks of the period down to about 450 B.C. Homer was a real person who had lived at latest in the early seventh century and had composed a large number of narrative poems of the highest quality which were still being recited by professional rhapsodes" (1963: 235). Then, as a prelude to surveying ancient authors' and scholars' comments on Homer, he notes the disparities that arose concerning the master poet's origins (235): "By the early fifth century several different cities were already claiming to have been Homer's birthplace, and conflicting accounts of his pedigree were no doubt current."

Just how disparate the earliest biographical attestations were can be illustrated by a glance at the nine extant Lives of Homer as summarized by T. W. Allen.[58] While the Herodotean account does not cite a father, for example, the *Certamen* proposes Telemachos as one possibility, with Nestor's daughter Epikastê as one candidate for mother. Where the lineage is traced further back, the results show some consistency in the nearer generations, but Homer's ultimate ancestors vary from Apollo to Orpheus. Smyrna is a popular choice for the great bard's birthplace, winning mention in seven of the nine biographies, but we also hear frequently of Chios, Cyme, Ios, Argos, and Athens. The ancient Lives are equally at odds with one another over Homer's actual date, usually assigning him a relative historical niche on the basis of proximity to a famous event or person: for example, the *Certamen* makes him a contemporary of Midas, while Life VI places him before Hesiod. The name "Homer" is consistently taken as "blind" (a synonym for *tuphlos*) or "hostage" (the common noun *homêros*),[59] but this unity of explanation may stem as much from a legendary parallel to the blind bards of the *Odyssey* as from any other source. In other words, the oldest extant attestations yield a familiar contradiction: a real singer who was the tangible source of the best songs, but whose own origins and history seem to have been uncertain, contradictory, or at least dependent on local allegiance.

And what were these finest songs for which Homer was ultimately responsible? The answer to this question depends largely on the particular ancient source consulted. For some the repertoire extended beyond the *Iliad* and *Odyssey* to the no longer extant poems of the so-called Epic Cycle, preserved now only in occasional small fragments and sketchily summarized by the fifth-century B.C.E. Neoplatonist philosopher and critic Proclus.[60] For certain commentators Homer was considered to be at the root of poems as various as the *Thebais*, ascribed to him but more frequently pronounced anonymous; the *Epigoni*, cited by Herodotus with skepticism about its authorship; the *Cypria* (eleven books), attributed by some to Stasinus of Cyprus or Hegesias of Salamis rather than Homer; the *Little Iliad* (four books), with Homer and four other authors proposed; the *Aethiopis* (five books), by Homer or Arctinus of Miletus; and the *Nostoi* (five books), by Homer, Agias of Troezen, or Eumelus.[61] Other poems in the Cycle seem to have included the supposedly non-Homeric *Titanomachy*, said to be the creation of Eumelus of Corinth, Telesis, or Arctinus; the *Oedipodeia*, putatively by Cinaethon; and the *Telegony* (two books), by either the same Cinaethon or Eugammon of Cyrene. The Homeric Hymns, a collection of thirty-three poems addressed to various gods and goddesses and including four substantial narratives of about 300–600 lines as well as much briefer panegyrics, were thought by some to deserve the customary attribution, but ancient sources also name Olen, Pamphos, Musaeus, Orpheus, and Hesiod as possible authors.[62]

What do we make of such a highly inconsistent pattern of authorship? Were this a modern literary lineage, we might be dismayed or at least suspicious of its integrity and usefulness. But it is not a modern lineage, either in fact or in function. All in all, as Robert Lamberton puts it (1997: 39), "there is every reason to believe that these disagreements concerning authorship stemmed from changing models of literary production and the retrospective accommodation of the body of Greek hexameter poetry stemming from oral traditions to criteria of authorship alien to the conditions of their production."[63] In other words, the Cycle and the Hymns represent poetry that is sung within the larger tradition of the *Iliad* and

Odyssey, that is, within the tradition that generations have eponymically called "Homer." We need not wonder at, or be disappointed with, the lack of consistency in listings of his compositions; for a legendary figure, such variability is not only expectable but desirable. The very plasticity of the ascribed repertoire from one source to another illustrates how the anthropomorphization functions: each poet or commentator appropriates "Homer" as the source of all that is valuable in the poetic tradition, and derives an individual authority and position from that legendary attribution. From the perspective of our comparison with the South Slavic *Guslar*, the variant ascriptions in repertoire as well as in parentage and geographical origins are a natural feature of a figure such as Homer, who must be multiform in order to play his role as an anthropomorphization of the poetic tradition.

This scenario of the legendary singer meshes with what Gregory Nagy has described as a process of *retrojection* within the Panhellenic tradition of Homeric oral poetry, a process by which the individual poet is appropriated by the larger tradition, "potentially transforming even historical figures into generic ones who represent the traditional functions of their poetry" (1990b: 79).[64] Like the *Guslar* in his various manifestations, and like Homer in the sum total of ancient witnesses, Nagy's singer is "retrojected as the original genius of heroic song, the protopoet whose poetry is reproduced by a continuous succession of performers" (1996a: 76). In other words, we cannot know with certainty about Homer's birthplace, repertoire, or other biography simply because his identity is a composite representation of tradition, consistent enough to be meaningful to the audiences of Homeric poetry and varied enough to satisfy the particular local milieu in which "his" songs are performed and reperformed. Retrojection and idealization remove this master *aoidos* from the matrix of time and place that defines all subsequent singers, so that he is placed at the origin of the bardic lineage, understood as the primogenitor. One could say that Nagy's Panhellenic model calls for the erasure of actual, individual details in favor of foregrounding traditional status, and indeed that is precisely what the Stolac *guslari* are accomplishing with their invocations of Hasan Ćoso and Isak as legendary singers.

Singer as *Sêma*

If the *Guslar* and Homer are essentially anthropomorphizations of the poetic tradition, then their trademark multiformity mirrors the structure and dynamics of the epic compositions that are attributed to them. Just as the legendary singer and his repertoire take different shapes in each appearance—Isak with Bašić and Kukuruzović, Hasan Ćoso with Bajgorić; the *Nostoi* included in Homer's own repertoire for some ancient commentators but not for others—so the language and narrative patterns he uses to make his poems show the same kind of mutability. Neither the figure of the legendary singer nor the poem can ever have a single fixed form until he or it is instanced, whether in a certain singer's individualized account of his famous forebear or in a single given performance of a song. And even then the biography and the performance will be ephemeral as things in themselves unless texts or other kind of records intervene to fossilize them, to transform the events they represent into factual accounts. Each item is itself an instance, informed by tradition; collectively they illustrate the principle of variation within limits.

This principle proves more than a descriptive feature typical of both legendary singer and song, more than simply a way to understand how the figure and the performance proliferate. It is also at the core of their continuing viability as traditional *sêmata*. To put it almost aphoristically, only by remaining plastic can the singer and song also remain ubiquitous and idiomatic. Only by retaining the quality of multiformity can the legendary singer serve his many bardic progeny (each with a singular set of expectations) and the Homeric or South Slavic epic register suit its many applications (each with a situation-specific dimension as well as a generic relationship to the epic tradition at large). With the advent of fixation and historical certainty the *Guslar* becomes a mere *guslar*, caught in the web of geography, temporality, and "standard" biographical detail. At that point it becomes possible to speak with customary modern precision about this or that figure or event, but the price paid is considerable: the "protopoet" is removed from the lineage, the *imprimatur* he provides is deleted from the proceedings, and the individual bard's virtually genealogical link with tradition is severed. When the idiomatic diction of epic-making, a register of language dedicated to one purpose only, loses its characteristic and empowering pliability, the same thing happens. This specialized language lives through its rule-governed variability, not by fossilization. Like the legendary singer, it is necessarily both individual and traditional.[65]

What is true of composition is also true of reception. Telltale phrases and resonant scenes are not only tectonically useful to the poet building an epic narrative; they also function as signals to the audience(s), as keys that unlock the word-hoard of context and association and point toward traditional referentiality. As has been illustrated at length elsewhere,[66] South Slavic singers also employ recurrent phraseology not *metri causa* but *artis causa*, as when they turn to one of a group of lyrical expressions to describe the period of time during which some threatening and unrelenting action takes place. They may say "three white days," "two white days," or "a month of days" with essentially equal force; although superficially these phrases differ, idiomatically they are absolutely equivalent ways of urging the importance or intensity of any situation to which they are applied. Or *guslari* may sound the familiar knell of the typical scene of a captive "Shouting in Prison," customarily keyed by some form of the verb *cmiliti* ("to cry out") and following a familiar narrative pathway that involves the prisoner's noisy rousing of the ban's child, the banica's complaint, and an attempt at bargaining for release of the prisoner.[67] Each phrase or scene is a *sêma*; each instance is a complex web of expressive possibilities; and each "slots" the differentia of individual epic figures, actions, and situations within familiar and resonant traditional categories.

As we have seen in Chapter 1, Homeric epic likewise depends upon *pars pro toto* signification, with the poetic idiom that is employed for composition also serving as a guide for reception of the poetry. In order to highlight this typical strategy I emphasized the use of the word *sêma* in the *Iliad* and *Odyssey*, a term the poet employs to name a sign that points not so much to a specific situation, text, or performance as toward the ambient tradition, that serves as the key to an emergent reality. Each actual *sêma* also mimics a central expressive strategy of Homeric poetry: traditional referentiality. As we discovered, *sêmata* include many of Zeus' omens, Teiresias' prophecy of the oar and winnowing shovel, Odysseus' identifying scar, and not least the olive-tree bed shared by Penelope and Odysseus. Although superficially diverse, each of these signs has a common thrust: it signals an emergent reality that would otherwise remain hidden. As keys to what is to happen, each of these traditional signs marks a prolepsis, a connection from what is present and explicit to what is immanent and implied, and each of them is uniquely effective because it charts a unique revelatory pathway. *Sêmata* index traditional meanings: the omens mark divine warning, the oar summons the sea (and Poseidon),[68] the scar identifies the veteran of the boar hunt, and the bed symbolizes the Return fulfilled, the *telos* of the *nostos*. To put it another way, by encoding worlds of implication in simple, tangible signs, the *sêmata* work like language itself, only more so.

The image of the legendary singer is no different in this regard. In an important sense the *Guslar*—Isak, Hasan Ćoso, or whatever he is called— indexes as well as names the South Slavic epic tradition. From the same perspective the designation "Homer" amounts to a *sêma* of the ancient Greek poetic tradition. Milman Parry was very close to this same conclusion when he wrote in his field notes more than a half century ago, "from our literary point of view this is almost startling: the singer embodies the tradition, and what is true of the one is true of the other" (1933–35: 450). I would prefer to identify the legendary singer, that is, the *Guslar* or Homer rather than their real-life descendants, as the embodiment of the tradition, the figure who serves this *pars pro toto* function. As an anthropomorphization, he offers generations of bards and audiences both an idealized projection and a dependable, economical way to refer to the mythic context and background that they share. To invoke his name is to speak directly of the ongoing tradition of verbal art that on the one hand supersedes all individual poets and on the other cannot function without their active, idiosyncratic instancing of the common inheritance. Understood on his own terms, the legendary singer can perform a similar significative function for readers of texts, even for scholars who, attempting to root out legend in a vain search for biographical truth, have falsely interpreted an anthropomorphization as an *anthrôpos*. Segregating the *sêma* from its referent forces a choice no more promising than Solomon's infamous proposal; instead, let us accept the merger of individual with tradition in the *Guslar* named Isak and Hasan Ćoso and in the *Aoidos* named Homer.[69]

Epilogue: A Parallel from Inner Mongolia

In late September 1997 I had the opportunity to gather information about a North Asian analogue to Homer and the South Slavic *Guslar*. During a field trip to Tong Liao and Zharut Banner in Inner Mongolia I interviewed an active, practicing epic singer, Losor by name, about his craft and his bardic genealogy.[70] In response to my questions about the source of his songs, Losor recounted tales of a prior singer, Choibang, whom he and his fellows saw as the greatest of all bards. The figure he described was strikingly similar to the legendary singer who has been the major subject of the latter part of this chapter.

Losor placed Choibang three generations back in time, characterizing him as his teacher's teacher's teacher, and set his life span at approximately ninety to one hundred years. Although he never actually met this epic paragon, our informant was able to provide quite a lot of personal data about his life and exploits via stories told by his grandparents and by other singers. Choibang was, he said, an extraordinarily tall man of noble blood ("people called him 'your majesty'") who was descended from a wealthy family.[71] Though his precise village of origin remained obscure, he traveled everywhere, had a great love of hunting, and was a champion at many athletic endeavors; his nickname, in fact, translates as "Official Wrestler." Along with his outstanding physical gifts, Choibang possessed a superior intelligence, as evidenced both by his fluency in four languages— Mongolian, Tibetan, Mandarin, and Manchu—and by the immense respect shown him by other epic poets, who often walked twenty Chinese miles and more to listen to him perform.

Choibang's own repertoire of epic was unique in at least three ways. He knew a tremendous number of songs, he created numerous new compositions (against all standard procedure), and his words were so famous that they eventually became proverbial. On this last point, Losor assured us that many widely circulating expressions and stories are even today cited by their speakers with what amounts to a kind of oral-traditional footnote: "these are Choibang's words." All of the best songs thus came ultimately from him. Nonetheless, like the *Guslar* and Homer, the transmission of these narratives was shrouded in uncertainty and even mystery: for example, Losor claimed to have known a very old woman who had learned a song directly from Choibang but who died before she could reveal to our informant more than an outline and a few phrases.

In short, this legendary Mongolian singer followed a familiar pattern. He was far enough removed in time and space to serve as an effective anthropomorphization of epic tradition, a kind of *sêma* for Mongolian epic. He was larger than life—in his age, pedigree, physical abilities, intelligence, and accomplishments. To put it simply, he more closely resembles the heroes of the epics he sang than he does the "real-life" singers who are his supposed bardic descendants.

Although Choibang has been historicized by singers and folklorists in the Tong Liao region, much in the same way that Alois Schmaus historicized the South Slavic *Guslar* Ćor Huso[72] and generations of textual scholars have historicized Homer, the "facts" of his biography prove elusive from one account to the next. Even the carefully drawn genealogy of epic poets published in Sampulnorbu's compilation of field-elicited biographies cannot be taken as an authoritative document, since the "data" shift as one biography about Choibang is compared to another.[73] This is certainly not to say that the various sources (oral or written) are confused or corrupt, but rather to observe that the life story of this greatest of Mongolian epic singers is after all a traditional story, and traditional stories are characterized by their multiformity, by their variation within limits. A final anecdote about the great man's demise will illustrate the traditional nature of the singer as a legendary figure.

Speaking of course through the filter of "another singer's father," who in turn had "a friend who knew Choibang," Losor described how this greatest of bards enjoyed special privileges beyond those accorded normal citizens of the region. He was not only a professional craftsman free to go anywhere he wished, but he was also permitted by the political leader of Zharut Banner to carry a gun. How mysterious, Losor continued, that such a brave, well-respected community figure should be covertly murdered and then beheaded. Stranger still was the episode that followed: in keeping with the folktale belief that a bard's head would do wonders for a batch of wine, Choibang's detached head was actually dropped into an ongoing fermentation process, and "people said" that the yield was indeed improved in quality. Like his South Slavic and ancient Greek brethren, Choibang was a bard beyond all others, a truly legendary singer.

In the following two chapters we will continue our examination of the South Slavic epic tradition as an analogue for the Homeric poems, shifting our attention from singer to song, from the *guslar* to the *epske pjesme* ("epic songs") that he performs. Our major points of comparison will be a natural pair: the poetic register that supports composition (Chapter 3) and the traditional referentiality inherent in that specialized way of speaking (Chapter 4).

3

HOMER AND THE
SOUTH SLAVIC *GUSLAR*
Traditional Register

πολυφλοίσβοιο θαλάσσης
"of the loud-sounding sea"
—Traditional

Ovčijem te zadojila mlekom
"She began to nurse you with sheep's milk"
—Traditional

Our focus in this and the following chapter shifts from the singers to their songs—specifically to the distinctive poetic language employed by the South Slavic *guslar* and his epic tradition and the extent to which it mirrors the equally distinctive Homeric language, or *koinê*. We will, in other words, be examining these two specialized song-making idioms as *registers*, or "major speech styles associated with recurrent types of situations."[1] To put the matter as directly as possible, we will be asking a version of the same question posed at the beginning of Chapter 2: *Is the South Slavic epic register a useful, apposite comparison for the Homeric register?* And once again the answer will necessarily be mixed: Yes, it is; and no, it isn't. The two ways of speaking can be profitably compared in a number of dimensions, but that does not mean that they are wholly congruent, any more than any two languages, specialized varieties or not, can ever be wholly congruent. Differences exist, and they should be neither overestimated nor underplayed; rather we should seek a measured, mutually illuminating comparison that sheds light on both registers without reducing their complexity and therefore their capacity for verbal art.

Let us start by posing a series of questions. (I) Is Homeric formulaic phraseology similar to the formulaic phraseology of South Slavic epic? (II) Does enjambement function similarly in the two poetries? (III) Do metrical irregularities of the Homeric type also characterize South Slavic epic? (IV) Is South Slavic epic composed in an "artificial language" like Homer's? Along the same lines, do dialect variation (IVa) and archaisms (IVb) play a role in the *guslar's* language as they do in Homer? How comparable are the larger patterns of typical scene (V) and story-pattern (VI) in the two epic traditions? Carefully considered answers to these questions will help Homerists to judge the extent to which, and the particular ways in which, the *guslar's* epic *koinê* compares to that of the *aoidos*.[2]

Those interested exclusively in the implications of the *guslar's* language will find a discussion of South Slavic *sêmata* in Chapter 4. However, I consider the comparability of the two poetic languages an important enough matter—and one that has never been carefully treated—that I devote this chapter to a straightforward analysis of the chief linguistic and structural features of these two traditional ways of speaking. In short, Chapter 3 serves as a philological basis for the interpretive program espoused in Chapter 4.

The Language of South Slavic Epic: "Word" and Register

Any responsible comparison depends upon an acknowledgment of both similarities and differences, and the special poetic registers of *guslar* and *aoidos* are certainly no exception. In that spirit I turn now to an examination of South Slavic epic diction in terms of a series of questions that must be answered *both* yes *and* no. To settle for either answer alone would be, as we shall see, actively distorting: Homer's poems and the South Slavic performances are indeed very much alike in some ways, and in some other ways they are quite disparate. Hopefully, the process of sorting out differences and similarities in their special languages will help us to gain a clearer idea of how each idiom functions as a medium for composition and reception, and to construct a sturdier because more realistic foundation for their comparative study as verbal art.

Question I. Is Homeric formulaic phraseology similar to the formulaic phraseology of South Slavic epic?
    Answer 1: *Yes, it is.*

The poetic language of the *guslar* exists in symbiosis with the epic decasyllable (*epski deseterac*) line that has some features in common with the Homeric hexameter.[3] Because the meters are similar, so are the phraseologies. The most important of these shared metrical characteristics is colonic structure, that is, regular, constituent subunits within the line. This phenomenon leads in both cases to an encapsulated phraseology, a diction consisting of verbatim and substitutable phrases that Milman Parry called "formulaic." Thus both dictions demonstrate systems of noun-epithet or noun-adjective formulas; for example,

πόδας ὠκὺς Ἀχιλλεύς	swift-footed Achilleus
οἴνοπα πόντον	wine-dark sea

alongside

Musa kesedžija	Musa the beheader
knjiga šarovita	multicolored letter

Both traditions also include a large number of phrases that can vary by one or more words, providing compositional flexibility in these specialized languages. Examples include certain introductions to speeches; for instance, consider the following partial lines, each of which can be completed with a variety of subjects (ordinarily noun-epithet formulas):

τὸν δ᾽ ἀπαμειβόμενος προσέφη	But answering he addressed him
τὸν δ᾽ ἄρ᾽ ὑπόδρα ἰδὼν προσέφη	But looking darkly he addressed him

alongside

I govori	And [he/she] spoke
A govori	But [he/she] spoke
Ali reče	But [he/she] said
I reče mu	And [he/she] said to him

Many more illustrations could be of course summoned from both poetries, along the whole range from exact to highly variable repetition, but the point is that encapsulated phraseology, a reflection of colonic meter, is typical of them both.[4]

One way to underline this basic correspondence is to let the *guslari* themselves contribute to the discussion. Time and again during conversations with Nikola Vujnović, Parry and Lord's native assistant, the singers construed their performances in terms of *reči*, "words." But these were not at all words in our sense of lexical entries or root morphemes, a presumption that has caused serious misinterpretation of what the singers were saying about their art and craft. What they meant by a *reč*, it becomes clear from repeated exchanges, was an increment that satisfied two major requirements: (1) it must be at least a metrical unit in length (a minimum of a colon or line) and (2) it must constitute a speech-act.[5] In fact, singers used this ethnolinguistic term *reč* to designate units of utterance as extensive as a speech, a scene, and even a whole tale. The necessary quality of *reči*, whatever their size, seemed to be their identity as complete, unitary speech-acts.

At the level of phraseology, this concept has the effect of raising the threshold on what a "word" could be.[6] For example, when pressed to subdivide the *reč* to take account of its constituent parts, singers resisted doing so, maintaining in effect that the special language of epic performance had its own rules and definitions. Thus, when challenged to explain how a four-word poetic line could actually be a single "word," Mujo Kukuruzović responded: "It can't be one in writing. But here, let's say we're at my house and I pick up the *gusle*—'Pije vino lički Mustajbeže' ['Mustajbeg of the Lika was drinking wine']—that's a single *reč* on the *gusle* for me."[7] Kukuruzović was describing an entry not in a conventional printed lexicon but in the unprinted lexicon of traditional idiom.

Another *guslar* from the Stolac region, Salko Morić, responded to the challenge of defining a singer's "word" in a similar way. Here is a series of questions posed by Nikola Vujnović (himself a singer), together with Morić's answers:[8]

> *N*: For example, "pije vino" [he/she was drinking wine]—is that a *reč*?
> *S*: Yes.
> *N*: So then is "Salko," "Salko," is that a *reč*?
> *S*: Yes.
> *N*: It too?
> *S*: Yes.
> *N*: But what would this be—"Na *h*Udbini u pjanoj mehani / Sjede age, redom piju vino" ["At Udbina in a drinking tavern / Sat the agas, they were drinking wine one after another"]? What's that?
> *S*: "Svi ukupno redom piju vino" ["They were all drinking wine together, one after another"].
> *N*: So that's a *reč* too?
> *S*: Well, it's also a *reč*, yes.

This exchange provides telling evidence of how a *guslar* views the special language of epic singing. To begin, Vujnović asks whether an extremely common formula—"pije vino"—can be construed as a "word." Morić says that it can. Next the interviewer selects an example from outside the epic register, where the rules for words are different: is "Salko," the *guslar*'s own name, a "word"? Yes, he is told, although we should emphasize that the target has shifted: the context is now everyday conversational language, and not the epic *koinê*. On these grounds "Salko" qualifies as a unit of utterance. Finally, Vujnović poses what is for us the most interesting of the three questions. He recites two common formulaic lines from the South Slavic epic tradition and asks Morić whether this entire couplet—fully two decasyllables and a total of ten of our lexical units in the original language—is also one "word." Morić responds not only by confirming that the two poetic lines amount to a single "word" or speech-act, but also by translating the two decasyllables into a single decasyllabic line of his own. By rendering the two-line *reč* with a one-line "word" of his own, he illustrates the pliability and multiformity of the epic language.

From an internal, "emic" point of view Kukuruzović, Morić, and their colleagues from the Stolac region were articulating something very similar to what Parry and Lord discovered through external, "etic" analysis. The South Slavic epic language, as opposed to the everyday idiom in which four words were still four words, features phrases in capsule form, both exact repetitions and variable patterns, that function as larger "words."[9] Singers did not think of them or utilize them as collections of parts but rather as indissoluble units, much in the same way that we learn to interpret lexical entries as meaning-bearing wholes rather than collections of phonemes (e.g., "sat" rather than $[s]+[æ]+[t]$ or "lucky" rather than $[l]+[ə]+[k]+[i]$). Because Homer's formulaic "words" seemed very similar to these *reči*, it was natural to compare, and perhaps even to equate, the poetic languages they constituted. Homeric formulaic phraseology is in some ways quite similar to South Slavic epic phraseology.

Answer 2: *No, it isn't.*

Although the hexameter and decasyllable share a number of properties, they are far from identical, and their differences are reflected in the two phraseologies. Most basically, the *deseterac* is made up of only two possible cola, according to the following scheme ("s" stands for "syllable"):

	1	2	3	4		5	6	7	8	9	10
	s	s	s	s		s	s	s	s	s	s
ex.	I	go-	vo-	ri		Mus-	taj-	be-	že	lič-	ki
	And	spoke				Mustajbeg				of the Lika	

The sole caesura occurs between syllables 4 and 5 with virtually absolute regularity, dividing the line into two unequal parts. Thus only four- and six-syllable increments are permitted.[10] On the other hand, the hexameter comprises four cola per line; with variable caesura positions, cola can thus take a total of twelve different individual shapes.[11] This disparity alone means that formulas and formulaic phrases can be encapsulated in significantly more ways in the *Iliad* and *Odyssey* than in South Slavic epic. Or, to put it another way, there are more different kinds of metrical sites for "words" in ancient Greek epic.

Other consequences of the decasyllable's simpler colonic structure in-
clude the segregation of syntax and a complete lack of metrical "thrift"
in the *guslar*'s diction. The first segment in the line is customarily devoted
to short verb phrases, adverbial and prepositional phrases, abbreviated
echoes from the latter part of the preceding line, and the like. A good rule
of thumb is that this opening colon, limited to only four syllables, houses
the syllabically shorter and grammatically subordinate increments of the
sentence, including most function words, enclitics, and proclitics. The sec-
ond colon, by contrast, offers a roomier six-syllable capsule, and therefore
serves as the natural site for longer verb and noun phrases, including all
but a very few noun-epithet combinations. To borrow the *guslar*'s own ter-
minology, different kinds of *reči* tend to occupy the first and second cola in
the decasyllable.[12]

Furthermore, disparity in colonic structure is the basis for one of the
sharpest divergences between the two traditional phraseologies. Among
Parry's strongest arguments for the utility of Homeric diction was the doc-
trine of thrift, the considerable degree to which the language of the *Iliad*
and *Odyssey* tends to be "free of phrases which, having the same metrical
value and expressing the same idea, could replace one another" (1930:
276). In respect to noun-epithet formulas, he showed, Homer usually has
only one phraseological solution for each metrical problem.[13] Poets were
thrifty, Parry argued, because they were composing orally; more than one
solution to a problem would only prove a hindrance to rapid, fluent per-
formance. Significantly, however, since virtually every noun-epithet for-
mula in orally composed South Slavic epic must be precisely six syllables
long, exactly fitting the second colon in the line, no such feature as metri-
cal thrift can exist. Different appellations for a character cannot be selected
by differing metrical extent, since they all occupy the same slot.[14] On this
point Homeric epic and South Slavic epic are wholly at odds, with thrift
plainly a feature of hexameter diction in particular rather than of "oral po-
etry" in general.

In summary, if we are willing to view each formulaic phraseology on
its own terms, remarking differences alongside similarities and avoiding
generalizations not supported by analysis, a truer analogy emerges. Both
the hexameter and the decasyllable are founded on colonic structure,
and their dictions are therefore comparable. But comparable does not
mean identical, and they diverge on a number of points, most significantly
the precise nature of that colonic structure and the important issue of
thrift.[15]

Question II. Does enjambement function similarly in the two poetries?
    Answer 1. *Yes, it does.*
    The additive nature of the South Slavic line, which is well marked by
syllabic definition and a typical closing rhythm,[16] makes for enjambement

much like that found in the *Iliad* and *Odyssey*. Just as Homer tends to avoid periodic (necessary) enjambement, wherein the sentence is incomplete at hexameter's end and must be finished in the following line, so the *guslar* shows a marked preference for either unperiodic (unnecessary) or no enjambement. Lord's and my analyses of songs by three different singers from two separate regions—Salih Ugljanin from Novi Pazar and Mujo Kukuruzović and Halil Bajgorić from Stolac—measured that preference at between 85 percent and 93 percent, respectively, leaving only 7–15 percent of the *deseterac* lines that overran the end of the verse by necessity.[17] If anything, the tendency to avoid necessary enjambement is somewhat stronger in South Slavic epic than in Homer: Parry's and Carolyn Higbie's figures for the *Iliad* are between 73 percent and 76 percent with either unperiodic or no enjambement.[18] Although the *guslar* very often does continue his thought beyond line-end in a supplementary clause, there is seldom the absolute syntactic need to do so. This paratactic style of South Slavic epic goes hand in hand with its vocal and instrumental dimensions of performance: the two melodic lines, described as "heterophonic" by George Herzog, reveal a regular formulaic structure and whole-line integrity of their own that reinforce the decasyllabic diction.[19] The primacy of the line as a self-contained, additive unit is evident in both poetic traditions.

Answer 2: *No, it doesn't.*

Of course, the precise figures for enjambement preference are in part a function of the individual tradition and thus not subject to any universal, archetypal ratio. The tendency toward completeness within a single line may well be characteristic of many oral traditions, but once again linguistic diversity should caution against expecting absolute quantitative equivalence. Likewise, exactly how and under what conditions the thought and sentence are continued beyond a single line varies from one tradition to the other.[20] In South Slavic various kinds of appositive constructions regularly serve as vehicles for incremental, unperiodic extension. Such constructions may entail iterations of nouns, verbs, or other elements:

1. Oj! Rano rani Djerdjelez Alija, *v*Ej! Alija, careva gazija, Oj! Djerdjelez Ailja arose early, Ej! Alija, the tsar's hero,	*6699*: 1–2	Repeated Noun
2. Kad sve beže knjige rasturijo, Rasturijo na četiri strane, When the beg sent out all the letters, Sent them out in the four directions,	*6699*: 369–70	Repeated Verb
3. More biti neko *v*od Stambola, *v*Od Stambola, Stojna Carigrada. It must be someone from Istanbul, From Istanbul, Stojan's Tsarigrad.	*6699*: 165–66	Repeated Prepositional phrase

In addition, each of these examples exhibits the typically South Slavic epic feature of *terracing*. Also called pleonasm, this rhetorical and tectonic figure involves partial or complete repetition of a phrase from the preceding line: *Alija* for the full noun-epithet formula *Djerdjelez Alija* in (1); *rasturijo* for the full verb phrase "sent letters" (*knjige rasturijo*) in (2); and the entire prepositional phrase in (3). None of these continuations is syntactically necessary; instead, each one of them glosses what precedes with what amounts to an optional enrichment of the main thought.[21] From the point of view of traditional poetics, both the style and the individual phrases used as optional continuations have the effect of slotting the particular instances along familiar expressive tracks.[22] Both general style and actual phrase serve as *sêmata*. In such cases the function of enjambement is not to fill out incomplete syntax, nor simply to conform to a stylistic or compositional desideratum, but rather to invoke traditional referentiality.

Question III. Do metrical irregularities of the Homeric type also characterize South Slavic epic?

Answer 1: *Yes, they do.*

The *epske pjesme* contain numerous instances of so-called metrical irregularities, some of them similar to phenomena that Parry observed in Homer and linked to compositional style as early as his supplementary doctoral thesis (1928b).[23] By far the most common such phenomenon is vowel hiatus, which may occur in as many as 25–50 percent of the lines in a given *guslar's* performance and occasionally more than once per line.[24] Most often, vowel hiatus coincides with the break between lines or, as in Homer, with the juncture between formulaic phrases, which in the *deseterac* always occurs between the fourth and fifth syllables. Consider the following examples, drawn from *The Death of Marko Kraljević*, collected and published by Vuk Karadžić in the mid-nineteenth century (vol. 2: no. 73), with points of hiatus underlined. The reason for choosing this transcribed and edited text instead of one of the Parry-Lord performances from Stolac will soon become obvious:

1. pokraj mora Urvinom planinom   3
on Mount Urvina beside the sea.

2. posrtati i suze roniti   6, 14
to stumble and to shed tears.

3. što je njima ostalo od Marka   85
which was left to them by Marko

All three first cola and all three second cola recur with alternate partners throughout the tradition, in some cases avoiding and in some cases engendering hiatus. Thus it appears that Parry's theory—namely, that hiatus marks points of linkage between phraseological units that have lives of their own in the tradition at large—certainly applies to the *epske pjesme* as well. As in Homer, hiatus exposes compositional seams where smaller "words" have been combined to form larger "words" within traditional diction.

Answer 2: *No, they don't.*

Unlike the manuscript records of traditional oral poetry from the former Yugoslavia or ancient Greece, however, acoustic records of South Slavic epic reveal a compensating strategy for handling vowel hiatus. As part of the specialized language of verse-making, the *guslar* in performance is able to deploy a selection of nonlexical and otherwise meaningless consonantal sounds that bridge the gap between vowels and thus avoid interruption by an intervening glottal stop. Here are some examples of hiatus and its bridging from Halil Bajgorić's *The Wedding of Mustajbeg's Son Bećirbeg* (*6699*), with the inserted consonants italicized:[25]

1. Prije zore *v*i bijela dana—	4
Before dawn and the white day—	
2. Samo sebe *j*i svoga dorata.	18
Only himself and his horse.	
3. Ćebe preže, bojno sedlo bači,	
*v*A po sedlu četiri kolana,	
*h*I peticu svilenu kanicu.	30–32
He hitched the blanket, threw on the war-saddle,	
And four girths on the saddle,	
And fifth a woven sash.	
4. Dok se svane *v*i sunce *v*ograne,	6
When it dawned and the sun rose,	

As we can appreciate visually, Bajgorić uses [v], [j], and [h] to smooth the aural pathway over these few lines, most often at the caesura between formulaic line-parts or cola (example [1] above, from *zore* to *i*; also examples [2] and [4]). The same device is likewise enlisted to avoid hiatus between whole lines (example [3]) and even within cola (example [4], between *sunce* and *ograne*). As would be expected, the interlinear bridges appear only when a line both begins with a vowel and immediately follows a line that ended with a vowel.[26] The reason for such "performatives," as we may call these bridging consonants, is simply to allow the *guslar* to maintain a steady stream of vocalization as he sings the melodic phrase. Instead of having to interrupt the flow of song with a glottal stop, he can maintain spoken and sung continuity from the end of one unit to the beginning of another.

At least three characteristics of such performatives should be emphasized. First, they tend to mediate breaks between cola or whole lines; hence the instances of hiatus they mark are usually diagnostic of formulaic phraseology. To put it another way, performatives very often delimit a metrical and phraseological unit of utterance, a "word" (*reč*). Second, they are features of performance—created for fluent sung delivery and meaningful only within that context. For this reason they translate poorly if at all to textual transcriptions, and indeed virtually every published collection of South Slavic epic silently eliminates them from the textual representation.[27] Taken together, these first two characteristics beg the question of whether Homer and his tradition might have employed a similar phonological strategy to bridge hiatus between formulaic elements that, like the *guslar's* larger "words," also had lives of their own in the poetic tradition at large. The question is probably unanswerable, since we can reconstruct neither the acoustic reality nor the editorial history of the Homeric poems with any certainty, but it does suggest how much can be lost when we move from the aural experience of a performance to the silence of a textual libretto.[28] Third, performatives are one of the telltale signals that the poetic transaction is taking place in a special register, a dedicated *koinê*, and therefore that a certain kind of composition and reception are mandated.

Question IV. Is South Slavic epic composed in an "artificial language" like Homer's?

Answer 1: Yes, it is.

Like the *aoidos*, the *guslar* employs a special idiom marked not only by formulaic phraseology, certain enjambement habits, and metrical irregularities but also by multiple dialects (IVa) and archaisms (IVb). Together such features alert the audience or reader that the singer is using a particular version of the South Slavic language devoted solely to the performance of epic poetry, one among a sizable cultural repertoire of registers for verbal art.[29] I have measured these dimensions of the epic register in South Slavic by contrasting the song-performances of four singers from the Stolac region (Mujo Kukuruzović, Ibro Bašić, Halil Bajgorić, and Salko Morić) against the speech they employed during their conversations with Parry and Lord's assistant Vujnović. By this measurement, the traditional epic register departs significantly from the unmarked conversational standard.[30]

Answer 2: No, neither of these special languages is "artificial."

As compared to registers used by individuals for casual conversation, scholarly discussion, or reading and writing in modern media like newspapers, books, and most other printed sources, the *guslar's* language may sound "artificial," just as Homer's distinctive, multidialectal, archaized language has often been characterized.[31] But South Slavic epic diction is no more inherently artificial than those other registers; it is differently configured simply because it has a particular history and ongoing social function. In fact, one could say with as much justice that, from the viewpoint of the epic phraseology, many of the quotidian registers seem artificial. The truth is that each idiom plays its own role in the overall ecology of discourse, as reflected in their divergent combinations of verbal signs.[32] Each way of speaking is a viable linguistic instrument in its own right, and to understand any of them as artificial or eccentric is to dilute its expressive force. If the South Slavic and Homeric epic registers demonstrate features atypical of dialectally and chronologically streamlined versions of the language, then their very linguistic constitution is making a statement about how they are to be interpreted. Within the specialized arena designated by these "unusual" varieties of language, a certain kind of transaction is licensed. Homer and the *guslar* speak to their audiences in a highly economical because uniquely empowered idiom, not an artificial dialect.[33]

As both South Slavic and Homeric epic illustrate, the traditional nature of this kind of register—its usage over time and place as a dedicated expressive medium—thus exerts at least two trademark influences on a system of diction. First, it acts as a selective brake on linguistic change within its domain.[34] Indeed, both archaic features themselves and analogical adaptations or extensions based on archaisms characterize these two traditional registers. Second, it tolerates, preserves, and even promotes dialect mixture, which is also the result of a register's life history. On the one hand, South Slavic shows that a conversational standard used in a given area, for example, or even one of the more cosmopolitan registers of novel writing or scholarship, participates in a feedback loop of usage that continuously "updates" the phonology, morphology, and lexicon, subject to the requirements of the genre. On the other hand, both epic dictions demonstrate that traditional idioms necessarily harbor individual words and forms that either have long passed out of everyday currency and are therefore perceived as obsolete, or that cannot be justified in terms of a homogeneous, synchronically defined dialect. In short, they fossilize words within "words," prolonging the natural lifetime of whatever the *reči* have comprised.

These features of the diction could be seen as symptomatic of an artificial language, something unreal or aberrant. But oral epic tradition does not share that frame of reference. What we might choose to call "wrong" dialect and "archaic" or "borrowed" words and forms (basing our judgment on impertinent standards) are simply verbal signs that perform a function. Indeed, their continued usage is the clearest possible evidence for their full partnership in a highly idiomatic medium, in what Maximilian Braun, referring to the language of the *guslar*, has called "eine Schriftsprache für Analphabeten."[35] Regardless of their currency outside the epic, these signs are uniquely functional within it.

Question IVa. Are the South Slavic and Homeric epic registers actually mixtures of geographically defined dialects?

Answer 1. *No, they aren't.*

I begin in this instance with the negative response, in order to emphasize that within the epic register *guslari* keep *mainly* to the geographical dialect they use for everyday speech transactions. Nonetheless, departures from the usual local dialect, although much less numerous than "appropriate" words and forms, are both recurrent and systematic: they participate crucially, as we shall see, in the creation and maintenance of formulaic phraseology. This situation is directly parallel to Homeric diction, wherein "Ionic provides the predominant dialect base and . . . the Aeolic forms appear routinely only where they offer an alternative metrical shape to their Ionic equivalents."[36] Once again, we gain a true perspective not by referring to lexicons and grammars that epitomize a historically and geographically streamlined version of the language, but by focusing on the special dynamics of the epic *koinê* or way of speaking.

Answer 2. *Yes, they are.*

For a start, consider the analogous mixtures of geographically defined dialects that constitute the poetic dictions. Just as Homer's mainly Ionic language also draws from Aeolic Greek to answer compositional needs, so the *guslar*'s idiom combines two more or less distinct dialect sources to meet the challenge of composition in performance. When making their songs, as opposed to undertaking other speech-acts, South Slavic singers use both ijekavski (chiefly Bosnian and Croatian) and ekavski (chiefly Serbian) forms, not seldom in the very same line.[37] The major phonological difference between these two dialects amounts to the ijekavski preference for *ije* where ekavski favors long *ē*, and *je* for short *e*. Thus, the ijekavski word for "child," for example, is *dijete* as opposed to ekavski *dēte*. Another such pair would be the words for "milk": *mlijeko* as opposed to *mlēko*.[38] The two dialects are of course mutually intelligible, since neither this nor any other difference between them constitutes a true impediment to understanding. But although native speakers normally use only the forms appropriate to their particular geographical context in most registers, South Slavic singers customarily and systematically have recourse to forms and syntactic features from both dialects when they code-switch to the traditional performance idiom. For this reason, trying to explain the diction used in their songs as either ijekavski or ekavski runs roughshod over the inescapable fact that, strictly speaking, it is neither.

In many instances, as with the examples of *dijete/dēte* and *mlijeko/mlēko* cited just above, one form is a syllable longer than the other—a negligible consideration in everyday spoken or written language but often a crucial matter within a diction that cooperates symbiotically with a ten-syllable poetic line.[39] From a synchronic, compositional perspective, the syllabic flexibility afforded by being able to turn to either form (*dijete* or *dēte*, for example) can be very useful to poets employing a metrical idiom. From the complementary diachronic perspective, an encapsulated formula that depends on either *dijete* or *dēte* is unlikely to substitute one dialect form for the other, since the new unit would immediately become unmetrical. One is reminded of built-in Homeric options like the genitive singular *-oio* ending for o-stem nouns and adjectives, once understood as an Aeolicism but now shown to have a parallel in the Mycenaean dialect of the Linear B tablets.[40] This two-syllable inflection provides an option for the monosyllabic *-ou* ending and thus a compositional flexibility. In fact, a well-known formula in the epics and hymns that features this option alongside a quite different ending memorably illustrates the principle of metrically selected forms: πολυφλοίσβοιο θαλάσσης ("of the loud-sounding sea"), which combines an earlier adjectival ending with an Ionic noun ending.[41] Various other doublets, which combine certain Aeolicisms and Ionic forms, include θεά (nom./voc.) alongside θεός/θεέ, coexisting forms of "goddess."[42]

To illustrate a similar kind of dialect mixture in the South Slavic register, in which "foreign" dialect forms can replace standard forms if they offer an alternative metrical shape, consider two examples, both of them drawn from the Stolac singers' performances. The first involves the deployment of the doublet *dijete/dēte*, the ijekavski and ekavski forms of the word for "child" discussed above. Within the sample of six epic songs, Kukuruzović has occasion to use this word fourteen times, and the dialect form he employs depends strictly on the metrical and phraseological environment. That is, when he is naming the hero Halil, he turns to the ijekavski *dijete*, fashioning a six-syllable noun-epithet formula, *dijete Halile* ("child Halil"). This *reč* or larger "word" thus consists of the three-syllable version of "child" accompanied by the vocative inflection of Halil, constituting a relatively common kind of phrase that can serve as either a pseudo-nominative or the vocative that it is.[43] In all other instances, however, Kukuruzović resorts to the two-syllable ekavski *dēte*, as in phrases like "A sjede mu dēte besjediti" ("But the child began to address him") or "Dēte, si mi rezil učinijo" ("Child, you have shamed me"). None of these phrases, neither the six occurrences of *dijete Halile* nor the eight occurrences of various other patterns, will tolerate substitution of the alternate form. Such substitution would render them unmetrical. The singer speaks the poetic language fluently by speaking it multidialectally, and according to the rules of the register for fashioning verbal signs.

The second example involves the other of our doublets, *mlijeko/mlēko*. In this case Kukuruzović employs only the shorter, two-syllable form within his recorded repertoire. But alongside the ekavski *mlēko* he uses ijekavski-like adjectives inflected with an extra syllable, as in the following two lines:

Ovčijem te zadojila mlēkom   1868.1279
She began to nurse you with sheep's milk

A tvojijem mlēkom zadojila   1287a.638
But you nursed [him] with your milk.

Although one would not expect to find such concatenations as *ovčijem* . . . *mlēkom* or *tvojijem mlēkom* in conversational speech or any other register of South Slavic, they are perfectly natural and unartificial in the epic diction.[44] Indeed, because the contrasting forms occur in the very same line, as partners in a single noun phrase, there can be no question of "different sources" or imitation of an alternate geographical dialect.[45] In both lines, and in epic performance as a whole, the dialect that the *guslar* speaks is neither ijekavski nor ekavski, but rather the traditional register.

Of course, such "decisions"—as well as other kinds of adjustments like those examined below—are based on options inherent in the register and are thus no more "conscious" or intentionally strategic than making subjects agree with verbs. It is a matter of what linguists call "competence,"[46] or simply fluency in the register. What is more, many such combinations come to the *guslar* as encapsulated phrases—as *reči* or larger "words," according to the singers' own conception of the most basic increments that make up their way of speaking. Especially given the contemporary political situation in which ethnicity has become cause for cruel displacement and outright slaughter, it must be stressed that the South Slavic epic register can and does supervene ethnic or geographical affiliation. While ekavski or ijekavski speakers naturally favor their "home" dialect to a large degree, traditional epic phraseology always and everywhere entails a utilitarian mixture of forms, sorted not according to the singer's individual speech habits but rather *metri causa*.[47] As we shall see in Chapter 4, *metri causa* ("for the sake of meter") implies the more fundamental principle of *artis causa* ("for the sake of art").

Closely allied to the matter of dialect is the set of syllabic adjustments used by the *guslar* and his poetic tradition to mold and maintain the ongoing symbiosis between prosody and phraseology.[48] These adjustments do not stem from alternate dialect forms, but they do provide the same kind of compositional flexibility. For descriptive purposes, and again basing our distinctions on the language used by the Stolac *guslari* in conversation, we can separate strategies that "subtract" from those that "add" syllables to the expectable form.[49] On the subtraction side of the ledger we list those features that entail compression: aphaeresis, dropping an initial syllable; syncope, suppressing a medial syllable; and apocope, deleting a final syllable. Common examples include:

> *Aphaeresis* ovako > 'vako [thus]:
> Pa mu 'vako mlada govorila   *6617.134*
> Then the young woman spoke to him thus
> *Syncope* obećao > obeć'o [promised]:
> Obeć'o sam nebrojeno blago   *6617.404*
> I promised uncounted wealth
> *Apocope* evo > ev' [here]:
> Ev' zemana dvadeset godina   *6617. 73*
> Here it's been twenty years' time.

Adjustments like these can become institutionalized features of the epic register for an individual singer, for a region, or more widely. Some are linked to specific words, such as *ovako* and *evo* in the first and third examples above, and some affect a whole class of words or forms, like the generalized reduction of the masculine past inflection of verbs from the disyllabic *-ao* to monosyllabic *-o* in the second example.[50] These and many other elements, like the personal pronouns and function words that can occur as disyllables, monosyllables, or unvocalized phones,[51] offer compositional plasticity. Diachronically, many of these reduced words and forms are already part of encapsulated phrases learned as *reči* by the singers, so that metrical accommodation has become part of a unit that functions at a higher level. Additionally, a *guslar* may apply the principles of variation derived from "regular" syllabic reduction to a "new" situation, thus generating a form that may not already be common coin in the traditional register.[52] Aphaeresis, syncope, and apocope greatly smooth the singer's—and the tradition's—compositional path, providing malleable constituents with which to construct encapsulated formulas as well as set phrases that exist within the register as larger "words."

The same is true of strategies for syllabic flexibility that "add" to standard, expectable forms. Of the corresponding modes for syllabic expansion—prosthesis, epenthesis, and proparalepsis—only the last occurs with any regularity. That is, at least within the Stolac songs, syllables are never added to the beginning of a word in the South Slavic epic register, and very seldom, except in the case of dialect forms as analyzed above, do they expand a word from within. But proparalepsis is a relatively common adjustment that as a rule operates on the level of the *reč*, or larger "word," adding a syllable to the end of a colonic or linear unit. A case in point is the frequent and systemic strategy that substitutes a vocative for a nominative inflection, with no change in overall sense or syntax. Since the vocative of many nouns, especially proper names, is one syllable longer than the nominative, the alternate inflection provides a metrical bi-form, just as many "foreign" items from the Aeolic dialect conventionally offer alternative metrical bi-forms for the basically Ionic dialect of Homer.

This is the situation with two of the most famous, and infamous, heroes in South Slavic epic, Mustajbeg of the Lika and Prince Marko. The simple nominative forms of these names, *lički Mustajbeg* and *Kraljević Marko*, both produce five-syllable increments, one syllable shy of fitting the assigned slot for noun-epithet formulas. One of the tradition's solutions to such metrical quandaries—and the regularity of the "irregularity" throughout many repertoires and regions ensures that it is genuinely a property of a register shared by many individuals—is to press the vocative inflections into service as the nominative subjects of sentences: thus the six-syllable forms *lički Mustajbeže* and *Kraljeviću Marko*. To these vocative names, which function precisely as if they were nominatives, the singers customarily prefix four-syllable verb phrases, with results like the following from both the Parry-Lord and the Karadžić songs:[53]

Sejir čini lički Mustajbeže	Mustajbeg of the Lika gazed around	6699.532
Progovara lički Mustajbeže	Mustajbeg of the Lika spoke forth	6617.417
Kad to začu Kraljeviću Marko	When Prince Marko heard this	57.90
Poranio Kraljeviću Marko	Prince Marko arose early	73.1

Like the deployment of different dialect forms, these vocative replacements offer the *guslar* an alternative that, once made part of a *reč*, will tend to become fossilized within that larger "word" and thus resistant to change. As we shall see in the next chapter, the crucial feature of this kind of sign, as with all South Slavic and Homeric *sêmata*, is not its superficial appearance but rather the traditional referentiality it so economically encodes.

Question IVb. Does the South Slavic epic register, like that of the Homeric poems, depend upon archaisms?

Answer 1: *No, it doesn't.*

Far the greater part of the traditional register, both lexicon and morphology, is coincident with the everyday speech used by the Stolac *guslari* in their conversations with Nikola Vujnović. In that sense the words and syntax used by the singer in performance are largely "contemporary."

Answer 2: *Yes, it does.*

Because the special language used by South Slavic singers operates according to traditional rules, it also includes phrases inherited from earlier times, phrases with features that have not survived in more streamlined, thoroughly contemporary registers. Again like the *aoidos*, the *guslar* thus depends upon a certain number of archaisms, both words and grammatical forms, that are no longer a part of the singers' conversational language but remain an integral feature of their traditional register.[54] In most such cases "modernizing" the lexicon or morphology would destroy the metrical integrity of the unitary phrases so vital to fluent communication between singer and audience. Even when modernization does not simply render the "words" unmetrical and thus compositionally useless, it reorganizes or replaces their internal architecture. In those cases where archaisms are constituents of *reči*, that is, they are unlikely to be replaced.

One of the most common sources of archaic words in South Slavic Moslem epic is the extensive inventory of Turkicisms. During the five-hundred-year Ottoman reign over the Balkans, from the fourteenth century onward, Turkish words entered the general language in significant numbers, and many of them became part of the specialized poetic language still employed by the Stolac singers in the 1930s and beyond.[55] Today some of these earlier borrowings remain part of the singers' conversational register, but most seem to be confined to the epic way of speaking. For example, Turkish terminology associated with wedding ceremonies persists in the highly conventional scenes of ritual bride-stealing and procession traditionally associated with marriage in the epic (*6699.550–57, 564–68*):

Kad su bili dobro podranili,	When they had risen early,	550
Sve naprijed careva gazija,	The tsar's hero was ahead of them all,	
*v*Ej, gazija Djerdjelez Alija,	Eh, the hero Djerdjelez Alija,	
Pa za njime silan Osmanbeže,	And after him Osmanbeg the powerful,	
*v*Osmanbeže, starosvat svatovim',	Osmanbeg, eldest witness among witnesses,	
Pa za njime Mujo buljubaša—	And after him commander Mujo—	555
Buljubaša bješe selambaša—	The commander was the greeter—	
Pa za njima paša sa Budima. . . .	And after them the pasha of Budim. . . .	
Kad su bili do Kanidže bil*i*,	When they were at white Kanidža,	
*v*A dobro *ji'* tamo dočekaše;	They awaited them there for a while;	565
Dočeka *ji'* kanidžki *v*ajane	The Kanidža leader awaited them	
Na *v*alaju i turskom selamu,	With a troop and a Turkish greeting,	
Poglavare na gornje *v*ahare.	The chieftain in the upper rooms.	

Aside from the sheer density of Turkicisms in this passage, most of them not in common usage in everyday vocabulary, their fossilization in larger phraseological "words" provides an interesting parallel to archaisms in Homeric diction. For example, fully ten of the seventeen occurrences of *gazija* ("hero") in the Stolac sample are lodged in the colonic formula *careva gazija* ("tsar's hero"), and the remaining seven all participate in figures of leonine (in-line) rhyme.[56] When one adds the terraced repetition at lines 551–52, it becomes clear that the network of traditional structure makes "updating" of this Turkicism difficult if not impossible. The same is true of the noun-epithet phrase *Mujo buljubaša* in line 555, the rhyming and terraced Turkicisms in 556 (*Buljubaša / selambaša*), and the noun-epithet

phrase *paša sa Budima* in 557.[57] Especially telling in this regard is the co-
lonic formula *kanidžki vajane*: although we find four additional instances of
the whole phrase in the Stolac performances, the Turkicism *ajan* ("leader")
never occurs outside the context of this composite, colonic "word." The
epic register has constructed a *reč* that contains this archaic item, and in
preserving the whole phrase it also preserves an otherwise long-outdated
constituent.

But not all archaisms in the South Slavic epic register are lexical. One
of the more widespread anachronisms is morphological in nature: the
frequent usage of the aorist verb tense, largely outmoded in present-day
conversational and written genres.[58] Again our primary comparison is
against the Stolac singers' conversations with Nikola Vujnović, and in this
unmarked register—so different on many scores from the epic "way of
speaking"—the aorist is almost nonexistent. The many instances of the
aorist in the Stolac poetic performances, on the other hand, clearly reflect
the principle of syllabic diversity and metrical bi-forms examined and il-
lustrated above. Here is a set of examples from Bajgorić's *The Wedding of
Mustajbeg's Son Bećirbeg* (6699.804–9):

*v*A zavika lički Mustajbeže:	And Mustajbeg of the Lika began to shout:
"Svi *j*imami na dovu stanite,	"All you imams start up in prayer, 805
*v*A kurbane sinu *v*oborite."	And slaughter the animals for my son."
Tada njemu padoše kurbani,	Then the animals were felled for him,
*v*A na dovu stadoše *j*imami,	And the imams started up in prayer,
Bećirbegu moliše za zdravlje.	Prayed for Bećirbeg's health.

In this brief passage Mustajbeg orders the Moslem priests, or imams, to
slaughter the *kurbani*, the sacrificial animals, for his son's sake just as the
young man is about to enter a life-or-death duel with a certain Baturić ban.
In all three cases the underlined aorist verbs describe the actions taken in
response to Mustajbeg's orders, and each helps constitute a unique phrase
in our sample of South Slavic epic from Stolac. Nevertheless, although we
cannot point to recurrence of these particular phrases for prima facie evi-
dence of traditional character, we can note that the aorist forms offer a
metrical alternative to either the historical present or simple past forms
that might have been used.[59] Leveling the inflections to agree with the
conversational standard would thus make these lines unmetrical and com-
promise their integrity as larger "words," just as replacing the Turkicisms
would have done in the phrases examined above. It thus seems safe to in-
terpret *padoše*, *stadoše*, and *moliše* as archaic verb forms frozen inside *reči*.
The fact that they occur together and in a unifying ritual context, again in
parallel with the group of Turkicisms examined above, strengthens that
interpretation.

Aorists can also be frozen into other contexts, one of the more common of which is the leonine rhyme that matches the two colon-ends in the deca-syllable. This aspect of acoustic architecture tends to fix phraseology and limit variation; because the lines it undergirds are more tightly organized, both by sense and by sound-patterning, they tend to resist change even more stubbornly than other "words" in the traditional register. Additionally, in-line rhyme is often the site for proverbial phraseology of one kind or another, maxims that may also be freestanding proverbs outside the epic and that index traditional ideas of yet wider applicability.[60] Such is the case with the following example, which combines the stabilizing influence of leonine rhyme with a unifying semantic idea (*6699*.519–20):

*v*Ej klanjaše, *v*onda večeraše,	Eh, they prayed, and afterward ate their evening meal,
Pa legoše Turci da spavaju.	Then the Turks lay down to sleep.

The ritualistic connection between praying and eating meshes with the sound-patterning in *klanjaše / večeraše*, and the sleep that follows can also be understood as semantically linked. Like freestanding proverbs, this grouping indexes a cultural idea. The same combination of acoustic design and proverbial meaning underlies another phrase that depends on in-line rhyme of aorist verbs (*6699*: 549):

Tu noćiše, dobro podraniše.	Here they spent the night, they arose early.

It is significant that all other usages of the verb *podraniti* in the Stolac sample employ the simple past to indicate that a certain person or people "arose early."[61] Only this particular instance, because of the stability imposed by morphological rhyme between the forms in *-iše*, retains the aorist. In short, as these examples illustrate in various ways, the aorist, while moribund in the singers' conversational register and elsewhere, seems alive and well in the traditional idiom.

Question V. Are the typical scenes of South Slavic epic similar to Homeric typical scenes?

    Answer 1: *Yes, they are.*

    As Albert Lord was the first to point out, the *guslar* relies on standard action-sequences that resemble the typical scenes that underlie Homeric narrative.[62] Both the South Slavic and the ancient Greek units are pliable multiforms rather than memorized data, and both show variation within limits, with details shifting from one occurrence to the next to fit the particular narrative situation.[63] The South Slavic typical scene is most clearly understood as another level of *reč* or "word," a unit of utterance and a speech-act that is an important part of the *guslar*'s register. As we shall see in Chapter 4, it is also a *sêma* with its own range of traditional implications and its own expressive role as a slotting device.

Within the Stolac songs a number of typical scenes recur with some regularity, none with more frequency than the "Shouting in Prison" multiform.[64] In songs performed by *guslari* from the area, this sequence comprises four major actions: (1) the prisoner cries out loudly and continually; (2) the captor's wife complains to the captor that the terrible noise is threatening their infant son's life; (3) the captor refuses to help, threatening eventual desecration of the prisoner's remains; and (4) the wife enters the prison herself to bargain for the prisoner's release. This basic story is embroidered in many different ways, with differing emphases according to the individual tale, the individual singer, and, with respect to versions from outside Stolac, different regions. For example, some performances elaborate the desecration with a memorable capsule like the following from Mujo Kukuruzovic´ (*6618*.62–67):

"*h*A mu duša iz kostiju izidje,	"But when his spirit leaves his bones,
Njegove ću kosti pokupiti,	I will gather the bones up,
Pa ću kosti ložit' u odžaku,	Burn the bones in a chimney,
Pa ću kosti u dibeku tući,	Grind the bones in a mortar,
Palicu i' moru na širinu—	And shoot them into the wide sea—
Nek od vraga ne ostaje traga!"	Let there remain no trace of the devil!"

Others emphasize the wife's desperation or her dismissive attitude toward her husband, and not a few employ the cultural as well as epic reality of "bloodsisterhood" to explain how the Christian wife manages to strike a bargain with the enemy Moslem captive.[65] But all instances are recognizably the same typical scene, with the standard pattern and situation-specific details counterbalanced in the *guslar*'s act of composition. As with all traditional *sêmata*, the audience or reader must accordingly take account of what lies both behind and between the signs.

Other commonly deployed typical scenes within the performances recorded in Stolac include arming the hero, caparisoning the horse, writing letters (as summons to battle or marriage or often both), arrival and assembly, and the disguised hero's contests with suitors, all of which exhibit the trademark variation within limits, taking slightly different forms in each performance as well as in the repertoires of different individuals (idiolects) and, outside Stolac, in different regions (dialects). What is more, each of these examples participates in the grander design of the Return Song story-pattern, the story of the *Odyssey*, which will be treated briefly below and at length in Chapter 5.

Answer 2: *No, they aren't.*

Just as the smaller *reči* of phraseology show differences from as well as similarities to Homeric "words," so the larger units of narrative—which must, after all, be expressed through phraseology—also show some incongruities. Since on available evidence the abstract idea-patterns of typical scenes from the two traditions are comparable,[66] we can cover most of these differences by recounting the areas of comparison from questions I–IV: formulaic structure, enjambement, metrical irregularities, dialect mixture, and archaisms. Both poetries feature encapuslated formulas, but the rules for the structure and morphology of the capsules are different. Enjambement figures are nearly the same, but the South Slavic line seems to avoid necessary continuation somewhat more regularly and via a different set of compositional strategies. Metrical "flaws," especially hiatus, mark both registers, but the *guslar* smooths the acoustic pathway with a phonological kit of inserted consonants. Both phraseologies draw from more than one dialect and turn occasionally to an archaic lexicon and morphology, even though the greater part of their way of speaking stems from a single "home" dialect and a current vocabulary and syntax. What is more, the usage of multiple dialects and archaisms marks both registers as specific kinds of communicative instruments. In both cases we saw that the two dictions had many resemblances, but that they also exhibited points of divergence, due chiefly to the fact that the Homeric and South Slavic epic registers are based on two distinct natural language systems and partnered by two similar but not wholly congruent meters.

As a rule, then, we can say that alongside the parallels in these areas stand differences: the *guslar's* typical scenes are not identical to Homer's, any more than their traditional dictions are simply superimposable. And from this balanced judgment derives an important theorem: we cannot expect any linguistic feature of the typical scene to be universal. Consider the long-standing controversy over the requirement of verbal correspondence among instances of a theme, an argument that has focused on just how much has to be repeated from one occurrence to the next for a passage—or an entire poetry—to qualify as traditional. If a comparative examination of a single theme's instances produces only a modest overlap, some have asked, are we truly dealing with a traditional unit?[67] Part of the misunderstanding on this score arises from viewing the typical scene, and all "words," as merely tectonic and mnemonic devices, building blocks that are deployed *metri causa* rather than idiomatic strategies that operate *artis causa*.[68] But even at the compositional level, variance among traditional registers means that no one scene or tradition can serve as the standard by which all others are measured; Homeric feasts and South Slavic instances of "arming the hero" are examples, not standards. "Words" in different traditions will always be both similar and different.

It is important to note another aspect of variety as well. Even within the South Slavic epic tradition, not all typical scenes are cut from the same cloth. Within the repertoire of a single *guslar* some are repeated practically verbatim, while others retain very little in the way of specific phrases from one occurrence to the next.[69] Moving from the idiolectal to the dialectal level, from the performances of one singer to those recorded over an entire region, only multiplies differences among themes. Given this much variation in verbal correspondence within the *epske pjesme* themselves, we certainly cannot expect overall congruency with Homeric typical scenes. In fact, the variability inherent in typical scenes in the living, well-recorded tradition should alert us to the possibility that the narrative "words" of the *Iliad* and *Odyssey* might reveal the same kind of spectrum. By analogy, we might expect not one but many sorts of typical scenes, each with its own kind of phraseological component. In fact, actual analysis has proven this to be the case: some Homeric scenes seem to depend on regular phraseology, while others are much more open to individual invention.[70] This inequivalence is what one would expect of the traditional register in general, if indeed it works like language, only more so.

Question VI. Does story-pattern function similarly in the two epic poetries?
     Answer 1: *No, it doesn't.*
     I begin with the negative response in order to provide a realistic background for the comparison. Because of both the paucity of evidence on the Homeric side (two extant poems with different overall patterns) and a presumed divergence in the two repertoires of storytelling, we must be cautious about comparing the Stolac songs with the *Iliad* and *Odyssey* at this macrolevel of "word." For these reasons, story-patterns, which Lord defined as "narrative patterns that, no matter how much the stories built around them may seem to vary, have great vitality and function as organizing elements in the composition and transmission of oral story texts,"[71] must to some extent differ in South Slavic and ancient Greek epic.
     Answer 2: *Yes, it does.*
     The major point of comparison here is the *nostos* tale, or Return Song, which survives in a single witness from ancient Greece but in many hundreds of versions in South Slavic, as well as Albanian, Bulgarian, Russian, and other traditions.[72] Lord discussed this story-pattern as a sequence of five stages through which the hero passes: Absence, Devastation, Return, Retribution, and Wedding.[73] That is, the protagonist, whatever he may be named, is unnaturally absent from his homeland for a long time, during which period he undergoes various ignominies in captivity and encounters various challenges en route back home. In the meanwhile his abandoned family suffers parallel, linked miseries, as rivals for the hero's position usurp the household in a sustained and abusive occupation. The hero

then returns, always in disguise, and takes vengeance on the usurpers, first in the ritual combat of athletic contest and then, if necessary, by killing one or more of them. An important part of the hero's reestablishment is an extensive series of loyalty tests that involve family members and cohorts, most centrally his wife or fiancée. The Return Song comes to closure rather quickly if that most important test proves positive, but if the wife or fiancée turns out to be unfaithful it continues into a sequel pattern in which the hero runs off to join the enemy before eventual revenge and return are secured.

This is of course the story of the *Odyssey*, but it is also the story of, for example, *Alagić Alija and Velagić Selim*, as told by Stolac singer Ibro Bašić, which features not one but two Return heroes. And it is the story of *The Captivity of Ograšćić Alija / Alagić Alija*, performed by his colleague Mujo Kukuruzović, whose protagonist finds a Klytemnestra rather than a Penelope figure awaiting him. These correspondences place any one South Slavic Return Song in the context of an entire tradition, and provide evidence for a compositional "word" at the macrolevel of tale-type. Story-pattern—and here specifically the Return sequence—is thus another kind of *reč* or *sêma*; it exhibits characteristic variation within limits and is an essential aspect of the traditional register. It is another way in which oral tradition works like language, only more so.

For the moment we will be content with having pointed out the unmistakable parallels between the *Odyssey* and the South Slavic Return Song.[74] Of course, alongside similarities are the ever-present differences: Odysseus and Alagić Alija are no more identical than their experiences, the central female figure is handled in some singular ways by each tradition, and so forth. But there are also a remarkable number of correspondences: some of the South Slavic Penelopes even weave, and some of their husbands bear telltale scars on their thighs. As always, one must read both behind and between the signs.

Conclusion

To summarize, the analogy between the special epic registers employed by the *guslar* and the *aoidos* presents a viable avenue for investigation: upon careful examination their similar features bear out the original comparison forged by Milman Parry and Albert Lord and carried forward by others. At the same time, it would be an error—in both philology and comparative research—to assume simple congruency between the two traditions. As we have seen, each register manifests certain idiosyncrasies; each exhibits characteristic features not found in the other. To put the matter telegraphically, each register is a living, functional variety of language with its own rules for composition and reception. Because these two languages serve parallel compositional and communicative purposes, it can prove profitable to set them side by side and observe how they mutually illuminate one another. In this way the living tradition can in some ways help us better understand the tradition that survives only as a relatively small group of texts. Nonetheless, part of that illumination must always consist of an unblinking awareness of differences as well as similarities. In fact, the entire South Slavic analogy is most helpful to readers of Homer only when it is properly attenuated, only when we are willing to move beyond reductive claims of absolute congruency or incongruency and toward the kind of detailed, nuanced comparison that both poetic languages and both epic poetries deserve.

More precisely, we have identified a number of parallels, all of which can be traced to the fact that the two registers represent *traditional* ways of speaking. Both epic poetries demonstrate a formulaic phraseology that follows traditional rules for the formation and maintenance of large "words," unitary speech-acts that the South Slavic singers refer to as *reči*. Likewise, we find similar patterns of enjambement and metrical irregularity in the two epic poetries, patterns directly traceable to the incremental nature of their dictions. While not really "artificial," each idiom juxtaposes archaisms and multiple (geographically defined) dialects alongside the forms one would expect in a nonspecialized register. Finally, the larger *reči*, the typical scene and story-pattern, function similarly in the epic idioms of *guslar* and *aoidos*.

As we have also observed, the two registers are by no means entirely congruent. Their formulaic structures differ because of disparities in meter and traditional rules; perhaps the most dramatic consequence is the complete lack of Parryan thrift in South Slavic epic. Additionally, necessary enjambement is if anything more strongly avoided by the *guslar*, who has his own repertoire of interlinear strategies, and the major metrical irregularity in South Slavic epic, vowel hiatus, is mitigated by consonantal bridges or "performatives." Likewise, when examined closely, each poetry demonstrates its own particular mixture of dialects and archaisms. Finally, the larger narrative "words," while certainly comparable, also demonstrate a number of differences, due mainly to their idiosyncratic phraseological dimensions.

In this chapter we have been concerned primarily with the nature of the *guslar*'s register and its structural and dynamic comparability to Homer's way of speaking. In the following chapter we will shift our focus from the "words" themselves to the problem of how and what such "words" mean, how the South Slavic *sêmata* engage traditional referentiality.

4

HOMER AND THE SOUTH SLAVIC *GUSLAR*
Traditional Referentiality

kukavica crna
the black cuckoo
—Traditional

San usnila, pa se prepanula.
You've dreamed a dream, so you're frightened.
—Traditional

At a functional level, traditional registers enable the *guslar* and *aoidos* to compose fluently in performance and to express themselves idiomatically. In that sense they offer fine-tuned linguistic instruments dedicated to a single purpose: the ready composition of epic verse. But these specialized languages are extraordinary in another way as well—in their traditional referentiality. In the preceding chapter we saw that both the ancient Greek of Homer and the South Slavic spoken and sung in performance by the Stolac bards depart significantly from the sort of language to which we are more accustomed, and indeed from the language used by *guslari* in conversations with Nikola Vujnović. Now we turn to the implications of this kind of singularity. For it is precisely such regular and expectable departures that serve as a crucial cue for the audience and later the reader: they signal the nature of the poetic event, prescribing the communicative channel and keying response. According to the model developed in Chapter 1, we can say that traditional registers create a recurrent performance arena and make possible a unique kind of communicative economy. These special poetic registers work like language, only more so.

Let us begin by restating the core concept of traditional referentiality from the South Slavic bards' point of view. According to Mujo Kukuruzović, Salko Morić, Ibro Bašić, and Halil Bajgorić, the "words" they use are also speech-acts; we may reasonably conclude, then, that every act of composition implies a corresponding act of reception. Or, as our homemade proverb advises, composition and reception emerge as two sides of the same coin. Indeed, as we shall see, the epic language resonates with implications at many different levels, implications that derive from its usage as an enriched idiom. To put it in Homeric terms, South Slavic epic language also depends heavily on the power of *sêmata*; to grasp the range of meaning and the possibilities for verbal artistry in such a medium, we must therefore learn to read both behind and between the signs. The challenge issued to us by the *guslar*—as well as by the *aoidos*—is clear enough: nothing less than fluency in the traditional register.

In this chapter we will be concentrating on the implications of an epic way of speaking, from the most basic and general level of simply using the register as a channel for communication through the recurrent South Slavic *sêmata* of phraseology, typical scene, and story-pattern. Of course, other aspects of the performance are relevant and constitutive here, even if we cannot address them directly: the vocal and instrumental music cooperates with the verbal component to signal that a certain kind of event is taking place.[1] Performances without vocal or instrumental music, as well as performances that are edited into textual format, will lack some of these features, but that is no excuse to leaven the speech-act to a conventional textual register.[2] All of these cues indicate that the epic channel is being opened, and that not just the *guslar* but also his audience, listeners, and even readers must tune to the same frequency if they are to communicate successfully. Only if all parties to the performance are "speaking the same language" can the exchange succeed. If audience or readers choose not to do so, or are by their training or experience unable to do so, then the communication must fail, to one degree or another. With this fundamental requirement in mind, it is easy to understand why perusing a few lines of a translation of South Slavic epic will always be an inadequate, reductive, and distorting approach. We need to learn the language and—more to the point—the register.

The Most Basic Signal

In plainest terms, performing in the decasyllabic poetic diction of South Slavic epic is itself a speech-act, and a speech-act rife with associations.

Even apart from the specialized units of utterance, this is a living idiom that creates a recurring and expectable frame of reference. It works like a language, only more so.

What does this mean for the *guslar* and for the audiences and readers who in their various capacities attend his performances? For one thing, the mere prescription of the decasyllabic idiom, with or without its musical and vocal dimensions, amounts to what Dell Hymes (1981, 1989) has termed a "breakthrough into performance." Nowhere is this more evident than in the conversations between the Stolac singers and Nikola Vujnović, which contain not only the kind of question-and-answer exchange studied above in Chapter 3 but also actual epic songs, performed in whole or in part. These performances are embedded within the interview context, sparked in some way by the exchange that precedes them, and yet quite separate. Once the *guslar* shifts to the act of singing, his code-switching to the epic register brings into play another frame of reference, another set of implications. No longer is the discussion about personal history or a particular character or situation in a song as someone or something detached; now the exchange is both narrowed and enriched, as the implicit background of South Slavic epic tradition is summoned as a referent. The singer's way of speaking modulates from an unmarked conversational style to the marked and dedicated language that is the vehicle employed solely for epic performance, and with that shift in composition must come a corresponding shift in reception. The language of epic performance is not as generally serviceable as the language of conversation, which can be used for many more purposes and situations than can the highly focused traditional register. But the trade-off is significant: the restricted, metrical idiom of epic performance is heavier with specific implications, more resonant with overtones, more demanding of a specialized reception.

Thus, along with examining the assortment of *sêmata* that serve as specific links or pathways to traditional referentiality, we should take full account of what amounts to far the most important sign in the *guslar*'s repertoire: the decasyllabic idiom of performance as a whole. It is the radical shift to this medium that makes everything else possible, that cues the "breakthrough into performance" in South Slavic epic. According to the terminology evolved in Chapter 1, it sets the performance arena, brings into play the signs that constitute the register, and enables communicative economy. Indeed, unless the phrases, typical scenes, and story-patterns occur within the context invoked by this most fundamental level of the register, they will seem opaque, abstruse, merely repetitive and unimaginative, or even infelicitous. The *sêmata* are, after all, units within a language, and the intelligibility of any language depends upon a shared knowledge of the rules and the referent.

The examples of traditional signs given below are organized into three categories: story-pattern, typical scenes, and formulaic "words." These

brief examinations correspond to the longer discussions of parallel Ho-
meric *sêmata* in Chapters 5–7 below, where a chapter each is devoted to the
Return Song pattern, the Feast and Lament scenes, and a variety of signals
at the level of phraseology.[3]

The Largest *Reč*: Story-Pattern

With this background, then, let us turn to the largest of the *guslar*'s "words"
or *reči*, the *story-pattern*. Remembering that this is not just a compositional
tool but a guide for reception, we can partially simulate an informed au-
dience's reaction by proceeding through the easily recognizable Return
Song, stopping at a few major junctures to take account of what is implied
as well as what is explicit. We will be interested not in any one realization
of the pattern, that is, but in the traditional context to which any single ver-
sion institutionally refers. Reception will amount to decoding the signals
that the poet and audience exchange to negotiate meaning.[4]

Conventionally, the *guslar* starts a Return Song—no matter who or what
the hero(es), captor, or location may be—with the Shouting in Prison
scene mentioned in the fifth section of the last chapter. More precisely, in
the Stolac region such songs begin with some form of the verb *cmiliti* ("to
moan, grieve, complain").[5] From this scene and even from this initial verb
onward, a map for the narrative journey begins to take shape. The rough
outlines are as follows. A Turkish hero, called away to a battle in which he
has little or no personal stake, is captured by forces under the command
of a Christian ban (political head of a city) and imprisoned. He screams
loudly for release, and the ruckus he raises will sooner or later cause a bar-
gain to be struck for his release. In the meantime we are aware, via the im-
plications associated with *cmiliti* and the opening scene, that his absence
has wrought great hardship for the family he left behind, which always in-
cludes a wife or fiancée and often a son.

But how will the expectable drama play out? Under what conditions
will he be released? What form will the quarrel over his shouting actually
take? Even within the Stolac region these and other questions will be
answered differently in different songs, within different performances, by
different singers, and so forth. The narrative sequence is hardly set in stone
but shows characteristic variation within limits, and it is the possibility of
that variation that engenders two complementary dynamics for interpre-
tation. First, the sameness of the pattern—its recognizability as an idio-
matic element or *sêma*—brings traditional referentiality into play. From the
opening signals on, the song-map begins to take shape, roughly and with
very little detail. As more signals appear, the resolution improves, and the

smaller topographical features come into view. We start to understand how this particular Return Song will realize the potentials inherent in the story-pattern. While we know from the start the background behind the imprisonment and the inevitability of release, only as events actually develop do we see precisely how that always-certain goal is reached this time around. Familiar cues slot this particular performance—and its apparently singular events—by bringing into play the network of possibilities within which they are always poised. Instance meshes with implication.

Second is the matter of individualized details and the dynamic of suspense. Unlike the kind of suspense that involves wholly unknown circumstances, wherein the reader is prevented from knowing much at all about how the future will turn out until it actually unfolds, the Return Song map designates a pathway right through to the final destination from the moment the performance starts. The hero's absence and the devastation it causes will dependably give way to his return, some form of retribution against his rivals, and a potential (re)wedding. Nonetheless, two types of uncertainty remain, one that affects the closure of the story and one that affects its progress all the way through. As for the closure, it is an inescapable fact that such tales of return balance on the fulcrum of the wife or fiancée, and not the hero. He will sooner or later find his way home and, while in disguise, will conduct a series of tests for faithfulness, the last and most important of which involves his mate. If she passes the test, the story ends at or near that point with their reunion; if not, it continues into a sequel adventure before revenge is eventually achieved. These are the only possible outcomes, and, what is more, the two song-types are indistinguishable up until the point of the hero's final test.

The other kind of uncertainty has to do with the "fine print" or detailed topography of a map that in its broad outlines is unambiguous. For while there is no mystery about what will happen in the most general terms, there is no certainty whatever about how this particular song will evolve. How demanding will the protagonist's journey home prove to be? What or whom will he encounter on the way? Will the disguised hero challenge the suitors in running, throwing, jumping, or other ritual contests? Will it be necessary to kill one or more of them or will his self-revelation be enough to drive the cowards off? Will his sister or mother or servants be given the same test of loyalty he later administers to his mate? And, most significant by far, will he find a Penelope or a Klytemnestra awaiting his return?

As a feature of the South Slavic epic register, story-pattern is thus a window that opens onto traditional referentiality and a *sêma* that keys an emergent event. The Return Song is of course a good story in itself; who could resist this tale of the triumphant reappearance of the long-absent hero, the long-suffering mate, and the hard-won reestablishment of the community? The outrageous suitors are finally repaid for their unseemly depradations and order is restored. Even an unfaithful wife cannot derail the satisfaction of narrative closure forever: the hero may stray to the enemy camp for a time, but all will eventually end appropriately (as far as the pattern is concerned). In the meantime, and whatever the challenge he meets at home, that same protagonist will have to demonstrate considerable physical and intellectual prowess just to accomplish his return. We are naturally intrigued by such a story, even if we are hearing it for the first time.

But the traditional audience is of course not hearing it for the first time, and neither is the reader of texts who knows the tradition and can read behind the signs. Any particular hero occupies a character slot that has enough definition to be recognizable and therefore to foreground traditional implications, but not so much that the individual story suffers or that the singer forfeits his own role in the making of the story.[6] The captor and location—familiar as types even if not by their actual names—may be handled differently by one *guslar*, or even in successive performances by the same singer, but not so differently that the clear, strong traditional signal modulates to static on the channel. There is a balance between traditional referentiality and individual craft, and between the general directions provided by the story-map and the measured suspense of precisely how one gets from here to there on that map. There is variation within limits. From the chemistry of individual and tradition, of instance and implication, of part and whole emerges the art of the *guslar*.

Narrative *Reči*: Typical Scenes and Other Brief Patterns

Since according to the Stolac *guslari* Mujo Kukuruzović, Salko Morić, and their peers the "words" they employ are also speech-acts, we may observe, as noted above, that every act of composition implies a corresponding act of reception. This will be as true for typical scenes as for story-patterns or phraseology. For this reason we must pay close attention not only to the tectonic features of recurrent narrative units, but also to their traditional referentiality.

1. *Arming the Hero.*   For the first example I have chosen a frequently occurring typical scene from the Stolac songs, Arming the Hero, in order to illustrate in greater detail how such narrative *reči* participate in the poetics of epic performance. A great many more examples could of course be brought forward,[7] but this scene suggests as well as any how the charac-

teristic variation within limits acts as a double axis for the evolving narrative. Like other kinds of "words," the typical scene ties the individual song-performance into the traditional network of meaning at the same time as it leaves room for situation-specific variation according to individual song, singer, and realization. Instance meshes with implication.

Arming the Hero has been studied extensively elsewhere, most often in ancient and medieval traditions.[8] In South Slavic epic its form varies widely from region to region, so I limit my remarks to the Stolac area and its local dialect of the poetic register. In fact, even within this relatively well-defined area Arming shows more variety than do most other scenes. Here is a brief excerpt from a dictated performance by the *guslar* Halil Bajgorić, whose versions of this "word" prove considerably more elaborate than those of his peers. The subject of this particular arming episode is the celebrated Turkish hero Halil (6703.368–82):

Skoči neva na odaju š njime,		The bride rushed to the room with him,
Pa mu stade birat' odijelo.		Then she began to pick out clothing for him.
Dok mu jedne bila odabrala,	370	When she had chosen him some things,
Po izboru najbolje haljine,		According to her selection the best clothes,
Kad se Halil stade preoblačit':		Then Halil began to get dressed:
Najpre' meće gaće i košulju,		First he put on drawers and a shirt,
Po gaćama od saje čakšire—		Over the drawers some red-silk trousers—
Čakšire mu kraja bugarskoga,	375	His trousers were in the Bulgarian style,
Veli da su veza stambolskoga,		It's said they were embroidered in Istanbul style,
Kudgodj šavi sve harčevi zlatni—		The seams had golden braid everywhere—
A na pleći fermen od kadife,		And on his shoulders a velvet vest,
Na kom stoje troje toke sjajne.		On which stood three shining silver plates.
One toke koje gornje bjehu—	380	The plates that were up above—
Na nji' puce dvades' i četiri,		On them were twenty-four buttons,
Dvades' srme a četiri zlata.		Twenty of sterling silver and four of gold.

This passage happens to be drawn from Bajgorić's performance of *Halil Rescues Bojičić Alija* (6703), but similar passages occur in other songs by him and his fellow Stolac singers. I will not rehearse the details of their structure and morphology here; descriptions of the characteristic multi-formity of typical scenes are available elsewhere.[9] For present purposes I am principally interested in the "map" projected by the Arming scene. What implications does it contribute to the process of reception for an audience schooled in traditional referentiality?

Most basically, of course, the donning of clothes, armor, and weapons formally readies the hero for whatever adventure he is to undertake. Although in some traditions, like the Anglo-Saxon, the next step is usually battle,[10] in the Stolac songs that is not the case. Instead, the hero so carefully dressed and armed departs on a journey, and a specific kind of journey: he will ride his horse not into immediate combat but to a distant, foreign locale where he will eventually embark on a dangerous mission. Furthermore, as part of the mission he will always have to deal with a duplicitous character with divided loyalties. None of these implications is transparently a part of the Arming as such; there is no clue in the assortment of clothes, armor, and weapons or any other literal dimension of the scene that these subsequent actions will take place. Nonetheless, they always do occur, in some form or other, and the well-prepared audience will therefore expect them.

In the performance from which the excerpt above was quoted, *Halil Rescues Bojičić Alija*, Halil arms and then rides off to the Christian town of Kotar. The journey in this song-version is memorably perilous, as the hero encounters wolves, bears, and ravens en route, but he eventually arrives and enlists the aid of his mother's bloodbrother,[11] the *haiduk* (highwayman) Malenica, in freeing Bojičić Alija from enemy captivity. Malenica fits the bill of an ambiguous figure in a number of ways: he is a *haiduk*, living outside the law and conventional society, and though he now resides among Christians he has a history of allegiance to the famous Turkish hero, Mustajbeg of the Lika. It becomes apparent that the highwayman's double identity will aid his Turkish comrade in the undercover mission on which he is embarked. In fact, as we follow out the finer points of the traditional referentiality associated with this sequence, we find that Malenica is himself one version of a *sêma*, a stereotyped figure who lives on the border between cultures and is thus uniquely positioned to aid in such secret projects. The highwayman-bloodbrother thus occupies not one but two familiar "slots," with his individuality played off against two recognizable profiles with encoded associations. These generic cues, along with the larger map associated with the Arming scene, alert us to certain broad expectations, which are then realized in an idiosyncratic, even unique fashion by the singer Bajgorić in this particular performance of this particular song.

In another of Bajgorić's songs, *The Wedding of Mustajbeg's Son Bećirbeg* (*6699*), the action evolves along the same general pathway but with a quite different combination of characters and situations. In this case the protagonist doing the arming, the famous Turkish stalwart Djerdjelez Alija, will head for the fortified tower of Mustajbeg of the Lika, whose son Bećirbeg is about to be married. Marriage in this tradition happens on a grand scale, with a ritual bride-capture supported by a handsome array of allied forces; in epic practice it is often indistinguishable from a battle, into which the bride-capture frequently modulates. So the dangerous, life-threatening adventure lies very clearly on the horizon for Djerdjelez Alija, just as the Arming-scene map would lead us to expect. What is more, Mustajbeg is one of the most duplicitous, undependable figures in the tradition at large: he will sometimes act the proper Turkish patriot, but he can just as easily lock his own ally outside the city gate, effectively offering him up to a besieging enemy, or play the South Slavic Antinoos by leading the suitors' attempt to win the Return Song hero's wife or fiancée during the latter's prolonged absence. In short, what this second song-performance illustrates is another way in which the trail blazed by the Arming *reč* can be traversed: once again the suitably prepared hero undertakes a journey that must lead to an ambigous character and a risky mission.

As a third illustration of the traditional referentiality associated with the Arming pattern, consider its unusual application to a female character in multiple performances of *Alagić Alija and Velagić Selim* by the Stolac singer Ibro Bašić (*6597, 291b*, 1283). What stands out is not the fact of the heroine Fata's femininity, which entails only a minimal adjustment, but the overwhelming extent to which the unit and its implications remain the same. Like the male heroes, she depends upon her mother to prepare the food that will sustain her en route; also like her masculine counterparts, she goes to the stable to find and caparison the horse that will carry her on the journey. And like all the others she dons clothing and arms herself (1283.972–94):

Vid' djevojke Muminove Fate—		But you should have seen Mumin's daughter Fata—
Ona pade u šikli odaju;		She fell upon the gold-adorned room;
Sjede svlačit' žensko odijelo		She began to take off her women's garb
A oblačit' madžar' djeisiju.	975	And put on Hungarian clothes.
Kad obuče madžar' djeisiju,		When she had donned Hungarian clothes,
A ra'plete devet pletenica		She wove nine hair-braids
Kao nose po gradu Madžari;		Like Hungarians wear in the city;
Više vrata tri krsta o' zlata.		Around her neck hung three crosses of gold.
Pa udari krila i čelenke,	980	Then she put on the wings and feathers,[12]
A opasa kajišer silaha,		And she girded on herself a belt of arms,
Za nj' zadila dva čifta pušaka,		On which she hitched two pairs of pistols,
Dva ingleza i dva venedika,		Two English and two Venetian,
Medju njima handžar od čelika—		Between them a long steel dagger,
Iz njeg' jesu četiri sindžira—	985	From it hung four chains;
Potkićen je rušpam' mljetačkijem		It was studded with Venetian ducats
(Ljudi veli pe'stotina ruš'pa);		(People say five hundred ducats);
Uteže se tri, četiri puta.		She encircled herself three, four times.

A pripasa oštru ćemerliju,		And she put on a sharp saber,
Što je isk'o od Zadarja bane,	990	The one that the ban of Zadar sought,
Što siječe pod oklop		The one that cut through the Hungarian's
Madžara.		armor.
Kad se cura hazur učinila,		When the maiden finished her
		preparations,
Primače se rafu i dolapu		She approached the shelf and the closet
A nasipa žute madžarije.		And filled [her pockets] with golden
		coins.

Restricting our survey to formulaic correspondences in the Stolac songs cited above, we find male-centered parallels as follows. The "taking off and putting on" phrases are reflected in the full form of both Halil's and Djerdjelez Alija's arming, as are the feathered headgear, the paired English and Venetian pistols, and the three- or fourfold encirclement. Djerdjelez Alija also straps on a belt of arms and a long steel dagger with four chains and fills his pockets with golden coins. Numerous heroes gird themselves with a sharp saber.[13] These features are juxtaposed to the specifically feminine features of plaited hair and golden crosses with which the passage begins.

What stands out in this third Arming, then, is its combination of a few obviously feminine and many more conventionally masculine details, as well as the scene's slotting of the young woman Fata as the traditional hero about to undertake a dangerous mission. She prepares for her role as sub-stitute—taking the place of the imprisoned Alagić Alija, the fiancé whom she intends to free from captivity—by appropriating this narrative signal, this heroic *sêma*. The workings of traditional referentiality are quite trans-parent here, as the *guslar* uses the idiomatic power of the register to con-vert the young woman into the substitute champion and hero of the song. From the time she dons the armor and adopts his identity, she effectively becomes the protagonist of the Return Song, bearing on her shoulders the considerable weight of the story's narrative momentum as well as of the prisoner's liberation. For this reason, I would argue, the attribution made by the Arming scene is basically genderless: the important dimension is that she assumes the role of hero, not that she merely imitates masculine behavior. With the conversion accomplished, we now expect her to em-bark on a substantial journey leading to a life-threatening mission asso-ciated with a character (or characters) with divided loyalties. This is pre-cisely what happens, as she rides to the Christian town of Zadar where her fiancé Alagić Alija is being held prisoner by the enemy ban. She joins forces with innkeeper Mara, a kind of double agent who favors the Turks, and Andjelija, the ban's own daughter, in a bold plan to secure her future mate's eventual freedom. Once again the map designates a familiar narra-tive route, although precisely what and whom we encounter along the way always remain to be realized.

2. *The Unexpected Answer.* Of at least equal frequency, and of much more modest compass, is a small pattern we may call the Unexpected Answer.[14] This recurrent sequence consists of a number of questions, usually two or three, posed by the narrator in an attempt to account for some as yet unexplained phenomenon, followed by a string of responses in the same order.[15] But whatever the query and however many of them he may pose, the responses are always in the negative, until at the very end of the series an unexpected solution to the quandary is appended. The substance of the questions, which varies from one occurrence to another depending on the song and the local situation, is given a traditional, resonant context by the recognizable frame. From the beginning, then, the audience or reader fluent in the register understands the rhetorical sequence and awaits the solution to that sequence in the coda.

Mujo Kukuruzović employs this traditional *sêma* to particular advantage in the opening lines of his dictated version of *The Captivity of Alagić Alija* (1868.1–6):

Šta no nešto u Zadarju cmili?	What in the world was shouting in Zadar?
Da je vila u gori bi bila?	Could it be a mountain nymph?
Da je guja u kamen' bi bila?	Could it be a snake under a stone?
Nit' je vila, nit' je šar'a guja,	It was neither a nymph nor a striped snake,
Nego jadan Alagić Alija.	But the wretched Alagić Alija.
Turčin cmili tri bijela dana.	The Turk shouted for three white days.

This performance begins without the signal of a proem or *pripjev*,[16] but the "unexpected answer" pattern provides an idiomatic momentum of its own. The very first line focuses on earsplitting shouting (always with some form of the verb *cmiliti*), the trademark activity of the incarcerated Return hero, and thereby unmistakably designates the subgenre of epic to ensue. At the same time, the line as a whole signals the onset of a figure of speech that is rife with traditional referentiality. By suggesting and then disqualifying a few possible explanations for what is avowedly a curious and important phenomenon (so the frame certifies), the singer postpones explicit identification of the specific hero. We are told that someone has been captured (one of the Turkish "good guys") and, by implication, that his unceasing noise will sooner or later force a negotiation with the ban's wife to secure his eventual release, but we are not yet told precisely who the captive is. A well-prepared audience could quite accurately describe the prisoner's physical appearance (dressed in rags, with a beard to his waist and nails grown out "like those on a winged horse," etc.) and immediate surroundings (his cell filled with water to his shoulders, complete with scorpions and snakes), but could not at this point name him. We recognize the traditional slot; we just don't yet know the particular person. Waiting for the final solution in the coda to the series only increases the tension, opening an area of indeterminacy for the audience or reader and paving the way for the eventual divulging of the prisoner's actual identity. Via this South Slavic *sêma* the narrative tracks along a familiar trajectory—from slotting by traditional type or pattern to actually naming the particular individual or action. The "unexpected answer" serves as a guide in the melding of implication with instance.[17]

3. *Journey Home.* At various points and for many different reasons in South Slavic epic, whether as part of a Return Song or of some other subgenre, a hero must undertake a journey back to his place of origin or residence. Many of these adventures are fraught with dangers, whether from an enemy force, highwaymen, wild animals, or simply the challenge of a substantial trek that must be managed by a weakened protagonist suffering from many years' imprisonment. It is precisely at such points that the *guslar* has great flexibility in his performance. He may choose to recount the journey expansively, detailing every challenge the hero faces; he may opt for a medium-length exposition; or he may sing a telegraphic version of the trip, bringing the protagonist from point of departure to destination in the matter of a few lines. This natural flexibility in the performance register is parallel to the rhetorical figures of diminution and augmentation that became a consciously deployed staple of the medieval European poet's stylistic repertoire.[18]

In his dictated version of *The Captivity of Alagić Alija*, Kukuruzović employs a familiar sequence of lines to send his hero from incarceration in the Christian city of Kotar to his home in Udbina with all possible speed (1868.160–65):

Kad rekoše da se pozdraviše,	When they had bid each other farewell,	160
Podje Ale od kršli Kotara.	Ali departed from red Kotar.	
Kudgoj idje, na granicu sidje.	Wherever he went, he came to the border.	
Tu j' Alija konak učinijo,	Here Alija made his overnight stay,	
Pa ujutru rano podranijo.	Then he arose early the next morning.	
Kudgodj idje, svojoj kuli sidje.	Wherever he went, he came to his tower.	

Not unlike the speech introduction lines to be examined in the next section, these verses perform a homely but necessary function: they move the protagonist from place to place under idiomatic sanction, and almost telegraphically. No sooner are the good-byes uttered and leave taken than Alagić Alija reaches the border of Christian and Turkish lands. After an overnight rest and early awakening that require only a couplet to describe, he swiftly arrives not merely in his home region of Udbina but right at his tower, the tangible symbol of his family and local power that has become decrepit in his absence. It is hard to imagine a more expeditious journey from the faraway enemy jail to one's own special corner of the world. But the important point is that these lines serve more than a functional purpose. They also constitute a ready *sêma* for such homeward treks, deriving their authority from regularity of usage and implication. Precisely because the singers employ them, or some close idiolectal variant, for this singular purpose only, their appearance slots whatever particular trek is under way within the familiar category of heroic journeys back. Because they have the force of idiom, the *guslar* can deploy this shorthand strategy for bringing the hero home with all of the poetic force inherent in other dimensions of the specialized register. Just as surely as Arming the Hero or Unexpected Answer provides more than a literal meaning, eking out the narrative process via the word-power of the traditional register, so Journey Home contributes its own measure of idiomatic implication. Although sometimes remarkably terse in sheer number of decasyllabic verses, it is in no way expressively inadequate. Traditional referentiality fills out the picture keyed by these resonant phrases, aligning Alagić Alija's trip with those undertaken by many other heroes, whatever their actual itineraries. Journey Home amounts to a humble but serviceable *reč*, a word and speech-act that implies much more than it seems to state, and it offers another bit of evidence in support of the overall case that the South Slavic epic register works like language, only more so.

Phraseological *Reči*: Formulaic "Words"

In addition to the larger levels of *reči* and the general cue for code-switching furnished by the decasyllabic diction as a whole, the *guslar* draws upon numerous phrases that have a wide range of idiomatic implications in epic performance. Like the higher-level units, they project a more than literal meaning, linking this particular song and situation to the poetic tradition at large and thereby enriching the local proceedings with traditional referentiality. Many times the singer's phrases slot a given action, otherwise unique in itself, within a recognizable frame of reference, acting as *sêmata* that key emergent associations. As a rule, although as we shall see not without exception, the superficial, literal meaning of such phrases harmonizes easily with the surrounding story, with the overtones contributing a supplementary poetic value. By plugging into the network of traditional signs, these *reči* become speech-acts, with the nominal part standing for an implicit whole.

The present section reviews a small selection of such phrases, employed by the Stolac *guslari* (and in most cases outside that region as well) not simply to support composition but also to guide reception. As we have seen, the register is first and foremost a language rather than a collection of items: accordingly, formulaic phrases must be as much instruments that foster communication with an audience or reader as mere building blocks for the composer. In the analysis to follow, I will emphasize what the examples denote lexically (their literal meaning) in contrast to what they connote via convention (their traditional referentiality).

1. *Noun-Epithet Formulas.* I begin with the most obvious kind of *reč*, the formulary names for specific principal characters like Halil but also for general character types like the "black cuckoo" (*kukavica crna*). Taken together, these examples demonstrate a range and variety of coding typical of the register's broad spectrum of signification. Both perform an important poetic function, and each stands for more than its literal meaning can indicate. As we shall see, the performance is richer because of their contributions.

Within the Stolac sample, Halil is named in four ways, all of them matched as usual to the six-syllable second colon of the line: *ugojak Halile* (the stout one Halil), *Mujagin Halile* (Mujo's [brother] Halil), *dijete Halile* (child Halil), and *goješna Halila* (stout Halil [gen. case only]).[19] As noted in Chapter 3, Parryan thrift is not a feature of South Slavic epic verse. Nonetheless, within its own register this system of naming accomplishes the same referential task as Homer's metrically more diverse system: it indexes the given character through the use of assigned *sêmata*. That is, by deploying one of the sanctioned designations for Halil, each of which is used in myriad other songs and situations throughout the networked epic tradition, these *reči* summon the figure they name to narrative present. What is more, this slotting procedure amounts to an extremely economical kind of characterization. Because the singer uses a "word" familiar from other occurrences, it indexes a large inventory of background information, representing not just the boiled-down "essential idea" of Halil but the living mythic figure complete with his epic biography. Far from just getting the compositional job done, that is, these *sêmata* strike a resonant chord, driving reception by tapping into traditional referentiality.

The nonspecific "black cuckoo" is also a *reč* that drives reception, in its case by slotting whatever female character is given this metaphorical name in a recognizable traditional category. Lexicographer and collector of epic songs Vuk Karadžić explained that this bird-name became a generalized noun for "miserable one" via the embedded folktale of a woman who so mourned her brother's death that she turned into a cuckoo.[20] Beyond this metaphor lies the traditional implication of *kukavica crna*, which is consistently and exclusively applied to a woman whose conjugal or kinship status—and therefore her entire social existence as pictured in the epic— hangs in the balance. Employed exclusively by Mujo Kukuruzović in the

Stolac sample, this phrase appears a total of seven times in two songs, a version of *The Captivity of Alagić Alija* (1868) and a version of *The Captivity of Ograšćić Alija* (6617).

Within *The Captivity of Alagić Alija*, the first three instances designate the central hero's sister Fata and point toward family and community dysfunction and evil days ahead now that he has returned and found his supposedly faithful wife to be false. Thus Alija calls Fata "black cuckoo" just after she recognizes him (330) and again as he tells her that he is now forsaking the Turks to join an enemy Christian army (545). In between these signals lies another hint of trouble, as Alija's mother refuses to believe her daughter's report that her son has returned, calling Fata "miserable one" (376),[21] and at 769 a minor Turkish stalwart, Gojenović Ibro, foretells disaster by applying the phrase to the beg's daughter Zlata as he rides off for help. Later on in the same song-performance, the ban of Janok assures another female character, Andjelija, that she will not remain a *kukavica crna* for long, since he will engineer a marriage to Djulić, son of the beg of Ribnik (2126). This is especially welcome news for Andjelija because she has just lost out on one prospective mate due to his capture during a daring adventure. Within the thoroughgoingly patriarchal and patrilocal context of South Slavic epic, "black cuckoo" has especially clear and threatening implications for the women to whom it is applied.

The remaining two instances of this *sêma*, from Kukuruzović's *The Captivity of Ograšćić Alija*, illustrate in complementary ways the kind of difference that such idiomatic meaning can make. Toward the end of the story the dispirited and long-detained captive Velagić Selim, comrade to the main hero Ograšćić Alija, asks Halil to deliver a message to his wife: he implores her not to remain a "black cuckoo," mourning him forever, but to go ahead and remarry. His usage of the traditional phrase indicates not only abject despair, but also the linked problems that his absence has caused at home. As a *kukavica crna* for many years, his wife has had to persevere in the most perilous position possible for an adult female in South Slavic epic, with her ever-shrinking corner of the world continually under threat. It is from this social incarceration that her husband seeks to free her. The last and most unusual application of this *reč* occurs some three hundred lines later. Here Mujo, in disguise as a female servant to the banica (the ban's wife), contrives to win her confidence as part of an undercover plan to liberate Turkish prisoners. In order to unsettle his captor's wife, he pretends to be an engaged bride-to-be whose wedding party is being held hostage by Mujo (really himself)! The wording of his complaint urges the seriousness of the situation with special force—"she" claims to fear that Mujo's intervention will make "her" a *kukavica crna*. The implications of the phrase harmonize well with this gender-switching trickery, as the male hero, representing himself as a female for the purpose at hand, slots himself in the recognizable role of a helpless, downtrodden woman facing what amounts to elimination from society. Moreover, the ruse works as planned: the banica fairly explodes with indignation over "her" peril, due in no small part to the power of traditional referentiality, and the liberation is under way.

2. *Speech Introductions.* Like their familiar analogues in Homeric epic, these workaday phrases have no deep resonance but fulfill a basic function: they simply slot whatever follows as a speech, equating the immediately subsequent passage with numerous other such passages of direct discourse. What may interest us here, however, is another perspective on the disparity between lexical and traditional meaning. To put it crudely, this family of phrases often entails a subtraction rather than an addition of meaning. Whereas many speech introductions resort to generalized verbs for vocal performance and exchange, as in the expression *Onda kaže* ("Then he/she said"), others actually bend the semantics back, diluting the particular lexical force of the verb in the interest of promoting the introductory function of the phrase as a whole. Thus we find such constructions as *Pa besjedi*, literally "Then he/she announced, orated" but within the register merely "Then he/she spoke"; and . . . *iz grla povika*, literally ". . . shouted from his/her white throat" but within the epic way of speaking again no more than "he/she spoke."[22] This paring back or generalizing of a verb's specific literal sense—within a larger traditional "word"—illustrates how the register may favor simple function over complex semantics. It is also a reminder that the lexicons we use are for the most part constructed from unmarked varieties of the language, and that marked varieties such as the epic register can deflect meanings in a number of different directions according to the requirements of the speech-act.

3. *Boundary Lines.* Like speech introductions, boundary lines mute the semantic content of their individual parts in order to fulfill a simple but important collective function as *sêmata*, in this case the separation of one narrative entity (scene, speech, or the like) from the next. By traditional fiat, these *reči* also act as transitions between units, providing a familiar signal that something has ended and something else is about to begin.[23] As such, they also smooth the interstices in what has long been understood as a paratactic, additive style.

Two kinds of boundary lines are extremely common in the Stolac songs. One is the "But you should have seen X" ("Pa da vidiš X") frame, with X being a formulaic noun phrase identifying the focal character in the next unit. Thus, for example, when Ibro Bašić finishes describing the servant Huso's readying of the horse and wishes to shift attention to the substitute hero Fata's arming scene, he interposes "But you should have seen the beautiful young woman" (*6597.1078*), and the job is done.[24] The speech-act conveyed by this line has little to do with the act of seeing, of course, or with how beautiful the young woman may be; the literal meaning of the words is downplayed in favor of the overall poetic function of the "word."

The same is true with the "position change" signal, the other type of boundary line frequently deployed throughout the Stolac performances. It can take many forms, but the basic thrust is always the same: to locate a character at or move a character to the site of the next action. Read according to the wrong criteria, this kind of phrase can seem like an unmotivated interjection, an unwarranted imposition on the story. But once again semantic content is secondary to the function of delimiting units and effecting a transition from one unit to another. Thus the audience or reader interprets the very next line in the same performance by Bašić—"She went into the gold-adorned room"[25]—in two ways, as both a logical enough precursor to the Arming scene and a "position change" signal that helps to smooth over the narrative seam between Huso's and Fata's complementary but separate activities. Both types of boundary lines are common and useful "words"—that is, *sêmata* or speech-acts—in the epic register. They are signs behind which we must read.

4. *Traveling "Words."*   Also very useful to the composing poet and his audience and readership are the small-scale *reči* that make up the narrative pattern called Journey Home, examined above. Two of these deserve special attention, both for their telltale shape and for the implications they bear.

The first of them, "Kad rekoše da se pozdraviše," literally translated as "When they said that they bid farewell," belongs to a large family of phraseology used only by Mujo Kukuruzović among the Stolac singers. The idiolectal item in question could be described as the formulaic system "Kad rekoše da [verb in aorist tense]," or "When they said that they [verb in the aorist tense]," where the particular verb used may describe a wide range of actions, including repentance, prayer, division, capture, conciliation, loading, gathering, remembering, covering, and nourishing.[26] Whatever the highly variable content of the phrase, it is stabilized acoustically by the grammatical rhyme or near-rhyme of aorist endings (-*oše/-iše* in the present example) and syntactically by the overall structure of the "When they said that . . ." pattern with its two linked verbs. As so often happens in hierarchies of traditional diction, however, there is a further specification within the general pattern: "When they said that they bid farewell" not only belongs to the general family of diction that can be used in virtually any narrative situation, but also specifically signals the onset of Journey Home. In each of three additional occurrences over three different song-performances, Kukuruzović also uses this *sêma* for that particular, dedicated purpose. In a dictated version of *The Captivity of Ograšćić Alija* (1287a.146), it brings the named hero home to Turkish lands; in an acoustically recorded version of that song (6617.148) it does the same; and later in a dictated version of *The Captivity of Alagić Alija* (1868.1434) it moves a Christian enemy leader, General Pero, to his residence in Kara Bogdan. None of the other related phrases perform this function; only "When they said that they bid farewell" can serve as the traditional sign announcing Journey Home.

Once the pattern is announced, the *guslar* turns to another phrase to get the actual job done. This modest "word" can be described as "Kudgodj idje, [to a place] sidje/dodje," or "Wherever he/she went, [to a place] he/she came," and it is employed dialectally in the Stolac region by both Kukuruzović and Bajgorić.[27] There is considerable variety in the heroes to whom the phrase is applied, as well as in their individual destinations: Turks and Christians alike travel to the Udbina area, Ribnik, Kladuša, Makara, Prevala, Jabuka, Karlovo, the border (the Lika), and their own towers over the fourteen instances of this boilerplate pattern in our song sample. But whoever the character and whatever the actual site to which he or she is traveling, the traditional force of the "word" is the same: it certifies the journey as idiomatic and slots it alongside countless other journeys portrayed within the epic register. Such is the estimable traditional force of this simple sign.

5. *Proverbs and Proverbial Expressions.*   As noted in the Introduction to this volume, proverbs and epic *reči* are difficult to distinguish; both are speech-acts that align variant moments and situations via the linchpin of traditional referentiality. Of special interest, then, are those traditional phrases that qualify as freestanding proverbs outside the epic and also have managed to enter the register to serve as signals that guide reception. Of related concern is the substantial number of expressions that, while not documented in standard collections of proverbs, closely imitate their formal structure and function within the epic genre. Let us consider one example of each type.

The first bit of wisdom is attested as a freestanding proverb in Vuk Karadžić's *poslovice* collection (1849): "Njema leta bez Djurdjeva dana, / Niti brata ne rodeći majka" ("There is no summer without St. George's Day, / Nor a brother without a mother giving birth"). The literal thrust of the message is to affirm universal verities, one cultural and one biological: St. George's Day marks the onset of the summer season through the Mediterranean region and is of special ritual significance in the South Slavic lands,[28] while the second line emphasizes an inarguable truth about consanguineal kinship. As a capsule account of the inevitability of natural process, this proverb proves very useful to Mujo Kukuruzović toward the end of *The Captivity of Ograšćić Alija* (6617), for example, as the disguised hero counters innkeeper Mara's caution to remain undercover rather than reveal himself too early and spoil their secret rescue plan. He insists that he must go to his brother Halil right that moment, whatever the consequences, emphasizing the urgency by adding that his action is as instrumental to Halil's release as St. George's Day is to the start of summer or as a mother's giving birth is to her son's gaining a brother. The vehemence of the hero's argument and his willingness to risk his life to save Halil are impressive, and the poet's application of the proverb adds another level of insistence by reference to a traditional index. The *sêma* acts as an independent yardstick to measure this (and potentially any other) particular situation.

Just as the St. George's Day proverb deepens the context of this and other encounters, acting as a recurrent sign that slots each singular, immediate event within a timeless frame of reference, so proverbial expressions also provide interpretive maps for many regions of the epic landscape. A phrase need not necessarily qualify as an attested proverb outside the epic, that is, to simulate its aphoristic function as a traditional linchpin within the epic. The Stolac songs contain many instances of such expressions, which are acoustically patterned like proverbs and add resonance through their idiomatic implications. A prominent example is the relatively common line, "San usnila, pa se prepanula" ("You've dreamed a dream, so you're frightened"), which on the surface portrays a recurrent, quotidian situation: comfort for the terror induced by a nightmare. In practice, the Stolac *guslari* use the expression for the specific purpose of discrediting a report of impending disaster. Conventionally, the report comes from a young woman, herself uninvolved with the masculine concerns of waging war, who glimpses the enemy army on the horizon. She is patronizingly dismissed by the minor hero to whom she conveys this reconnaissance, and the *reč* he speaks in dismissing her is precisely the proverbial expression, "You've dreamed a dream, so you're frightened." But this is not the end of its implications: soon thereafter her report comes ironically and tragically true, and the Turks she tried to warn are decimated. An audience fluent in the traditional register will sense an irony greater even than this particular catastrophe, as the proverbial expression helps drive reception of a highly charged exchange between a hero who should have known better and a maiden who did.

6. *The "Truelove": Penelope or Klytemnestra?*   As hinted above and discussed at length in Chapter 5, the narrative fulcrum of the Return Song proves to be not the long-lost husband and father but rather the long-persevering, much-courted wife or fiancée. Moreover, this focus on the woman is imaged memorably in the most frequent of the formulaic signs that name her in the Stolac songs: *vjerenica ljuba* and *vjerna ljuba*, both of which literally mean "truelove."[29] So far, so good, but in practice there is

another, crucially important layer to this traditional *reč*. To wit, the test administered by the disguised hero can go either way; she may prove faithful or unfaithful. Thus "truelove" will dependably, and sometimes very ironically, identify not just the Penelopes of South Slavic Return Songs, but also the Klytemnestras. One might expect the phrase to be used of those figures who deserve its literal meaning, but interestingly that is not the end of its application. Even as the scheming woman's faithlessness is being revealed and even as she is recognizing her husband with her dying breath, the Stolac singers will still call her *vjerna ljuba* or *vjerenica ljuba*. From the onset of the story-pattern right up through its dénouement, that is, the character who serves as the rhetorical balance-point for the action retains this coded name.

Thus it is that the *sêma* warrants not her fidelity but rather her identity as this pivotal character; it slots whatever woman is given the label as one whose faithfulness hangs in the balance, along with the story. In the event, such a wife or fiancée is "true" only *potentially*, only if she actually turns out to have waited for her husband, held the suitors at bay, and so on. That may indeed happen, in which case she is implicitly compared to as many South Slavic Penelopes as are known to the audience or readership, and played off against the Klytemnestras. But then again her potential fidelity may just as well give way to infidelity, in which case the process of resolution will take a very different turn. The irony of the situation derives not from the individual poet's invention, then, but from the interplay between this song-performance and the much larger traditional background of the Return Song. When in Parry no. *6617* Ograšćić Alija's wife reacts to the (false) report of her husband's death by laughing, the "truelove" signal rings hollow; her response is ironic because it contradicts her formulaic name even as it points away from the narrative path that leads to Penelope and closure of the song. Her laugh means that the song will continue by following the other of two possible paths, toward the hero's temporary alliance with the enemy and subsequent events that would never have taken place had he not found Klytemnestra waiting at home. Traditional referentiality radically deepens the irony of the faithless "truelove," making her conjugal betrayal all the more poignant.

7. *"He/she jumped from the ground to his/her feet."*　Within the epic register spoken by the Stolac *guslari*, this phrase signifies much more than sudden verticality. Beyond the literal sense of the *reč* lies its implicit sense of "an honorable response to an unexpected or threatening turn of events that demands the principal's immediate attention."[30] Thus, for example, the minor hero Gojenović Ibro, mentioned earlier in connection with the dream proverb, is at one point in Kukuruzović's *The Captivity of Ograšćić Alija* (*6617*) called upon to undertake a suicide mission to deliver a crucial message to an ally. Not hesitating for an instant, Ibro "jumped from the

ground to his feet." The singer's use of the formulaic phrase slots this mission as an honorable action that demands the individual's exclusive attention, one that responds to an unforeseen threat of sizable proportions. Traditional referentiality helps us understand the nature of Ibro's heroism by providing a resonant and recognizable context for his alacrity, even as he faces certain death.

The same *reč* indexes numerous other moments as well, none of them more tellingly than a crucial juncture in Bašić's *Alagić Alija and Velagić Selim* (6597). The central hero, Alagić Alija (AA), has written a last will and testament from prison, releasing his betrothed Fata from her marriage contract and instructing his mother to distribute or sell his possessions as appropriate. A messenger now brings this document to the two women, who as the scene opens are pictured in the upper story of AA's tower. The messenger's ringing knock echoes on the outer door below, and Fata "jumps up from the ground to her feet" (837). Taken literally, the singer's choice of this line at this particular point appears to be evidence of "nodding" on Bašić's part; at minimum, Fata is a full story *above* the ground, huddled with her future mother-in-law in a room overlooking the courtyard. Nor would the epic equivalent of collecting the mail seem reason enough for such a strong, immediate reaction, and this is to say nothing of its unusual application to a (conventionally) docile and domestic fiancée. But while the literal content of the *reč* seems awkward or impertinent, its idiomatic content turns out to be absolutely appropriate, as fiancée modulates eventually to substitute hero and liberator of AA. Fata's is most certainly an honorable response, the letter from AA is unquestionably both unexpected and threatening, and the emergency that presents itself will without doubt require her immediate attention. Once again, we can appreciate the slotting effect of the "word" or *sêma*, as it emphasizes her duty to the old woman and loyalty to her fiancé as well as furnishes a traditional context for the heroism she is about to demonstrate by riding off to AA's rescue as the stand-in Return hero. Within the register the plain act of jumping up from the ground to one's feet, when phrased canonically as a recognizable signal, has definite and important implications.

8. *"Below accursed Markovac."* The traditional register abounds with *reči* at every level, but let us be satisfied with one final example. I choose the phrase "below accursed Markovac" ("niz Markovac kleti") because it illustrates as dramatically as any phrase in the Stolac performances how crucial a role traditional referentiality plays in the art of the *guslar*. If we try to make literal sense of this formula and its usage, we are faced with a dilemma. The town Markovac takes its name from the chief Serbian hero in South Slavic epic, Prince Marko.[31] Local legend had it that he visited there, perhaps spending some appreciable amount of time; thus the toponym and eponym.[32] But then how do we explain the decidedly pejora-

tive adjective *kleti*? Calling such a revered place "accursed" seems contra-
dictory, and yet the phrase is repeated intact throughout the epic songs of
the Stolac region.

Here the singer's own viewpoint—from inside the register—comes to
the rescue. Consider the following excerpt from Nikola Vujnović's conver-
sation with Stolac *guslar* Halil Bajgorić, in which the problem of apparent
contradiction is addressed:[33]

> *Nikola*: This Markovac, where is it?
> *Halil*: Markovac is a little hill town over there on the mountain; that
> particular place is called Markovac.
> *N*: But why is it called Markovac?
> *H*: Because [Prince] Marko came by there.
> *N*: And it wasn't named Markovac before that?
> *H*: It wasn't named Markovac before, only afterward.
> *N*: But why then do you say in a song, "Then there he was *below
> accursed Markovac*" ["Pa eto ga *niz Markovac kleti*"]?
> *H*: Because that's the way it must be said.

In the terms we have been developing, the singer is explaining that a *reč*
cannot be dismembered, that it is a unit of utterance and a traditional sign
that conveys meaning as a whole. If the literal sense of the constituent ele-
ments is muted, or in this case actually overridden and reversed, such is
the natural process of making "words" from words in the traditional reg-
ister—which works like language, only more so. "Below accursed Marko-
vac" performs an unspectacular but useful function in the Stolac songs, in-
dexing an epic site via a unique place-name, and in doing so it actually
celebrates that place rather than damns it. No misapplication here, no un-
fortunate error committed by a poet imprisoned by his language; within
the *guslar*'s way of speaking, Bajgorić was trying to explain, that's just the
way it must be said. As for the singer, so also for his audience and reader-
ship: that's just the way we must read behind the signs.

Conclusion

The preceding three chapters have in various ways concentrated on a
single core question: *Is South Slavic epic a useful, apposite comparison for
Homer?* In Chapter 2 I began by considering some of the unexamined as-
sumptions behind this comparative approach, paying special attention to
the positive and negative aspects of the "strong thesis" developed by
Parry and Lord. In particular, I discussed the arguments over general qual-

ity and over length and complexity, insisting on a fair evaluation of a substantial sample of South Slavic epic in the original language and on its own terms (at minimum). At the same time, it has become apparent that it is time for a "second growth" in Oral Theory that moves beyond the typology of oral versus written to an appreciation of the complexity and diversity that folklorists and anthropologists have illustrated, prima facie, in living oral traditions. Against that background we then listened to what the Stolac *guslari* had to say about their craft, and especially about the legendary singer, or *Guslar*, who in his multiformity bears a striking resemblance to Homer.

In the two chapters that followed, the focus shifted from the history of the theory and the singers themselves to the poetic language and its implications. Chapter 3 considered some basic structural questions that have long gone without satisfactory responses. How do South Slavic and Homeric epic really compare in terms of formulaic phraseology, enjambement, and metrical irregularities? Do both traditions use an artificial language, marked by archaisms and multiple dialects? How do the two registers compare at the levels of typical scene and story-pattern? Forthright engagement of each of these questions called for both yes and no responses: the epic registers are alike in some ways, and unalike in others. A focus on shared features must include a recognition of inevitable differences.

This philological analysis paved the way for perhaps the most crucial part of the three-part sequence—the present chapter's examination of the traditional referentiality that distinguishes the *guslar*'s epic way of speaking. By merely designating the special decasyllabic language as the expressive channel, and then by deploying the *sêmata* of story-pattern, typical scene, and phrase, the South Slavic singers "slot" the particular and momentary within the traditional, deepening the singular epic performance by engaging a naturally resonant context. Thus, whether the analysis treated the Return Song, the scene of Arming the Hero, or the "truelove" phrase, we saw that the various *reči* serve not only as structures but also as *sêmata* or speech-acts. As in the *Iliad* and *Odyssey*, these "words" not only support composition but also drive reception, guiding the audience's or reader's responses via a map "inscribed" with traditional signs. Like Homer's specialized *koinê*, the *guslar*'s register works like language, only more so.

PART III

READING HOMER'S SIGNS

5

STORY-PATTERN AS *SÊMA*
THE *ODYSSEY* AS A RETURN SONG

> *Vjerna ljuba svijet mijenila.*
> The truelove changed worlds.
> —Traditional

> οἱ μὲν ἔπειτα
> ἀσπάσιοι λέκτροιο παλαιοῦ θεσμὸν ἵκοντο.
> Then [Odysseus and Penelope]
> gladly reached the site of their long-standing bed.
> —the *telos* of the *Odyssey*, 23.295–96

Comparison, Methodology, and a Caveat

Over the opening four chapters of this book I hope to have established two basic premises about Homer and oral tradition. The former, explored in Part I, concerns the importance of traditional referentiality and Homeric signs or *sêmata*, and specifically the necessity of crediting the oral traditional background that informs not only the composition of the *Iliad* and *Odyssey* but also their reception, whether by ancient or by modern audiences. The latter, examined in Part II, holds that the analogy of South Slavic oral epic can be useful as a comparative tool, shedding light on such matters as the structure and meaning of the poetic register, the vexed issue of poetic quality, and not least the traditional poet himself. The usefulness of the comparison always depends, however, on clearly recognizing the limits of the analogy and thus the inevitable differences between Homer and the *guslar*; as argued above, only against the realistic background of incongruencies can points of congruency emerge in proper perspective.

With both of these premises in mind, I now put the thesis of traditional referentiality to a series of further tests by closely considering selected signs or "words" from the Homeric poems. Over the following three chapters, cumulatively the third part of the book, we will be considering the implications of *sêmata* at the levels of *story-pattern*, specifically the overall narrative structure of the *Odyssey*; of *typical scene*, emphasizing the Feast in the *Odyssey* and the Lament in the *Iliad*; and of *phraseology*, or "words" at the level of a line or partial line, in both epics.

In general, our approach will be as much as possible the same as that employed in the opening chapter to investigate the meaning of the word and term *sêma*. Because we are interested primarily in traditional implications, we will be closing the dictionary, as it were, in favor of learning the language. Of course, the fact that this language-learning must take place with only the surviving textual remnants of ancient Greek epic to guide us makes the enterprise more challenging in a number of ways. In addition to the inherent problem of teasing idiomatic meaning out of the specialized register of epic diction, the relatively modest size of the Homeric corpus limits our options. Not only the finite limitation of approximately twenty-eight thousand verses, but yet more the fact that we have only two songs (and those two songs quite dissimilar in epic subgenre) makes an analytical approach more difficult. But even if we had more Homeric verses or poems or texts to support the investigation, unlocking the traditional referentiality networked in Homer's signs would still present a formidable obstacle. Not all *sêmata* yield up their secrets as easily as the Grimm brothers' "Once upon a time."[1]

For this reason we need to prescribe and to practice a straightforward methodology that promises the best results possible. In pursuing what Homer implies, let us direct our primary attention to the idiomatic meaning of recurrent signs. That is, let us consider multiple instances of each signal—at whatever level—and inquire whether they collectively index any traditional implications that are not a part of their literal significance. What else, if anything, does a given "word" mean? Does any idiomatic meaning lie beyond the plain denotative sense enshrined in lexicons and dictionaries? If so, how do we incorporate such additional associations into our reception of the poems? This procedure of collating multiple instances will foreground the indexical meaning of the story-pattern, typical scene, or phrase, and help to explain how traditional compositional structures are also, and crucially, maps for construing Homer's art. Aspiring to fluency in the register, with an emphasis on idiomatic meaning, will help us read behind the signs as well as between them.

Obviously, this approach will work best with signs that recur many times and in a variety of situations; such cases will foster the broadest possible view and thus reveal the presence or absence of traditional implication. It would be more accurate to say that it will reveal the *degree* and *kind* of such value-added meaning, since even the most workaday item—the invariant noun-epithet formula or the boilerplate speech introduction, for example—performs a useful indexical function. Thus frequently deployed typical scenes (Chapter 6) and formulaic phraseology (Chapter 7) offer convenient and dependable footholds for our purposes. Gathering the instances together and ascertaining their traditional implication is one route to learning the bard's (and audience's) language; with relatively common *sêmata* this kind of collation can lead to rewarding results. But we should also acknowledge the potential handicap inherent in this approach. Just as the most frequently occurring "words" offer the best chance for recovering traditional referentiality, so the rarest of signs must present us with a quandary. The Homeric corpus is, as already noted, quite limited, and there will naturally be many phrases, scenes, and larger patterns that occur too infrequently to divulge much if any of their indexical meaning via the collation method.

This is especially the case with the first of our three *sêmata*, the story-pattern. As discussed elsewhere, the *Odyssey* follows a narrative path well known throughout central and eastern Europe over many thousands of years—the track of the so-called Return Song.[2] Exactly what that pattern consists of, and the precise role it plays at the foundation of Homer's poem, will be the major burden of the present chapter. But before investigation of those matters can begin, we need to confront a formidable limitation: the fact that we have only a single surviving Return Song from ancient Greece. Other returns, or *nostoi*, are certainly implied, as constant Odyssean references to the Agamemnon story and the remains of ancient sources indicate; but none of these reported stories actually survives.[3] Moreover, the *Iliad* follows another story-pattern, distinct from that underlying the *Odyssey*, and the two epics cannot profitably be compared at this level of traditional structure.[4] Thus, while we will be able to study multiple instances of Feasts and Laments in Chapter 6 and numerous iterations of selected phrases in Chapter 7, the available sample of ancient Greek epic precludes using the same internal method to study story-pattern. We cannot learn anything about this largest of *sêmata* via collation within the Homeric epic corpus.

But that does not mean that we must entirely abandon the search for traditional referentiality in the *nostos* story-pattern, for, with proper calibration, the South Slavic analogy can provide an alternative referent. As briefly previewed in the preceding chapter, the epic tradition of the *guslari*, in particular the Moslem songs collected by Parry and Lord, features as its most prominent subgenre a strikingly similar story of the returning hero.[5]

Like Homer's tale, these South Slavic Return Songs portray protagonists striving to reach their homelands after a great battle, fighting their way through challenging adventures, competing in disguise against rival suitors, secretly testing their mates, relatives, and servants, and generally trying to regain the positions they long ago left behind. Some heroes bear telltale scars on their legs; some are recognized by favorite animals; some wives or fianceés even weave. Whether this tale-type, recorded in Greece more than 2,500 years before its first recorded performance in the former Yugoslavia, is traced to a common Indo-European origin or to some direct chain of transmission is finally beside the point.[6] What matters is that the South Slavic tradition does provide us with an extremely close and therefore useful parallel to the *Odyssey* and its long-lost kindred songs, an analogy that will foster a comparative examination of works that share the same or a remarkably similar story-pattern. We have no recurrence of this largest of "words" within the Homeric corpus itself, but we can collate *sêmata* across the two traditions.

A Traditional Morphology and Three Questions

Since the *Odyssey* is unique in the ancient Greek tradition, I will begin by turning to the well-collected South Slavic tradition of Return Songs in order to establish the kind of context only a traditional morphology—an inventory of variability—can provide. By summarizing the main action of three different but genetically related tales, each performed by a different *guslar*, I will draw some rough outlines for the multiform narrative of the returning hero. In this fashion we can gain at least some awareness of both the inherent plasticity and the recurrent idiomatic structure of this largest of *sêmata*. It will become apparent that the typical, constitutive events that make up the Return Song guide both the singer in his composition and the audience or reader in their reception of the story. Because the implied story-pattern contextualizes all individual tales, it provides a natural background for each one by built-in reference to what they share. Because it is also a flexible expressive instrument, it gives the singer adequate opportunity for variation within limits. In the process it leaves room for the audience to participate, to help constitute the work of art by bringing into play their knowledge of traditional implications. The South Slavic examples will illustrate, in short, that the *nostos* pattern works like language, only more so.

  With this morphology in hand, I will then turn to the most important section of the present chapter: the significance of the "word" and *sêma* of Return as applied to the *Odyssey*. Placing the unique story of Odysseus against the multiform background of the Return Song from the South Slavic tradition, I will confront three fundamental questions of interpretation. Each of these challenging questions has been under discussion from ancient scholarship onward, and each of them can, I believe, be profitably addressed anew from the fresh perspective of traditional referentiality.

In order to focus as clearly and directly as possible on the fundamental issues to be raised, let us phrase the three core inquiries as follows: (1) What is the narrative sequence of the *Odyssey*, and why does it begin "in the middle"? Here we will be interested in the nonchronological order of the poem's core events, including the inserted tale told by Odysseus to the Phaeacians in Books 9–12. (2) Why does Penelope think and act as she does, often behaving mysteriously toward both the suitors and her husband? With this question we will be investigating her ambivalence, stubbornness, close counsel, and overall role in the tale. (3) Where does the *Odyssey* really end? Should we agree with the ancient and modern critics who argue that the poem reaches some kind of conclusion at Book 23, line 296? How do we explain the "continuation" beyond Odysseus' and Penelope's reunion in the olive-tree bed?[7] With relation to all three of these inquiries, it will become evident how the historical accident of a single surviving *nostos* tale from ancient Greece, and furthermore one that happens to lead toward Penelope (rather than Klytemnestra, for example), has predetermined our reception of a story that could just as easily have followed a quite different path. To this singular tale we propose to restore a measure of its natural multiformity—and its traditional referentiality—by recourse to the South Slavic analogy.

The Story of Return in South Slavic Epic Tradition

In broadest terms, the Return Song opens with a hero's long-standing absence from home and the devastation that both he and his family have suffered as a result.[8] Customarily, and usually before the story starts, he has abandoned a new bride or fiancée, sometimes a son as well, in order to join a large army embarked on a mission aimed at a goal that strictly speaking is not his personal concern. As a member of that composite force he encounters trouble either during or after the battle, falling victim to imprisonment by the enemy or some third party. Much of this background is often implied, either coming to light explicitly somewhat later on in the narrative or "filled in" only via the tacit implications of the story-pattern *sêma*. The actual tale, at any rate, usually picks up with the hero suffering in captivity and bemoaning his fate, his journey homeward indefinitely suspended. In the events that follow, the action will take place against the background of the long, unrelieved estrangement between man and woman, and the inescapable fact that they have spent much of their adult lives apart from one another.

The early lines of a South Slavic Return Song thus assume a fait accompli: the captive hero in a miserable state, long separated from his wife/fiancée at home and waiting to die in a far-distant land. By convention, this Turkish stalwart then begins to lament so loudly and incessantly that he threatens the life of his Christian captor's infant son(s), and thus the health of the entire royal lineage. His unbearable racket causes the child's mother, the banica, to take matters into her own hands and demand the release of the offending prisoner, something her husband the ban is reluctant to allow. Nevertheless, she manages to strike a bargain for the captive's permanent or temporary freedom, sometimes conducting the negotiations herself and not seldom forging a bond of synthetic kinship (bloodbrotherhood or -sisterhood, godparenthood) across the otherwise unbridgeable gap between Turk and Christian.[9] It is only in this fashion—through the superficially unexpected intercession of a powerful female—that the hero eventually gains release and has a chance to complete his *nostos*.

Once having escaped confinement, the hero then proceeds as directly as possible to his home, undertaking a journey that may be either accomplished with alacrity or lengthily protracted. Whatever the case, he finds on arrival that things have changed markedly during his absence: his wife/fiancée is now being courted by his countrymen, his son (if he has one) has reached adulthood but has not assumed authority, and the material aspects of his homestead have suffered considerably without his stewardship. Remaining in the disguise of long-term captive and for the moment unrecognized by any of his family, servants, or rivals, he proceeds to test many of them before revealing himself through some key strategy. In quite a few songs he defeats the suitors in the ritual combat of athletic competition, and then resorts to a special signal to alert selected allies—often mother, sister, son, or serving-woman, and inevitably his wife/fiancée—of his presence. This unmistakable South Slavic sign not seldom consists of a lying tale in which the disguised hero slyly reports his own death and measures people's reactions, or it may take the form of a special object or possession known only to the small family circle, such as a musical instrument that the long-lost hero plays in an inimitable style or a horse that only he can ride. Whatever the particular *sêma*, his mate is always the last to be tested, and the riddle of her fidelity or deception is solved once and for all in the process.

In the simplest form of the Return Song, the action moves from absence to an eventual wedding (or rapprochement), with the wife/fiancée passing the test and proving her faithfulness. If she has been true to her husband/fiancée and successfully held the suitors at bay, the song can end there. Diagrammatically, the narrative thus moves through a series of five stages or elements:

A (Absence) > D (Devastation) > R (Return) > Rt (Retribution) > W (Wedding)

But many variations are also possible within the limits of this traditional pattern. For one thing, the song can continue into a brief, linked rescue expedition that takes the now-reestablished hero on a short sequel adventure. For another, the action can be doubled by involving not one but two heroic protagonists who cooperate in various ways, with the culminating stages of the return accomplished by stand-ins or proxies. Or, more dramatically, the wife/fiancée may prove a Klytemnestra rather than a Penelope figure. In this case the narrative necessarily veers off from its hoped-for conclusion in a (re)wedding to an extensive sequel that involves a traitorous episode of fraternizing with the enemy before the final heroic return brings the overall story to a close.

In what follows I will briefly rehearse the basic plots of three Return Songs from the South Slavic tradition in order to provide a glimpse of the traditional morphology of this pattern and subgenre of epic narrative.[10] In concert with the overall aim of the chapter, emphasis will be placed not simply on the general flexibility of the sequence, which is of course an important dimension, but also on three particular areas that have special pertinence for our understanding of Homer's *Odyssey*: (*a*) the major constituent actions of return and the conventionally nonchronological order of narration, (*b*) the ambiguous identity of the wife/fiancée and her uniquely powerful and determinative role in the story's outcome, and (*c*) the troublesome question of closure.[11]

Alija Fjuljanin's *The Captivity of Četić Osmanbey*

I begin with a very short and simple Return Song of 708 lines, *The Captivity of Četić Osmanbey*, as performed for Milman Parry and Albert Lord on 21 November 1934 by Alija Fjuljanin of the Novi Pazar district in the former Yugoslavia. It was recorded acoustically, transcribed by Nikola Vujnović, translated by Albert Lord, and published in the first two volumes of the *SCHS* series;[12] it is thus readily available for the reader to consult in its entirety. This performance conveniently illustrates, with unusual terseness and in almost schematic form, the main features of the South Slavic story-pattern of return.

After the generic proem or *pripjev* that is optional for epic performances in this tradition,[13] the song opens quite characteristically with the Turkish hero, Četić Osmanbey, having fallen into captivity at the hands of the Christian ban, here named Tasević, in the enemy city of Zadar. The audience familiar with this kind of narrative will have a general idea of how that imprisonment came about, and will naturally expect the round-the-clock shouting and screaming that has followed, stimulated in this instance by the ban's wife, who cruelly taunts the miserable Turk by throwing a bouquet of flowers into his wretched cell. She soon regrets her thoughtless action, however, and, fearing for her sons' health if the clamor does not cease, urgently petitions her husband to release, execute, or ransom the prisoner. Her earnest plea causes the ban to send a servant, Djuro the turnkey, down to the prison to fetch the woebegone hero in an effort to rectify what has become an intolerable situation.

Četić Osmanbey's audience with Ban Tasević offers the singer the opportunity to describe the captive's memorably sorry condition: dressed in rags, with hair to his waist and iron shackles having worn through to his wrist- and leg-bones, the hero has in effect donned the disguise he will be wearing until the subsequent testing and recognition process, to be conducted back home in Udbina, is complete. The ban sets the ransom for his captive's release at a thousand ducats, a patently unrealistic request for someone in Osmanbey's state, and is about to throw him back into jail when the banica intervenes and implores her husband to free him now and await a deferred payment of the designated sum. Thus, as usual, a powerful female secures the hero's return by channeling authority in a productive direction.

But freedom does not automatically mean immediate homecoming, as the Turk and so many of his counterparts in other Return Songs learn through bitter experience. Even with the "passport" issued him by the ban, Osmanbey encounters highwaymen (hajduci) on the way back to his native Udbina, outlaws who seek to relieve him of his valuables and even his life. The last of these, Haiduk Milutin, in fact proves his superior in hand-to-hand combat, and only through a prayer and a ruse does Osmanbey survive and eventually get the better of his adversary. Indeed, trickery is a common and usually successful strategy in this type of song and should be correlated with the hero's characteristic lying tales; both types of ruses show how the Return Song tends to privilege cleverness and mental agility over brute force and superior strength. At any rate, just as the Turk is about to put an end to the beaten Milutin, the outlaw begs for bloodbrotherhood, the institution of synthetic kinship that figures so commonly as a link between natural enemies in the epics, and the two become fast comrades. They continue the trek together and reach Udbina safely.

Although the physical return has now been achieved, the Turkish champion's reassumption of his proper identity has really just begun. He administers the initial test to his servant Husein, asking the unsuspecting fellow whether the nearby tower (really his own, of course) boasts any master. Husein loyally responds that the tower belongs to Četić Osmanbey, who disappeared into captivity some twelve years ago. Until recently those whom his master left behind had received letters assuring them he was alive, the servant goes on, but later a message arrived indicating that he had "changed worlds"—a traditional index for a pitiable, useless death.[14] Attributing the prisoner's condition and appearance to his recent incarceration, Husein then asks whether he has any inside information on the condition or whereabouts of his master. Quite expectably, this query prompts a lying tale from the disguised hero, who, posing as Osmanbey's former co-prisoner, proceeds to report his own death four years prior. Nonetheless, and presumably as a reward for this sad information, he asks Husein for the hospitality owed a bloodbrother, calling himself a "guest from the wilderness."[15]

This plea for help leads to consultation of Osmanbey's elderly mother, who like her servant seeks whatever news she can get of her long-absent son. After mother and disguised son eat, drink, and enjoy coffee and tobacco, Husein readdresses their pauper guest, searching for anything the beggar can tell them about the reportedly deceased Osmanbey. In typical fashion, the returning hero responds by posing a number of questions supposedly based on what he learned in prison but cleverly designed to uncover the present condition of what are actually, as only he is yet aware, his own family and possessions. What of Osmanbey's chestnut horse, he asks, and his dogs and falcons? Has his "truelove" (*vjerna ljuba*) remarried while still young? The news is promising: he is told that the horse and dogs survive, and that his truelove has waited the full twelve years—and would wait twenty-four—for her husband's reappearance.

The process of testing and recognition then reaches a critical point as the disguised master poses a further, carefully pointed question concerning the whereabouts of Osmanbey's mother-of-pearl tamboura, an instrument associated with epic performance and the *sêma* that will eventually unlock his identity. Taking the tamboura in hand and looking about for a moment, he starts to play and sing a song of recognition, gently chiding his mother, the servant Husein, and finally his faithful wife for failing to guess his real identity. His truelove reacts by joining her mother-in-law in weeping, the logical and expectable response in songs of this type and usually a cue that the story is drawing to a close. With order reestablished and fidelity secure, the absence and devastation that began the song are repaired and the basic Return pattern has run its course. The story has reached its climax, equivalent to what the ancient commentators identified as the *telos* of the *Odyssey*.

But in this instance the hero presses the point even further, inquiring whether his wife's weeping might indicate that she has committed herself to another man and even offering her a letter of release from their own marriage contract. From this proposed reinterpretation of the truelove's genuine sorrow derives the impetus for continuing the story, a continuation that illustrates the inherent flexibility of the Return Song sequence, its variability within limits. The wife goes on to say that the reason for her sadness has to do not with any shift in loyalty (she repeats the "twelve and twenty-four" phrase that idiomatically indexes her fidelity) but rather with the fate of a son, Ahmetbey, who was conceived on their wedding night so many years ago. It seems that a band of Hungarian raiders kidnapped the boy four years before, and since that time she has heard nothing except a secondhand report that he had been captured by the ban of Janok, who was trying to convert him to the Christian Orthodox religion.

The brief sequel then addresses this "loose end," which of course needs attention if order is to be truly and completely restored in Udbina. At first, the rescue goes poorly, with scrupulously honest Osmanbey insisting on going back to Zadar to pay his promised ransom to Ban Tasević. Reimprisonment proves his only reward for honoring that agreement. With the help of Haiduk Milutin and his wife Latinka, however, who reappear from "offstage" to turn the tables by kidnapping the ban's son Mihail, Osmanbey once again secures his freedom as well as that of his missing son Ahmetbey. The story closes with the ban powerless and awaiting Mihail's release, while the reunited Turks ride homeward to their native borderland, the Lika. With this last set of actions the story is now complete.

Although Fjuljanin's performance of *The Captivity of Četić Osmanbey* is so telegraphic that some of the major actions are elided and the usual flashback episode does not appear, most of the Return Song paradigm is visible enough. The hero is missing for an extended period of time, here twelve years (Absence), while both he and his family undergo privations of various sorts (Devastation): he is incarcerated and neglected, and his wife suffers without hope against the aggressive advances of suitors. Although this extremely terse performance does not explicitly portray her plight, the hero's multiple questions about her marriage status and the context implied by the story-pattern fill in the background. Osmanbey manages to find his way home (Return) and proceeds to test his family and servants to determine their faithfulness during his absence. If suitors were explicitly mentioned, instead of left at the level of an implicit threat to resumption of the marriage, an athletic or martial Retribution (or both) would have accompanied his testing procedures. With the discovery of his wife's fidelity, Osmanbey has reached the end of the primary Return story (Wedding or Re-wedding). Both the Milutin episode and the rescue sequel are thus illustrations of ancillary directions beyond the fundamental story, optional pathways that a given song may follow. It is accurate to say, here and elsewhere in the poetic tradition, that the Wedding element provides the *telos* or culmination of the story; it is also accurate to say that, such closure notwithstanding, the story may go on to confront a related problem.

What is not optional, here or in any other South Slavic Return Song, is the endemic and persistent uncertainty associated with the figure of the hero's wife/fiancée. Until he reaches home, weighs the situation he finds there, and completes a series of testing strategies capped by his self-revelation through a key detail or strategy, the hero just cannot know whether he will find a faithful or an unfaithful mate. Indeed, this fundamental and active ambiguity is memorably etched in the very phrase "truelove" (*vjerna ljuba*), the formulaic and traditional title always accorded the wife or fiancée in the Return Song, wherever her loyalty may lie.[16] As discussed in Chapter 4, slotting the hero's mate in this familiar category is both automatic and functional. The "truelove" *sêma* begs the question of whether specific figures in specific songs will in fact be "true," or whether their infidelity will in the end prove the epithet ironic. As we shall see in the synopses of other Return Songs below, it is absolutely central to the nature of the *vjerna ljuba* that she remain mysterious and uncertain—that her "disguise" remain just as impenetrable as her husband's—until the hero somehow shows his hand. She thus serves as the most important narrative pivot in the overall story, and as such cannot be judged before the defining moment of the hero's revelation. At the level of story-pattern neither he nor we can know in advance whether he has reached Ithaka or Mykenae, Penelope or Klytemnestra, "truelove" or not.

Ibro Bašić's *Alagić Alija and Velagić Selim*

The Stolac *guslar* Ibro Bašić performed three versions of the *Alagić Alija and Velagić Selim* for Parry and Lord in 1935, one a dictated text and the other two sung versions that were later transcribed by Nikola Vujnović. It is the earlier of the sung versions, no. *6597*, recorded on 7 June and the longest of the three at 1,558 lines, that I have selected for summary here.[17]

After the optional and generic proem, Bašić begins his tale in the chronological "middle," the customary starting point for Return Songs of any length, by portraying the ban of Zadar's celebrations over the prisoner he has just captured—the Turkish hero Alagić Alija. The train of events that led up to his capture will await explanation via the equally customary flashback. Cast into the familiarly forbidding confines of a Turkish jail, with its indexical garnish of scorpions, snakes, and shoulder-high water, Alija suffers terribly in an environment so foul and far removed from everyday reality that inmates are unaware even whether it is summer or winter unless someone throws them a flower (as in the story of Četić

Osmanbey). Things look extremely bleak with such an accomplished Turkish stalwart mired in the narrative depths of Absence and Devastation, but of course the story-pattern "map" promises a smoother road ahead, eventually.

From this juncture the *Alagić Alija and Velagić Selim* follows a direction superficially different from many other related narratives, although it is as we shall see a direction clearly linked to the traditional morphology and network of Return Songs. Alija is surprised to find another prisoner in his cell, and even more surprised that this longtime captive turns out to be Velagić Selim of Udbina, the very hero whom he has been seeking without success for twelve years. The two champions then embrace and "ask after each other's heroic health," after which Selim immediately begins a litany of questions designed to update him on the status of the family and possessions he left behind so long ago in Udbina.[18] These include general queries about whether life goes on as usual (Do the agas still drink wine at the inn? Does the sentry still stand guard at his tower?) and more pointed inquiries about whether his mother is still living and his truelove has yet remarried. Alija's responses are generally positive but discouraging on the crucial points: Udbina at large remains as it always was, but Selim's own residence is overgrown with ivy, his mother has declined with age and lack of care, and, most significant, his fiancée has planned a new marriage with Halil, whom we know from other sources as an estimable Turkish hero in his own right.

At this point Alija launches into a retrospective biography of nearly two hundred lines, a substantial flashback making up more than one-tenth of the entire epic and filling in the background of his own past and capture by the enemy. Like his sorry fellow prisoner Selim, he was about to be married when a summons arrived from Mustajbey of the Lika reporting a momentous attack by a Christian foe, General Pero, and pleading with him to join the composite force opposing that threat. Alija at first refused but was eventually drawn into the fray, and subsequently taken alive and deposited in the ban of Zadar's jail. This retold part of the adventure is of course chronologically preliminary to the prisoners' present discussion and the ensuing action, but its nonchronological placement at this location in the tale is in fact predictable and idiomatic. The fluent audience expects the flashback to occur here. The singer Bašić is describing the two heroes' present Devastation and the events that led up to their meeting by proceeding along a well-worn traditional pathway.

The next step along that familiar narrative route must be the physical Return, and toward that goal the song moves directly to a characteristic bargaining scene with the ban of Zadar. The Christian captor offers Alija the chance to return home and tend to his truelove Fata, but there are conditions attached to the release. In quick succession he asks Alija for one hundred ducats, special religious clothing, his sharp saber with the pure silver hilt, a decorated cape, and three shining silver plates; to these demands the captive agrees without objection. But the additional ransom to which he will not consent is the gift of his sister Ajkuna, and negotiations founder on the spot. The angry ban reacts by promising never to free Alija, and, in a memorable capsule used by many *guslari* in the Stolac region, pledges to grind his bones in a mortar and use them for cannon fodder.[19]

The captor's intransigence softens, however, when his wife the banica approaches him with the archetypal problem conventionally associated with South Slavic songs of return: the prisoner's (here Velagić Selim's) shrieking has so disturbed their child, causing the infant to stop nursing, that the royal lineage is imperiled. She demands that her husband remedy the situation by either freeing or selling off the offending Turk. After a cursory interview, the ban accepts Selim's proposal that he be released for one month in order to attend to affairs in Udbina that have gone unaddressed during his twelve years' absence. Well aware that he has not escaped imprisonment permanently, Selim begins the arduous trek homeward. The trip is made more difficult by his extremely run-down condition, which is also—and significantly—his disguise; we hear that he has only rags to wear, that his hair reaches to his waist, and his nails are grown out "like those on a winged horse" (499). His disguise is a standard feature of the Return Song, and operates as a *sêma*.[20]

In this conventionally unrecognizable state Selim finally reaches Udbina, only to find Mustajbey of the Lika, most duplicitous of all Turkish heroes,[21] his henchman Mujo of Kladuša, and an army of prospective wedding guests encamped below his tower. These interlopers quiz the woebegone prisoner first about his own identity, a question he deflects, and then about whether he ever encountered their colleague Velagić Selim in jail. His negative response elicits alms from the suitor Turks, since it amounts to (misleadingly) welcome news for them, and over the next few scenes the hero successfully continues to line his pockets while maintaining his apparently impenetrable disguise. Then, during the confrontation with Halil, his fiancée's bridegroom-to-be, Selim requests permission to enter their athletic contest of stone-throwing, at which he handily outdoes all present. A subsequent challenge to single combat sends the chief suitor Halil packing.

Selim then turns to what is always the heart of the matter for the Return Song hero: the testing of his truelove. Once he admits to having been incarcerated in Zadar, she of course asks him for some word of her long-lost fiancé, and he just as expectably meets her anxious query with the (false) news that Selim died in prison. On hearing that this sorry fellow before her was responsible for preserving her husband's dignity by burying the body, the truelove shows her gratitude by rewarding him with ten *madzharijas*.

Pressed further with the explicit question of whether she is honoring Se-
lim's soul or the suitor Halil's health with her generosity, the truelove tear-
fully affirms her fidelity to Selim. Note that until this final declaration her
status is characteristically ambiguous, framed in the very alternatives the
prisoner offers her, and that only in her outright declaration of faithfulness
does she resolve that endemic uncertainty. After revealing his identity to
his mother, Selim discards his prisoner's rags (together with the disguise
they constitute), and spends his month of freedom setting things right in
Udbina. At the end of this period he announces that he must fulfill his
pledge to return to Zadar and to captivity, and so leaves the two women
as *kukavice crne* ("black cuckoos" or "mourners"),[22] effectively consigning
all three of them to reentering the Devastation stage of the story-pattern.
From a conditional Return and Retribution, the story moves in reverse, as
it were, back to an earlier moment in the traditional sequence.

With this retrograde development the scene then shifts back to the other
Turkish hero, Alagić Alija, still detained in Zadar with no hope of escape.
Now begins his own loud lamentation, predictably engaging the ban's at-
tention if only to furnish the prisoner writing materials for a last, dispir-
ited message to his mother.[23] He instructs her to disperse his possessions
and release his truelove Fata from their betrothal agreement, and the ban
hires a Hungarian messenger to deliver the *knjiga šarovita* ("decorated
letter") to Udbina, the homeland shared by both Alija and Selim. After
some days' travel the messenger reaches his destination and knocks on the
courtyard gate; Fata "jumps from the ground to her feet" and answers the
summons.[24] She eventually reads the letter's sad contents to her prospec-
tive mother-in-law, who sees the impending loss of not only her son but
also his fiancée as nothing less than catastrophic and totally disabling.

Fata has other ideas, however. She promises the old woman that she will
lose neither her son nor his future wife, and sends an urgent missive to her
father, Muminaga, asking him to gather his forces and help her to free
Alija. The bearer of that message, their servant Huso, succeeds only in en-
raging Muminaga, who is shamed by this turn of events and threatens to
punish his daughter. He later relents, as we shall see, but his change of
heart takes place offstage, at the level of expectable traditional context
rather than explicit description. For the moment, it seems to Fata that
she must take matters into her own hands, and so she proceeds to don
her bridegroom's identity by performing the customary rituals of heroic
preparation for a journey: asking his mother for provisions, having Huso
ready Alija's famous horse, donning heroic costume complete with wea-
ponry,[25] and taking a highly ritualized leave of (his) loved ones and home-
land. The trip to Zadar proves fraught with dangers, none of which she
has experienced before but none of which deter her; at one point, Fata-
become-Alija even sings to the wolves, bears, and ravens, calling them her

companions and urging friendship and conversation. These are actions and responses normally the province of the South Slavic (male) hero himself, whose identity and responsibilities the young woman has wholly assumed in this Return Song variant.

Her perilous journey to Zadar accomplished, Fata arrives at the city walls and is challenged by the gatekeeper Mato, who wants to know who she is and where she is from. If there were any doubt about the young maiden's new status as a substitute Turkish champion standing in for the imprisoned Alija, her dissembling response actually clarifies the situation: she claims to be Vide, young standardbearer to the ban of Janok, a Christian ally to the ban of Zadar. In short, she is for the purposes of the story (and the story-pattern) fully a hero, here telling a lying tale and masquerading as the enemy in order to gain admittance to the fortified town. Her ruse succeeds, and, in a popular strategy mirrored in innumerable other narratives, she relinquishes her personal control of the search and asks Alija's horse to find the way to the inn as a first step toward discovering his whereabouts. Tradition warrants that this strategy cannot fail, and the horse brings her to innkeeper Mara, a stock go-between in the epic tradition and here as elsewhere bloodsister to the missing Turkish champion. She quickly guesses Fata's true identity and characteristically offers her help in securing his release.[26]

Typically, that help takes the form of an undercover operation that involves the young daughter of the ban of Zadar, "beautiful Andjelija" (*dilber Andjelija*) as she is formulaically indexed. Mara leads Fata, now disguised in Hungarian women's clothes, along a secret passage to the young woman's chamber, where the three of them hatch a plan to rescue both Alija and Selim. Quite disloyally, Andjelija proposes to ask her father to allow the prisoners a few hours' liberty in order to pull her coach to church, and Fata promises to be ready and waiting with horses and her father Muminaga's troops.[27] When the next day dawns, their plans are enacted: Andjelija, her father the ban, and Captain Ivan accompany the coach drawn by the two prisoners, while Fata—still standing in for her betrothed hero—meets her father Muminaga with his five hundred soldiers and swoops down upon the unsuspecting Christian force. Alija of course immediately recognizes his horse and his clothes, now being employed by Fata in her role as his substitute and savior, but mistakes the rider; weeping, he tells his comrade and bloodbrother Selim that it is a "sharp Hungarian" speeding to their aid.

Still in disguise, Fata quickly beheads both the ban of Zadar and Captain Ivan. She then turns her attention toward the captives, slicing through the bonds that tie Alija and Selim to the coach like draught animals, and furnishes them sharp swords to wield and war-chargers to ride. Now transformed into armed warriors, the two former prisoners reassume their heroic roles and heartily attack the ban's remaining soldiers. With the rescue achieved and the enemy destroyed, Fata turns her mount over to its owner Alija, Muminaga gathers up his wounded, and the now-orphaned Andjelija is quickly betrothed to Halil, the otherwise honorable Turk who had courted Fata in Alija's absence. This amounts to the second Retribution in this particular Return Song, as the stand-in hero(ine) removes the remaining obstacles to fulfillment of the narrative sequence. A double Wedding element then closes the epic, as Alija and Fata are reunited and the way is cleared for Selim to make his unqualified, permanent return to a long-delayed marriage. Through the agency of a substitute hero—the hero's fiancée herself—the long-anticipated final scene prescribed by the Return Song paradigm takes place. Here at last the song reaches its *telos*.

Bašić's *Alagić Alija and Velagić Selim* thus offers a comparative perspective on all three of the main issues addressed in the present chapter. Its nonchronological sequence of events is typical of a Return Song of appreciable length: beginning in the middle, the story uses the flashback—two of them in this case—to fill in the events prior to the heroes' detainment in Zadar. These inset tales, in which the focal characters take over the narration in order to relate incidents to which only they have been witness, are a regular and important feature of the story-pattern as *sêma*. The mere onset of a Return Song implies this idiomatic, "out of order" presentation and flashback, and the well-prepared audience expects this sequence of events, just as surely as they know that Absence eventually leads to Wedding.[28]

As for the pivotal truelove figure, in this song there are two: Selim's unnamed fiancée and Alija's Fata. The former takes the classic female role in this kind of story; Selim tests her fidelity rigorously and finds her faithful. Although he must resume his incarceration after the month of freedom, he has succeeded in dispelling the suitor Halil and the wedding guests, and at least preliminarily in reestablishing himself back in Udbina. If and when he secures permanent liberty, his own return will be complete. Fata's situation is somewhat different, in that Alija sends a message instructing his mother to cancel the betrothal, but in another way it is quite familiar. By traditional convention the *vjerna ljuba* is an icon of uncertainty or indeterminacy, and in Fata's case the offered letter of release from the marriage contract amounts to Alija's test of her fidelity—a test she passes in nothing less than heroic fashion. Whereas the classic response to the hero's probing is a tearful confirmation of her love and commitment, Fata reacts by going a major step further. With her bridegroom imprisoned in an enemy city rather than standing disguised before her, she manifests the depth of her devotion by taking matters into her own hands. Resolution of the truelove's inherent ambiguity takes center stage in a forceful way as she dons her mate's identity and rides off to save him. While tearful confirmation is the appropriate response in most such cases, it just does not apply in this particular instance. Here testing, reaction, and retribution take on different dimensions. When words won't suffice, the truelove turns to action.

This performance of *Alagić Alija and Velagić Selim* thus demonstrates a number of ways in which the basic Return Song morphology can accommodate different kinds of variation. Instead of a single hero, we have two. Instead of a return that leads straight to retribution and wedding, we have the conditional and temporary release of Selim. The retrograde movement within the song means that the story does not end with Selim's return, and also that Alija will not be available to test his fiancée in the customary fashion. Finally, instead of a male hero leading the narrative toward its expectable closure, we have a young woman assuming heroic disguise and acting as a substitute champion.

The most important point to make about these variations, however, is that they are unified, contextualized, and given meaning by the idiomatic pattern of the Return Song. The main events and their order, the truelove's ambiguity, the inherent plasticity of closure—all three of these features signal the traditional pattern on which all such individual tales and performances are based, and through which they should therefore be viewed. Because the story-pattern functions as an overarching *sêma*, the Return Song evokes numerous associations, including numerous constituent *sêmata*. We expect shouting in prison, one or more extensive flashbacks, the hero Selim's arrival home in the impenetrable "disguise" of a prisoner, and his testing of his fiancée. We expect the same of Alija. The fact that these actions take intriguingly different forms in this song should not obscure the fact that the speech-act as a whole takes its shape from the narrative map of Absence—Devastation—Return—Retribution—Wedding. We must recognize and give due weight to the traditional referentiality of the *nostos* sequence, a pattern that not only supports composition but also drives reception. We must read behind the signs as well as between them.

Mujo Kukuruzović's *Captivity of Ograšćić Alija*

As a third example of the traditional morphology of the South Slavic Return Song, I have selected another performance recorded by Parry and Lord in the region of Stolac. This instance of the returning-hero narrative, titled *The Captivity of Ograšćić Alija* by the collectors, is one among a family of closely related performances sung or dictated by the *guslar* Mujo Kukuruzović.[29] For summary here I choose Parry no. *6617*, at 2,180 lines the longest of the four similar song-versions; it was recorded acoustically on 10 June 1935 and afterward transcribed by Nikola Vujnović.[30]

This one of Kukuruzović's performances happens to begin without the optional proem, moving straight into the prisoner's intolerable shouting, the banica's complaint, and the expectable scene of her bargaining with the strident and naturally inimical Turkish hero, named Ograšćić Alija in this particular tale. As with other Return Songs, the sequence starts far from the Turkish homeland in an enemy Christian city, this time called Janok. The initial exchange between the captor and his wife reveals more outright bickering than many such scenes, with the ban initially intransigent and the banica countering cleverly by ruthlessly emphasizing his old age and impotence, but their intense war of words has a familiar enough ring because it is waged on a recognizable interpersonal battlefield within standard traditional limits.

Having received the ban's grudging permission to negotiate with the offending captive herself, the wife then enters the prison and begins deliberations with Alija, who soon creates the special relationship of synthetic kinship typically shared by these figures by addressing her as "foster mother" (*majka na mjestu*). In the highly conventional flashback he complains that he has received word of his son's impending marriage in the Turkish Krajina, a son he has never met due to his long imprisonment. In response, but only after requiring of him the "bridging" institutions of bloodbrotherhood with herself and godfatherhood to her son Nikola, as well as a solemn oath never to fight against her husband's army, the banica agrees to release her one-time deadly foe and to furnish him with clothing and provisions for the trip home.

After many nights and much demanding travel, Alija, dependably incognito like all Return Song heroes in his "disguise" as a prisoner, encounters en route a large force headed by the ever-duplicitous Mustajbey of the Lika. Our protagonist wonders whether this is in fact the wedding party attending his son Hadžibey, embarked according to social mandate on the preliminary ritual of bride-stealing. But before he can ascertain their identity and purpose, a young bey who is part of the company asks him the inevitable questions about who he is, where he was imprisoned, and whether he knew their comrade Ograšćić Alija. The prisoner predictably responds that he buried Alija, and is rewarded for that professed service with a few *madzharijas*. In the course of this first test Alija also learns some other things: that it is in fact his son's wedding party, and that he must not reveal Alija's supposed demise to anyone else lest the bridegroom, hearing the sad news, feel that he must put a stop to the ceremony.

Nonetheless, the disguised hero goes ahead and administers the same test to many members of the assembled company, most prominently the trickster figure Tale of Orašac and Hadžibey himself. Tale responds as did the unnamed young bey a few moments earlier, but the loyal son reacts as feared and summarily halts the festivities. After some confusion over whose horse he will take, Alija proceeds toward his tower, ostensibly to report his own last words to his wife, assigned the name Alibegovica by her position as his duly wedded wife. In the process, of course, he intends to test her fidelity. Meanwhile, this same Alibegovica angrily inquires of Mustajbey why the joyous proceedings have suddenly come to a halt. Even after his cogent explanation—here strategically abbreviated[31]—she demands that the festivities resume immediately. This is the first hint that all may not be right at home, but it is a subtle clue; the innate ambiguity of the truelove remains intact as the story moves forward.

But not for long. Alija arrives at his homestead, greets his *vjerna ljuba*, and reports his own death via the same key lines he has earlier employed to test other characters. Her response to this news, and most strikingly to her husband's supposed final words of love and devotion as conveyed by the prisoner, is hardly Penelope-like: she laughs heartily in celebration of his reported demise, and she and her attendants handsomely reward the bearer of such welcome tidings. Then, contrary to all but traditional expectation, the miserable prisoner, presumably weakened by years of incarceration, asks to compete against the one hundred ablest men from the wedding party in a two-hour footrace. According to what we must now recognize as a convention, he defeats them all, though he is ungraciously refused the prize normally accorded the winner.

At this point Alibegovica, still unaware of the prisoner's real identity, sets her own contest for the assembled wedding guests. She offers the prize (and *sêma*) of her husband's most important possession, his famous horse, to whoever can mount it successfully, cautioning that during his twelve-year absence no one has managed to groom, water, saddle, or even bridle the animal.[32] The bey of Ribnik summons his finest young retainers and challenges them to try, but all are quickly dispatched by the dark steed's fury. Then the sorry captive asks permission to try his luck, and Alibegovica agrees. Although the horse initially confronts him with the same forbidding show of bared teeth and ears bent backward, Alija soon calms him and embarks on a full-blown typical scene of Readying the Horse, a traditional sign that the prisoner is transforming himself into a Turkish hero by preparing his horse for a heroic deed.[33]

From this stage the newly reestablished Ograšćić Alija rides to his mother's tower, where the old woman lies weeping, clothed in the funereal black of a *kukavica crna* as she mourns her son's presumed death. While still out of her sight, he plucks his long-neglected tamboura from a peg, and through his unmistakable singing and playing acoustically alerts his mother to his return. The same signal, a dependable because traditional portent of what is to come, plunges the nearby Alibegovica—her real nature now exposed as ironically opposite to her formulaic designation of "truelove"—into loud, incessant lamentation. Soon she will die, although in the present version her actual death will not be so graphically portrayed as in many other performances.[34] This Klytemnestra-type figure then reports Alija's unwanted return to Mustajbey of the Lika, the bey of Ribnik, and the others who are gathered as both her son's wedding party and her own suitors. They are savvy enough to flee without delay, abandoning her to her fate.

At this juncture the Return Song is complete, at least in one dimension. Absence and Devastation have given way to Alija's Return and Retribution. But the discovery of the truelove's faithlessness precludes simple closure in a Wedding element, and so the reemergent Turkish hero traitorously rides off to join the enemy General Pero in the Christian stronghold of Kara Bogdan. The song has come to a climax without reaching its *telos*, and so it continues.

Alija's express aim in falling in with the enemy is to wage a war of terror against his Turkish brothers, as revenge for the injustices perpetrated on him by Mustajbey, the bey of Ribnik, and most of all his scheming wife. His initial plans are fulfilled, as the turncoat Turk joins the Christian army assembling to attack Ribnik. Before long, however, Alija's original loyalties supersede his momentary treason, and the sequel story modulates into another standard subgenre of Moslem epic, the Rescue Song. This second story-pattern provides a final return of imprisoned Turkish heroes, a last act that serves as a coda for the composite song as well. This time the performance really does come to closure, with a final scene that is doubly expectable: it fits both the immediate context of the Rescue sequel and the long-term context of the overall, composite epic.[35]

This performance of Mujo Kukuruzović's *The Captivity of Ograšćić Alija* thus illustrates other ways in which the Return Song *sêma* can accommodate different directions in plot development and yet preserve basically the same plastic structure that guides both composition and reception. Within the first section we note the customary nonchronological sequence: the narrative begins in the middle, with Alija in jail and raising the typically intolerable ruckus. Here the flashback emphasizes the length of the hero's imprisonment; he has been absent from his home for so long that the son he never met is now about to be married. The remainder of this first part of the performance then chronicles his return in the customary fashion, with a perilous journey leading to disguised entry into his homeland, victory over his peers, and a series of loyalty tests.

But the Wedding (or rapprochement) scene toward which all of these events lead just never happens. Instead of the faithful *vjerna ljuba* always sought by returning heroes and found by many of them, Alija encounters a South Slavic Klytemnestra who openly rejoices over the report of her husband's demise. To put it another way, and this will be of crucial importance for our discussion of the Return Song *sêma* in the *Odyssey*, it is hardly a foregone conclusion that the hero will find a faithful truelove at the end of the journey and testing process. The well-trodden narrative pathway leads not to certainty, but to a persistent ambiguity that can be resolved either way, for good or for ill. Implicit in the truelove figure from the start is a mysterious and stubborn duality or indeterminacy that amounts to her own "disguise." What is more, the key to her discarding that disguise—the fork in the path where ambiguity yields to mutual acceptance or its opposite—depends upon some sort of special understanding shared between man and woman. Whether this amounts to a musical feat, as with the hero's idiosyncratic tamboura-playing, or some other action or reaction, the unmistakable signal dissolves the characteristic tension suddenly and authoritatively—because traditionally.[36]

Kukuruzović's song also sheds light on the general question of ending or closure in the Return Song. Precisely because the *vjerna ljuba* proves herself to be committed to a rival, the song obviously cannot reach its *telos* or fulfillment in Alija's long-sought reunion with his wife. Of the three examples considered in our overview of the South Slavic Return Song, this last performance departs furthest from the Odyssean pattern in its continuation of the story.[37] In this case we must deal not simply with the Milutin adventure and brief rescue that capped Alija Fjuljanin's *The Captivity of Četić Osmanbey*, or even the double-prisoner sequence and substitute hero of Ibro Bašić's *Alagić Alija and Velagić Selim*, but with an entire second story-pattern of Rescue that is actually about twice the length of the first section of the performance. In other words, the flexibility of the Return Song allows the *guslar* to build a composite story based on two well-known patterns, and, as it happens, corresponding to two freestanding songs from within his own repertoire.[38] Clearly, the traditional morphology of the Return Song is anything but confining or predetermined; its recognizable shape modulates from one song to another, one singer to another, and even one performance to another. Like all traditional *sêmata*, it varies within limits. It furnishes a map for reading behind as well as between the signs.

Agamemnon and the Two Return Songs

Our principal aim in this chapter is to understand the significance of the "word" and *sêma* of Return as applied to the *Odyssey*. With a traditional morphology now in hand, let us start our examination of Odysseus' *nostos* by yielding the floor to Agamemnon, whose own counter-Odyssean experience provides him a unique point of view on what can await the hero returning home. Midway in the twenty-fourth book, Agamemnon's ghost listens to Amphimedon's account of the suitors' slaughter and then comments as follows (192–202):

"ὄλβιε Λαέρταο πάϊ, πολυμήχαν' Ὀδυσσεῦ,
ἦ ἄρα σὺν μεγάλῃ ἀρετῇ ἐκτήσω ἄκοιτιν·
ὡς ἀγαθαὶ φρένες ἦσαν ἀμύμονι Πηνελοπείῃ,
κούρῃ Ἰκαρίου· ὡς εὖ μέμνητ' Ὀδυσῆος,   195
ἀνδρὸς κουριδίου. τῷ οἱ κλέος οὔ ποτ' ὀλεῖται
ἧς ἀρετῆς, τεύξουσι δ' ἐπιχθονίοισιν ἀοιδὴν
ἀθάνατοι χαρίεσσαν ἐχέφρονι Πηνελοπείῃ,
οὐχ ὡς Τυνδαρέου κούρη κακὰ μήσατο ἔργα,
κουρίδιον κτείνασα πόσιν, στυγερὴ δέ τ' ἀοιδὴ   200
ἔσσετ' ἐπ' ἀνθρώπους, χαλεπὴν δέ τε φῆμιν ὀπάσσει
θηλυτέρῃσι γυναιξί, καὶ ἥ κ' εὐεργὸς ἔῃσιν."

"O fortunate son of Laertes, Odysseus of many devices,
surely you won yourself a wife endowed with great virtue.
How good was proved the heart that is in blameless Penelope,
Ikarios' daughter, and how well she remembered Odysseus,   195
her wedded husband. Thereby the fame of her virtue shall never
die away, but the immortals will make for the people
of earth a pleasing song for prudent Penelope.
Not so did the daughter of Tyndareos fashion her evil
deeds, when she killed her wedded lord, and a song of loathing   200
will be hers among men, to make evil the reputation
of womankind, even for one whose acts are virtuous."

As in so many other places throughout the poem, the Klytemnestra-Agamemnon-Orestes paradigm emerges as an explicit contrast to Penelope-Odysseus-Telemachos. We sense the faithfulness of the long-abandoned wife in Ithaka the more keenly because of Agamemnon's stark comparison with his parallel homecoming in Mykenae. Indeed, the tragic denouement represented by this latest unraveling of the House of Atreus never seems far from the main story of the *Odyssey* up through the long-sought reunion in Book 23, as if it were furnishing not merely a distant comparison but an actual implied alternative.[39]

Moreover, with this brief speech Agamemnon goes far beyond a simple contrast between the two different women or the two different situations to a sustained contrast between two diametrically opposite songs of return. He specifically juxtaposes the "pleasing song" (*aoidên . . . chariessan*) that the gods will accord Penelope to the "song of loathing" (*stugerê . . . aoidê*) destined to circulate about Klytemnestra. These are the two tales, the two paradigms, that the poetic tradition will create and maintain—one of praise and one of blame. And he is just as specific about why the tradition will treat the two women in this way: Penelope honored her husband, earning *kleos,* "glory in song," while Klytemnestra chose Aigisthos and killed her husband, earning nothing but ignominy for herself and her gender by her evil deeds. These eleven lines thus amount to a tour de force, as the ghost sets one woman's qualities against the other's liabilities with a rhetorical skill that echoes traditional distinctions. Penelope will earn a "pleasing song" and Klytemnestra a "song of loathing" specifically because the former "remembered Odysseus, her wedded husband" (195–96) while the latter "fashion[ed] her evil deeds" and "killed her wedded lord" (199–200). On account of these disparate actions, one is fated to receive the everlasting fame of *kleos* for her virtue and the other only *chalepên . . . phêmin* ("evil reputation").[40]

But Agamemnon is also doing much more. He is in effect providing a traditional morphology of the ancient Greek *nostos* tale that looks very much like the forked pathway of the South Slavic Return Song. Interpreted in this fashion, Agamemnon's ghost's commentary can be understood as distinguishing the possible outcomes of the same widely distributed story that Milman Parry and Albert Lord recorded in the Balkans in the present century. That is, he comments from inside the tradition on the same network of events that they studied, as fieldworkers, from outside the tradition. Will the ancient Greek "truelove" turn out to be faithful or treacherous? After requisite loyalty tests have been administered and the athletic contest(s) won, will she welcome him home or take advantage of his death to establish or continue a relationship with a rival? Will any given performance, in short, be a Penelope-song or a Klytemnestra-song? Even within the only surviving *nostos* epic, our *Odyssey*, which of course portrays only one possible outcome, Agamemnon's own words provide dramatic, parable-like evidence of what the journey would have entailed had the story followed the road not taken.

Question 1: Events and Sequence

Based on the traditional morphology of the South Slavic Return Song and Agamemnon's parallel typology, can we now offer a fresh perspective on the *Odyssey* story? In particular, can we shed any light on its constituent events and their nonchronological order? I believe we can.

Although generations have understood the shorter of Homer's epics as a stylized exercise in beginning a poem "in the middle of things" (*in medias res*), we are now in a position to see that the *Odyssey* does nothing of the sort. It starts "where it should," proceeds "as it should," and ends "where it should." Even the extended flashback—Odysseus' own song-within-the-song in the so-called Apologue of Books 9–12—amounts to a customary, even expectable feature of the Return Song *sêma*. In short, by offering an alternative to the presumed archetypal form in which one action or event succeeds another in tidy chronological sequence, the comparative morphology and Agamemnon's commentary point in another direction. They allow us to glimpse a deeper and more fundamental pattern to Odysseus' adventures, a pattern with a vital expressive life of its own.

Consider first the opening gambit on Ogygia. It is here that Kalypso has detained the hero for many years since his departure from Troy, here that he has languished in captivity, powerless to change his circumstances until Hermes' visit catalyzes Zeus' (and Athena's) plan. As with the South Slavic songs, much lies behind the scenes, some of it to be revealed later on as the hero recounts his prior adventures before the Phaeacians and some of it left at the level of mythological implication and traditional referentiality. For example, we never hear explicitly in the *Odyssey* itself about the origin and dynamics of the Trojan War. Nonetheless, in company with other audiences we know from alternate sources that, like the usually undescribed Turkish conflicts implied in the Moslem Return epics, it involved Odysseus' participation in a composite force fighting a far-off battle in which the hero himself had no personal stake. Such expeditions unfailingly lead to a lengthy, disabling separation of husband and wife, and in this case, as in many South Slavic songs, to the hero's effective ignorance of the son who comes of age during his time away.

In terms of the Return Song story-pattern analyzed and exemplified above, the *Odyssey* thus begins quite canonically with the hero's Absence and with the Devastation that has resulted for both him and the family and community left behind. Because even this first part of the traditional sequence or *sêma* brings into play a unique, focused set of implications, a map now begins to unfold before the audience or reader. The story as it is told neither lacks coherence because it fails to follow chronological order nor is merely falling victim to a convention that happened to become a stylistic staple of literary epic. Rather the Return pattern imposes its own constitutive order on the proceedings, directing attention toward a familiar horizon of expectation at the same time that it slots the immediate events within larger traditional categories. From this perspective the trek homeward is foreordained from the initial book of the *Odyssey*: there is no question that the hero will inevitably reach Ithaka after requisite trials and tribulations. But what he finds there must always to some degree hang in the balance. Even if the names of Odysseus and Penelope themselves forecast a successful reunion of long-suffering hero and his equally long-suffering faithful wife, the expressive force of the Return *sêma* introduces a palpable tension. Agamemnon's testimony indicates that reading behind the signs must produce a sharply defined ambiguity: fidelity and a happy homecoming or infidelity and a disastrous homecoming. Only the particular, between-the-signs fabric of the given song or performance can resolve this projected duality. Indeed, as at every level throughout the *Odyssey*, from phrase through scene to story-pattern, the poem's richness stems in large part from the interaction of traditional *sêma* with particular moment or event, from the characteristic meshing of idiomatic implication with singular instance.

According to the *nostos* map, Devastation implies a twofold challenge. On the one hand, the wife or fiancée, as we will remember from the South Slavic songs, faces usurpation of her mate's position by a ruthless band of unruly suitors, former allies of her fiancé or husband who are now taking full and ruthless advantage of her powerless situation. Their leader regularly proves an especially pernicious individual, who combines innate cowardice with external bravado, and she usually has all she can do to hold him and his cohorts at bay.[41] On the other hand, the absent hero experiences his own parallel devastation, held in captivity far from the homeland to which he has so desperately been trying to return. Before the third element of the story, the actual Return, can begin, the hero must tell his own tale and, where possible, seek inside information about the state of the family and community he left behind.

Odysseus accomplishes both of these narrative prerequisites, although in much more extended and complex form than is typical of South Slavic epic. Just as Alagić Alija rehearses for his cellmate Velagić Selim the tale of how he came to be the prisoner of the ban of Zadar, so Odysseus recounts for his Phaeacian hosts the perilous encounters with Polyphemos, Kirke, Helios, and the rest as a precondition to his magical journey home. But whereas Alija's tale-within-a-tale covers a few hundred lines, the ancient Greek song devotes four books or some 2,200 lines to this major exposition. Still, against the background of the Return *sêma*, the major consideration must remain the relative importance of the flashback for the story-pattern as a whole, and by this measure the two poems are closely comparable.[42] In this fundamental sense, the retrospective episode is not at all "out of order," but rather follows the traditional sequence mapped out from the start. Indeed, any other order would diminish the art of the *Odyssey*, countering traditional referentiality by frustrating expectations and violating the expressive rules of the register.

Furthermore, just as Velagić Selim quizzes his fellow inmate Alija about the condition of his wife, mother, horse, and tower, so Odysseus spends a fair amount of time making similar inquiries of Teiresias' and his mother Antikleia's ghosts during his extraordinary sojourn in Hades in Book 11. In addition to asking why she died, he tries to ascertain the latest information about Penelope, Telemachos, and Laertes. Teiresias provides him a virtual blueprint for the homeward journey and revenge, noting the threat under which the suitors have placed his family and possessions, while Antikleia reports Penelope's overwhelming grief, Laertes' pauperlike existence, and her own death brought on by her son's protracted absence.[43] Very similarly to Velagić Selim and so many other South Slavic return heroes, Odysseus discovers to his sorrow how great a devastation his absence has visited upon Ithaka. This kind of "early news" from the home front, delivered through an unlikely interview with a person possessing special knowledge, functions as an integral part of the traditional sequence, a prerequisite to the physical return. This is one more way in which the overall momentum of the story depends on its telltale lack of ordinary, linear chronology.

Unlike any of the South Slavic songs with which I am familiar, the *Odyssey* then goes a step further by previewing the hero's strategy of disguise and testing through Agamemnon's warning to his comrade (the exchange at 11.387–466). Via this irruption of the "other" Return path into the Odysseus-Penelope story, the audience thus has the opportunity to compare the dysfunction and ignominy of a reunion gone terribly wrong, a *nostos* capped not by faithfulness and (Re-)Wedding but by infidelity and murder. Agamemnon underlines Klytemnestra's insult by poignantly noting her failure to observe even the merest of obsequies; turning her back while he was expiring, she refused even to close his eyes and mouth as his spirit headed for Hades. But most important of all for our present purposes, Agamemnon counsels Odysseus not to reveal himself fully until he has tested Penelope (441–43), and further, to enter Ithaka secretly (455–56). As an audience well aware of Odysseus' penchant for trickery, we may justifiably respond that he hardly requires any extra encouragement to proceed with stealth. But we should also read behind the signs: another Return hero who found himself going down the wrong fork in the narrative road is insistently recommending caution. Even as he criticizes the hateful woman who brought him down, Agamemnon urges a more suspicious approach on his comrade. Until the ambiguity of the Greek "truelove" figure is finally resolved one way or the other, he warns, Odysseus had best keep close counsel.

At this juncture the hero's physical return to Ithaka, appropriately preceded and signaled by the flashback, can appropriately take place. It amounts to the next stop on the narrative itinerary projected by traditional referentiality. Odysseus completes his tale-within-a-tale by bringing the skein of his adventures up to date (singing the episodes of revisiting Kirke as well as encounters with Skylla, Charybdis, Helios' cattle, and Kalypso), and, with the help of the unmatched Phaeacian rowers, he soon finds himself home. But *nostos*—whether in ancient Greece or twentieth-century Bosnia or elsewhere—entails one crucial qualification, a characteristic that unfailingly marks the reentry of Return Song protagonists: a durable, even impenetrable *disguise*. Like the South Slavic beggar-heroes who come back to their native lands as long-incarcerated prisoners fully confident that their real identities remain hidden, Odysseus' ragged appearance dependably shields him from discovery.[44] This disguise enables him to conduct the testing procedure consonant with his personality, recommended by Agamemnon, and, most fundamentally, required by the story-pattern. From within an anonymity that serves at the same time to protect his identity from other characters and to make him transparently identifiable to any audience or reader familiar with the Return story, he will administer the tests that lead to the next stage—a series of recognitions.[45]

From Absence, Devastation, and Return, the story moves toward Retribution, the vengeance meted out to the suitors by the returning hero as recompense for the indignities they perpetrated on his family and community. As we learned from the South Slavic songs, this activity can take one or both of two forms: the ritual skirmishing of athletic competition or actual mortal combat. Odysseus partakes of both forms of vengeance by outdoing the suitors' pick, the beggar Iros, in fisticuffs and by winning the contest of the bow just before he carries out the well-planned slaughter of the suitors in Book 22. We might also recall that the Phaeacian episode, in so many ways an early reflection of the eventual Ithakan homecoming, had prefigured this aspect of *nostos* as well. While still an unrecognized guest-stranger just recovering from his bout against Poseidon in Book 8,[46] Odysseus had met the rude challenge of the young Phaeacian Euryalos by far outdistancing him in the discus competition. Now the battle has modulated from ritual contest to bloody reality via the *sêma* of the bow, and the hero does what the Return Song hero in general, and Odysseus in particular, must do.[47]

Although she at first refuses to believe Eurykleia's report of the suitors' grim fate, Penelope, as we have seen in Chapter 1, employs secret *sêmata* to convince herself that Odysseus has beyond doubt returned. This most crucial of recognitions makes possible the *telos* of the *Odyssey* at Book 23.296, and it also marks the climax of the Return Song, the (Re-)Wedding. We will have more to say below about the process of Penelope's recognition and her role in the overall narrative (Question 2), as well as about the "continuation" of the poem beyond this point (Question 3).

For now let us emphasize that the *Odyssey* is first and foremost a Return Song, an instance of a widely distributed tale-type that at least until recently could still be collected in eastern Europe. As such, its sequence of events is not only explicable and structurally logical; it is also idiomatic. The fact that the *Odyssey* proceeds from Absence through (Re-)Wedding along a traditional route, a predictable trajectory that happens not to be chronological, is an essential feature of the work's expressive force. For the narrative to proceed in any other sequence would be unidiomatic.

On the other hand, outside the *sêma* and speech-act of Return, linear chronology may well be the order of the day, as Odysseus shows in Book 23

(306–43) when he recapitulates his story before Penelope. Here the tale proceeds from the Kikonians, Lotos-Eaters, and Kyklops through Aiolos, the Laestrygonians, and Kirke on to Hades, Teiresias, the Sirens, Skylla and Charybdis, Helios, Kalypso, the Phaeacians, and home. For us this revised itinerary may seem to be the "correct" one, with the various adventures described as they "actually happened." But the truth is that Odysseus' tale-telling before Penelope is not itself governed by the epic story-pattern, which as we have seen mandates another, register-specific kind of narrative logic. Indeed, from the perspective of the Return Song, it is the small reprise in Book 23 that begins "out of order" or "in the middle."[48] The contrast between the larger epic and its brief recapitulation is therefore instructive: each has its own rules for composition and reception. Odysseus tells his story to Penelope *as it happened*; Homer tells the story to us *as it was told to him*.

Relying on a few scraps of ancient evidence, a modern narrative morphology, and Agamemnon's own words, I have suggested that the *Odyssey*, far from merely starting "in the middle" (*in medias res*), is told "all in order," *panta kata kosmon*, as Homer is fond of saying.[49] To do anything else—whether to attempt to "straighten out" the chronology or adopt an alternate narrative sequence—would be to shatter the idiom, to insist on a vehicle that lacks traditional referentiality. Composition would suffer, as would reception. *Nostos* is a *sêma* "writ" large, and to ignore its contribution is to fail to read behind the sign.

Question 2: Penelope's Indeterminacy

Over the centuries many have observed that Penelope, the prudent, sharp-witted daughter of Ikarios, presents a genuine quandary for any audience or readership of the poem, ancient or modern. Not seldom her words and actions seem puzzling and unmotivated. Although our sympathies are ever with her plight as an abandoned wife in a dire situation not of her own making, we must wonder why she sometimes seems to resist hoping for Odysseus' return and waits so long to accept her husband's presence. Or does she? Indeed, Penelope's delays have often prompted critics to suggest that she "knows" much earlier—well before the trial of the bed or even before the contest of the bow—who the stranger is, and that she chooses for whatever reason not to reveal that knowledge. Her inaction has always been a riddle.

As with so many other aspects of Homeric art, the challenge is to read behind the signs as well as between them. Just as the Return Song morphology sheds light on the *Odyssey* as a whole by providing multiple parallels for its sequence of events and thus a context for its reception, so the particular dramatis personae of this widely distributed story-pattern can help us better understand the chief players in the ancient Greek epic drama. Such assistance is especially important in the case of Penelope. For while Odysseus is center stage for most of the twenty-four books, explicitly living through or retelling his *nostos*, his equally long-suffering mate remains offstage, silent and out of sight, for the majority of the time. While we have the opportunity to experience practically every detail of Odysseus' adventures and encounters in his personal company, the narrative focus that so prominently features him necessarily tends to ignore Penelope's moment-to-moment thoughts and responses, leaving her desperate struggle largely at the level of implication. This imbalance—foregrounding the hero's adventures explicitly and portraying the heroine's experiences chiefly as implied background—is not at all unusual; in fact, it reflects the typical division of narrative emphasis in the South Slavic Return Songs as well. And while the *Odyssey* offers us only one such heroine, the redoubtable and apparently unique daughter of Ikarios, the South Slavic epics present scores of wives and fiancées who await their mates with one of two distinctly different agendas in mind. Collectively they offer us the chance to glimpse something of the Return Song heroine's dilemma and response. It will be the burden of the present section to tap into the traditional referentiality associated with this figure in order to open up Penelope's behind-the-scenes invisibility to plainer view.

I will argue here, based on the comparative morphology sketched above, that Penelope's recognition of Odysseus is anything but a secret she keeps to herself. She delays because delay is functional; she avoids early closure because early closure would violate her character and subvert the *nostos*; she insists on doubting her husband because any other reaction would be dangerously premature—for him, for her, and not least for the *Odyssey* as a tale of return. Holding the suitors at bay is the more obvious dimension of her weaving and unweaving, a strategy that accords memorably with the poet's and tradition's emphasis on her indeterminacy.[50] But I will also be suggesting that Penelope really does not and cannot know for certain who stands before her until that man has expounded the riddle of their bed, as no other man could ever do. Along the way we will have reason to affirm her indecision, to stress that her supposed delay or failure to proceed as directly as possible toward closure is actually a fundamentally positive and even heroic achievement. It is the source of her *kleos*, as Agamemnon stipulates. For Penelope's indeterminacy—both the ambiguity she experiences and the ambiguity she represents—not only saves her and her returning husband; it also keeps the song alive.

That is one side of her indeterminacy, the extent to which she both confronts and projects uncertainty. Just when Penelope seems to be on the verge of finishing her weaving, the fabric unravels and the almost-solved questions loom anew. Marilyn Katz has studied this aspect of her epic role in detail, stressing the functional "disruption of fixity" in her character.[51] Much of what Katz derives from a close examination of Penelope and a consideration of the alternative narrative route that leads toward Klytemnestra harmonizes well with our comparative approach through the South Slavic Return Song. Both analyses point toward a central, pivotal figure around whom the rest of the epic revolves, a heroine whose resilient ability to keep options open saves the *nostimon êmar*, the "day of return," for her husband, family, community, and not least herself.

But there is another side as well. In what follows I also use *indeterminacy* in the additional sense employed by Receptionalist critics such as Hans Robert Jauss and Wolfgang Iser, and as adapted to the interpretation of works from oral tradition.[52] In this sense the term names the open or "undetermined" space left in the work for the reader or audience to participate in the making of the given work. As Jauss and Iser demonstrate, texts (and by extension performances) do not supply every last signal and detail; verbal art is not a laundry list or a computer-software manual where total explicitness is the goal. Rather they provide well-integrated blueprints for what will always remain an individual experience, stimulated and maintained by the text or performance but necessarily incomplete and therefore open to the reader's or audience's personal "take."

Thus when we speak of Penelope's indeterminacy we also speak of the space she provides the audience or readership of the *Odyssey* in which to form their own opinions of her action and inaction. Each of us evolves an internally consistent explanation for exactly why she weaves and unweaves, for example, or precisely when she knows the stranger is truly Odysseus. We base our explanations on the text as it has reached us, of course, but, because that text also leaves gaps of indeterminacy, not all of Penelope's auditors and readers will speak with a single voice. The history of criticism makes that point very strongly: no challenge or issue in Homer has met with a greater variety of solutions, and with less agreement, than those that surround the redoubtable mistress of Ithaka. She has constituted a problem in reception since ancient times, prompting myriad different readings or hearings.

Far from being a handicap, this stubborn indeterminacy, this resistance to a final and singular solution, functions as a crucially important force driving the composition and reception of the *Odyssey* story. If Penelope does not yield to facile rationalization, if she fits no mold but her own, so much the better for the dynamics of the epic. We are drawn to her uncertainty, at pains to have it all make sense, intrigued enough to try to walk through her experience with her. In practice this means she is a focal character—perhaps *the* focal character in the epic, even more so than her husband, who also harbors his share of indeterminacy.[53] If Odysseus' "polytropism," the shape-shifting with which he is credited in the very first line of the *Odyssey*,[54] is the ultimate source of his much-celebrated *kleos*, then Penelope's heroic indeterminacy, another brand of polytropism, is the foundation for her fame, the *kleos* that Agamemnon's ghost so ruefully celebrates. As we shall see below, from the perspective of the Return Song story-pattern, Penelope is the linchpin character, the fulcrum on which the entire epic balances. Indeed, Odysseus' wiliness, which allows him to adapt to all challenges and eventually to find his way home, is more than matched by his wife's ability to suspend narrative development, to stave off the suitors' advances and the pressure of societal reality.[55] Were it not for her heroic performance at home, his efforts—no matter how deserving of *kleos* in the poetic tradition—would be for naught. She is the center of the story; even if she presides over its unfolding from offstage.

With this double understanding of indeterminacy in mind, let us establish a comparative traditional context by considering Penelope's South Slavic sisters. Of what does the Return Song heroine's vital and functional ambiguity actually consist? Drawing chiefly from the synopses of Stolac songs given above, let us construct a set of typical actions and characteristics that is echoed much more widely throughout the traditional network of South Slavic epic.[56]

For one thing, the heroine customarily loses her mate early in their relationship, soon after marriage or betrothal and before the couple has had a chance to spend much time together.[57] Almost always this separation has taken place before the song begins. It is not so much that their relationship is incipient or immature as that the two principals have been and will be deprived of a shared existence for most of their adult lives. This reality of one-time unity and long-term estrangement can also be signaled by the presence of a son (and emphasized by his coming of age or impending marriage) whom the hero may never have known, or at least has not known since infancy. Since any possibility of a future shared with her mate remains under threat throughout most of the story, the Return Song heroine both faces and embodies uncertainty. The cognate problem of her being actively courted by suitors, former countrymen now turned merciless usurpers, only intensifies her indeterminacy. The truelove is an icon of ambiguity at this juncture and throughout the rest of the story, in that neither her pursuers nor the tale's audience know whether or when the suit will succeed. We may presume she is deflecting the advances of the suitors, but in truth we just don't know.

The *Alagić Alija and Velagić Selim* sung by Ibro Bašić, and many other South Slavic Return Songs as well, spotlight the heroine's indeterminacy with a sign steeped in traditional referentiality: the series of anxious questions typically posed by her absent mate as he languishes in captivity.

Above and beyond all other concerns (mother, father, children, posses-
sions, community, and so on), the hero expresses the most disquiet over
whether his wife has remarried. What is more, the response he receives is
always conditional, at best amounting to "so far, so good, but no guaran-
tees." In a real sense the hero strives toward home to resolve that ambigu-
ity, to convert his mate's necessary, functional ambivalence to certainty,
one way or the other. The *Alagić Alija and Velagić Selim* illustrates how
pressing that task can be, as Velagić Selim confronts a particularly de-
manding version of this trying situation: Alija plainly reveals to him the
impending (but as yet unaccomplished) remarriage of his wife.[58]

It is of course the hero's cleverly administered loyalty test that dispels
the heroine's celebrated indeterminacy and helps to make evident which
fork the narrative will take—toward resolution in (re-)marriage or toward
death and ignominy. Among the songs examined above, both Velagić
Selim and Ograšćić Alija conduct their covert examinations by maintain-
ing their disguise as prisoners even as they report their own deaths. With
this kind of cataclysmic announcement and the finality it portends, both
the uncertainty the heroine faces and the uncertainty she represents fall
away. The more immediate, face-to-face version of this strategy, used to
make trial of other people as well, can involve the hero's pressing her with
ever more deliberate questions, even asking whether she rewards him for
burying her mate or for the possibly welcome news of her certain loss and
consequent freedom.[59] In other words, the examination process may be
protracted in various ways and for various reasons. For example, the let-
ter of release from betrothal, written from prison by the despairing Alagić
Alija, constitutes a long-distance test, one that could allow the heroine
to take up with another man but in the case of the story of *Alagić Alija and
Velagić Selim* transforms her into a substitute Return champion. Finally, the
unmistakable sign of the hero's tamboura-playing also serves as an effec-
tive means to reduce the heroine's indeterminacy to a singular, unambigu-
ous personality. It forces her to commit, one way or the other. Like the
other testing *sêmata*, this musical sign divulges her allegiance, for good or
for ill,[60] and prescribes the hero's actions from that point forward.

Among such traditionally transparent signs, all of them ubiquitous
ploys in both Penelope- and Klytemnestra-songs in South Slavic epic, it is
not unusual to view the truelove conducting a test—really a contest—of
her own. Whether she seems consciously aware of the ultimate importance
of the competition or not, any reader or audience familiar with this idio-
matic strategem will recognize it for what it is: a dependable way to iden-
tify the disguised hero in front of his rivals and to cue the onset of his retri-
bution. In Mujo Kukuruzović's *The Captivity of Ograšćić Alija*, Alibegovica
offers Alija's horse to whoever can ride it and, as surely as Excalibur selects

the stripling Arthur from more promising peers or Odysseus' bow unfailingly reveals its owner, the horse refuses everyone but its disguised master.[61] On the one hand, the heroine's action seems superficially unmotivated; she gives no explicit indication that she is seeking to cull her disguised mate out of the throng, or even that she suspects he is among the competitors. But the contest *sêma* has a life of its own and a necessary implication for all who recognize the telltale sign. Every audience member or reader fluent in the traditional register knows that her setting of the contest must inexorably lead toward the hero's identification and revenge. In the process it will also dissolve her double indeterminacy, both the ambiguity she confronts as an apparently helpless woman besieged by suitors and the ambiguity she projects by deftly managing the ever-inchoate relationships with her present pursuers on the one hand and her once and future mate on the other. Indeed, in respect to the contest and all of the challenges that face her, the Return Song heroine's seeming powerlessness is, paradoxically, the source of her considerable power. In contrast to her mate's high-profile adventures and celebrated actions, she is most characteristically defined by low-profile indeterminacy and inaction.

In summary, then, the South Slavic truelove's heroism consists most essentially of her persistence. Performing offstage and largely by indirection, she nonetheless exists at the geographical and narrative center of the Return Song, defending against the incursion of hostile suitors by virtue of her patience and cleverness. Abandoned for the greater part of her married (or betrothed) life, the *vjerna ljuba* has had to fend largely for herself, often with the added responsibility of caring for the hero's mother, their son, or both as well as trying to manage whatever property and goods he has left behind. Her main weapon in this battle, and it is a battle fully as demanding as the hero's more celebrated deeds, is her indeterminacy. Neither the suitors nor her mate—nor for that matter the audience or readership of the epic that revolves around her—can be sure of the truelove's allegiance and status until she reveals herself through the two-way medium of the testing process.

Indeed, as noted above, the truelove represents nothing less than the fundamental narrative pivot in the Return Song, for it is she, and not her mate, who ultimately directs its course. Consider their roles and responsibilities. There is never any question about whether the hero of the story-pattern will succeed in actually reaching his homeland; all such heroes always do. But that is not the end of the story, for everything depends on what he finds there. To put it another way, from the very first line the Return genre absolutely ensures the male protagonist's physical arrival back home, while leaving tantalizingly open the question of whether he will be greeted by a South Slavic Penelope or Klytemnestra. Only time, test, and contest will tell. The ultimate course of events takes final shape very late, with the durable sign of her indeterminacy remaining two-sided until the moment of revelation.

For these reasons I would propose that the Return Song heroine is at least as important a figure as her mate: it is she, not he, who drives the development of the narrative at the deepest and most fundamental level. Indeed, we could as easily and as accurately assign titles like *Alibegovica's Devastation* or *Fata's Revenge* to the epics that Parry and Lord chose to name *The Captivity of Ograšćić Alija* and *Alagić Alija and Velagić Selim*, respectively.[62] Even when the heroine does not assume the identity of substitute hero (and such stand-in behavior is relatively rare), she is still the fulcrum on which the entire story balances. This is the functional core of the truelove's indeterminacy, a persistent ambiguity shared, I believe we can see, with the heroine of the *Odyssey*.

Even the most superficial overview of Penelope's often puzzling actions, especially over the defining course of Books 19–23, reveals her kinship with this truelove figure from the South Slavic epics. In broadest terms we cannot doubt her persistence, as she struggles daily against the latest indignities of the suitors with nothing to support her but her own cleverness and stubborn indeterminacy.[63] For much of the poem she remains out of sight, yielding narrative prominence to her husband's many adventures, but that invisibility does not translate to diminished importance. Penelope exists at the very core of the *Odyssey*, at both its geographical hub in Ithaka and its teleological center in Book 23; indeed, she personifies the *telos*, or fulfillment, toward which the hero strives from a time well before the song begins.[64]

What is more, her function as narrative pivot or fulcrum also parallels the role of the South Slavic truelove. Even though we receive many clues that it is a faithful wife who awaits the hero in Ithaka, two dimensions of the *Odyssey* story qualify that interpretation and keep the issue in doubt. One is the question of whether she will eventually be forced into giving up her socially anomalous position in Ithaka, that is, required by Telemachos to go back to her father's house and submit to remarriage under his aegis. Odysseus worries over this possible development, and so does she.[65] Such a remarriage could very well happen in spite of her fidelity and her personal wishes, spurred on by the suitors' impatience and the realities of a patriarchal society. The other aspect of the *Odyssey* that induces a tension in her characterization, that suggests the threat of an unhappy return despite her avowed faithfulness, is the recurrent comparison of Odysseus and Penelope's situation with that of Agamemnon and Klytemnestra. Whether the source of the frequently drawn analogy is Agamemnon or the poet himself, the two possible endings for the Return Song resonate throughout the poem.[66] This is Penelope, we are told, and there is every reason to expect she will earn her *kleos* as the unassailable defender of indeterminacy until her husband comes home. At the same time, we are never allowed to forget the treachery of Klytemnestra and Aigisthos, and the ignominious end of Agamemnon, for very long. Everything depends on whether Penelope's faithfulness and strategic inaction can both survive the severe social pressures under which she labors and defuse the tension induced by the unwelcome parallel from the House of Atreus.

Her performance as a Return Song heroine within this context is crucial to the overall dynamics of the *Odyssey*, as the South Slavic analogy indicates. If she succeeds, we may expect effective closure once the *telos* is reached, with some allowance for tying up any loose narrative threads that might remain after that coda. But if circumstances do not allow her to succeed, that is, if either social pressure or the Agamemnon-Klytemnestra parallel somehow wins the day, then we may anticipate a prolonged continuation, a sequel story, to set things right.[67] She alone determines whether the hero succeeds or not; she alone determines whether the song ends or goes on. As with the epic tales performed by Ibro Bašić and Mujo Kukuruzović, which could with some justice be renamed after their heroines, the *Odyssey* (or at least its last handful of books) could with equal justification be retitled the *Penelopeia*. Odysseus may seem to be the sole or at least the far more prominent agent in completing his return; it is after all he who slaughters the suitors and thereby regains his position, securing Ithaka for Penelope and his family. But it is she who weaves and unweaves, she who earns *kleos* by her indeterminacy, she who hands Odysseus the bow and later forces his hand via the riddle of the bed.

To appreciate the subtlety with which she operates, let us take a closer look at a few of Penelope's explicit heroic actions in what, for the sake of convention, we will continue to call the *Odyssey*. Her capacity for suspending or deflecting action, for introducing a special kind of narrative inertia, manifests itself as early as her very first appearance in Book 1, where she seeks to silence Phemios' own *nostos* song. We have learned a few lines beforehand (11–15) that Odysseus' homecoming is the last one left unaccomplished; all his Greek peers who did not die at Troy or on the journey back have reached their destinations, for better or for worse.[68] Only too apparently, then, a performance of the "miserable return of the Achaeans" (*Achaiôn noston . . . lugron*, 326–27) is preemptive: it has no place in the Ithakan palace at this point, with Odysseus still unaccounted for. In the only truly applicable context, that of the narrative logic associated with the story-pattern *sêma*, here is an element that is truly out of order. In putting a stop to the performance, Penelope safeguards the progress of the only actual *nostos* that is still under way—both as a "real" journey and as a traditional song.

More immediately, singing the *Achaeans' Return* cannot but exacerbate

Penelope's singular woe, reminding her as it must of the harsh reality of Odysseus' absence. Complementarily, her profession of deep sadness over the singer's choice of topics harmonizes with the South Slavic truelove's characteristic and frequent protestations of fidelity in the face of hopeless despair.[69] From that perspective, it is Penelope's apparent powerlessness—always the core of the wife's or fiancée's devastation in the storypattern—that Phemios is unwittingly foregrounding, juxtaposing it to the usurped power wielded by the suitors before whom he is forced to sing. But consider who really possesses the power in this traditional scenario. Halting the performance of the *Achaeans' Return*, and in the process affirming her fidelity and momentarily deemphasizing the suitors' hold on her, certainly amounts to a logical, even aggressive goal for the Return Song heroine. Although the newly assertive Telemachos dismisses his mother's objections and sends her off to her room and the release of "sweet sleep,"[70] she effectively silences the *nostos* song just as her son incites the suitors to an unprecedented level of debate. Penelope's intervention has succeeded; the *Achaeans' Return* is unwoven. It will be rewoven when the time is right.

At the end of Book 4 the Return Song heroine confronts another potential loss, the suitors' plan to ambush Telemachos, and the way in which she reacts says much about the functional nature of her indeterminacy—again, both the ambiguity she experiences and the ambiguity she represents. As the result of a prayer to Athena, the goddess casts "sweet sleep" upon Penelope and appears in a dream as her sister Iphthime, bearing the assurance that her son will survive the trap. But Penelope's further inquiry about Odysseus is rebuffed as the dream-image stubbornly forecloses on discussion (4.836–37):

"οὐ μέν τοι κεῖνόν γε διηνεκέως ἀγορεύσω,
ζώει ὅ γ' ἦ τέθνηκε· κακὸν δ' ἀνεμώλια βάζειν."

"As for that other one, I will not tell you from beginning to end whether he lives or has died. It is bad to babble emptily."

Why should Athena not grant her wish to learn more about her husband's status, especially since the goddess has already disclosed Telemachos' safe return? Simply because, as with Phemios' song, the time is not yet right; for now the signs point away from the security of certainty and toward a necessary uncertainty. Against the background of the developing *nostos* tale, Penelope's inquiry after her husband amounts to a question that if forthrightly answered would short-circuit the narrative. By reducing the heroine's ambiguous lack of knowledge to factual certainty one way or the other, any definite answer would foreshorten the Return Song and damage the precarious balance of its traditional referentiality. The truelove's continuing doubt, the pain of not knowing with which she wakes every day, is both her essence as a character and her most effective tool against the suitors' encroachments. Thus, whatever consolation the story can allow her in relation to Telemachos' journey and its outcome, Penelope must be kept in the dark about Odysseus. Her very life—as a focal character in the Return Song paradigm and more immediately as Odysseus' *vjerna ljuba*—depends upon it.[71]

Just as she remains both the victim and the beneficiary of her own indeterminacy, so Penelope is also the touchstone of ambiguity for virtually everyone to whom she is linked. During his trip to Hades, for example, Odysseus prompts his mother's ghost for some news of what is transpiring at home—typical behavior, as we have seen, for the Return hero as he seeks inside information to "fill in the blanks" during the expectable flashback. Their question-and-answer series, so similar in form and traditional referentiality to parallel series in South Slavic epic, consists of a five-part ring structure: Odysseus poses questions about Antikleia's death (171–73), his father (174), his son (174), his inheritance (175–76), and Penelope (177–79); Antikleia responds with answers treating Penelope (181–83), his inheritance (184), his son (185–87), his father (187–96), and her own pitiable death (197–203), in that annular order.[72] All of these are important, but at the very heart of his concern—and not circumstantially at the very center of the ring—lies the riddle of Penelope. Here is the most crucial segment of their exchange (11.177–83):

"εἰπὲ δέ μοι μνηστῆς ἀλόχου βουλήν τε νόον τε,
ἠὲ μένει παρὰ παιδὶ καὶ ἔμπεδα πάντα φυλάσσει
ἦ ἤδη μιν ἔγημεν Ἀχαιῶν ὅς τις ἄριστος."
῾Ως ἐφάμην, ἡ δ᾽ αὐτίκ᾽ ἀμείβετο πότνια μήτηρ·   180
"καὶ λίην κείνη γε μένει τετληότι θυμῷ
σοῖσιν ἐνὶ μεγάροισιν· ὀϊζυραὶ δέ οἱ αἰεὶ
φθίνουσιν νύκτες τε καὶ ἤματα δάκρυ χεούσῃ."

"Tell me about the wife I married, her plan and her mind,
and whether she stays fast by my son, and guards everything,
or if the best man among the Achaeans has married her."
So I spoke, and my queenly mother answered me quickly: 180
"All too much with enduring heart does she wait for you
there in your own palace, and always with her the wretched
nights and the days also waste away with weeping."

Like the South Slavic Return hero, Odysseus is consumed by wondering whether Penelope has been able to persevere or not, whether devastation has broken their covenant, whether she has survived as the person he left. Also analogously with other *nostos* tales, the reassurance he receives is qualified and conditional. Yes, he is told, she waits for you, but the toll exacted on her is cruel and unremitting; left unsaid is the obvious implication that Antikleia's report from the underworld is now out of date, that Penelope's heroic resistance may have reached its limit. What the Return hero in general, and Odysseus specifically, is being told is that all aspects of the home situation are under heavy siege.[73] Much has already given way (Antikleia has died from longing, Laertes struggles in wretched poverty) and much hangs perilously at risk. There is no escaping the fact that the hero's absence has already brought terrible deprivation, and no guarantee that wife, son, and inheritance are still salvageable. Only Penelope's stubborn indeterminacy—her ability to weave and unweave—prevents an Ithakan collapse and keeps the *nostos* alive.[74]

Like the Return Song heroine she is, Penelope turns eventually to questioning the recently arrived "stranger" in Book 17 (507f.), or at least she attempts to do so. But the suitors' boorishness and Eumaios' caution delay the interview, and she is not able to pursue news of her husband immediately.[75] Instead, soon after the Iros episode in Book 18, she undertakes what seems a curious action: at Athena's urging she tells her nurse Eurynome that she wishes to show herself before the suitors. And why? A number of answers present themselves.[76] The narrator states explicitly (160–62) that Athena wishes her to "open the suitors' hearts" and to "seem the more precious to her husband and son," and for this reason transfigures her, increasing her beauty. For the bemused Penelope herself, unaware of the stranger's identity or the goddess' motivation, this divine initiative translates to wanting simply to counsel Telemachos against trusting the suitors (164–68). From the perspective developed in this chapter, however, Athena's manipulation is transparent enough. She is fostering Penelope's indeterminacy, heightening the ambiguity that the heroine both faces and represents, by stirring all competitors to prize her more highly. From her usual position offstage the unattainable heroine moves for a brief moment into full view of all concerned—usurping suitors, long-absent mate, loyal son, and not least the song's audience. With this action she comes no nearer to choosing any one course; if anything, she is further postponing resolution for herself and all concerned by stretching the narrative string yet tighter. Even though she does not consciously realize the complex chemistry that she is catalyzing, Penelope is fulfilling her role of heroic inaction.

Book 19 amplifies and articulates that role, portraying Penelope as unquestionably committed to Odysseus but obstinately dismissive of the stranger's earnest attempts to convince her that her husband has at last arrived. Echoes of the South Slavic truelove abound, as when—in the lying tale typical not only of this but of all Return heroes—the stranger claims to have known Odysseus in Crete (185f.) and to have established a relationship of guest-friendship with him (194–95).[77] This avowed relationship compares in narrative force and function to the putative bloodbrother-

hood, godparenthood, or provision of funeral rites that the disguised pris-
oner often claims as his link to the missing hero in the South Slavic Return
Song. Moreover, in these and other instances the appeal to a prior social
debt also amounts to the hero's conventional test for loyalty, administered
most importantly to his mate. He is seeking to accomplish what Agamem-
non recommended in hindsight and what the Return Song hero does as a
generic matter of course: to peer behind her veil of ambiguity.

In keeping with its general richness of character development, the
Odyssey then goes a step further, beyond the limits of any South Slavic tale
in my experience, in complicating the heroine's personality. Penelope does
not immediately show her hand, but, with the remarkable presence of
mind that has kept both her and the song alive to this juncture, presses the
supposed Cretan refugee for a precise description of the man he claims
was Odysseus. When he provides details of Odysseus' clothing, with
special attention to the unique golden pin with the hound and fawn (226–
31), she accedes as would any Return Song heroine but in unmistakably
Homeric fashion (249–50):

> Ὣς φάτο, τῇ δ' ἔτι μᾶλλον ὑφ' ἵμερον ὦρσε γόοιο,
> **σήματ'** ἀναγνούσῃ τά οἱ ἔμπεδα πέφραδ' Ὀδυσσεύς.

> So he spoke, and still more aroused in her the passion for weeping,
> as she recognized the sure *sêmata* Odysseus had given.

Such signs can be read only one way; they point, as observed in Chapter 1,
toward an emergent reality and cannot be gainsaid. Since the stranger has
furnished *sêmata*, Penelope has no choice but to credit his story, and her
tears of recognition—here precisely parallel to those of the faithful *vjerna
ljuba* in the South Slavic songs—warrant her fidelity and long-standing
commitment. She will not be plotting her husband's death nor willingly
seeking remarriage.

In many if not most Return Songs, such a highly recognizable and idi-
omatic scene would dissolve the truelove's indeterminacy, but not so in the
Odyssey. Counterpoised to Penelope's obvious and ongoing fidelity is her
equally stubborn refusal to believe that Odysseus has already reached the
region of Ithaka, or that he ever will. When the stranger continues his ly-
ing tale with the promise that her husband has indeed reached nearby
Thesprotia and will be home "either at the waning of the moon or at its on-
set" (19.307), she steadfastly dismisses his assurance (true in its major if
not its minor narrative points) and shifts the scene's impetus to readying
her guest for a peaceful rest and the next day's feast. It is within this im-
mediate and long-term context of uncertainty that Eurykleia will very
soon recognize the unmistakable *sêma* of Odysseus' scar as she washes his

feet. Things are beginning to happen, and potentialities are precipitating into palpable realities: Penelope has openly cursed the suitors and revealed her continuing loyalty, and the old nurse has discovered her disguised master. But the mistress of Ithaka, of the *Odyssey*, and of the story-pattern *sêma* maintains her controlling grip on the proceedings, braking the accelerating narrative with the persistent indeterminacy we have come to expect of her.

The remainder of Book 19 only sharpens the contrast between the two opposing forces of Penelope's intransigence and the epic's drive toward dénouement, a dichotomy deeply embedded in the traditional character of the Return Song heroine at large. Penelope begins the conversation, admitting that she cannot decide whether to try to hold out as Odysseus' wife or bend at last to the suitors' will and remarry. With the poles of possible action stipulated—the same options she has successfully kept open for twenty years without foreclosing on either—Penelope then moves the discussion to the level of her dream of the eagle and her pet geese, marking her request for the stranger's interpretation with the traditional sign "But come . . ." (*all' age . . .*, 535).[78] Of course, it is a dream with clear symbolic meaning, and the stranger gives her the obvious reading of this virtually allegorical story: the eagle is her avenging husband, and the slaughtered geese are the suitors finally furnished their comeuppance.

But that reading, so transparent to Odysseus and to the audience and readership of the *Odyssey*, is not so obvious for the woman who has survived this far only by her willingness to suspend certainty, by her refusal to accept even the most patent reality without qualification. I would argue that Penelope is not being coy here, not consciously baiting a man she suspects may be her husband; she is simply being Penelope, the Return Song heroine who cannot yet afford to behave in any other way.[79] When she launches into the "dream science" of horn versus ivory, then, she is not trying to force her husband's hand but rather keeping her distance from a final decision one way or the other. She is resolutely affirming that this may be a true dream, issuing through the gates of horn, or it may be the false variety from the gates of ivory. Given the "map" of the story-pattern according to which she and the other major figures are navigating the territory of the *Odyssey*, and keeping in mind her present progress on the path toward its *telos*, what else can she possibly do?

Even the minor details of Penelope's oneiric narrative amplify this characteristic indeterminacy and provide insight into her continuing dualism and ambiguity. Although the eagle must represent Odysseus taking his (and her) revenge, presumably a welcome and long-overdue relief from decades of torment, her allegorical dream also pictures the geese as her pets, as animals she enjoys watching (537) and whose death she and her servants mourn (541–43). Is this a conscious ploy designed to stimulate the man she suspects to be her mate, to test his identity? Against the background of the Return Song *sêma*, I believe it is more accurate to understand the curious attitude toward her "pets" as reflecting the dualistic behavior by which she held the suitors at bay, encouraging them only to discourage them, weaving only to unweave. If the tableau of grief over her pets also serves, like Athena's transfiguration of Penelope, to heighten the tension between husband and wife, so be it. But the quality that drives that result is once again her unwavering indeterminacy.

Things come to a head in a predictable way when, as the Return heroine often does, Penelope proposes a contest. Like Alibegovica in Mujo Kuku-ruzović's *The Captivity of Ograšćić Alija*, she sets up a competition that su-perficially appears to offer any one of the eligible suitors a realistic chance at winning an inestimable prize, but which idiomatically can select only the person whom nobody believes can be present.[80] It all boils down to an-other masterful equivocation, for while the contest seems to be open to all, in fact no one can win—at least to the best of the heroine's present knowl-edge. If Odysseus is the only one who can string the bow and send an ar-row through the axes, and Odysseus is missing, then by definition there is no danger in her posing such a challenge. Once again this icon of indeter-minacy has managed a strategy that encourages while it discourages, sum-mons while it dismisses.

But of course the hero knows better, both in the immediate Odyssean context and throughout parallel scenes in South Slavic epic. Reading be-hind the signs along with the audience, he supports her gambit for reasons of his own. Consider Odysseus' encouraging words (19.583–87):

"ὦ γύναι αἰδοίη Λαερτιάδεω Ὀδυσῆος,
μηκέτι νῦν ἀνάβαλλε δόμοις ἔνι τοῦτον ἄεθλον·
πρὶν γάρ τοι πολύμητις ἐλεύσεται ἐνθάδ᾽ Ὀδυσσεύς,   585
πρὶν τούτους τόδε τόξον ἐΰξοον ἀμφαφόωντας
νευρήν τ᾽ ἐντανύσαι διοϊστεῦσαί τε σιδήρου."

"O respected wife of Odysseus, son of Laertes,
do not put off this contest in your house any longer.
Before these people can handle the well-wrought bow, and manage   585
to hook the string and bend it, and send a shaft through the iron,
Odysseus of the many designs will be back here with you."

As already noted, this is a contest she (conventionally) expects to fail to produce a winner, precisely because it cannot select anyone except her husband, whom she believes to be lost or dead. At the same time, the con-test marks a point of convergence with the Return hero's agenda. He urges her rapid implementation of the contest because he knows, as does the au-dience fluent in the traditional register, that winning will do far more than simply divulge his identity. This resonant strategy will cue his retribution and reassumption of his place in the family and society, just as it will dependably lead toward the dissolution of her indeterminacy. What for Penelope portends stasis and inaction moves Odysseus' plans—and the developing *nostos*—forward along an expectable route. While the two strategies may seem contradictory, they are actually complementary when appraised against the backdrop of traditional referentiality. Each of the two figures has a distinctly different expectation, each of their perspectives being fully justified by prior history and present challenges. It is the chemistry of their varying points of view, coming into direct contact for the first time here, that will now drive the *Odyssey* toward its *telos*. From this juncture, they pursue parallel tracks toward a final convergence in the secret *sêma* of the olive-tree bed.

With the prodding of Athena, who can profitably be understood as nudging the focal characters along the Return pathway throughout the course of the epic, Penelope secures her husband's bow, orders the axes positioned, and issues the challenge.[81] With trademark dualism, she begins her challenge with unmitigated criticism of the suitors' arrogant, destructive behavior. Then, once again marking a rhetorical shift with the familiar traditional sign "But come," she appears to give in, weary of the intolerable situation and resigned to her fate (21.73–79):

"ἀλλ' ἄγετε, μνηστῆρες, ἐπεὶ τόδε φαίνετ' ἄεθλον·
θήσω γὰρ μέγα τόξον Ὀδυσσῆος θείοιο·
ὃς δέ κε ῥηΐτατ' ἐντανύσῃ βιὸν ἐν παλάμῃσι   75
καὶ διοϊστεύσῃ πελέκεων δυοκαίδεκα πάντων,
τῷ κεν ἅμ' ἑσποίμην νοσφισσαμένη τόδε δῶμα
κουρίδιον, μάλα καλόν, ἐνίπλειον βιότοιο,
τοῦ ποτε μεμνήσεσθαι ὀΐομαι ἔν περ ὀνείρῳ."

"But come, you suitors, since here is a prize set out before you;
for I shall bring you the bow of godlike Odysseus.
And the one who takes the bow in his hands, strings it with the greatest   75
ease, and sends an arrow clean through all the twelve axes,
shall be the one I go away with, forsaking this house
where I was a bride, a lovely place and full of good living.
I think that even in my dreams I shall never forget it."

Maintaining her ambivalence to the last, Penelope couches what seems to be a straightforward, uncomplicated offer in characteristically two-sided language. On the one hand, how could the task be clearer? The contest is to replace her husband. On the other hand, she spends the final two and one-half lines of her offer reminiscing over the house she must leave and the memories that will always remain vivid for her.[82] Nonetheless, the initial reading of this sign must amount to: "simply string the bow and win my hand."

Or so the suitors think—both the *mnêstêres* of the *Odyssey* (Antinoos,

Eurymachos, and company) and their brother suitors in the cognate tradition of South Slavic Return Songs. As noted earlier, the heroine on whom this story-pattern pivots never really expects a winner to emerge in this kind of competition, which from her point of view is best understood as a crafty prolongation of the status quo rather than a climax. Nonetheless, with his stringing of the bow and successful shot, signaled by Zeus' thundering *sêmata* (21.413), things change utterly: the stranger modulates to her husband Odysseus and the ritual battle of athletic contest modulates to all-out, life-or-death combat.

As the arrow zips through the axeheads, the various realities converge. No longer is the stranger a Cretan refugee in search of a temporary harbor; he is the hero at last returned, the hero who has finally accomplished his *nostos*. No longer will the suitors plunder his home, threaten his family, and batter him at will; now they will pay the ultimate price for their shameless depradations.[83] Even Penelope will eventually have to acknowledge his return. And all of these new realities stem directly from the implications of the arrow-shot. Odysseus' feat is an inimitable act, made possible only by his archer's genius in tracing an arc, in finding a path through the gamut of individual axeheads. Were he less skilled, were he not the Return hero, were he not in fact Odysseus, the shot would fail.

In this respect the arrow-shot mirrors the traditional poetic act of slotting individual situations via the *sêma*. Homer and his tradition proceed not by distinguishing among disparate moments but by aligning them, not by foregrounding their separateness but by tapping into a unity that resides in the larger poetic tradition. And they do so in effect by shooting a *sêma*-arrow through the series of individual narrative targets.

Odysseus' feat of archery thus stands as a metaphor for a feat of poetry, as Homer reaches into his quiver of traditional signs and miraculously sends a carefully tailored shaft through the otherwise segregated episodes of his poetry. Suddenly the axeheads are no longer singular items, individual targets, *things* in themselves, but rather partners in a brilliant and unifying *action*. And with that shift from thing to action, from concrete item to experienced event, comes a profound shift in how we understand the *Odyssey* as a traditional work of verbal art. What matters is neither the arrow nor the axeheads but the genius of the shot and its immanent implications—for Odysseus the archer and for Homer the poet.

Question 3: Where Does the *Odyssey* Really End?

From Odysseus' famous *sêma*-shot to the equally famous *sêma*-bed is but a short distance, by any measure. After the slaughter cued by the hero's triumph in the contest of the bow, the story moves rapidly through a dense series of traditional signs to its *telos*, which I translate as "fulfillment," at 23.295–96:

οἱ μὲν ἔπειτα
ἀσπάσιοι λέκτροιο παλαιοῦ θεσμὸν ἵκοντο.

Then [Odysseus and Penelope]
gladly reached the site of their long-standing bed.

Since we have devoted Chapter 1 to examination of the *sêmata* in Books 19–23, let us pass directly to the olive-tree bed and the question it has occasioned since antiquity. Given the obvious prominence of this symbol and moment in the *Odyssey* as a whole, does the poem for all practical purposes end here? Do the rest of the twenty-third and all of the twenty-fourth books amount to a "continuation," something added on to the core structure by either the poet or an editor? To what extent are the final episodes organic to the epic, and to what extent are they less than central to the poem? These are important questions, since they bear on how we interpret the memorable events of the last part of the epic, especially the hero's testing of Laertes, the revenge sought by the slaughtered suitors' families, and the concluding Peace of Athena. In short, does post-*telos* necessarily mean inessential?

The Oxford *Commentary* offers a sensible perspective by weighing the relevant scholia and cautioning that *telos* and *peras*, the two terms used by ancient scholars to describe the reunion of Penelope and Odysseus, did not designate "the end."[84] For one thing, there remains considerable doubt over whether Aristarchus really advocated athetizing Book 23, lines 297 and following, and indeed whether such an opinion would have had much effect on the complex history of fixation and transmission of the *Odyssey* as we have it.[85] In addition, and much more basically, we may observe that there is no reason why a poem cannot reach its *telos* or *peras* without coming to a complete halt or stoppage in the sense of absolute silence or closure. This is clearly true whether the poem in question is a performance or a text, and on the face of it equally applicable to Milton's *Paradise Lost*, Keats' *Endymion*, or any work of verbal art from oral tradition.[86]

Indeed, the differences between "fulfillment" and "end" only multiply as we hear or read the oral or oral-connected work against its ambient tradition.[87] What is *the story*, after all? If no single song or song-version exists alone outside the vital network of tradition, and if multiformity is the lifeblood of oral tradition, is "end" really a meaningful concept? More precisely, if all songs and song-versions are implicitly informed by a context enormously larger and more resonant than any one text can ever be, then seizing upon a single moment in any version as "final" must prove a lost cause. Consider the analogy of the South Slavic Return Song. As our morphology illustrated, the *sêma* of story-pattern points toward the reunion of husband and wife—joyful or tragic—as the climax of the epic, the ultimate goal of the foregoing story. This much is true of all Return Songs, of the *Odyssey* as well as each of its numerous South Slavic kindred. But we also saw that each of the three songs summarized for our traditional morphology had its own particular trajectory, its own idiosyncratic narrative development. No one of them could be tidily superimposed on either of the other two. As with every level of "word" or speech-act in the epic register, the story-pattern depends on variation within limits for its structural pliability and expressive force, for its viability as language. To speak of any situation or event as final—even if it is the last situation or event in that particular version—is to cut the version off from its tradition and to denature its structure, idiom, and art.

Placing the last episodes of the *Odyssey* against the background of our traditional morphology will help to bring such observations into greater relief, as well as begin to indicate just what the *telos* at 23.296 really represents. As noted above, while all three South Slavic performances—Alija Fjuljanin's *The Captivity of Četić Osmanbey*, Ibro Bašić's *Alagić Alija and Velagić Selim*, and Mujo Kukuruzović's *Captivity of Ograšćić Alija*—are Return Songs sharing the same basic sequence of Absence through Wedding, they are also quite different. More to the point for our present concerns, their most salient points of incongruity are their "endings." Taking the last song first, we remember that Ograšćić Alija wends his way homeward only to find a Klytemnestra rather than a Penelope awaiting him; by definition, no *telos* of happy reunion can be reached with Alibegovica, and the epic must complete a second story-pattern of Rescue before closure can take place. For all of its *nostos*-driven action, Bašić's song about Alagić Alija and Velagić Selim also has its share of idiosyncrasies, including two protagonists, a temporary return, and a substitute champion. Of the three performances only Fjuljanin's reaches a positive *telos* directly, with a single and focal hero, Četić Osmanbey, and a "truelove" who earns her formulaic epithet. But even so this is not the whole story: Milutin the highwayman plays a supporting role, and resolution does not occur until after the kidnapping episode is completed.

Two observations should be made. In each case the epic song plainly depends upon the general story-pattern of Return for its structure and expressive force, and in each case the particular identity of the characters and shape of the story follow familiar lines. This consistency can be easily verified outside the three summarized narratives; all three song-types are multiply attested in the Stolac material and elsewhere.[88] So there can be no doubt that the performances by Kukuruzović, Bašić, and Fjuljanin represent realistic, natural variations on the *nostos* pattern. From their opening lines all three performances point idiomatically toward a potential *telos*, the reunion of man and woman after a prolonged separation, without divulging how things will turn out until the critical moment.

But none of the stories "ends" with the implicated reunion, successful or not. Each continues in one way or another, and, very significantly, the individual variations on the basic pattern are inherently logical, internally motivated, and themselves traditional. Četić Osmanbey encounters Milutin the *hajduk* on his way home, and later the highwayman and his wife Latinka are instrumental in releasing Osmanbey's son from his kidnapping by Ban Tasević. If circumstances had forced us to treat this song as something unique, a singular text isolated from its context, we might well have concluded that the episodes involving Milutin are somehow inessential, that like the final scenes of the *Odyssey* this post-*telos* material is not organic to the central epic action. It would then be considered, via whatever textual mechanism one imagines, as something "added on."

And yet these episodes are clearly linked to, even generated from, the main *nostos* story. Return heroes frequently meet with life-or-death challenges as they seek their homeland; rare is the protagonist who has an easy road back to his tower, megaron, or whatever. Although to my knowledge no South Slavic song can match the *Odyssey* in the number or variety of such challenges, they are certainly a customary and expected feature of the tale-type. Against this backdrop Osmanbey's battle against *hajduks*, and even his consequent befriending of one of the enemy, are hardly unusual events. One can say with confidence that the *sêma* of story-pattern slots the Milutin episodes, contextualizing them within its familiar confines, and that the highwayman's role in freeing the young boy toward the end of the epic is therefore integral to this Return Song.

I say "this Return Song" because the *sêma* allows and even promotes the singularity of individual instance alongside the generic structure and expressive force of the *nostos* pattern. Just as the legendary singer figure— Isak, Hasan Ćoso, or Homer—makes it unnecessary to choose artificially between individual and tradition, so the story-pattern melds foreground with background, instance with implication. In the case of Bašić's *Alagić Alija and Velagić Selim*, it is the double captivity and substitute champion that are slotted within the traditional network. Attempting to detach either one of the captive heroes or their female stand-in on the grounds that they are unusual or somehow unwarranted, or even relegating any of them or their deeds to secondary status, would violate the traditional unity of the song. And where does Bašić's performance "end"? Surely no one would argue that Velagić Selim's temporary freedom constitutes closure; after setting things straight at home, he willingly reenters jail and the Devastation element. There has been a *telos* of sorts, but the song is not "over." Only with what might be regarded as the second and final return does the performance reach its true closure.

The most dramatic example of a post-*telos* continuation of a Return Song is of course Kukuruzović's *Captivity of Ograšćić Alija*. As illustrated above, this is the story of meeting Klytemnestra rather than Penelope, and so the recognition and encounter of husband and wife constitutes a different kind of climax. Positive narrative fulfillment must await a sequel story. Overall, this song-performance explicitly figures forth what the *Odyssey* as a specific story frequently hints at and the Return Song as a story-pattern always implies: the ever-present possibility of an unhappy homecoming and of compensatory action that will have to be taken. Like the other two Stolac songs, it realizes some of the potentials inherent in the *sêma* of Return, giving concrete evidence of an alternate direction in which the story can develop.

In terms of the traditional morphology assembled from South Slavic witnesses, the *Odyssey* certainly reaches its *telos* at 23.296, as the ancient commentators maintained, but just as certainly it does not end there. Furthermore, the chief events that follow the reunion and its *sêma* of the olive-tree bed are strongly and naturally linked to what precedes that culminating moment. They are logically generated, as we shall see, from this Return Song.

As with the South Slavic analogues, I carefully stipulate "this Return Song." For the final episodes demonstrate an obvious link not to *Nostos* in general but to this particular *nostos* story, leaving open the possibility that they would have proven inappropriate for other Return epics, if indeed such other epics had survived.[89] After all, the episodes in question—the testing of Laertes, the revolt by the suitors' relatives, and the Peace of Athena—are not part of the Return paradigm at large but rather associated specifically with Odysseus and Penelope's particular saga. If as in most South Slavic Return epics the hero lacked a living father, for example, or if the suitors' deaths somehow failed to inspire revenge, the Odyssean final moments would obviously be out of place. We thus distinguish between, on the one hand, mandated narrative events that are always a part of all stories of this type (such as the hero's detention, his adventures, and his disguised reentry into the community) and, on the other hand, events associated with certain specific realizations of the story-pattern. The former actions and reactions constitute a traditional "blueprint" and carry with them an idiomatic force far greater than that of any one song, version, or performance. They are the signs we must read behind. The latter events elaborate the compelling features of what is a single or a very limited number of tales, highlighting what is memorable and noteworthy about the actual narrative presently under way. They occur between the signs.

Odysseus' polytropic trek from Absence through (Re-)Wedding at 23.296 thus traces the well-worn *oimê* (path) of the Return hero at large, just as Penelope's even more pivotal campaign of indeterminacy and ambiguity parallels her husband's more visible and celebrated exploits. He confronts a fantastic array of mortal threats trying to win his way back; she wages war against certainty and foreclosure on possibilities at home. Both are central actors in the *nostos* drama, playing roles shared by hundreds of male and female pairs across the South Slavic and numerous other Indo-European epic traditions. *Nostos* is without doubt the core of the *Odyssey's* narrative structure. In contrast, what follows the sign of the bed must belong specifically to the Ithakan couple. These later episodes make perfect sense for them and their situation, and are in that sense organic to *this Return song*. As story-specific features they are folded into the larger network of the Return Song story-pattern, as this particular man and woman operate within the traditional frame of structure and expectation. It is to that vital interaction of individualized events and ambient context that we now turn in the remaining moments of this chapter.

After husband and wife exchange their recent life histories, the hero recounting his story in the order in which it happened rather than via the Return Song *sêma* employed by Homer, Book 23 closes with Odysseus' warning that more trials still lie ahead of them. Book 24 then opens with Amphimedon's ghost's account of the revenge and of Penelope's weaving-and-unweaving strategem, leading toward confrontation with Antinoos' father Eupeithes and other outraged relatives of the slain suitors. But before the trouble can come to a head, Agamemnon's ghost issues his denunciation of Klytemnestra's perfidy and celebration of Penelope's *kleos*, providing not just a memorable contrast between the two women but an explicit typology of Return Songs. Immediately afterward, Odysseus goes off to see Laertes, a natural enough next step in that it promises at last to close the family circle. But of course he could not undertake such an apparently unexceptional mission without being his exceptional self.

It is in many ways quite painful to watch the disguised son bait his decrepit and long-suffering father, but we should remember that it is not only Odysseus, son of Laertes, but also the naturally polytropic Return Song hero who is doing the baiting. Indeed, on both levels he could proceed in no other fashion; the consistency of his characterization—both the individual and the traditional facets—demands maintaining such duplicity. He could no more abandon that tactic than Penelope could relinquish her indeterminacy before the time is right.[90] Consider how, even though driven to tears on first viewing the old man's misery, Odysseus the Return hero finds himself at a very familiar, highly traditional fork in the road (24.235–40):

μερμήριξε δ' ἔπειτα κατὰ φρένα καὶ κατὰ θυμὸν   235
κύσσαι καὶ περιφῦναι ἑὸν πατέρ', ἠδὲ ἕκαστα
εἰπεῖν, ὡς ἔλθοι καὶ ἵκοιτ' ἐς πατρίδα γαῖαν,
ἦ πρῶτ' ἐξερέοιτο ἕκαστά τε πειρήσαιτο.
ὧδε δέ οἱ φρονέοντι δοάσσατο κέρδιον εἶναι,
πρῶτον κερτομίοις ἐπέεσσιν πειρηθῆναι.   240

and he deliberated then in his heart and spirit   235
whether to embrace his father and kiss him and tell him
everything, how he was come again to his own dear country,
or to question him first about everything, and make trial of him.
In the division of his heart this way seemed best to him,
first to make trial of him and speak in words of mockery.   240

In addition to the resonant language, which itself provides a *sêma* to guide the audience or readership through the typical balancing of alternatives,[91] the testing process has another crucial implication. As with earlier, pre-*telos* encounters, testing plus some sort of duplicity (usually in the form of misrepresentation) serves as the idiomatic precursor to the act of recognition. The one implies the other via traditional referentiality. In Book 16 (91–111), the disguised Odysseus had baited Telemachos, ingenuously asking why he was tolerating the suitors' behavior, before Athena signals him to reveal his real identity to his son. Three books later (19.383–85) Odysseus directly counters Eurykleia's remark about his similarity to the master of the house just before her discovery of the scar *sêma* certifies her observation. The hero's treatment of Eumaios and Philoitios is no different in this regard: as the stranger he queries them on their willingness to take up arms in defense of Odysseus before identifying himself (21.193–98). The contest of the bow provides one of the grandest misrepresentations for the stranger, serving the double traditional purpose of keying revenge at the same time that it acts as prologue to Odysseus' recognition by the suitors (21.404f.). And of course the grand *sêma* of the olive-tree bed, as figured forth in the misrepresentation to which only wife, husband, and a single serving-maid hold the key, cinches his apotheosis before Penelope. It is precisely here that his trickery and her indeterminacy meet and merge. Even poor Argos' feeble but willing recognition of his long-lost master proves the linkage of misrepresentation/testing and recognition, as in Book 17 Melanthios' scornful words, together with the stranger's own probing remarks to Eumaios about whether this is Odysseus' house, set up the dog's last, pitiable gesture of faithfulness.

Inasmuch as these elements collectively make up a recurrent and idi-

omatic sequence in the *Odyssey*, the very sequence clearly generates ex-
pectation; beyond its compositional usefulness lies its expressive force.
But the implications run deeper yet. As we recall from the traditional
morphology of South Slavic epic, the very same sort of idiomatic sequence
of misrepresentation/testing and recognition governs the disguised hero's
activities as he reinserts himself, bit by bit and with extreme caution, back
into the community. What the *Odyssey* and the South Slavic songs together
indicate is a larger traditional pattern, not limited to any one song or even
poetic tradition but more extensive in scope.

In general, then, how does the Return hero conduct himself as he man-
ages his own reaccession? Precisely as Agamemnon's ghost advised him
during the visit to Hades (11.441f.)—by trusting no one, by keeping close
counsel, by testing the waters before plunging in. This is the way not only
of Odysseus but of all his South Slavic Return counterparts as well: reduc-
ing family members to tears by questioning their loyalty, telling false tales,
and acting in a fashion that outside of the traditional network of impli-
cation we might describe as cruel or unnecessary. What is more, as with
all *sêmata*, this traditional sign of testing and recognition slots all of the
scenes it helps describe, adding resonance to each instance. Each such
scene thus has a double force: its uniqueness plays out against its tradi-
tional referentiality.

So it is that Odysseus *must* approach his father in this ruthless way.
Although he ponders which path to follow, his choice is actually fore-
ordained: he must *kertomiois epeessin peirêthênai* ("make trial of [Laertes]
with mocking words," 24.240) before identifying himself. To operate other-
wise would be to abandon the epic register, to introduce an unmotivated
shift in the tale-telling idiom. It would amount to both a compositional
faux pas and static on the channel of reception. In the terms employed
earlier in this chapter, the recognition scenes are naturally lined up for
Homer's (and the *Guslar's*) *sêma*-shot; if Odysseus were simply to drop his
disguise and embrace Laertes without testing him, he would have failed
the poetic equivalent of the contest of the bow. Since the only route to
recognition is through testing, ignoring the rule of idiomatic expression
means precluding recognition and thereby denying Laertes membership
in the reunited group of family and community. Instead he brings his fa-
ther into the fold with his mocking words and lying tale. That is simply
how it must be. There is nothing unwarranted in Odysseus' last test; both
he and Homer know how he must proceed.[92]

Let us reiterate the formulation offered above for the final episodes of
the *Odyssey*. While these post-*telos* events are not inherently a part of the
Return Song story-pattern in general, they do harmonize logically with
this Return Song. The testing of Laertes simply reflects Odysseus' (and all
Return heroes') conventional practice as they operate undercover, seeking

to discover whom they can trust by confronting each person—no matter how intimate or nonthreatening the relationship they used to share—with the same strategy of challenging, aggressive words and lying tale.[93] The revolt by the suitors' families responds, of course, to the wholesale slaughter of the most promising young men in the community. We are accustomed to viewing them, again through the lens of the Return Song, as idle, usurping conspirators, but from their families' perspective they are victims of mass murder. Although revenge for the slain suitors never figures as a motive or event in the South Slavic Return epics, to the best of my knowledge, it is plainly a reasonable and logical reaction. The same can be said of the Peace of Athena, less an externally imposed kind of proceeding than it might seem because of the frequent interplay of gods and mortals in this epic tradition.[94] As with the Atreus myth, to which the *Odyssey* constantly adverts, the revenge cycle once initiated requires divine intervention in order to come to an end. In this respect the *Odyssey* shares an ending with Aeschylus' *Oresteia* trilogy.

To the question posed at the beginning of this section of the chapter—Where does the *Odyssey* really end?—we can thus provide a two-part answer, one response true to the pattern and the other true to this particular poem, one that reads behind the signs and the other between them. On the one hand, the Return Song paradigm, the core of this and so many other poems in other traditions, ends with the reunion of husband and wife. In the *Odyssey* that *telos* is reached at Book 23, line 296. On the other hand, the poem does not end there, and what follows is most certainly not additional or superfluous. As the traditional morphology illustrates by analogy, the final episodes of the *Odyssey* are an essential part of *this Return Song*. Just as Četić Osmanbey's story is not itself complete without the participation of Milutin the highwayman, just as Velagić Selim must go back to prison and later be rescued by a female stand-in, just as Ograščić Alija finds his wife unfaithful and rides off to join the enemy; so the *Odyssey* moves toward its true "end" via the testing of Laertes, the revolt of the suitors' families, and the Peace of Athena.

As the various strands of the epic converge, another *sêma* helps to unify the particular story via traditional referentiality. This pattern, which operates throughout the *Iliad* as well and is thus not linked solely to the *nostos* sequence, is smaller than the Return Song and yet larger than the testing and recognition sequence. It consists of a linked series of actions: Assembly (sometimes involving mourning), Anointment, Feast, and Mediation. Within the *Iliad* this traditional sign participates in the composition and reception of numerous scenes, none of them more striking than the final reconciliation between Priam and Hektor. In that remarkable instance the old man and his son's killer come together and mourn, and the anointment of Hektor's corpse leads to the feast that both men have so long deferred and the mediating funeral that closes the poem so quietly in advance of Troy's eventual destruction. In the *Odyssey* this *sêma* takes a number of different forms, but the inherent momentum of the sequence is quite similar. Of all six examples perhaps the most resonant instance of the pattern is the last, begun at 24.365–71, where the modest Assembly of Laertes and Odysseus gathers for the hero's planned trial of the old man. Laertes's hopes for word of his long-lost son seem dashed by the lying tale he is told of pseudo-Alybas, and, in the traditional expression of newly experienced grief, he defiles himself in the dust. Only after Odysseus reveals his identity does the servant Dolios anoint Laertes, preparing him for the healing Feast (ending at 489) and eventual Mediation of the apparently irreconcilable conflict in the Peace of Athena.[95]

As the poem reaches its final stages, considerably past the *telos* that ended its core, it is once again traditional referentiality that undergirds its structure and unity. The *Odyssey* ends with a series of events entirely appropriate to this Return Song, and well within the logical and idiomatic limits of the poem and the poetic register as a whole. Odysseus' testing procedure is nothing other than the one prescribed for him and for all Return heroes, the revolt is a logical consequence of the slaughter (itself the expectable Retribution), and the Peace of Athena amounts to the Mediation we are led to expect by a common pattern in both Homeric epics. We can thus render a two-part judgment on the poem's closure. The *Odyssey* as Return Song ends with the final stage of the reunion of Odysseus and Penelope at 23.295–96, which stands as the epigraph to this chapter on story-pattern as *sêma*:

οἱ μὲν ἔπειτα
ἀσπάσιοι λέκτροιο παλαιοῦ θεσμὸν ἵκοντο.

Then [Odysseus and Penelope]
gladly reached the site of their long-standing bed.

The *Odyssey* as *this particular Return Song* ends with the last few lines of Book 24 (541–48), which can now stand as a postlude to the chapter and the discussion:

δὴ τότ' Ὀδυσσῆα προσέφη γλαυκῶπις Ἀθήνη·
"διογενὲς Λαερτιάδη, πολυμήχαν' Ὀδυσσεῦ,
ἴσχεο, παῦε δὲ νεῖκος ὁμοιΐου πολέμοιο,
μή πώς τοι Κρονίδης κεχολώσεται εὐρύοπα Ζεύς."
    Ὣς φάτ' Ἀθηναίη, ὁ δ' ἐπείθετο, χαῖρε δὲ θυμῷ.   545
ὅρκια δ' αὖ κατόπισθε μετ' ἀμφοτέροισιν ἔθηκε
Παλλὰς Ἀθηναίη, κούρη Διὸς αἰγιόχοιο,
Μέντορι εἰδομένη ἠμὲν δέμας ἠδὲ καὶ αὐδήν.

Then the gray-eyed goddess Athena said to Odysseus:
"Son of Laertes and seed of Zeus, resourceful Odysseus,
hold hard, stop this quarrel in closing combat, for fear
Zeus of the wide brows, son of Kronos, may be angry with you."
    So spoke Athena, and with happy heart he obeyed her.   545
And pledges for the days to come, sworn to by both sides,
were settled by Pallas Athena, daughter of Zeus of the aegis,
who had likened herself in appearance and voice to Mentor.

Is it really any wonder that these final four lines of the poem are more a closure for the post-*telos* train of events than for the epic as a whole? It is always in the interplay of story-pattern and actual story, of implication and instance, of traditional referentiality and narrative singularity, that we may most fully locate Homer's and his tradition's art. According to the wisdom indexed by our homemade proverb, we must read both behind and between the signs.

Over the following two chapters we will continue examining the role of *sêmata* in Homeric art, turning our attention to typical scenes in Chapter 6 and to phraseology in Chapter 7. Throughout the ongoing discussion our goal will be to highlight the traditional referentiality of these various kinds of speech-acts, to understand not just their compositional usefulness but also some of what they imply as features of a highly expressive poetic register. All of them are indisputably deployed by an individual, and just as indisputably they all bear an idiomatic, more than individual meaning crucial to the reception of Homeric epic. Whether the "word" or sign in question is a story-pattern, typical scene, or phrase, oral traditions work like languages, only more so.

6

TYPICAL SCENES
OF FEAST AND LAMENT

οἱ δ᾽ ἐπ᾽ ὀνείαθ᾽ ἑτοῖμα προκείμενα χεῖρας ἴαλλον.
αὐτὰρ ἐπεὶ πόσιος καὶ ἐδητύος ἐξ ἔρον ἕντο,

They put their hands to the good things that lay ready before them.
But when they had cast off their desire for eating and drinking,
—*Odyssey* 1.149–50, and so on

"ἆνερ, ἀπ᾽ αἰῶνος νέος ὤλεο, κὰδ δέ με χήρην
λείπεις ἐν μεγάροισι· πάϊς δ᾽ ἔτι νήπιος αὔτως,
ὃν τέκομεν σύ τ᾽ ἐγώ τε δυσάμμοροι, οὐδέ μιν οἴω
ἥβην ἵξεσθαι·"

"My husband, you were lost young from life, and have left me
a widow in your house, and the boy is only a baby
who was born to you and me, the unhappy ones, and I think
he will never come of age."
—*Iliad* 24.725–28

In this chapter we turn our attention to a second species of Homeric *sêma*, another kind of speech-act that contributes a set of traditional implications to its every localized instance. In this case the traditional sign to be examined is the "word" at the level of narrative increment—what has often been called a *typical scene* or *theme*.[1] As with the Return Song story-pattern examined in Chapter 5 and the examples of phraseology to be treated in Chapter 7, this middle level of *sêma* is another aspect of the specialized idiom, the traditional epic register. As such, it cues idiomatic meaning and participates in the reception as well as the composition of Homeric poetry. It is another of the ways in which oral tradition works like language, only more so.

Two Thematic Patterns

Our two examples of thematic patterns offer the opportunity to track the morphology of easily identifiable, recurrent signs through a variety of realizations and in the process to illustrate both their pliability and their expressive force.[2] The Feast is a frequent event in the *Odyssey*, from Telemachos' embarrassed hosting of the disguised Athena in Odysseus' usurped palace in Book 1 through Laertes' memorable reception of his long-lost son in much humbler surroundings in Book 24. Between these bookends a litany of diverse figures extend their various brands of hospitality— Nestor, Menelaos, Kalypso, the Phaeacians, Kirke, Eumaios, the suitors, Penelope, and Autolykos, not to mention the perverse host Polyphemos or the unwilling provider-in-absentia Helios. Likewise, a variety of guests enjoy their sometimes sumptuous, sometimes modest fare, including Mentes, Telemachos, Hermes, and most often Odysseus (as both himself and the stranger). The local details are of course particular to the individual situation, but the traditional background of each feast derives from the idiomatic force of the speech-act that they share.

Although it appears less frequently than the Feast, the Lament also meshes instance with implication in complex and fascinating ways, as we shall see. Like other traditional *sêmata*, it operates on the principle of variation within limits, allowing for compositional flexibility at the same time that it delivers a resonant context that frames each of its occurrences. There are six principal laments in the *Iliad*, involving Briseis, Andromache (twice), Hekabe (twice), and Helen; all but the first, in which Briseis reacts to Patroklos' death, mourn the loss of Hektor.[3] But such is the nature of Homeric poetics that we must also consider a seventh threnody, a lament that strictly speaking is preemptive, even jarringly out of sequence. I speak here of Andromache's first lament in Book 6, spoken by a wife who, we are being told idiomatically and by implication, is already bereaved though her husband stands living before her. As much as any moment in the two epics, this scene demonstrates the power of traditional *sêmata* and their vital role in Homeric art.

Strategy for This Chapter

Our strategy for learning to read behind the Feast and Lament signs will differ from that employed in the preceding chapter in two ways. First, because both thematic patterns are amply attested in Homer, we need not resort to comparisons with South Slavic epic in order to construct traditional morphologies. With thirty-two examples in the *Odyssey* and three more in the *Iliad*, our basis for determining the structural outline and idiomatic value of the Feast is quite extensive.[4] Likewise, the seven full-blown examples of the Lament in the *Iliad* provide rich evidence of how local situation combines with traditional sign to produce a singular and yet resonant effect.

The second aspect concerns the actual presentation of the evidence. From the very beginning of our discussion of thematic "words," I will be aiming to simulate fluency in the register and to activate pertinent traditional contexts. Thus, instead of deducing the shape and implications of these two thematic patterns by carefully collating their instances, as we did with the Return Song, I will be providing that information from the start and then applying it to selected occurrences. In that way we will be encountering nine instances of the Feast and the single instance of Andromache's proto-lament with the proverbial connotations of their respective *sêmata* already in hand. Like the audience or reader who fluently "speaks the language" of Homeric epic, we will then be in a position to read each passage in its natural context, enriching the individual scene or speech with whatever the signal conventionally implies. Via this strategy we can directly engage Homer's art, reading both behind and between the signs.

The Feast and What It Signifies

The Feast sequence, chiefly an Odyssean rite and commonplace, involves several key features: a host and guest(s), the seating of the guest(s), actions that constitute feasting, the satisfaction of the guest(s), and some kind of mediation that follows the scene in question.[5] Some of these features are marked by specific words or phrases with which an audience or reader can soon become familiar, while others are more variable. For example, as noted above, hosts and guests vary widely throughout the *Odyssey*. On the other hand, the act of seating, the narrative prerequisite to the actual sharing of a meal, almost always finds expression with one of three verbs— *hezdomai*, *hêmai*, or *hidruô*—all of which mean "to sit" or "to cause to sit." That is, this introductory aspect of the Feast pattern depends on a particular lexical signal (one of *our* words).[6] Just how clear and unambiguous a lead-in it provides is most strikingly illustrated by the single Homeric instance in which this formal invitation to the Feast is declined. When at *Iliad* 24.553 Priam refuses Achilleus' offer of a chair (522) in his understandable impatience to bear his son's body back to Troy, the old man is effectively refusing the Achaean hero's hospitality and short-circuiting the consequent mediation that this *sêma* institutionally implies. Just as the

Feast cues mediation, so seating cues the Feast, and by failing to cooperate Priam runs the risk not simply of seeming ungracious but of undoing the hard-won truce and temporary peace between him and Achilleus.[7] His is no mere faux pas; the *Iliad* threatens to unravel over this breach of etiquette and traditional referentiality.

The preparation and serving of food constitute the heart of the Feast and can take one of a number of shapes. The most stable and recognizable form is the following five-line increment:

χέρνιβα δ' ἀμφίπολος προχόῳ ἐπέχευε φέρουσα
καλῇ χρυσείῃ, ὑπὲρ ἀργυρέοιο λέβητος,
νίψασθαι· παρὰ δὲ ξεστὴν ἐτάνυσσε τράπεζαν.
σῖτον δ' αἰδοίη ταμίη παρέθηκε φέρουσα,
εἴδατα πόλλ' ἐπιθεῖσα, χαριζομένη παρεόντων.

A maidservant brought water for them and poured it from a splendid
and golden pitcher, holding it above a silver basin
for them to wash, and she pulled a polished table before them.
A grave housekeeper brought in the bread and served it to them,
adding many good things to it, generous with her provisions.

This exact cluster of verses appears six times in the *Odyssey*, with different hosts, guests, and locales each time (Telemachos and Mentes on Ithaka, Alkinoos and the stranger on Scheria, Kirke and Odysseus on Aiaia, Telemachos and the stranger on Ithaka, and Menelaos and Telemachos in Sparta twice).[8] Although these are six manifestly different situations, involving disparate people and places and even including a divine meal, the formulaic sequence helps to identify the proceedings as a Feast and to conjure the appropriate traditional context. Of course, this section of the pattern may also find expression in alternate actions, such as libation or sacrifice, or be conveyed telegraphically in a generalized line or two.[9]

The third, very consistently realized aspect of the Feast is the idiomatic notation that the diners have eaten heartily and satisfied themselves. By far the most common form of the signal for closure is this couplet—

οἱ δ' ἐπ' ὀνείαθ' ἑτοῖμα προκείμενα χεῖρας ἴαλλον.
αὐτὰρ ἐπεὶ πόσιος καὶ ἐδητύος ἐξ ἔρον ἕντο, . . .

They put their hands to the good things that lay ready before them.
But when they had cast off their desire for eating and drinking, . . . —

or its second line alone.[10] It is worth noticing that even a barbaric meal of human flesh as enjoyed by Polyphemos closes with a variation of this cue, as does the forbidden and catastrophic meal that Odysseus' comrades make of the cattle of the sun. We will be returning to both of those instances below. For our present structural purposes, however, let us emphasize only that this pliable verse or pair of verses—what we will call the "satisfaction" marker—serves as a syntactic and logical transition between scenes. That is, the "But when they were sated" element, whether the most common version as cited above or some equivalent, signals the end of the meal, bringing the ritual to a close and projecting a sequel scene that is in some way dependent on the Feast. Satisfaction of the diners thus acts as a pivot or fulcrum in the narrative process, a cue that directly implies certain further developments, as we shall see.

Just as the Feast itself allows room for variation within limits, so it may occur as either a freestanding element or as part of a more extensive pattern. In its most elaborate form, this resonant sign participates in a substantial sequence of scenes, identified elsewhere as Assembly/Mourning—Purification—Feasting—Mediation. That is, the act of sharing a meal may be imbedded in a string of traditional actions, leading from a formal assembly or rite of lamentation through anointment and cleansing to the Feast itself.[11] At the other end of the compositional spectrum, things are much smaller and simpler: the guest's seating may be elided, the actions of preparation and serving may receive an extremely brief treatment, and only the narrative pivot of satisfaction may be fully realized. In keeping with our emphasis on the epic register as first and foremost a species of language, it is important to observe that all of these instances—large or small, complex or simple—prompt traditional implications. They do so with varying degrees of specificity or explicitness, of course, responding in part to the individual demands of the local situation and in part to the poet's own sense of art and balance, but within the performance arena the Feast dependably acts as an idiomatic as well as lexical "word" in all of its appearances. More than a static dictionary entry, it promotes the active negotiation of meaning in traditional context. The lesson here is simple but far-reaching: we should not mistake the sign, always variable within limits, for its signification—whether that sign is the Return Song pattern, the Feast, or a "byte" of resonant phraseology like "swift-footed Achilleus" or "green fear."[12] Within restrictions imposed by the rules of the register, the *sêma* always does its job. It cues the tradition.

So much for the traditional morphology of the Feast *sêma*, then: hosts and guests vary widely, and the pattern consists chiefly of seating, the actions of preparation and serving, and satisfaction of the participants. This outline illustrates the compositional usefulness of the Feast and suggests an expectable structure. But what about the traditional referentiality of the pattern? Does it contribute idiomatically to the ongoing narrative and, if so, how? To what extent is the Feast not simply a tectonic convenience but also an expressive strategy?

In order to guard against claiming too much, let us start by acknowledging the scene's literal implications, that is, by asking what can be discerned without recourse to traditional referentiality. We can remark, for example, the relative peace and welcome respite that the sharing of a meal customarily provides, or the social commerce it supports. Whether the participants give and accept hospitality in a grand setting like Menelaos' incomparable palace or in the much humbler environs of Eumaios the swineherd's hut, the exchange forges some sort of human bond, some linkage that can potentially stand as permanent social networking.[13] The breaking of bread—wherever it takes place and whomever it involves—certainly harbors such basic presumptions; this much is apparent from any one instance in isolation, and in no way depends on an awareness of the scene's idiomatic meaning. But this general and unidiomatic reading also lacks any sense of the traditional referentiality inherent in the speech-act, any grasp of the implications that accompany each instance. It makes acceptable sense, but it sells Homeric art short. If we are to read behind the sign, we must go further.

Simply put, collation of the thirty-five instances of the Homeric Feast sign reveals that it betokens *a ritualistic event leading from an obvious and pre-existing problem to an effort at mediation of that problem.* The signal itself is protean: the initial disruption takes many different forms, the pattern itself is structurally quite flexible, and the outcome is quite unpredictable in its specifics. Indeed, even a character's best and most promising efforts at mediation may just fail. But what typifies each and every Feast scene is at minimum the promise of improvement or remedy, and it is this hoped-for trajectory that provides a recurrent, expectable context for the many individual dramas played out over the course of the *Odyssey* and *Iliad*. To read behind the Feast sign with understanding is to recognize that, from the telltale detail of seating (or, if present, from the foregoing assembly or purification) onward, this is an event that offers a real chance for wholesale change, for moving beyond a difficult or compromising situation or at least improving it. This is the conventional idiomatic thrust of the Feasting *sêma*, the implication borne by the traditional structure. Like other Homeric *sêmata*, its meaning lies beyond—as well as at—the literal, textual level, and faithful reception requires meshing instance with implication.

Rereading Some Feasts

As with any approach to verbal art, the proof must emerge in the application. Awareness of the typical structure or the traditional referentiality of a Homeric *sêma* is of little use if it does not make us a better audience for the *Odyssey* and *Iliad*. For this reason I now propose rereading a "sampler" of Homeric Feasts from the perspective of their shared context, inquiring what if any difference the idiomatic meaning of this pattern makes to our reception of the poetry. Are the individual moments reinforced, enriched, qualified, or even contradicted by the implied frame in which they occur? Does traditional implication mesh with local instance in any discernible and productive fashion? In order to answer such questions, I have selected nine of the thirty-two feasts in the *Odyssey* for closer examination.[14] We will proceed by striking flint against steel—by glossing the uniqueness of each separate event with the unspoken context implied by the register, attempting to demonstrate the role played by the *sêma* as a speech-act. We will, in other words, be rereading each scene by consulting not an *apparatus criticus* but rather an *apparatus fabulosus*, not a critical handbook that glosses one text by reference to another text but a story-based companion that brings into play the resources of the poetic tradition.[15]

Will this procedure produce entirely new readings of these passages, readings that share little or nothing with conventional, text-based interpretations? Of course not: as remarked earlier and often throughout this volume, no absolute contrast of orality versus literacy or oral tradition versus text can be sustained. Homer's traditional art isn't that one-dimensional. But the perspective from traditional register can illuminate Homer's art in complementary and important ways, adding idiomatic frames that would otherwise be lost. It is to reawaken these echoes that we are investigating the role of oral tradition, the interplay of *sêmata* and what lies between them.

Book 1: Telemachos as Interim Host.   The first feast in the poem provides a handy blueprint for one kind of interaction between traditional context and immediate situation. The specifics are as follows (113f.). Telemachos serves as the host for his guest pseudo-Mentes, the putative lord of the Taphians and hereditary guest-friend of Odysseus, who is of course Athena in disguise. This prior relationship entitles Mentes to reciprocal hospitality, which Odysseus' son endeavors to arrange without hesitation. What is more, all of the conventional signals are there: Telemachos seats him (130) and sees that the often-repeated, canonical ministrations are carried out (the maidservant washes their hands, the housekeeper and carver supply the food and drink, 136–42). As they finish eating, the expectable satisfaction marker appears in its most frequent and recognizable form: "They put their hands to the good things that lay ready before them. / But when they had cast off their desire for eating and drinking, . . ." (149–50). On the structural surface all seems ordinary enough.

But a closer look indicates that this is far from an ordinary feast, as the unpredictable details associated only with this particular instance are woven in and among the recurrent, resonant features of the traditional *sêma.* Telemachos is manifestly embarrassed over the suitors' usurpation of his father's authority and possessions, a takeover he seems at this point virtually powerless to contest. Indeed, as the scene starts, we find him silent and grieving among the suitors, roused from his reverie about Odysseus' possible revenge only by the appearance of Mentes and the social imperative of guest-friendship it entails.[16] Although he rushes to receive his visitor and thoughtfully makes a place for him apart from the din of the usurpers, within a few lines the young man's inmost thoughts and shame-motivated actions will give way to an explicit complaint to his guest about the suitors' intolerable behavior (158f.). The overall proceedings thus high-light disarray and dysfunction against the background of the order and civility that the traditional signal idiomatically leads us to expect. There are a host and guest, yes, but Telemachos is a poor shadow of the absent Odysseus and the paternal "guest-friend" he tries his best to honor and entertain is a goddess in disguise. In other words, the host is not really in charge and the guest is not really a guest. Mentes is seated, yes, but at a distance from the others involved in the feast. The servants wash and feed the diners, to be sure, and the ritual closes appropriately with the satisfaction marker, but all this appropriate feast-related activity clashes with Telemachos' own blushing critique of the present chaotic situation.

In addition to examining the warp and woof of unique detail and traditional structure, we should consider the contribution of traditional referentiality. If the Feast *sêma* prescribes a route from *an obvious and preexisting problem to an effort at mediation of that problem,* then we should ask just how such a dependable, idiomatic context participates at this early but crucial moment in the *Odyssey.*[17] The long-standing problem at one end of the implied route or trajectory is easy enough to locate: it is of course Odysseus' twenty-year absence, the incipient stage of the Return Song, that has led to devastation not only for himself but also for the loved ones and the community he left behind. Into this vacuum the suitors have inserted themselves, establishing and maintaining an illegitimate, alternate community characterized only by disorder and imbalance. Misery has reigned ever since Odysseus left for Troy, and will remain in the ascendancy—as the overall story-pattern continuously reminds us—until his *nostos* is complete. It is clear enough that the specific impasse faced by Telemachos and pseudo-Mentes as they break bread in Book 1 is a symptom of a much deeper social, familial, and political disarray.

But that hardly exhausts the implications of this *sêma.* There are always two interdependent dimensions to the Feast as a traditional sign, and they point in opposite directions. As much as the Feast proceeds out of initial discord or misery, it also looks ahead toward potential mediation of those troubles, and this particular instance in *Odyssey* 1 is no different in that regard. After identifying herself as the lord of the Taphians and flashing the credential of prior guest-friendship between their families, Athena as Mentes undertakes the predictable amelioration. By arguing that Odysseus is alive and will return, by urging Telemachos to find a method of forcing the suitors out of the household, and most patently by advising him to call the offenders into assembly for an immediate dressing-down, Athena does what she announced as her intention during the council on Olympos (88–89): she instills courage into the young man. For it is solely on Mentes' advice that Telemachos will undertake the mini-*Odyssey* to Pylos and Sparta to search for news of Odysseus. We remember the instructions: if he discovers that his father lives, says Mentes, then patience must sustain him; if he learns that Odysseus is dead, however, then it will be up to Telemachos to marry off his mother and kill the suitors. If his father lives, he must await his reaccession; if not, Telemachos must become master of Ithaka. Both of these plans constitute mediation of the problems at hand, as the Feast signal always implies, whatever the situation. The *sêma* furnishes a traditional vehicle for transition, helping in this instance to key Telemachos' voyage of discovery in Books 2–4 as well as to foster his maturation from a helpless boy to a more self-sufficient man who will attempt to take some charge of his own (and his father's) affairs. The sign works cooperatively with the specifics of its local environment—like language, only more so.

Book 5: Kalypso's Divine Fare.   Cognate changes of status and situation are keyed by a pair of feasts over which the goddess Kalypso presides in the fifth book of the *Odyssey*, one for Hermes (85f.) and the other for Odysseus (192f.). Both events follow the familiar pathway from seating (86, 195) through preparation and serving of food and drink (92–93, 196–99) and on to satisfaction (94–95, 200–1), tracing the horizon of expectation in both cases. But since these are also divine feasts, they depart somewhat from what we experience on Ithaka and elsewhere when humans are in charge. Instead of the maidservant, housekeeper, and carver or their equivalents, Kalypso herself distributes the consumables to her guests; and instead of the mortal staples of bread in baskets and sliced meat, she puts nectar and ambrosia before her divine peer and a great smorgasbord of human delicacies before Odysseus. As always, the Homeric sign varies within limits, its morphology accommodating a spectrum of realizations.

What then of the idiomatic implications of the Feast *sêma* in each of these two instances? In the first sequence, Hermes is delivering a message from Zeus, a command to the nymph to release the long-detained hero that will mediate the present situation by starting him on the final stage of his trek homeward.[18] The absence and devastation implied by the Return Song story-pattern set the larger context and define our perspective: although Odysseus is being entertained by a goddess who offers him immortality, he is just as surely suffering over the loss of all that is dear to him as a human being.[19] Homer makes this suffering absolutely explicit by twice showing the miserable captive sitting on the beach in abject despair and mourning his fate, once before each Feast (81–84, 151–58). Both scenes testify that the hero's return and poem's momentum are similarly stalled. But Kalypso's idiomatic reception of Hermes marks an initial step toward amelioration of the hero's plight: after they eat and drink their fill, Hermes delivers the message and the goddess grudgingly agrees to comply. As the pattern prescribes, a preexisting and obvious problem has been addressed in a promising way. It is important to stress that neither the immediate instance in particular nor the traditional speech-act in general guarantees an easy or complete solution to the hero's troubles, and indeed Poseidon's thirst for vengeance will delay Odysseus' homecoming further, almost killing him in the process. But at least, so warrants the *sêma*, potential progress is forthcoming.

The second of the Feast signs in Book 5 describes the same arc, supporting resumption of the hero's voyage home by promising a path leading from present troubles toward mediation. Here, of course, the guest is Odysseus himself, and Kalypso is thus responding directly to him rather than to Zeus' divine emissary. She warns the hero of the hardships he will face en route and after a last night together provides him with tools and materials to build the remarkable raft as well as provisions for the journey and tips on star navigation. Paired with the earlier Feast in Book 5, this sequence puts Zeus' plan into action, moving Odysseus toward Phaeacia and the eventual completion of his return. Hero and poem are back on track. Kalypso thus participates importantly in both the mediation prescribed by the Feast signal and the larger-scale "intervention by a powerful female" that always happens early in the Return Song.[20] Typically, then, two complementary forces are driving the narrative forward at this juncture. Traditional referentiality glosses and enriches the presentation, meshing the real-life details of Odysseus' departure from Ogygia with the idiomatic implications of both the Feast scene and the Return Song story-pattern. Although Poseidon has other ideas, Odysseus' future looks brighter than it has in many years. A significant dimension of that potential improvement derives from the referentiality of traditional signs.

Book 9: Polyphemos' (In)human Meal.   With the perverse Feast in the ninth book we take a step back in actual chronological sequence—a customary interlude in the *nostos* song as we saw in the last chapter—and learn firsthand about the origin of Poseidon's enmity toward the Ithakan hero. And what memorable dysfunction the ogre's cannibalistic meal represents. Polyphemos' horrifying feast on human flesh emphasizes as no other action could the utter lack of human rules and categories informing his idiosyncratic existence. As Steve Reece has thoroughly documented (1993: 123–43), all usual practice is starkly reversed in the monster's unique brand of "hospitality." Here the host, posing the expected questions about identity and homeland, but before rather than after a meal is offered, proceeds to eat his guests rather than entertain them. Here the chief guest discharges his ritual responsibility of self-identification by portraying himself fraudulently as "Nobody" (*Outis*). The rules of both human society and epic register are apparently suspended. Under such conditions it perhaps comes as no surprise that the preliminary ritual of seating never takes place, or that the satisfaction marker undergoes a grotesque mutation. Instead of the common feast-closing couplet,

οἱ δ᾽ ἐπ᾽ ὀνείαθ᾽ ἑτοῖμα προκείμενα χεῖρας ἴαλλον.
αὐτὰρ ἐπεὶ πόσιος καὶ ἐδητύος ἐξ ἔρον ἕντο,

They put their hands to the good things that lay ready before them.
But when they had cast off their desire for eating and drinking,

or some equivalent, we hear an eerily echoic perversion of that familiar signal (288, 296–97):

ἀλλ᾽ ὅ γ᾽ ἀναΐξας ἑτάροις ἐπὶ χεῖρας ἴαλλε, . . .
αὐτὰρ ἐπεὶ Κύκλωψ μεγάλην ἐμπλήσατο νηδὺν
ἀνδρόμεα κρέ᾽ ἔδων καὶ ἐπ᾽ ἄκρητον γάλα πίνων,

But springing up, he put his hands to my companions, . . .
But when he had filled his great belly,
eating man-meat and drinking unmixed milk,

The underlined correspondences and general similarity in sense only highlight the gross discrepancies. Instead of what amounts to a rite embodying peace and harmony at the same time that it forecasts mediation, this monstrous meal violates all our expectations for the Feast.

Dysfunction leads to dysfunction, as the positive change usually implied by the Feast *sêma* is compromised, or at least delayed. For while there can be little doubt that a threat exists, that is where the predictable sequence comes to a halt: the perilous position occupied by Odysseus and his men since their entry into the ogre's cave will see no immediate improvement. Having gorged himself with one unspeakable meal, Polyphemos will rise again the next day only to repeat his inhuman depradations before Odysseus can hatch a plan, bait the monster with wine, and eventually blind him. This instance of the Feast sign thus proves profoundly ironic, sounding an identifiable echo of a familiar pattern while at the same moment diametrically contradicting its implications. We sense something very much amiss within the structure of the signal itself, of course, but there is enough correspondence with a thematic pattern used thirty-one other times in the *Odyssey* that the idiomatic association presents itself. It is the register and its referentiality that beg the question: will the hero's problems somehow be resolved or lessened, notwithstanding the strange and perverse nature of this Feast? It would seem highly unlikely, and yet the signal suggests the ironic possibility. Even in such an extreme case, traditional implications figure significantly in the narrative process, sharpening the contrast between the fundamentally human culture of Odysseus and the culture of Polyphemos and his kin, which is just as fundamentally *athemistos* ("without *themis*"; "lawless," and thus by definition "not human").[21] Terror and irony reside in the malformed *sêma* itself and in the brutal discrepancy that contrasts the customary rhythm of the community-affirming rite against the monster's wholesale violation of everything it portends. Instance and implication are never more dramatically opposed in the *Odyssey*.

Book 10: Kirke's Delayed Feast. With the following example we return to what initially appears to be a much more conventional feast and set of implications. The scene opens (348f.) with Kirke's maidservants preparing the physical site and giving her guest Odysseus the purifying bath and olive-oil anointment that often precede and key the fullest version of this Homeric sign-sequence. Soon the goddess seats Odysseus (366), and the familiar actions of the maidservant and housekeeper, which occur in Book 1 and as part of four additional feasts, ensue (368–72). But at this point the characteristic rhythm of the pattern comes abruptly to a halt. In language that once again echoes the satisfaction phrase but flatly contradicts its function, Odysseus refuses to "put his hands to the food" until his companions are transformed back into human beings.[22] He interrupts the progress of the *sêma*, in other words, stopping its momentum and forestalling the mediation that it idiomatically implies. Much now hangs in the balance, at the level not only of instance but also of implication. Not until Kirke provides a remedy—literally by changing the companions back from pigs to men and then traditionally by putting them through the purification ritual (449–51)—does Odysseus relent and accept her hospitality. With his acquiescence the expected progression resumes and mediation is imminent.

The long-postponed satisfaction marker, this time in a somewhat different but still recognizable form, then brings to closure not only this particular feast but the entire year of splendid inaction—and dereliction of *nostos*—spent with Kirke (467–70):

ἔνθα μὲν ἤματα πάντα τελεσφόρον εἰς ἐνιαυτὸν
ἥμεθα, δαινύμενοι κρέα τ' ἄσπετα καὶ μέθυ ἡδύ·
ἀλλ' ὅτε δή ῥ' ἐνιαυτὸς ἔην, περὶ δ' ἔτραπον ὧραι,
μῆνων φθινόντων, περὶ δ' ἤματα μακρὰ τελέσθη, . . .

There for all our days until a year was completed
we sat there feasting on unlimited meat and sweet wine.
But when it was the end of a year, and the months wasted
away, and the seasons changed, and the long days were accomplished, . . .

After a brief reprise of the Feast sign (476–78), Odysseus asks his goddess-host to fulfill her promise to send him homeward. Kirke proves as good as her word, and, in harmony with the mediation proverbially implied by the traditional signal, instructs him in how to proceed. Here the poetics of instance and implication provide for an especially rich and complex presentation. On the one hand, the goddess does as he wishes, as she pledged, and as the *sêma* requires by releasing Odysseus and giving him the necessary information to continue his return. On the other hand, she advises him that his next step must be to consult the blind prophet Teiresias in the underworld, to undertake a journey no mortal has ever survived. Disturbing questions must arise. How does the hero complete his *nostos* to Ithaka and Penelope? Though it may seem counterintuitive, the answer is via the route through Hades. Even if he manages the first half of this most challenging itinerary, then, will Odysseus live to follow Teiresias' instructions? Other indications to the contrary, the mediation that traditionally accompanies the Feast would suggest that this is indeed the right course of action and that the hero will live to tell about it. The road ahead may prove remarkably challenging and dangerous, but it is the right road. Reading behind the signs once again frames what lies between them.

Book 12: Angering the "Host" Helios.   No feast is more deadly or more determinative than the forbidden meal that the doomed companions make of the sacred cattle belonging to Helios, the sun. This is the unforgivable transgression about which Teiresias warns Odysseus in the underworld, and which the returning hero tries mightily to prevent. But when "sweet sleep" overtakes him, the same disabling sleep that left Polyphemos vulnerable to blinding by his own olive-wood stake,[23] the men's hunger gets the best of them and another perverse feast commences.

Structurally this absolutely unique event has a curiously familiar resonance. Although the seating element is elided (naturally enough, given the unparalleled site and dynamics of the meal on Thrinakia), the preparations and serving take one of the customary forms: a sacrifice to the gods, intended as propitiation. Given that this unfortunate feast directly contradicts Teiresias' advice and constitutes a sin against Hyperion, there is considerable irony in the language associated with the slaughter. Indeed, the passage in question is a pastiche of traditional and untraditional language, with familiar phraseology interspersed with situation-specific diction. In what follows, repeated lines or phrases associated with sacrifice or feasting are designated by **boldface**; those simply repeated elsewhere in Homer and unattached to this *sêma* are underlined):[24]

αὐτίκα δ' Ἠελίοιο βοῶν ἐλάσαντες ἀρίστας
ἐγγύθεν· οὐ γὰρ τῆλε νεὸς κυανοπρῴροιο
βοσκέσκονθ' ἕλικες καλαὶ βόες εὐρυμέτωποι·   355
τὰς δὲ περιστήσαντο καὶ εὐχετόωντο θεοῖσι,
φύλλα δρεψάμενοι τέρενα δρυὸς ὑψικόμοιο·
οὐ γὰρ ἔχον κρῖ λευκὸν ἐϋσσέλμου ἐπὶ νηός.
αὐτὰρ ἐπεί ῥ' εὔξαντο καὶ ἔσφαξαν καὶ ἔδειραν
μηρούς τ' ἐξέταμον **κατά τε κνίσῃ ἐκάλυψαν**   360
δίπτυχα ποιήσαντες, ἐπ' αὐτῶν δ' ὠμοθέτησαν·
οὐδ' εἶχον μέθυ λεῖψαι ἐπ' αἰθομένοις ἱεροῖσιν,
ἀλλ' ὕδατι σπένδοντες ἐπώπτων ἔγκατα πάντα.
αὐτὰρ ἐπεὶ κατὰ μῆρε κάη καὶ σπλάγχνα πάσαντο,
μίστυλλόν τ' ἄρα τἆλλα καὶ ἀμφ' ὀβελοῖσιν ἔπειραν.   365

At once, cutting out from near at hand the best of Helios' cattle—
for not far from the dark-prowed ship
the handsome broad-faced horn-curved oxen were pasturing—   355
they stationed themselves around them, and made their prayers
to the gods, pulling tender leaves from a deep-leaved oak tree;
for they had no white barley left on the strong-benched vessel.
But when they had made their prayer and slaughtered the oxen and
     skinned them,
they cut away the meat from the thighs **and wrapped them in fat,**   360
making a double fold, and laid shreds of flesh upon them;
and since they had no wine to pour on the burning offerings,
they made a libation of water, and roasted all of the entrails;
but when they had burned the thigh pieces and tasted the vitals,
they cut all the remainder into pieces and spitted them.   365

The irony of this perverse feast stems most obviously from its being a sacrifice to honor the gods (a common variant in this part of the pattern) and concurrently a rash and irremediable insult of Helios. That same duality is imaged in the two contrasting modes of language—expectable versus unique—that the fluent audience or reader recognizes as traditional signs versus their individualized interstices. We hear one rhythm through the first half of the passage, where formulaic language makes for the general resonance of the Homeric register, reinforcing the performance arena and the "wavelength" in use by poet and reader or audience.[25] The latter half follows another rhythm and carries more focused implications: feast- or sacrifice-specific diction, which strongly summons the typical scene and its associations, alternates with unique, wholly unparalleled diction that contradicts the idiomatic force of the *sêma*. Thus the companions pray and begin the unprecedented and unholy slaughter with a line (359) related to no other in Homer, while the next two verses (360–61) seem to situate this aberrant act within the phraseological context of a bona fide feast. For this brief moment things almost sound right. But lines 362–63 reverse that impression by stressing the discrepancy between this sacrifice and any other, emphasizing what Odysseus' men did *not* have available and highlighting the distance between this atrocious act and an acceptable propitiation of the gods. The description of meal preparation and serving then shifts the focus one more time, closing with lines that—taken by themselves—betoken a successful and well-managed Homeric feast (364–65). At the levels of both structure and diction, then, this instance ironically undercuts the traditional impression it makes. Eating Hyperion's cattle is more than an incomplete or compromised meal, we are being told; it is a perverse violation of the feast ritual.

And what of mediation, the traditional sequel to that ritual? As with the Polyphemos episode in Book 9, the immediate yield of this sacrilegious feast is nothing but dysfunction. Just as the ogre's man-meal led only to another round of cannibalism before Odysseus could contrive a plan to escape, so the companions' consumption of the sacred oxen augurs only their loss of *nostos*, their permanent forfeit of return.[26] After the satisfaction signal marks the end of the illegitimate feasting at 397–400, they confidently set sail, where they quite predictably become victims of the great storm sent by Zeus in his vengeance. Odysseus alone rides out the meteorological fireworks, escapes Charybdis and Skylla, and eventually gains the sanctuary of Kalypso's island, Ogygia. The episode of Helios' cattle is, to say the least, far from an ordinary instance of the feast paradigm, and it follows that the implications of that instance will be just as aberrant.[27] The perverse feast has forecast not mediation but oblivion for the uninvited guests of the unwilling host Hyperion: instead of ameliorating the problem, their countertraditional, unholy rite has quashed any hope of returning to Ithaka—at least for themselves.

Book 17: Inside News of the Nostos.   At the other end of the structural and idiomatic spectrum lies the encounter between Telemachos and the stranger (84f.). Odysseus has revealed himself to his son one book earlier, but by this time has once again donned the conventionally impenetrable disguise of the Return Song hero—itself a *sêma*—and all that it signifies.[28] Now Telemachos (as host) and the stranger (as guest) enter the megaron and are accorded the washing and anointment that often precede the most elaborate feasts. After they are seated (90), the housekeeper and maid-servant perform their "classic" roles in providing the consumables (91–95). Throughout this instance of the pattern, only a single situation-specific detail emerges, but it is a crucially important one: Penelope is present, sitting by a pillar and turning yarn on a distaff. Even the satisfaction signal assumes the most familiar form (98–99), as the diners enjoy the wealth of provisions until they "cast off their desire for eating and drinking." In clear contrast to the companions' reckless and fatal actions on Thrinakia, this feast includes all of the structures and signals that regularly imply mediation, without qualification or subversion.

And we are certainly not disappointed by what happens next. Before Penelope can retreat to her upper chambers, two heavily portentous and encouraging observations are made. The first is by Telemachos, who reports on his mini-*Odyssey* and especially on what he heard from Menelaos in Sparta. Although Nestor could tell him nothing of his father, Menelaos both expressed his own wish for revenge against the suitors and passed along what he learned from Proteus, namely, that Odysseus had reached Ogygia but was being detained by the nymph Kalypso. This claim, of course, turns out to have been the truth, even if by now it is old news. The second observation comes from the prophet Theoklymenos, and rings true for the audience and others "in the know" even as he speaks it before Telemachos, the stranger, and Penelope (155–59):

ἴστω νῦν Ζεὺς πρῶτα θεῶν ξενίη τε τράπεζα
ἱστίη τ' Ὀδυσῆος ἀμύμονος, ἣν ἀφικάνω,
ὡς ἦ τοι Ὀδυσεὺς ἤδη ἐν πατρίδι γαίῃ,
ἥμενος ἢ ἕρπων, τάδε πευθόμενος κακὰ ἔργα,
ἔστιν, ἀτὰρ μνηστῆρσι κακὸν πάντεσσι φυτεύει·

Zeus be my witness, first of the gods, and the table of friendship,
and the hearth of blameless Odysseus, to which I come as a suppliant,
that Odysseus is already here in the land of his fathers,
sitting still or advancing, learning of these evil
actions, and devising evils for all of the suitors.

In short, the feast has keyed mediation of the long-standing problem of Odysseus' absence in the form of two extremely promising reports from separate and "inside" sources. Via Telemachos, Penelope hears of what Menelaos was told by Proteus, an eminently dependable advisor once he is subdued. Even more reliable is the reading she receives straight from Theoklymenos, the same person who will successfully interpret the suitors' blood-feast three books hence.[29] If the best that Penelope can muster in response is a wish that the seer's word could be believed, her recalcitrance is more a tribute to her thoroughgoing (and life-preserving) indeterminacy than the ineffectuality of the signs before her.[30] Feast has directly and idiomatically implied mediation, in this case nothing less than the eventual *nostos* of Odysseus.

Book 23: Penelope's and Odysseus' Feast of Reunion. The same pattern frames the poem's approach toward its *telos*, the culminating moment of Odysseus' and Penelope's reunion. As I have demonstrated elsewhere,[31] the Bath scene, wherein a person is cleansed with water and anointed with olive oil, leads unfailingly to a feast; characters who undergo the purification procedure regularly and idiomatically take part in the traditional Homeric meal and in all that it implies. There are six quite straightforward occurrences of this predictive linkage. In Book 3 (464–68) Bath precedes the elaborate slaughter and sacrifice at Nestor's palace, in Book 4 (48–50) it occurs just after Telemachos and Peisistratos arrive at Menelaos' home, and in Book 8 (449–57) it follows the laying out of clothes for Odysseus at the Phaeacian court. Likewise, in Book 10 (360–65) the Bath pattern introduces the feast that Odysseus will suspend until Kirke gives his men back their human form, in Book 17 (85–90) Telemachos and the stranger bathe before the meal after which Penelope will hear promising news of her husband, and in Book 24 (365–71) the purification ritual initiates the feast shared by Laertes and his long-lost son, a meal to be discussed below.[32]

But there is another, quite remarkable instance of Bath at 23.153–64:

αὐτὰρ Ὀδυσσῆα μεγαλήτορα ᾧ ἐνὶ οἴκῳ
Εὐρυνόμη ταμίη λοῦσεν καὶ χρῖσεν ἐλαίῳ,
ἀμφὶ δέ μιν φᾶρος καλὸν βάλεν ἠδὲ χιτῶνα·   155
αὐτὰρ κὰκ κεφαλῆς χεῦεν πολὺ κάλλος Ἀθήνη
μείζονά τ' ἐσιδέειν καὶ πάσσονα· κὰδ δὲ κάρητος
οὔλας ἧκε κόμας, ὑακινθίνῳ ἄνθει ὁμοίας.
ὡς δ' ὅτε τις χρυσὸν περιχεύεται ἀργύρῳ ἀνὴρ
ἴδρις, ὃν Ἥφαιστος δέδαεν καὶ Παλλὰς Ἀθήνη   160
τέχνην παντοίην, χαρίεντα δὲ ἔργα τελείει,
ὣς μὲν τῷ περίχευε χάριν κεφαλῇ τε καὶ ὤμοις.
ἐκ δ' ἀσαμίνθου βῆ δέμας ἀθανάτοισιν ὁμοῖος·
ἂψ δ' αὖτις κατ' ἄρ' ἕζετ' ἐπὶ θρόνου ἔνθεν ἀνέστη,

Now the housekeeper Eurynome bathed great-hearted
Odysseus in his own house, and anointed him with olive oil,
and threw a beautiful mantle and a tunic about him;   155
and over his head Athena suffused great beauty, to make him
taller to behold and thicker, and on his head she arranged
the curling locks that hung down like hyacynthine petals.
And as when a master craftsman overlays gold on silver,
and he is one who was taught by Hephaistos and Pallas Athena   160
in art complete, and grace is on every work he finishes;
so Athena gilded with grace his head and shoulders.
Then, looking like an immortal, he strode forth from the bath,
and came back then and sat on the chair from which he had risen,

From this resonant passage, complete with the washing and anointment phrases that key the Bath pattern, the narrative proceeds not to the usual breaking of bread but to another kind of feast—the epic *telos*.

But this is no blind alley, no traditional misdirection, no violation of register or of the implications conventionally associated with the Bath sign. Instead of keying the distribution of food and wine, this seventh instance of the Homeric purification ritual leads to an alternate but no less joyous feast, one that features the rapprochement of woman and man at its center and points unmistakably toward mediation. Traditional pattern resonates uniquely with situation-specific action here, as the idiomatic frame of Bath-Feast-Mediation deepens the singular moment, producing a familiar, echoic context even as the inimitable, one-time drama of reunion plays itself out before our eyes. This is a feast, we are being told, and yet more than a feast.[33] The satisfaction marker takes an appropriate shape— "When Penelope and Odysseus had taken their pleasure in lovemaking" (Τὼ δ' ἐπεὶ οὖν φιλότητος ἐταρπήτην ἐρατεινῆς, 300)[34]—and mediation assumes the composite form of the biographies they then exchange, bringing their identities up to date as it were, and of the surrender to a "sweet sleep" (*glukus hupnos*, 342) that finally comes without threat or qualification.[35] I have characterized this unusual instance of Bath and Feast as follows (1990: 287):

> It is a measure of Homer's profoundly traditional art, I suggest, that the Feast is this time a celebration not of eating and drinking but of long-sought reunion and fulfillment, not of consuming elaborately prepared foodstuffs but of finding once again the feast of love and tenderness that had been denied for twenty years. For in a vital sense, this instance of the pattern shows not a deviation from expectation but an augmentation of the conventional sequence, and its extraordinary make-up derives directly from the traditional expectation on which Homer, or his poetic tradition, has so brilliantly built.

We will find few combinations of instance and implication that can match this scene in its meshing of uniqueness with traditional referentiality.

Book 24: A Father's Humble Repast.   The final feast to be examined in this chapter forms part of the sequence that "ends" the *Odyssey*, as opposed to marking its *telos*. As we discovered in the preceding chapter, the so-called continuation of the poem consists of the kind of sequel often found in the Return Song tradition. Its entailed actions are thus neither extraneous nor superfluous, but rather constitute a natural (if optional) feature of the story-pattern.

As these post-*telos* actions play themselves out, and while trouble with the suitors' relatives brews in the background, Laertes and Odysseus share a meal and the *Odyssey* thereby gains a traditionally motivated momentum as it nears the end. All of the signals appear. Laertes undergoes the Bath ritual (365–71) in preparation for the feast, whose onset is unambiguously marked by the seating of both father and son (385). The actual description of the meal is very brief, even telegraphic (386, 412), but the satisfaction phrase rings loud and clear: "When the men had cast off their desire for delicious feasting" (Οἱ δ' ἐπεὶ οὖν σίτοιο μελίφρονος ἐξ ἔρον ἔντο, 489). What is more, the very familiarity and proverbial function of these traditional signs cast the singularities of the scene into sharp relief. Before the satisfaction marker can perform its function as a narrative pivot, shifting from feast toward mediation, we hear of the suitors' burial, Eupeithes' outraged call for revenge, and the earnest conference between Zeus and Athena on Olympos. Only after citation of these unique and ominous events—unparalleled disparities that stand out against the recurrent background of the pattern—does the story move toward resolution. Complementary to the tension between the hero's return and the suitors' revenge, between the lineage of Laertes and the lineage of Eupeithes, between order restored and further unraveling of the Ithakan community, is the tension between the traditional scene of the Feast on the one hand and the specific characters and actions particular to this singular situation on the other. We cannot afford to neglect either side of such fundamental dualities; Homer's art emerges from reading behind the signs as well as between them.

Just so with the foreordained mediation. As discussed in the preceding chapter, the brief pitched battle gives way quickly to the Peace of Athena. The problems highlighted during the feast scene are resolved by the goddess, who instills an unhinging "green fear" (chlôron deos) into Eupeithes and company.[36] Her intercession at this juncture is by definition a one-time occurrence (at least in the Odyssey), perhaps even a dea ex machina. Nonetheless, as highly untraditional as her intervention may seem, it is also a species of mediation, and as such is institutionally implied by the feast scene that precedes it.[37] Athena's actions here bear the same idiomatic sanction as her instilling of courage in Telemachos in Book 1, or the negotiations with Kalypso that allow Odysseus to leave Ogygia in Book 5, or Theoklymenos' encouraging prophecy in Book 17, or the final stage of Penelope's and Odysseus' reunion at the telos in Book 23. All of these and many more mediations are prefigured by the ritual event of the feast.

The Lament and What It Signifies

For another example of a "word" at the level of a typical scene, we turn to a sêma limited strictly to the Iliad. Here the set of signals that drives composition and reception is largely structural rather than phraseological, depending almost entirely on a sequence of actions rather than an array of particular lines or phrases.[38] Its basic pattern consists of three parts: (1) an address to the slain warrior indicating "you have fallen," (2) a narrative of personal history and future consequences for the mourner and those close to her, and (3) a readdress of the warrior for a final intimacy.[39] Individual laments can and do vary, of course, but this pattern counterbalances their diversity. By indexing a recognizable subgenre, it summons a definite set of expectations, identifying each lament as belonging to a category, as being a particular kind of speech-act with certain implications.

In what follows I will explore these implications in context by rereading a passage that presents a demanding but enlightening crux. During a pause in battle in Book 6 of the *Iliad*, we find Andromache sharing a rare domestic scene with her husband Hektor. As she speaks with him, she adopts the discursive posture of a woman singing a formal lament for a loved one who has died. Yet Hektor stands before her, quite alive. In disentangling this unique twist on a familiar pattern, we can see more deeply into the traditional resources of Homeric poetics.

Andromache's First Lament

Hektor's brief absence from the battlefield in Book 6 opens the way for some riveting human moments back in Troy, moments that vividly expose the awful price of the war. His mother Hekabe and his sister Laodike run to greet him, but, his hands stained with the bloody defilement of battle, he must refuse the libation his mother suggests.[40] Nor, visiting Paris' palace in search of his reticent brother, can he accept Helen's offer of a seat, the customary traditional prelude to the feasting and mediation that war has precluded.[41] He has time only to urge Paris to hurry on to battle, and to enlist Helen to convey the same message.[42] Martial and domestic rhythms prove everywhere absolutely at odds, as the glories associated with defending Troy and winning *kleos* are continually called into question by Hektor's inability to assume any but the most temporary of roles in the ongoing drama of the home or *oikos*. At every turn the men's world of desperate fighting, restless action, heroic relationships, and sudden death clashes with the women's world of domestic responsibilities, resigned reaction, familial relationships, and the nourishing of life. In their prominent juxtaposition a fundamental and terrible irony comes to the fore. Not only are these two worlds opposite and apparently incompatible; they also stand in a cruelly symbiotic relationship, each one necessary to the other's continuing existence.

This irony undergirds all of the *Iliad*'s action as an implicit contradiction, an irreducible problem of human culture, but it is nowhere so manifest as in glancing-helmed Hektor's exchange with Andromache, daughter of great-hearted Eëtion. In refusing Helen's hospitality, he cites the need to return to battle—from which frame of reference he has never really emerged—and to visit his wife and infant son en route. His reasoning behind the visit is compelling in its frankness: "I do not know if ever again I shall come back this way, / or whether the gods will strike me down at the hands of the Achaeans" (367–68). Indeed, Hektor endures each day burdened with this uncertainty, as does Andromache; the difference, of course, is that he takes the hero's proactive role in living out his fate, while she is assigned the woman's passive role of response. Thus, even though Hektor and Andromache laugh together at the baby Astyanax's startled reaction to the waving horsehair plume on his father's shining helmet, the discrepancy that prompts their shared laughter only underlines their separateness. The man must and will fight heroically to the death in defense of Troy; the woman must and will persevere in a much more immediate attempt to defend her family and eventually to pay for his heroism. Her nourishing and community-building concerns center around the *oikos*, the home, while he fights for the city by pursuing *kleos*, or glory.

The fatalism they both harbor about what will eventually become of Troy and of them finds resonant expression in the very form of Andromache's initial words to her husband. What she speaks amounts to a traditional Lament, the *sêma* or speech-act that she, Briseis, Helen, and Hekabe will employ another six times to mourn the actual demise of Patroklos and Hektor further on in the poem. Here are Andromache's traditionally prescient words (6.405–39), with the three sections of the lament pattern designated (A, B, C) and some smaller traditional signals marked by underlining and labeled in **boldface**:

Ἀνδρομάχη δέ οἱ ἄγχι παρίστατο δάκρυ χέουσα,   405
ἔν τ' ἄρα οἱ φῦ χειρὶ ἔπος τ' ἔφατ' ἔκ τ' ὀνόμαζε·   **Emotional speaker**
A: Address / "You have fallen" (407–10)
"δαιμόνιε, φθίσει σε τὸ σὸν μένος, οὐδ' ἐλεαίρεις   **Contest/Change; Ring 407/431**
παῖδά τε νηπίαχον καὶ ἔμ' ἄμμορον, ἣ τάχα χήρη   **Ring 408/432**
σεῦ ἔσομαι· τάχα γάρ σε κατακτανέουσιν Ἀχαιοὶ
πάντες ἐφορμηθέντες·
B: Narrative / Personal history and consequences (410–28)
                                    ἐμοὶ δέ κε κέρδιον εἴη   **Road not taken**
σεῦ ἀφαμαρτούσῃ χθόνα δύμεναι· οὐ γὰρ ἔτ' ἄλλη   411
ἔσται θαλπωρή, ἐπεὶ ἂν σύ γε πότμον ἐπίσπῃς,
ἀλλ' ἄχε'· οὐδέ μοι ἔστι πατὴρ καὶ πότνια μήτηρ.   **Ring 413/429–30**
ἤτοι γὰρ πατέρ' ἁμὸν ἀπέκτανε δῖος Ἀχιλλεύς,
ἐκ δὲ πόλιν πέρσεν Κιλίκων εὖ ναιετάουσαν,   415
Θήβην ὑψίπυλον· κατὰ δ' ἔκτανεν Ἠετίωνα,

οὐδέ μιν ἐξενάριξε, σεβάσσατο γὰρ τό γε θυμῷ,
ἀλλ' ἄρα μιν κατέκηε σὺν ἔντεσι δαιδαλέοισιν
ἠδ' ἐπὶ σῆμ' ἔχεεν· περὶ δὲ πτελέας ἐφύτευσαν
νύμφαι ὀρεστιάδες, κοῦραι Διὸς αἰγιόχοιο.   420
οἳ δέ μοι ἑπτὰ κασίγνητοι ἔσαν ἐν μεγάροισιν,
οἱ μὲν πάντες ἰῷ κίον ἤματι Ἄϊδος εἴσω·
πάντας γὰρ κατέπεφνε ποδάρκης δῖος Ἀχιλλεὺς
βουσὶν ἐπ' εἰλιπόδεσσι καὶ ἀργεννῇς ὀίεσσι.
μητέρα δ', ἣ βασίλευεν ὑπὸ Πλάκῳ ὑληέσσῃ,   425
τὴν ἐπεὶ ἂρ δεῦρ' ἤγαγ' ἅμ' ἄλλοισι κτεάτεσσιν,
ἂψ ὅ γε τὴν ἀπέλυσε λαβὼν ἀπερείσι' ἄποινα,
πατρὸς δ' ἐν μεγάροισι βάλ' Ἄρτεμις ἰοχέαιρα.

C: Readdress / Final intimacy (429–32)
Ἕκτορ, ἀτὰρ σύ μοί ἐσσι πατὴρ καὶ πότνια μήτηρ   Ring 413/429–30
ἠδὲ κασίγνητος, σὺ δέ μοι θαλερὸς παρακοίτης·   430
ἀλλ' ἄγε νῦν ἐλέαιρε καὶ αὐτοῦ μίμν' ἐπὶ πύργῳ,   Fulcrum: command;
          Ring 407/431
μὴ παῖδ' ὀρφανικὸν θήῃς χήρην τε γυναῖκα·   Ring 408/432
Addendum (433–39)
λαὸν δὲ στῆσον παρ' ἐρινεόν, ἔνθα μάλιστα
ἀμβατός ἐστι πόλις καὶ ἐπίδρομον ἔπλετο τεῖχος.
τρὶς γὰρ τῇ γ' ἐλθόντες ἐπειρήσανθ' οἱ ἄριστοι   435
ἀμφ' Αἴαντε δύω καὶ ἀγακλυτὸν Ἰδομενῆα
ἠδ' ἀμφ' Ἀτρεΐδας καὶ Τυδέος ἄλκιμον υἱόν·
ἤ πού τίς σφιν ἔνισπε θεοπροπίων ἐὺ εἰδώς,
ἤ νυ καὶ αὐτῶν θυμὸς ἐποτρύνει καὶ ἀνώγει."

Andromache stood close beside him, letting her tears fall,   405
and clung to his hand and called him by name and spoke to him: Emotional
                                                                    speaker
A: Address / "You have fallen" (407–10)
"Strange one, your own great strength will be your death,   Contest/Change;
     and you have no pity   Ring 407/431
on your little son, nor on me, ill-starred, who soon must   Ring 408/432
     be your widow;
for presently the Achaians, gathering together,
will set upon you and kill you;
B: Narrative / Personal history and consequences (410–28)
                    and for me it would be far better   Road not taken
to sink into the earth when I have lost you, for there is no other   411
consolation for me after you have gone to your destiny—
only grief; since I have no father, and no honored mother.   Ring 413/429–30
It was brilliant Achilleus who slew my father, Eëtion,
when he stormed the strong-founded citadel of the Kilikians,   415
Thebe of the towering gates. He killed Eëtion
but did not strip his armor, for his heart respected the dead man,
but burned the body in all its elaborate war-gear
and piled a grave-mound over it, and the nymphs of the mountains,
daughters of Zeus of the aegis, planted elm trees about it.   420

And they who were my seven brothers in the great house all went
upon a single day down into the house of the death god,
for swift-footed brilliant Achilleus slaughtered all of them
as they were tending their white sheep and their lumbering oxen;
and when he had led my mother, who was queen under wooded Plakos,   425
here, along with all his other possessions, Achilleus
released her again, accepting ransom beyond count, but Artemis
of the showering arrows struck her down in the halls of her father.

C: Readdress / Final intimacy (429–32)

Hektor, thus you are father to me, and my honored mother,	**Ring 413/429–30**
you are my brother, and you it is who are my young husband.	430
But come now take pity on me, stay here on the rampart,	**Fulcrum: command;**
	Ring 407/431
that you may not leave your son an orphan, your wife a widow,	**Ring 408/432**

Addendum (433–39)

but draw up your people by the fig tree, there where the city
is openest to attack, and where the wall may be mounted.
Three times their bravest came that way, and fought there to storm it   435
about the two Aiantes and renowned Idomeneus,
about the two Atreidai and the fighting son of Tydeus.
Either some man well skilled in prophetic arts had spoken,
or the very spirit within themselves had stirred them to the onslaught."

We have been prepared for what amounts to this "proto-lament" in
Book 6 by Homer's notation that Andromache has left her home and fled
to the wall, "mourning and weeping" (373).[43] This stage direction is but-
tressed by the familiar verse that introduces her speech, what I call the
Emotional speaker line—"And so she clung to his hand and spoke a word
and called him by name" (406). According to traditional convention, this
small *sêma* signals (1) a very positive and intimate or very negative and
hostile relationship between speaker and addressee; (2) the speaker's ear-
nestness; (3) a heightened emotional tension; and (4) a subsequent ques-
tion, command, request, or prayer.[44] But, in addition to these indications,
and much more subtly and powerfully, her speech to Hektor follows the
established traditional paradigm for the woman's speech-act of mourning:
a three-part sequence of

    A. Address / "You have fallen"   (407–10)
    B. Narrative / Personal history and consequences   (410–28)
    C. Readdress / Final intimacy   (429–32).

This tripartite speech-act identifies Andromache's words as a formal la-
ment, a specific and recognizable subgenre that according to epic conven-
tion confronts the reality of a loved one's actual death. As such, it moves
beyond the simple expression of sorrow to a frank examination of the con-
sequences for those left behind and, if only by implication, toward an

eventual process of community and familial healing, to the extent that these goals are possible.[45]

Consider first the opening to the latter of Andromache's two "real" laments (24.725–30), the beginning of which serves as an epigraph to this chapter:

"ἆνερ, ἀπ' αἰῶνος νέος ὤλεο, κὰδ δέ με χήρην   725
λείπεις ἐν μεγάροισι· πάϊς δ' ἔτι νήπιος αὔτως,
ὃν τέκομεν σύ τ' ἐγώ τε δυσάμμοροι, οὐδέ μιν οἴω
ἥβην ἵξεσθαι· πρὶν γὰρ πόλις ἥδε κατ' ἄκρης
πέρσεται· ἦ γὰρ ὄλωλας ἐπίσκοπος, ὅς τέ μιν αὐτὴν
ῥύσκευ, ἔχες δ' ἀλόχους κεδνὰς καὶ νήπια τέκνα."   730

"My husband, you were lost young from life, and have left me   725
a widow in your house, and the boy is only a baby
who was born to you and me, the unhappy ones. I think
he will never come of age, for before then head to heel this city
will be sacked, for you, its defender, are gone, you who guarded
the city, and the grave wives, and the innocent children."   730

As the traditional idiom demands, the mourner speaks directly to the fallen hero during the Address, stipulating his demise. To varying degrees, the immediately following laments by Hekabe and Helen, as well as the earlier songs of mourning by Briseis, Hekabe, and Andromache, do the same thing: they key the speech-act by initiating a fictive conversation made tragically one-sided by the hero's absence. Andromache speaks more fully of the implications of Hektor's death than does either her mother-in-law or her adopted sister-in-law in the Address section, and perhaps that is as it should be. Traditional forms create flexible frames for individualized actions, and the wife in her widowhood (and now single parenthood) naturally feels a kind of pain no one else can wholly share, no matter what the nature of their own relationship with the deceased.

But in Book 6 the *sêma* shows unmatched flexibility; the hero whom Andromache laments has not yet perished, and her mourning ritual is accordingly attenuated. Her Address substitutes a future certainty for a past fact, "you will fall" in place of "you have fallen" (407–10):

"Strange one, your own great strength will be your death, and you have no pity
on your little son, nor on me, ill-starred, who soon must be your widow;
for presently the Achaeans, gathering together,
will set upon you and kill you."

There is no condition, no qualification in her pronouncement, only plain fact. That pronouncement will soon lead, as do both of her later laments in Books 22 and 24, to a further, brutally frank delineation of what his death means to wife and child alike. That sober assessment will also include mention of a reality that renders her particular situation even more perilous: with her father and mother both dead, Andromache's option of rejoining her family of origin is forever gone.[46] She will return to this disabling reality later on in the final stage of her threnody (429–30). Alongside such singular details, the Lament sêma—customarily the consequent of death rather than its harbinger—emphasizes the inevitability encoded in her speech. Not only the bare bones of her speech but also the traditional referentiality implied in her speech-act argue the compelling force of her assertion: Hektor is effectively dead to her, and she and their son are lost.

Tellingly, Andromache's very first word to her husband is the salutation *daimonie* ("Strange one"), a feature of the epic register that stamps her proto-lament and the exchange to follow as a recognizable traditional *sêma*. Beyond its lexical sense of "possessed by a *daimôn*," this single *sêma* serves throughout Homer as a signal implying verbal contest and urging some kind of change, presuming all the while a substantial degree of familiarity between speakers.[47] It sets the stage for Zeus and Hera's quarrelsome exchange over Thetis' visit in *Iliad* 1 (561); it also keys the exchange between Odysseus and Penelope in the last stages of their testing and recognition in *Odyssey* 23 (166, 174, 264). Its idiomatic implications of verbal contest and mandated change serve to frame Hektor's two scolding speeches to his laggard brother Paris (*Il.* 6.326, 521), and even to add impetus to Antinoos' warning to his fellow suitors not to talk so loosely about their deadly plans for Telemachos (*Od.* 4.774). In all of these and the other instances of speeches indexed by "Strange one(s)," what is to follow involves some form of contest, supported by a prior relationship that may be familial or social. In this case that context is deepened by another traditional Homeric signal, the general structural index of ring-composition,[48] which emphasizes the *pity* she is begging (407/431) and the *son* and *widow* he will be leaving behind (408/432). These echoes link the Address (A) and Readdress (C) sections of the mourning song, framing the wife's treatment of personal history and consequences (B). Andromache thus begins her proto-lament—hardly an uncritical hymn of praise—in what is by traditional implication and situation-specific fact a context of contest, an agonistic performance arena.[49]

The second section of the Lament *sêma*, "Narrative / Personal history and consequences," typically treats the history of the mourner, the person mourned, and any family members who will be affected by the loss. Let us this time compare Helen's threnody for Hektor from Book 24 (763–72):

"ἦ μέν μοι πόσις ἐστὶν Ἀλέξανδρος θεοειδής,
ὅς μ' ἄγαγε Τροίηνδ'· ὡς πρὶν ὤφελλον ὀλέσθαι.
ἤδη γὰρ νῦν μοι τόδ' ἐεικοστὸν ἔτος ἐστὶν   765

ἐξ οὗ κεῖθεν ἔβην καὶ ἐμῆς ἀπελήλυθα πάτρης·
ἀλλ' οὔ πω σεῦ ἄκουσα κακὸν ἔπος οὐδ' ἀσύφηλον·
ἀλλ' εἴ τίς με καὶ ἄλλος ἐνὶ μεγάροισιν ἐνίπτοι
δαέρων ἢ γαλόων ἢ εἰνατέρων εὐπέπλων,
ἢ ἑκυρή—ἑκυρὸς δὲ πατὴρ ὣς ἤπιος αἰεί—,   770
ἀλλὰ σὺ τὸν ἐπέεσσι παραιφάμενος κατέρυκες,
σῇ τ' ἀγανοφροσύνῃ καὶ σοῖς ἀγανοῖς ἐπέεσσι."

"My husband is Alexandros, like an immortal, who brought me
here to Troy; and I should have died before I came with him;
and here now is the twentieth year upon me since I came   765
from the place where I was, forsaking the land of my fathers. In this time
I have never heard a harsh saying from you, nor an insult.
No, but when another, one of my lord's brothers or sisters, a fair-robed
wife of some brother, would say a harsh word to me in the palace,
or my lord's mother—but his father was gentle always, a father   770
indeed—then you would speak and put them off and restrain them
by your own gentleness of heart and your gentle words."

Here the woman who lacks both a home and a true champion examines
the extraordinary kindness and protection that Hektor afforded her, not-
withstanding her central role in the long war and its manifest destruc-
tion. What remains implicit and immanent—made present via traditional
referentiality—is her vulnerability now that he is gone. Whereas other
mourners use the Narrative element to explore their individual history
and impending future in further depth, describing the disabling conse-
quences of the departed hero's death more explicitly, all of the lamenters
share at minimum a brooding awareness that their own lives are about to
change utterly and irreversibly.

Andromache's proto-lament is no different on this score. Following her
assertion that she no longer has either father or mother, she expands in the
Narrative section on how that came to pass (6.410–28):

"and for me it would be far better   410
to sink into the earth when I have lost you, for there is no other
consolation for me after you have gone to your destiny—
only grief; since I have no father, no honored mother.
It was brilliant Achilleus who slew my father, Eëtion,
when he stormed the strong-founded citadel of the Kilikians,   415
Thebe of the towering gates. He killed Eëtion
but did not strip his armor, for his heart respected the dead man,
but burned the body in all its elaborate war-gear
and piled a grave mound over it, and the nymphs of the mountains,
daughters of Zeus of the aegis, planted elm trees about it.   420
And they who were my seven brothers in the great house all went
upon a single day down into the house of the death god,
for swift-footed brilliant Achilleus slaughtered all of them

as they were tending their white sheep and their lumbering oxen;
and when he had led my mother, who was queen under wooded Plakos,   425
here, along with all his other possessions, Achilleus
released her again, accepting ransom beyond count, but Artemis
of the showering arrows struck her down in the halls of her father."

This is of course the same Achilleus who, though it may presently seem impossible given his withdrawal from battle, will kill her husband, and the lament paradigm underlines the inevitability of that event. As with Helen's description of Hektor's protection, which foregrounds her helplessness now that her protector is no longer living, so Andromache's words make her new powerlessness yet more evident, adding the irony of a common slayer to the fatal danger of losing all family connections and therefore all social status. Here as elsewhere, the Narrative section offers a diachronic, developmental view of a woman's social and familial exile, an unavoidable descent into subjugation that the heroic code always holds in store for the loser's kith and kin. No matter how glorious the struggle, *kleos* belongs to the winners and the dead, and the Narrative element in the lament casts that reality into painful relief.

Within the second section Homer also uses two smaller rhetorical signals to invoke traditional meanings that complement and intensify the presentation. First, another figure of ring-composition underlines Andromache's lack of either a *father* or *mother* (413) and links that loss structurally to the plea she makes to Hektor in the Readdress section that follows. Because she has no living parents, so goes her pitiable petition, he is both *father* and *mother* to her (429), as well as brother and young husband (430). The other signal, which also intensifies the presentation of her grief by recourse to traditional referentiality, we will call "Road not taken." This open-ended and flexible sign—here "for me it would be far better . . ." (ἐμοὶ δέ κε κέρδιον εἴη . . . 410)—consistently identifies an action or event that will not or did not happen, and forecasts something dire as a result.[50] Among the many instances in the *Iliad* and *Odyssey*, three of the more arresting are Achilleus' rueful wish that Briseis had been killed before her forced exchange caused so much woe (*Il.* 19.63), Odysseus' recalling that his men had sensibly tried to persuade him not to seek guest-gifts from Polyphemos (*Od.* 9.228), and Andromache's poignant usage here. For Briseis was not killed, and the trafficking in prizes that involved her led directly to Achilleus' withdrawal and the deaths of many Achaeans. Nor did Odysseus heed his companions' counsel to take a few lambs and cheeses and escape while they could; many of those who urged caution then became victims along that other path their leader chose instead to follow. Likewise, she herself predicts, Andromache will not be spared, not be simply swallowed up by the earth when Hektor falls: her fate, and that of her son, must be the ongoing misery of slavery. In short, the traditional force of the ring-composition and "Road not taken" *sêma* help to reinforce an outcome already made inevitable by the more general implications of the Lament. They are signs that echo the larger sign.

This brings us to the third and final section of Andromache's speech of proto-lament. The traditional song of mourning, in every case a distinct and recognizable speech-act with a rhythm and purpose of its own, always closes with a coda in the form of Readdress / Final intimacy. Through this coda the lamenter reaches out for the last time, trying vainly to bring the loved one back within the compass of living discourse. As in the other parts of the threnody but more poignantly, the special relationship between lamenter and fallen hero reemerges to individualize the Readdress, as once again the indexical power of the *sêma* harmonizes with the singularity of the particular situation. For example, Hekabe's is unmistakably a mother's intimacy as she pitifully admires her dead son's lifelike appearance (24.757–59):

"νῦν δέ μοι ἑρσήεις καὶ πρόσφατος ἐν μεγάροισι
κεῖσαι, τῷ ἴκελος ὅν τ' ἀργυρότοξος Ἀπόλλων
οἷς ἀγανοῖσι βέλεσσιν ἐποιχόμενος κατέπεφνεν."

"Now you lie in the palace, handsome
and fresh with dew, in the likeness of one whom he of the silver
bow, Apollo, has attacked and killed with his gentle arrows."

With equal appropriateness, Andromache closes her immediately preceding lament with what can only be a wife's complaint—namely, that Hektor did not meet his end beside her in bed, that he did not leave her some "intimate word"[51] as a verbal keepsake (24.740–45):

"τῷ καί μιν λαοὶ μὲν ὀδύρονται κατὰ ἄστυ,   740
ἀρητὸν δὲ τοκεῦσι γόον καὶ πένθος ἔθηκας,
Ἕκτορ· ἐμοὶ δὲ μάλιστα λελείψεται ἄλγεα λυγρά.
οὐ γάρ μοι θνῄσκων λεχέων ἐκ χεῖρας ὄρεξας,
οὐδέ τί μοι εἶπες πυκινὸν ἔπος, οὗ τέ κεν αἰεὶ
μεμνῄμην νύκτας τε καὶ ἤματα δάκρυ χέουσα."   745

"Therefore your people are grieving for you all through their city,   740
Hektor, and you left for your parents mourning and sorrow
beyond words, but for me passing all others is left the bitterness
and the pain, for you did not die in bed, and stretch your arms to me,
nor tell me some last intimate word that I could remember
always, all the nights and days of my weeping for you."   745

These women's songs have the capacity to move and to begin to heal, a capacity that depends upon both their personal perspectives on an individual's death and their common invocation of a traditional speech-act. We must read both behind and between the signs.

Just so with Andromache's lament in Book 6. We observed that she opens the Readdress by emphasizing the unique relationship she shared with a husband who in the absence of her own parents has also been father and mother to her. This citation of special kinship not only echoes the history of her parents' death at Achilleus' hands in the Narrative section just preceding; as noted above, it also completes a typical Homeric pattern of ring-composition (413/429–30). Her plea for pity, which closes another ring with the Address section (407–8/431–32), is conveyed with all of the special referential force of the Lament's third section, and set off by the extremely common "But come" signal, which conventionally marks a rhetorical fulcrum followed by a command.[52] Here, at precisely that stage of the speech-act where tradition calls for the woman's final intimacy to her loved one, her brave but futile attempt to connect him to the living world, Andromache makes an extraordinary plea for Hektor not to rejoin the battle that must soon claim his life, effectively dooming her and their son to a living death of slavery. The final few lines of her speech (433–39), effectively not part of the *sêma* of Lament, simply ground that hopeless plea in the matter-of-fact details of the present situation: she suggests how the troops might best be deployed in his absence. That advice, like her larger petition, falls on deaf ears.

The meshing of traditional form with singular content in Andromache's first lament adds texture and depth to an already remarkable scene. Because Andromache enters into the speech-act and ritual of mourning, in one important sense her husband is as good as dead. Yet within that lament, and harnessing the rhetorical impetus of the *sêma*, she pleads with him to avoid the death she is already mourning. Her words—and her "word"—are thus both powerful and vain, making for an irresolvable contradiction in terms: she seeks to save Hektor by singing his mourning-song.

Andromache's speech thus represents a dirge for the living, a hymn for the husband she mourns as dead though he stands before her. The traditional sign effectively dissolves the distance and contingency between Hektor alive and Hektor perished, and makes ever more real the consequences for her and their son, consequences that are now as certain as the unmitigated fact of her prior losses. Andromache uses the highly evocative lament form to telescope events, to weave her past and future into a present fabric that she unrolls before Hektor and presents for his judgment. This verbal artifact is certainly a heartfelt plea for him to forgo battle, to stay with her, to go on living; but ironically its very form predicts that her words, so vital and effectual in the world of *oikos* (homestead) she inhabits, will prove tragically empty in his world of *kleos*.

Just how much distance separates their two worlds, which overlap for only a brief moment in Book 6, becomes graphically apparent in the speeches that ensue and in Hektor's return to the battlefield. Their parting amounts to a disattachment, a gender-based separation of duties, as the hero must leave his community behind in order to defend it. Father's and mother's perspectives diverge correspondingly, as Hektor prays to Zeus that his son may know the glory of killing and the bloody spoils that—so goes the heroic consensus—will warm his mother's heart. The harsh incongruity of these aspirations with Andromache's sad petition illustrates how mutually unintelligible are the languages they speak, even when they are speaking directly to one another. Hektor goes on to acknowledge his wife's unavoidable destiny as a Greek slave but hopes himself to be dead and unaware of her tribulations by the time that happens. To her desperate plea for him to remain he responds agonistically by calling her "Strange one" (*daimoniê*, 486), the same traditional signal for verbal contest that began her lament, and by admonishing her that death comes sooner or later to every man, hero or coward. Having issued this fatalistic premise, a useless and impertinent rationalization within the *oikos*, the defender of Troy then proceeds to order Andromache back to "the loom and the distaff," ending their conversation by prying their worlds apart, by reinvoking the separateness and symbiotic tension of two disparate value systems. And with that he marches off—shining Hektor with the horsehair-plumed helmet—back to the glory and the death of battle, while all his wife can do is to join the other Trojan women in continuing his dirge (6.497–502):

αἶψα δ' ἔπειθ' ἵκανε δόμους εὖ ναιετάοντας
"Εκτορος ἀνδροφόνοιο, κιχήσατο δ' ἔνδοθι πολλὰς
ἀμφιπόλους, τῇσιν δὲ γόον πάσῃσιν ἐνῶρσεν.
αἱ μὲν ἔτι ζωὸν γόον "Εκτορα ᾧ ἐνὶ οἴκῳ·   500
οὐ γάρ μιν ἔτ' ἔφαντο ὑπότροπον ἐκ πολέμοιο
ἵξεσθαι, προφυγόντα μένος καὶ χεῖρας Ἀχαιῶν.

And as she came in speed into the well-settled household
of Hektor the slayer of men, she found numbers of handmaidens
within, and her coming stirred all of them into lamentation.
So they mourned in his house over Hektor while he was living   500
still, for they thought he would never again come back from the fighting
alive, escaping the Achaean hands and their violence.

This is the present and future reality encoded in Andromache's first lament.

Coda

Both of these *sêmata*, then, the Feast and the Lament, offer us a brief tutorial on how to read behind and between the signs. By projecting the set of associations that each typical scene naturally carries with it idiomatically, the Homeric poems invoke traditional referentiality and mesh instance with implication. When a Feast happens, we may be sure that some sort of mediation is in the offing. Indeed, for this very reason perversions of the dining ritual strike the listener or reader with heightened impact—the traditional contract is voided and expectation is keyed only to be dashed. Likewise, we need not wonder long over the narrative logic for Andromache's preemptive lament for Hektor; as far as she is concerned, Homer and the tradition are saying, her infant son's father is as good as dead. But in neither case does the sign-language of typical scenes become a simplistic process. Each instance of Feast or Lament presents a manifestly different profile from all of its counterparts: the players change, as do the framing issues, the site, and numerous other between-the-signs details. Alongside such variation, however, the implications of the speech-act remain in force. Typical scenes offer a referential advantage; they are another way in which oral tradition works like language, only more so.[53]

In the following chapter we will be extending the principles illustrated above for the story-pattern and the typical scene to a third level of "word" or speech-act—the traditional phrase. In concert with the larger patterns, these smallest of *sêmata* promote an experience of the *Iliad* and *Odyssey* that balances the situation-specific with the global, the unique instance with its expectable implications. By supporting composition and driving reception, all of these signs enrich Homer's traditional art.

7

WORD, IDIOM, SPEECH-ACT
The Traditional Phrase as *Sêma*

words are not lacking in words,
tales in the telling don't fail
—*Kalevala* 21: 371–72

In this chapter we will be concerned with the smallest-scale Homeric *sêmata*, those "words" or speech-acts much more limited in size and structure than the typical scenes and story-pattern examined in earlier chapters. To be specific, these phrases range from part of a single hexameter verse to one or more entire verses. Most often the increment in question is an "atom" of phraseology, a "word" in the same sense meant by the South Slavic *guslari*: a unit of utterance. Such signs rarely coincide with the words that populate lexicons, enshrined in lists of freestanding items; or with our familiar model of a word in a written or printed text, so tidily delimited by white spaces on either side. Nor do they often coincide with what linguists call morphemes, segments marked off by minimal function and meaning. In fact, Homer's smallest units of meaning (one common definition of morphemes) very frequently turn out to be *phrases*, and to attempt to reduce them beyond that irreducible form is to cancel their idiomatic function and fracture their meaning. It is to read the wrong language.

With this notion of "word" in mind, we will be asking how such traditional phrases participate in the overall ecology of the Homeric register. Since Milman Parry's work and earlier as well, much attention has been directed toward the traditional structure of the diction;[1] as a result, we know that certain rules inform the specialized poetic language, and we are able to "parse" the hexameter lines of the *Iliad* and *Odyssey* and learn about their logical parts and compositional basis. Once aware of the complex dynamics of the meter and its interaction with phraseology, we can grasp the basic tectonics of Homeric verse-making.

But the same level of scholarly energy has so far not translated to the study of what the phrases actually mean on their own terms, and for a simple reason. In presuming that the basic cognitive units of Homeric language are always and everywhere the same as ours, we have made a fundamental mistake. We have asserted tacitly and without reflection that the language of the *aoidos* works precisely like ours. What I will be advocating in this chapter, in contrast, is that we must admit at least the possibility that Homer is speaking according to a somewhat different set of expressive assumptions. At times those assumptions happen to mirror the strategies we unconsciously use in our dealings with texts, and no stark misreading results. In such cases the registers happen to match, at least roughly, and thus call no attention to their differences. But not seldom the two sets of rules diverge enough to lead the unsuspecting modern reader down the wrong path, simply because an unexamined conviction about cognitive units has that reader "speaking" the wrong language.

This line of argument is no more than an extension of the *sêma* principle to the diction, the root principle developed in the first chapter of this volume and then applied to the legendary singer (Chapter 2), the story-pattern (Chapter 5), and the typical scene (Chapter 6). For example, by analogy to the legendary *guslar* in South Slavic epic we maintained that Homer is more an anthropomorphization than an *anthrôpos*, more a sign standing for the poetic tradition than a "real" singer. We also discovered how textual parallax has conditioned readers—not to mention many succeeding generations of epic poets—to think of the *Odyssey* as beginning "in the middle of things" (*in medias res*), with its most basic chronology turned inside out. But the tale of Odysseus needs no chronological straightening out. The *nostos* story-pattern actively and positively supports the order of the story as it stands, complete with flashback; indeed, to portray the hero's return in any other way would be to violate the rules of the register and destroy the idiomatic meaning of the *sêma*. The same is true, to recall another of our examples, of the Lament scene. Andromache's plea to Hektor in *Iliad* 6 to forgo battle and its terrible human price is powerful from any perspective, but it gains the special force of traditional referentiality once we realize she is speaking through the *sêma* of Lament to convey her message, namely that Hektor is as good as dead. We read the *Iliad* and *Odyssey* best when we recognize their cognitive structure and implications at all levels, when we read behind as well as between the signs.

Our present emphasis on the smallest of *sêmata* thus amounts to another application of the homemade proverb that "oral tradition works like language, only more so." In fact, here we can be quite explicit about the "only more so" dimension of the proverb. Within the traditional register an enhancement of words to "words" is the rule, as the signifying power of the smaller items that populate lexicons is amplified beyond their usual capacity. Instead of depending primarily on the meanings we unearth with dictionaries and other tools in the usual scholarly kit, these larger "words" can evoke associations that are nowhere to be found in the literal denotation of the smaller words that make them up. We will see, for example, that "green fear" (*chlôron deos*) designates something more than and markedly different from its component parts: green fear in Homer is the unhinging, helpless terror that can be inspired only supernaturally. It has nothing directly to do with the color green, and everything to do with idiomatic association. But while the signal is clear and unambiguous for those who are fluent in the register, it cannot work if the audience or reader is unaware of its special idiomatic force. Without a sense of the traditional sign—of the divine or otherwise supernatural agency at the root of *chlôron deos*— we are thrown back upon such handsome but inadequate metaphors as "pale fear," a rendering that does not actually falsify Homer's art but certainly sells it short. Within the epic diction there is much more to this particular phrase than that. Just as with the Return pattern or the typical scene of Lament, there is something additional going on, something crucial to the poetics of Homeric verbal art. To put it simply, the "more so" amounts to traditional referentiality.

Procedure

In discussing the Homeric phrase as a traditional sign, we will be proceeding in a manner suited to this level of structure and implication. After a brief discussion of what we can expect in the area of traditional phraseology, the body of the chapter will present a series of contextual analyses of about a dozen phrases and groups of phrases, selected for both their individual variety and their collective illustration of the spectrum of ways in which such *sêmata* imply the poetic tradition. We will thus have reason to consider signs as complex in their systemic networking as the celebrated noun-epithet phrase, as homely and workaday as the speech introduction, as widely applicable as rhetorical transitions, and as flexible in their morphology as the language associated with sleep.

During individual analyses and rereading, an occasional analogy to South Slavic oral epic will be made to provide a comparative perspective. But such parallels will remain largely in the background, since our chief goal here is to decipher Homer's own code and since the available textual sample is adequate for many analyses.[2] Indeed, the twenty-eight thousand lines of ancient Greek epic give us ample opportunity to investigate multiple instances of many signs. In parallel with procedures used in earlier chapters, we can collate the various occurrences and decide whether or to what extent traditional referentiality is involved, whether or to what extent the instances are as indexical as Odysseus' well-aimed bow-shot through the axes. Of course, the Homeric corpus also has limits, and there will always be cases in which even the most assiduous analysis falls short due to the paucity of available material. But let us concentrate not on (the myth of) a "complete" reading, but on making what incremental gains we can while at the same time developing the *sêma* principle at the level of phraseology. If the theory and method are successful in unlocking some of Homer's traditional implications, later work can easily extend them further into the phraseology as well as other aspects of the epic register. For the moment we are concerned primarily with opening a new perspective, with learning how the epic diction works like a language, only more so.

A Traditional Morphology of Phrases

Before embarking on the actual hunt, it is wise to have a solid idea of our quarry. And here we must keep in mind the idea of the *traditional morphology*, or structural profile, of the speech-acts at other levels in the Homeric register. Let us begin by remembering that oral traditional registers in general, and Homer's in particular, are first and foremost languages rather than collections of items or things. Just as the story-pattern and typical scenes we examined over the preceding two chapters take shape from a traditional morphology, so do the *sêmata* that make up the diction. Just as the larger units of utterance vary within limits, so do traditional phrases.

Most basically, and this is an aspect of language too often overlooked in studies of oral and oral-connected traditions, phrases are the products of ongoing processes. Such bytes of diction, no matter how uniform or multiform they may be, are not merely "things in themselves," stored like tangible inventory in the warehouse of a singer's mind and ready for delivery as needed. As earlier investigations have established, we can best understand the recurrent diction characteristic of Homer and many other poetries by realizing that the phrases are part of a language and thus derive from an ordered set of *traditional rules*.[3] Like the laws that govern other kinds of processes, these rules set boundaries on the shape and variability of the products whose making they oversee. Just as a subject requires a verb to constitute a sentence or a preposition requires an object to complete a phrase, so traditional rules put their stamp on the particular brand of phraseology used for the composition and reception of epic, or whatever genre one is considering.[4] It is because of their influence that the register assumes and maintains a recognizable form and a typical range of variation. In short, traditional rules govern the making and morphology of signs.

For this reason it is essential that we preface our search for *sêmata* and their meaning with an elementary but far-reaching stipulation: namely, that the most fundamental of all phraseological signs is not any single phrase but rather Homer's "way of speaking" as a whole. That is, there is a simple, very powerful signal resident in each and every line of the *Iliad*, the *Odyssey*, and the Homeric Hymns—a recurrent cue that the poet is following traditional rules for composition—and it performs a crucial service. This signal alerts and continues to remind the audience or reader of the register, performance arena, and communicative economy associated with Homeric epic. It sets and maintains the channel, keeping the referential resources of the poetic tradition alive and accessible. We hear this broad and generalized *sêma* in the characteristic pattern of long and short syllables, the dependable word-breaks at particular positions in the verse, the preferred placements for words (and "words") of given metrical lengths and textures, and so on.[5] Other traditions may use other cues, perhaps not all of them verbal, to accomplish the same purpose of creating the performance arena and setting the channel. The South Slavic *guslar* often marks the exchange to come with an instrumental prelude to his epic performance, the Rajasthani *bhopa* has his assistant point to a particular panel on the *par* or blanket that visually documents their Pabuji tradition, and the erstwhile performers of the Finnish *Kalevala* locked arms in preparation for their cooperative performance of a story.[6] As we have seen throughout this volume, it is not the signal itself but its signification that matters, not the sign per se but what lies behind it.

In what follows, then, we will be focusing on the often poignant phrases, the *sêmata*, that emerge in prominent fashion from the diction as a whole. But in doing so we should not forget the critically important background provided by traditional rules. Without that background, without the continuous signal identifying and reidentifying the medium and the rules for the transaction of epic poetry, even the most dramatic of phraseological flourishes would lack the ready context they need in order to be meaningful. The first and most fundamental phraseological *sêma* is Homeric diction as a whole.

These observations have important bearing on what constitutes a traditional sign at the level of the individual phrase. In the simplest case, the sign takes the form of a single "word" such as "green fear" (*chlôron deos*), "looking darkly" (*hupodra idôn*), or the "silently to silence" line.[7] No flexibility or alternate form exists, so the implications associated with such signs can be evoked only via these exact indexes, which appear in combination with any other diction licensed by traditional rules. In such cases the *sêma* is obviously restricted to a single shape; its morphology is narrow. But in other cases the sign may take a number of forms, constituting a broad morphology. Grammatical inflection to accommodate different syntactical functions is one source of variety. Very often such changes entail corresponding changes in the metrical pattern of the phrase, as when "discreet Penelope" occurs in the nominative (*echephrôn Pênelopeia*) versus the accusative (*echephrona Pênelopeian*). If, as in this example, the hexameter can accommodate the variability within its own flexible structure, the same phrase may occupy the same position in the line even though its shape and extent may vary from one case to another. More frequently, however, grammatical inflection leads to different word-placement, an alternate noun-epithet formula, or occurrence of the noun without any epithet.[8]

One way to understand this morphology is to observe that in certain cases the Homeric language offers not one but many routes to the same destination. Some *sêmata* have only a single shape, but others are more variable—within limits, of course. Many of the noun-epithet formulas sort themselves out by metrical type. Naming Odysseus in the nominative case, for example, is normally accomplished with the epithets *dios* ("divine"), *polumêtis* ("of many counsels"), *polutlas* ("much-suffering"), or *diogenês* ("Zeus-born"), depending not on the immediate narrative context but on the metrical situation. Should the poet wish to name him in the genitive case, he can turn to the epithets *talasiphronos* ("stouthearted") or *theioio* ("godlike"), again depending on the metrical context. Long ago Milman Parry demonstrated that such systems of diction demonstrated a collective thrift, with usually only a single solution for each compositional problem.[9] At the level of the sign itself—not, I emphasize, at the level of its meaning—such phrases work in clear symbiosis with the requirements of the hexameter. Their traditional morphology reflects that symbiosis.

Consider a grammatical analogy. In many languages, especially Indo-European tongues, the words we locate in a dictionary are regularly inflected to serve a variety of needs. Thus the ancient Greek *agros* ("field") in the nominative case can serve as a subject or predicate noun, while its genitive case, *agrou*, varies within limits to yield, for example, the meaning "of the field." If someone is plowing the field, the grammatical repertoire can specify a direct-object function with the accusative case, *agron*. Rules for these kinds of transformations are of course predictable because they are systematic; every speaker who uses the grammatical system observes them in order to achieve and maintain intelligibility, and every successful listener or reader redeploys them in agreement with the code shared by speaker and audience. The resulting repertoire of forms, all of them alternate pathways that allow "field" to play many different roles in discourse, makes up a grammatical morphology. Analogously, a *traditional morphology* amounts to the group of "inflections" that make it possible for a traditional sign to serve a variety of metrical functions while conveying the "word's" traditional implications.

Because traditional morphologies vary, because "words" are "inflected" differently, Homer's signs exhibit wide variation. As we shall see below with the *sêma* for sleep, multiple pathways can include not only a network of metrically alternate forms but also "words" formulaically or even lexically unrelated to one another. That is, the poet can signal sleep's binary implications of release and vulnerability via a collection of different noun-epithet formulas, by an unmodified noun ("all-conqueror"), or simply by the word "sleep" (*hupnos*). Despite their apparent diversity, all of these signs point in the same direction: toward traditional referentiality. Together they constitute a traditional morphology considerably more varied than that of "discreet Penelope" or even of the whole repertoire of ways of naming Odysseus. Nonetheless, our analysis will show that the "sleep" signal still invokes the same set of associations in all of its superficially disparate forms.

We should underscore that this last kind and extent of variation goes well beyond what was predicted by the initial version of Parry-Lord theory or by subsequent studies, which have advocated a much narrower view of the morphology of traditional diction.[10] The reason for this discrepancy is clear enough. In concentrating on the sign per se rather than its signification, these earlier investigations focused almost exclusively on the structural utility of the Homeric language. From seeking genetically linked phraseology it is but one step to diminishing or dismissing the possibility that apparently unrelated phrases could cooperate in serving the same poetic purpose. In emphasizing the nature of the Homeric register as a language, I choose instead to invert the process of investigation, first collating the various signs, then mapping their significance, and finally deciding empirically whether they constitute an expressive system. Traditional referentiality thus becomes the touchstone; structure as such follows in its wake. As our proverb puts it, *artis causa* supersedes *metri causa*. In this way we give the diction of the *Iliad* and *Odyssey* full credit for being a language, shared fluently by a poet and his listeners and readers, and, not incidentally, we also avoid the pitfalls of imposing our own frame of reference about how the traditional morphology works.[11]

In what follows, then, I consider the traditional implications of some example phrases from the Homeric epics, with a view toward ascertaining their *poetic* usefulness.

Traditional Phrases and Their Implications

1. Dramatis personae: Noun-epithet formulas for characters. I begin with the category of phrases that served as the site for Milman Parry's initial work on formulaic structure, and that have occasioned much discussion ever since.[12] In simplest terms, the argument has always hinged on the poetic value of these oft-repeated bytes of diction. Are they merely, as Parry contended, metrical solutions to emerging problems of composition in performance, bearing no meaning other than the "essential idea" of the god, human being, or thing they name? According to this view, "swift-footed Achilleus" means only "Achilleus," and "white-armed Hera" only "Hera"; the epithets have no poetic resonance because "Homer had inherited from his predecessors a language whose several elements were used solely in accordance with the needs of composition in hexameters."[13] Parry's theory further provided for *particularized* epithets that belonged to only a single character and *ornamental* epithets that were shared by metrically equivalent characters. But the origin and continuing basis of his explanation was his conception of hexameter phraseology as a prefabricated solution to the challenge of composing hexameter verse in oral performance.[14] Individual noun-epithet formulas were selected not for their poetic appropriateness, either in a given instance or more widely, but for their metrical appropriateness.

On the other side of the argument have stood those who felt that this model entailed too mechanical a process, that Homeric epic had to be much more than a clever fitting together of ready-made parts. It should be emphasized that what most enervated Parry's critics was not his careful demonstration of the system of Homeric noun-epithet formulae, a masterpiece of philological analysis, but rather the assumptions that he went on to derive from its existence. Because the system of diction revealed a large degree of thrift, with only a single solution for most compositional problems, Parry assumed that all elements of Homeric language were predetermined. Since they were predetermined and selected only by meter, then any poetic effect seemed impossible—at least the kind of poetic effect based on the original genius of individual authors and the play of intertextuality that the modern age has come to cherish. If the poet has no choice, no way to tune the lockstep idiom to his own sensibility or to the particular demands of a given narrative situation, then how can we talk about great art?

Much to their credit, many Homeric scholars just could not abide the notion of a Homer who merely got the hexameter job done. These cornerstones of Western literature must, they reasoned, have derived from a compositional method richer and more complex than that described by Parry, Lord, and their followers. Thus arose, for example, the idea that Homer must have been so much the master of his inherited language that he could escape its limitations, supersede its tectonic function, and use it as a poetic instrument in a modern, individualistic fashion. Commentaries are filled with instances in which the bard is credited with a masterful choice of epithet particularly suitable to the immediate situation, while relatively little mention is made of those legions of occurrences in which no such local pertinence can be detected. For decades, then, a chasm has separated Parry's undeniable demonstration of Homeric formulaic structure and literary critics' eminently reasonable demand that we find a way to restore what they see as Homer's lost art.

A crucial cognitive error mars both of these formulations, a crippling mistake that stems ultimately from both sides' failure to recognize the difference between a word and a "word," between an entry in a lexicon and what the South Slavic singers call a *reč*.[15] As I have maintained throughout this volume, there need be no contradiction between traditional structure and poetic art at any level; in fact, a special harmony and an inimitable gain often result from their natural meshing. As shown for the larger *reči* of typical scene and story-pattern, traditional structure projects its own kind of referentiality, its own kind of context for each local situation. The key lies in grasping the role of the signs—in reading both behind and between them—and in the process bringing into play the ambient epic tradition to which the Homeric register institutionally refers. To put it in the terms we have been employing in earlier chapters, Parry's noun-epithet formulas are *sêmata*, speech-acts with idiomatic implications. They are systematized and metrically defined, to be sure, but they are also indexical. They are concrete parts that stand for abstract wholes, "words" that imply large, often complex ideas. They help to support an oral-derived tradition that works like language, only more so.[16] Here is a spectrum of examples.

1a. *Podas ôkus Achilleus* ("swift-footed Achilleus")

Achilleus the swift-footed sulked in his tent;
Makes you wonder where all his fleetfootedness went.
(Elizabeth Foley)

No one would dispute the physical prowess of the hero so frequently stipulated as the "best of the Achaeans." He proves superior to his comrades and enemies in all aspects of battle; indeed, even the sight of his armor is enough to frighten the Trojan adversaries into retreat. But although Achilleus' fleetness of foot is a general and characteristic element of his mythic identity in epic, it is not often germane to the immediate situation. For example, his encouragement of the priest Kalkhas to tell the truth about Apollo's anger is introduced with a hexameter verse ending in *podas ôkus Achilleus* (*Il.* 1.84), as is his response to Odysseus' plea to end his withdrawal and rejoin the Greek effort against Troy (9.307). The former speech is delivered in assembly and the latter in his tent, both of them settings that depend on stasis rather than movement, so Achilleus' swift-footedness has no immediate pertinence in either case. To be sure, there are instances when citation of this aspect of his physical excellence may seem more appropriate to the business at hand, as when the great hero refuses Hektor's call for honorable treatment of the loser's remains just after their protracted chase around the walls of Troy (22.260). But such apparent examples of better "fit" are much in the minority, and are as we shall see mere accidents of a naming scheme that idiomatically complements rather than uniquely matches local action.

To put it telegraphically, "swift-footed Achilleus" is traditional epic code for the mythic entirety of the Achaean hero. It is an index for his character, a nominal part that stands by prior agreement for the whole of his personality. As a traditional "word," it obeys the metrical strictures uncovered by Parry, behaving as part of the noun-epithet system and cooperating with other ways to name Achilleus. But it conveys much more than an "essential idea," serving as much more than simply a compositionally convenient way to say "Achilleus." It summons the larger traditional identity of the best of the Achaeans, using a telltale detail to project the complexity of a character with a resonant and singular history in the epic tradition.[17] For the same reason that Hermes can meaningfully be called "mighty slayer of Argos" on the day of his birth, long before he ever encounters (never mind challenges) Argos,[18] Achilleus can always meaningfully be called "swift-footed"—even when seated in his tent. Both phrases are *sêmata*, signs we are asked to read behind.

Before passing on to the second of our examples of noun-epithet formulas, let us spend a moment on metrical thrift, an issue that bears on the naming of Achilleus and so many other characters in the Homeric epics. In Parry's view, thrift was proof of the traditional and oral nature of the *Iliad* and *Odyssey*, a feature indicating that the poet was relying exclusively on a tiered system of alternatives to compose his hexameter verses.[19] Having only one solution for each metrical situation, Parry reasoned, made composition in performance easier and more fluent. But later research has established two important counterindications. First, thrift seems to be a feature not of the specialized Homeric language in general, but of the noun-epithet formulas in particular, and even within that limited category of diction there are exceptions to be found.[20] Second, thrift turns out to be a feature not of oral traditional verse across the comparative spectrum, but of ancient Greek epic poetry specifically.[21] What thrift exists, then, must be understood as a characteristic of one category of diction within this particular register rather than as some wider diagnostic feature typifying all categories of diction, much less all traditional oral registers. But there are further implications as well. Even more important, we should be wary of reducing the poetic impact of all formulaic diction across the comparative spectrum on the basis of a characteristic limited to a single category of phraseology within a single poetic tradition. Thrift is a formal feature of *some* Homeric signs; it does not, I emphasize, speak *in any way* to their signification. The limited phenomenon of thrift has nothing to do with idiomatic meaning.

1b. *Amumôn*—"blameless" or not? The issues of word versus "word" and of thrift of sign versus thrift of signification also arise in the study of many other noun-epithet formulas. One celebrated example is the uncertainty over the meaning of *amumôn* in Homer, most obviously in its application to Aigisthos, lover of Klytemnestra and her co-conspirator in the murder of Agamemnon upon the Greek leader's return from the Trojan war.[22] On this account, at least, few would credit Aigisthos with being altogether "blameless," the usual definition of the adjective. What is more, even the poetic tradition seems to agree on the highly questionable nature of his overall character: of Aigisthos' three other epithets, two are hardly flattering—*analkidos* ("cowardly, unvaliant") and *dolomêtis/-n* ("cunning or crafty in counsel")—and the third is at best neutral—*Thuestiadês* ("son of Thyestes").[23] When one adds Zeus' criticism that Klytemnestra's lover acted "beyond measure" (*huper moron*, *Od.* 1.35), as well as the structural reality that the family dynamics surrounding Agamemnon are constantly counterposed to Odysseus' situation throughout the *Odyssey*,[24] the verdict seems irrefutable. Aigisthos is the furthest thing from blameless, and the application of the epithet at line 29 of the first book requires some explanation.

One proposal for solving this problem came from Anne Amory Parry (1973), who reviewed all instances of *amumôn* in the epics and argued against the widely accepted etymological reading from *mumar* that yields "blameless." Instead she suggested the meaning, accepted by the Oxford *Odyssey* commentary, of "beautiful, handsome" that evolves to "excellent, expert."[25] Since these alternate meanings are highly generalized and imposed empirically on the basis of actual occurrences, they do seem to fit. Indeed, they cannot fail: the variety of characters and peoples to whom *amumôn* is applied can all be understood as meriting the non-specific praise that the retooled definition confers, one way or another, perhaps even Aigisthos. Achilleus, Alkinoos, Glaukos, Patroklos, Menelaos, and the Phaeacians as a group are but a few of those so honored. This strategy of redefinition, of seeking to explain a contextually troublesome epithet by shifting attention away from the fact of its etymology and toward an expanded range of individual usages in the epics, is a familiar one in Homeric studies.[26] We will see another example of the same strategy in the following section on the epithet *dios*.

But does this strategy really work? Is it logically defensible and are its results truly illuminating? At a minimum, forsaking an accepted etymological meaning for a contextually based potpourri of more generalized meanings presents a dangerous opportunity for circular reasoning, and not all scholars have agreed with Amory Parry's procedures and results.[27] When we add to this procedural problem the special challenge associated with the difference between words and "words" in Homer, our doubts must increase. The reason is straightforward enough. If we focus on the epic register on its own terms, then the smallest meaningful unit in a noun-epithet phrase is neither the noun nor the epithet but their combination— neither one part nor the other but the phrase as a whole. That indivisible *sêma*, rather than the sense(s) that modern textual scholars unearth by concentrating on the individual morphemes that make it up, is what matters for both the composition and the reception of the poetry. To settle on any other unit as the bearer of traditional meaning is to misperceive the expressive rules of the traditional medium and ultimately to deny Homer's art.

Adjusting our perspective to avoid modern textual parallax, then, let us consider how this larger "word" functions in the Homeric register. First is the group of estimable figures named by *amumonos* (the genitive singular form) and exactly filling the second half of the hexameter line.[28] Joining Aigisthos in this category are Nestor's son Antilochos, the Phaeacian king Alkinoos, Aphrodite's lover and Aineias' father Anchises, Achilleus (called *Aiakidao*, descendant of Aiakos), and Demeter's first priest Eumolpos.[29] These characters all play prominent enough roles in the myths implied by and excerpted in the *Iliad*, *Odyssey*, and *Hymns*, but they are prominent for a host of different reasons. Antilochos performed heroically at Troy and learned a lesson in the chariot-race competition against Menelaos during the funeral games for Patroklos; later Memnon, son of the dawn goddess, cut him down. Alkinoos ruled graciously over the Phaeacians and provided transport to Ithaka for Odysseus. Anchises was the mortal beguiled by Aphrodite and father to one of the greatest of Trojan warriors. Achilleus, far too complex to be a universally admirable figure, nonetheless had no real peers by any purely heroic measure. Eumolpos ("beautiful singer") was the initial hierophant at Eleusis.[30] No single quality runs through the entire group; no one characteristic makes them all "blameless."

But what they do share is a traditional encoding. Each of them is named via a speech-act that provides an approved pathway to their individual characters—not by identification of a crucial shared quality but rather by idiomatic citation within the traditional way of speaking. They are named and understood according to the rules of the register because they are indexed according to those rules. *Amumonos Antilochoio, amumonos Alkinooio,* and even *amumonos Aigisthoio* are all "words," *sêmata* that point not to a single "blameless" or "excellent" behavior but to the various figures they idiomatically designate. In an important sense, the lexical force of *amumonos* is muted in any individual context, as the logic of the components gives way to the logic of the whole expression, as the "word"-parts give way to the entire "word." Aigisthos may well be considered to have been blameless at an earlier stage in his life; the sad reality that he was the bastard son of Pelopia, incestuously fathered by Thyestes, was after all not his fault. But that history is not the core issue here—nor would it be in any other particular situation, for that matter. The noun-epithet phrase is effective not because of his helplessness before the curse of the House of Atreus but because it has apparently become one of the traditional pathways to his most economical characterization.[31] To imply Aigisthos or Antilochos or Alkinoos in all of their complexity (and even their contradiction), Homer uses this traditional sign.

1c. The quality of *dios.* The simple epithet *dios* has occasioned much discussion among lexicographers and commentators. Cunliffe (1963) provides a spectrum of contextual applications, from "of Zeus" to "bright, shining" (when modifying the sea, rivers, etc.); "resplendent, glorious" (of goddesses); "noble, illustrious" (of men) or "noble, queenly" (of women); "well-bred" (of horses); and "famed, rich" (of cities).[32] The Liddell-Scott-Jones lexicon (1968) reflects a similar range of meanings and cites a Sanskrit cognate *div-yá* ("heavenly"). Speaking of this and other ornamental epithets, the Oxford *Odyssey* commentary observes that "the precise (or original) sense of *epitheta ornantia* is not easily determined, since their use by definition is independent of context" (Heubeck, West, and Hainsworth 1988: 256). Nonetheless, it offers three distinct senses: "of Zeus," "illustrious or noble," and "bright."[33] In short, the usage of *dios* cannot be taken as literally as its etymology from Zeus, and so scholars have devised a series of definitions to explain what seems to be its quite diverse deployment in the *Iliad* and *Odyssey*. Since the epithet cannot be forced into a uniform sense that solves all its appearances, they have settled for multiple meanings that match those occurrences empirically. This is a familiar strategy.

But what if *dios*, like *amumôn* and so many other epithets, were not simply a word but *part* of a Homeric "word"? What if it were not in such cases an element complete in itself but rather an integral part of a larger sign or *sêma*? If that were the case, then *dios* itself would have little or no significative status in the Homeric register (within this formula at least), no more individual status than any single phoneme would have in one of our lexicon-based words. As the Oxford *Odyssey* commentary explicitly notes, such ornamental epithets are always independent of any single context. More fundamentally, as our studies of traditional signs have shown throughout, the very first critical act must be to determine what the "word" actually is—in terms of the traditional register and not of some extraneous variety of language that happens to be more familiar to us and whose cognitive categories we customarily assume without reflection. In wrestling with the role of *dios* in Homer, then, we must start by inquiring into the phrases it helps to constitute.

One very common type is the group of phrases that always occur in the nominative case at the end of the hexameter line, occupying the last two feet or final colon, a primary site for such signs.[34] The most frequent of this group is *dios Odusseus*, which occurs 106 times over the two epics, with *dios Achilleus* the next most frequent at 55 occurrences. Each of these combinations fills an important metrical segment of the line and cannot be meaningfully subdivided: "divine" or "illustrious" does not stand by itself, but as a part of the code used to name and index these two characters.[35] Although it is not limited in its application to one specific figure like "swift-footed" (for Achilleus only) or "much-suffering" (for Odysseus only), *dios* nonetheless forms part of a unit of utterance, a speech-act, a traditional sign.

Of the other characters named with the *dios* sign,[36] only one appears more than a very few times: the decidedly undivine swineherd Eumaios, who is accorded this epithet no fewer than thirteen times.[37] And while we may choose to impute to Odysseus' faithful employee a nobility of character based on his hospitality, allegiance, and willingness to join the fray, he cannot qualify as *dios* on the basis of his prior achievement in heroic combat. Depending on how much of his autobiography we are prepared to credit as truth, we may or may not choose to grant him the royal lineage he claims,[38] but, whatever the case, we will need to recognize that his adult life has been spent in servitude rather than princely pursuits. For most of his days he has been a *huphorbos*, a keeper of pigs. Nevertheless, he is called *dios*—specifically, *dios huphorbos*—with greater regularity than anyone other than Odysseus or Achilleus, focal characters who spend much more time center stage in their respective epics than he does. This curious fact requires some explanation.

To emphasize the relative inactivity of the epithet and the integrity of the whole phrase as the smallest unit of utterance, I will resist actually translating *dios*. Let us rather think of a larger sign or "word"—*dios* X—where X can be one of a number of characters whose name takes the metrical shape u– – or u–u: *Achilleus, Odusseus, huphorbos*.[39] To employ this naming strategy is not only compositionally sound, forming a familiar unit at the end of the line that can combine with myriad other "words" from the beginning of the line onward. It is also idiomatic within the poetic register. That is, like *amumonos* X analyzed just above, *dios* X amounts to code for designating important, often principal figures within Homeric epic; when the code is used, not only the compositional but also the expressive job gets done. Like so many other combinations, this phrase stands as an approved pathway toward traditional characterization, an *oimê*, as Homer himself calls it,[40] and its word-power derives from its identity as a traditional sign, as a *sêma* in the Homeric epic way of speaking. In a sense it simply does not matter what definition we choose to assign *dios*. The crucial point is that we read behind the signs and recognize the speech-act inherent in *dios* X.

The same is true of two other *sêmata* that use *dios* to make up a larger "word." This pair of phrases idiomatically designates goddesses and mortal women as paragons among their peers, describing the divine female as *dia theaôn* (*dia* of goddesses) and the human female as *dia gunaikôn* (*dia* of women). Among the goddesses frequently named in this way are Kalypso, Kirke, Athena, Demeter, and Hera; the mortals so honored include Penelope and Helen. But once again we find an attribution that cannot be easily explained no matter how much we extend or generalize the connotation of *dios*. Like her menial equivalent the swineherd Eumaios, the serving-maid Eurykleia merits the same epithet assigned to goddesses and to the most beautiful and accomplished of high-born mortal women (*Od.* 20.147).[41] As in the case of "*dios* swineherd" and "*amumonos* Aigisthos," the formula *dia gunaikôn* (*dia* of women) as applied to Eurykleia is best understood on its own terms as an indivisible whole, an index, a pathway toward idiomatic characterization of the old nurse. Within the logic of the register, which supports both composition and reception, it is not the meaning of *dia* alone but the joint expressive force of *dia gunaikôn* that makes the difference.

What then do we conclude about the implications of noun-epithet phrases? First, these signs have primary allegiance neither to the demands of composition in performance nor to the particular moment in the narrative where they are deployed. They refer first and foremost to the poetic tradition at large, implying the totality of the named figure's personality.

As signs they follow Parry's rules of metrical placement and thrift to a large degree, but *their signification* draws on the deeper resources of the ambient poetic tradition.

Within this overall dynamic of "words" rather than words, noun-epithet phrases work in one of two related ways. Like "swift-footed Achilleus," they can name a telltale detail that is assigned exclusively, or nearly exclusively, to one figure. The epithet *podas ôkus* is in fact used of no other character, so the identification with Achilleus is sharply focused and automatic.[42] Or, like the combinations exemplified by *"amumonos* Aigisthos" and *"dios* swineherd," the detail may not be telltale for any single figure, but rather for a number of quite different characters.[43] In this latter case the most fundamental role of the traditional sign—to point idiomatically toward unstated implications—is perhaps more obvious. Because the root meaning of such epithets taken alone may seem to jar with the history or personality of a particular person, the necessity to tip the interpretive balance in favor of the larger "word" is easier for modern readers to grasp. But we must also remember those many instances in which "swift-footed Achilleus" seems contextually inappropriate, as when he is seated in his tent or otherwise unreliant on foot speed. We must recognize that they don't "fit," either. In the end both species of noun-epithet phrases reveal a common function: they are both composite "words." And these "words" are not merely metrical items; they owe primary allegiance to the principle of *artis causa*, not of *metri causa*. In indexing the tradition, they work like language, only more so.

2. Stock emotions and stage props: Noun-epithet formulas for feelings and things. Along with the noun-epithet formulas for people and gods, Homer and his tradition also use a number of unvarying noun-phrase formulas for feelings and things. Once again, these "stock emotions" and "stage props," as I call them here to emphasize their role as touchstones in the ongoing drama of traditional narrative, are neither constraints on poetic brilliance nor paragons of situational appropriateness. Rather they index poetic verities in the Homeric world—psychological states and tangible objects woven into the fabric of the narrative tradition that are singularly meaningful and recognizable to bard and audience alike. They do not speak only to their most immediate surroundings, but also help to "slot" the individuality of whatever character, scene, or action happens to occupy center stage, embedding that unique instance in the ready context of traditional referentiality.[44] In what follows I offer three examples of this resonant and useful feature of the Homeric register, another aspect of the special language that drives both composition and reception.

2a. Green fear. The small phrase *chlôron deos* ("green fear") occurs ten times in the epics and hymns, always as part of a larger "word" that also involves the verb *haireô*, "seize." Filling either the last two or three cola in the hexameter line, this proverbial phrase regularly reports that "green fear seized" one or more people.[45] But, other than the metaphorical force of the color and the ascription of agency to this paralyzing emotion, does the "word" bear any traditional referentiality?

If we collate the ten instances—three in the *Iliad*, six in the *Odyssey*, and one in the *Hymn to Demeter*—we find that nine of them clearly involve a specific kind of fear wholly beyond the literal meaning of *chlôron deos*. Each of these nine occurrences describes a situation in which a *supernaturally inspired fear* takes hold of a person or group of people. In *Iliad* 7, for example, the Achaeans and Trojans feast, but all night long Zeus devises evil things, thundering terribly, and green fear seizes the people (479). He visits an omen on the Achaeans a book later, and once again the proverbial phrase marks their reaction (8.77). Within the *Odyssey*, green fear grips Odysseus as the shades gather to drink the blood of the sacrificed sheep (11.43), while his men prove prisoner to the same emotion as they confront Charybdis (12.243). Beyond the sphere of the epics, Metaneira glimpses Demeter's divinity in the *Hymn to Demeter* and is idiomatically frightened out of her wits (190). The "green fear" *sêma* stands as a powerful signal in each of these quite disparate scenes, as it "slots" their variety by reference to a familiar traditional category, enriching the concerns of the momentary instance with the networked implications of the Homeric register. *Chlôron deos* is more than simply a powerful, disabling emotion; it is by traditional definition a superhuman, unconquerable force. It is a coded sign for something beyond mortal control.[46]

Only one occurrence of this idiomatic Homeric sign seems to lack the dimension of supernaturally inspired fear. In *Odyssey* 22, just after the slaughter begins with Antinoos shot through the neck, the suitors castigate the as yet unrecognized stranger for his catastrophic misdeed and promise him a quick death and mutilation of his remains as recompense. To their arrogant presumptions Odysseus responds by revealing himself as the wronged master of the household who will now bring about their certain and well-deserved destruction. Hearing this response, Eurymachos and the others react proverbially: "῝Ως φάτο, τοὺς δ' ἄρα πάντας ὑπὸ χλωρὸν δέος εἷλε" ("Thus he spoke, and green fear took hold of all of them," 42). Surely the threat of the returned Odysseus looms large for the usurping suitors, especially since (as we know even if they do not presently suspect it) the goddess Athena is assisting him. This alone might be enough to warrant the poetic code for supernaturally inspired fear. But the connection is yet more immediate. In the lines leading up to his climactic pronouncement of their doom, Odysseus recounts the suitors' crimes against him and his family: they despoiled his household, slept with his serving-women, and wooed his wife while he was still alive, "fearing neither the gods who hold the wide heavens / nor any blame that would come from men hereafter" (22.39–40). That is, the hero himself identifies their actions as violations that will inevitably trigger divine vengeance—presumably as embodied in the slaughter about to begin— and this stipulation lays the groundwork for the traditional *sêma* of "green fear." Even the single instance that might seem to lack a proper context for traditional referentiality in fact summons the meaning behind the sign.

2b. Wine-dark sea. Certainly every reader of (or listener to) Homer's poems will remember the formulaic citation of "wine-dark sea." Counting both its accusative (*oinopa ponton*) and dative (*oinopi pontôi*) inflections, this phrase occurs no fewer than nineteen times over the two epics and the hymns. Its traditional morphology is quite simple: both phrases are customarily the objects of prepositions, with the combinations then filling either the longer of the fourth cola at the end of the line or the entire second hemistich.[47] For example, Zeus is twice represented as having destroyed Odysseus' ship "in the middle of the wine-dark sea" (5.132, 7.250). There can be little doubt that this traditional sign serves a ready compositional function in the Homeric register. It is a handy "word."

But as frequent as this *sêma* may be, it harbors nothing like the special implications evident in the deployment of the "green fear" signal. Instead, its expressive role seems limited to serving as an effective traditional code for "sea." What it slots is not a complex emotion that results from supernatural agency but rather a static, identifiable "stage prop" in the continuing drama of Homeric representation.[48] Ships sail across this recognizably epic body of water, heroes gaze out over it, Crete exists in the middle of it. None of these actions or scenes is materially augmented by its noun-epithet name. Nonetheless, we must make a careful distinction here. The lack of complex overtones in "wine-dark sea" does not mean that we are justified, with Parry, in reducing *oinopa ponton* / *oinopi pontôi* to a metrically expeditious way to say "sea"; that would be to ignore the fundamental nature of the Homeric register as a language and a pathway to traditional referentiality. At the very least, any such sign reinforces the communicative medium, offering another indication that the verbal transaction will proceed idiomatically; it thus bears not only on composition but reception. Whatever the action that swirls around it, the "wine-dark sea" remains a still, immutable point of reference. It marks the other end of the significative spectrum from the dramatically resonant "green fear."

2c. Stout hand. The phrase *cheiri pacheiêi* ("stout hand," always in the dative singular form) occupies a privileged position in the Homeric line: in all nineteen of its occurrences, this "word" closes the hexameter verse, constituting the fourth and final colon in the line.[49] Moreover, like so many of the noun-epithet formulas for people and gods, it combines variously with other bytes of phraseology but remains itself invariable. These two features, regularly linked in Homeric phraseology, make "stout hand" an extremely useful formula, a standard increment that can serve many different purposes for the composing poet.

Notwithstanding this phrase's acknowledged usefulness, a few of its actual applications have puzzled scholars. Granted, most seem obvious enough. For example, many of the occurrences of *cheiri pacheiêi* in the *Iliad* are associated straightforwardly with battlefield heroics: Hektor lifts a great stone with his stout hand during the contest of champions against Aias (7.264), Aias uses his stout hand to drive a spear into Hippothoos during the fight over Patroklos' body (17.296), Achilleus defends himself against Aineias' spear by holding up his divinely wrought shield in his stout hand (20.261), and so forth. In accordance with the heroic code's customary emphasis on appropriate martial conduct over and above the secondary matter of winning or losing, the particular action described need not be victorious, successful, or even promising: the disabled Aineias drops to the ground and leans on his stout hand (5.309), as does the dazed Hektor (11.355), and Dolon extends his stout hand in trying to reach Diomedes' chin to beg for his life—the idiomatic posture for supplication (10.454). What most of the thirteen instances of *cheiri pacheiêi* in the *Iliad* share, in short, is a strong correlation with traditionally approved heroic action—in and of itself, with no certainty of success, lacking entirely any assurance that the character involved will prevail or even survive. The "stout hand" sign has little to do with manual size, strength, or dexterity; rather it seems to index a basic heroic context.

The three exceptions to this rule in the *Iliad* are no exceptions at all if we examine them from the perspective of traditional referentiality, rather than insist slavishly on mere local or literal meaning. In Book 14 Poseidon takes advantage of Zeus' capitulation to the All-conqueror Sleep[50] to inspire the Greeks; in leading them forward himself, holding a sword in his stout hand (385), Poseidon locates himself anthropomorphically in the same category as the human figures to whom this phrase more often applies. Likewise with Athena, who during her conflict with Ares in Book 21 grasps a stone in her stout hand (403) and subdues her divine antagonist with a single blow to the neck. As Aphrodite intercedes to lead the beaten god out of the fight, Athena uses that same stout hand (424) to deliver another blow, this time to Ares' beautiful savior.[51] That these three *divine* episodes mirror more commonly *human* actions is of little or no direct relevance; the point is that these unique combats involving the gods are contextualized according to heroic behavior and the traditional register by invoking *cheiri pacheiêi*. As with the fasting Demeter in the *Hymn to Demeter*, who as an immortal cannot starve but whose traumatic mourning is powerfully indexed by the traditional force of her abstinence from food and drink,[52] physical realities are not at issue here. What matters is the implication of the *sêma*; what matters is what lies behind the sign.

Within the less obviously martial narrative of the *Odyssey*, the phrase *cheiri pacheiêi* is, expectably, less often employed. Two of its five occurrences obviously answer the Iliadic definition of the "word," signifying actions undertaken in agreement with heroic principles, actions that are honorable and brave in their own right without necessary reference to eventual success or failure. Thus, in an embedded story explaining the telltale *sêma* of the scar, the young Odysseus sweeps in on the cornered boar, his spear held high in his stout hand (19.448), aiming to be the first to strike.[53] The painful result of his impetuousness—the wound that becomes the scar—exists between the signs, framed by this idiomatic invocation of heroic context. Later, in Book 22, Odysseus dismisses the suitor Leodes' groveling supplication and, grabbing a sword in his stout hand (326), dispatches him. This is of course well within his heroic role as agent of the retribution that the Return Song pattern has long led us to expect.[54]

Two of the remaining three Odyssean instances are easily enough explained as indexical of the same general connotation, but with a twist. At 6.128 the naked, brine-encrusted Odysseus emerges from his olive thicket to confront Nausikaa and her companions; in modesty before the young women he breaks off a leafy branch—with his stout hand—in order to cover himself. While this action is not in itself heroic, the resonant phraseology keys a heroic context: against all appearances, we are reminded, this is the same Odysseus who served so creditably at Troy and who now seeks, as the male protagonist in a Return Song, to find his way back to Ithaka and reestablish his identity. On his way toward that *telos* he will encounter many more obstacles, most dramatically the suitors who have usurped his domain. These outlaws include the violent Ktesippos, who breaks a long list of Homeric rules by using his stout hand to hurl an ox hoof at the disguised stranger (20.299). In this case it is the outrageousness of the *sêma's* application that catches our attention. As the cowardly usurper attacks his genuinely (but latently) heroic host, *cheiri pacheiêi* ironically emphasizes the discrepancy between what is and what should be, as well as prepares the way for what will soon happen to reverse the institutionalized inequity in Ithaka.

The final usage of the *cheiri pacheiêi* sign in the *Odyssey* has proven a stubborn crux in Homeric studies. Applied to Penelope in the sixth line of Book 21, this attribution has seemed awkward to many commentators, most obviously in its apparent non-fit in gender and sphere of activity. Why would this elegant, graceful woman be so clumsily burdened with such an inappropriately masculine physical feature? Is Homer nodding?[55] But if we are prepared to interpret this "word" as a Homeric sign that has more to do with traditional referentiality than with anatomical realism, then even Penelope can comfortably sport a stout hand. Indeed, assigning her this indexical feature at precisely the moment when she sets the contest of the bow only deepens the resonance of her heroism, of her continuing and crucial role in her husband's inexorable revenge. Homer stipulates as much a few lines earlier when he specifies that Athena put it into her mind "to place the bow and the gray iron before the suitors / in Odysseus' halls, the materials for the contest and the beginning of the slaughter" (3–4).[56] The fact that Penelope then proceeds to use her stout hand to unlock the weapons closet and procure those materials only underlines her inimitable brand of heroism, which here modulates from persistence and indeterminacy to active participation in the preparations for combat.

As the Return Song heroine, her previous contribution—inestimably important as the basis of Odysseus' eventual reaccession—had been to hold the suitors at bay through her cleverness and artful avoidance of certainty and decision. Now all that suddenly changes, and she takes a crucial part in the aggressive, long-awaited removal of the social cancer eating away at her family and homestead. We may debate how consciously aware she is of this change,[57] but via this unambiguous *sêma* Homer and his tradition leave little doubt that her preparatory actions in Book 21 are genuinely heroic. Penelope's stout hand, like those of Hektor, Aineias, Odysseus, and even the anthropomorphic gods, "slots" her setting of the bow-contest as a heroic deed, undertaken without foreknowledge of success or failure and idiomatically honorable and brave.[58] The fact that she happens to be female is in this regard quite impertinent, just as Athena's and Poseidon's divinity was poetically impertinent. On the surface, *cheiri pacheiêi* may seem to clash harshly with Penelope's femaleness and dependence on intellectual subtlety; once we read behind the sign, however, her "stout hand" fits her very well indeed.[59]

3. Traditional punctuation: Speech introductions. One of the homeliest but most functional "words" in Homer's traditional vocabulary is the boilerplate introduction to a character's speech. By virtue of this recurrent byte of diction the poet provides an aural punctuation mark, signaling the onset of direct discourse.[60] The speech introduction is essentially a predicate to a common sentence; as such, it can take many forms, most of them ready for combination with noun-epithet formulas that provide the subject.

3a. "And in turn addressed him/her." For example, consider τὸν δ᾽ αὖτε προσέειπε(ν) . . . ("And in turn addressed him . . ."), a *sêma* that occurs no fewer than twenty-four times in the *Iliad* and forty-eight times in the *Odyssey*. It contributes the predicate that combines with a whole host of subjects, both human and divine; among them are earthshaker Poseidon, long-suffering *dios* Odysseus, prudent Penelope, and goddess bright-eyed Athena. But this is not the end of this "word's" traditional morphology, or of its compositional usefulness in the Homeric register. By adding the optional nu-moveable to the end of the verb (*proseeipe[n]*) it can combine in approved metrical fashion with a host of characters whose noun-epithet designations begin with a vowel rather than a consonant: thus figures like godlike Alexandros (Ἀλέξανδρος θεοειδής) and Agamemnon leader of men (ἄναξ ἀνδρῶν Ἀγαμέμνων) can now be accommodated, and this flexibility adds twelve Iliadic instances to the collection.[61] Finally, the double possibility of *ton* ("him") or *tên* ("her") as the predicate's first element allows for variability in gender of the person or god(dess) addressed, accounting for nine more occurrences in the *Iliad* and eight more in the *Odyssey*. With a total of 101 usages over the two epics, there can be little doubt that the *sêma* we are translating as "And in turn addressed him/her" plays an important tectonic role in Homeric poetry.

That role, as noted above, is certainly modest by any artistic measure. It is one of the accepted traditional signs for an answering speech—idiomatically nothing more, but also nothing less. The force of *proseeipe*, which taken by itself means "speak to, address, accost" (Liddell and Scott 1968), is muted by inclusion as part of the larger "word." Together the phrase signals a response, a rejoinder that usually has nothing to do with "accosting" anyone.[62] Just as we cannot accuse Homer of nodding in his continuing characterization of Achilleus as "swift-footed" or in his application of *amumôn* to Aigisthos or *dios* to the swineherd or nurse, so we must recognize the way in which this ordinary byte of phraseology works—as a whole, with encoded traditional referentiality.[63]

3b. "And answering [he/it] spoke to him/her." Such is also the case with another of Homer's "words" for speech introduction, our second example of this kind of *sêma*: τὴν/τὸν δ᾽ ἀπαμειβόμενος/-ον προσέφη ("And answering [he/it] spoke to him/her"). Once again we are dealing with a modest but extremely frequent and useful sign, one that occurs thirty-eight times in the *Iliad* and seventy-three times in the *Odyssey*.[64] The major difference between the two examples is not their traditional signification; they are equivalent signs that identify what follows as a speech made in response. As idiomatic phrases they are almost interchangeable—almost, but not quite. The only quality that differentiates the two is their divergent metrical identity: "And in turn addressed him" falls between the beginning of the line and the midline caesura, while "And answering spoke to him" occupies the longer slot between line-beginning and the third caesura.[65] This divergence further means that the noun-epithet complements of the two speech-introduction "words" will be of two different lengths.

We can glimpse the adaptability of Homer's traditional style in this variability and its upshot: the collective accommodation of numerous noun-epithet subjects. At the level of composition, such combinations illustrate Parry's original principles of thrift and tectonic usefulness quite well.[66] But there is also the question of reception. Workaday as they seem, such *sêmata* do in fact perform the essential function of traditional signs: they mark a speech-act by reference to the tradition at large, and they "slot" each occurrence in a familiar category. In a sense these homely lines of speech introduction amount to the simplest case of "words" with more than lexical definition, in that they provide a broad and highly generalized cue—a kind of traditional punctuation—that also depends on an audience's or reader's idiomatic grasp of the register. We cannot read the parts in isolation; only the whole sign makes any sense.

3c. **Emotional speaker**. A few of the signs for speech introduction do substantially more than provide compositional flexibility and **Traditional punctuation**. In addition to the basic function performed by this type of "word," they also gloss the speech to follow and the relationship between the speaker and the addressee. They identify the ensuing speech-act as a particular kind of exchange.

One of the most poignant and focused of such *sêmata* is the group of phrases that share the component ". . . and spoke a word and called (him/her) by name" (. . . ἔπος τ᾽ ἔφατ᾽ ἔκ τ᾽ ὀνόμαζε(ν). The traditional morphology of the forty-five occurrences of this sign over the epics and hymns consists of three apparently related possibilities, which we can initially describe simply as follows:[67]

Type A, whole-line versions (17 instances)

> χειρί τέ μιν κατέρεξεν, ἔπος τ᾽ ἔφατ᾽ ἔκ τ᾽ ὀνόμαζε (6 instances)
> she stroked him with her hand and spoke a word and called him by name
> ἐν τ᾽ ἄρα οἱ φῦ χειρὶ ἔπος τ᾽ ἔφατ᾽ ἔκ τ᾽ ὀνόμαζε (11 instances)
> she took him by the hand and spoke a word and called him by name

Type B, half-line (hemistich) versions (20 instances)

> [X] ἔπος τ᾽ ἔφατ᾽ ἔκ τ᾽ ὀνόμαζε
> [X] and spoke a word and called him by name

Type C, whole-line system involving *enenipen* (8 instances)

> [Y] ἐνένιπεν ἔπος τ᾽ ἔφατ᾽ ἔκ τ᾽ ὀνόμαζε(ν)
> [Y] she reproached him and spoke a word and called him by name

All three versions share certain connotative features, embedded implications that an idiomatic reading (or hearing) automatically makes part of the proceedings. First, the two people involved are effectively "slotted," with the speaker expressing care and concern—or the opposite attitude of disgust and contempt—for the addressee. This depth of sentiment may be feigned, but the association is signaled traditionally and only the local context can overturn its reality. Second, the speaker is marked as extremely earnest in his or her conversation with the addressee; once this introductory line occurs, there can be no doubt that the speech to follow is of crucial importance for them both. Third, the exchange usually takes place in a state of heightened emotion when the stakes are high, when the balance of power or even some matter of life and death is at stake.

This much is characteristic of all forty-five instances, which notwithstanding their great variety are unified by inclusion in the same expressive category, keyed by the *sêma* of **Emotional speaker**. Making more precise distinctions, we can add that Types A and B are virtually identical, the only difference being that the shorter version of this "word" allows for more compositional adaptability. Many different half-lines combine with Type B, providing the poet with the best of both worlds: an idiomatic sign that is nonetheless pliable enough to serve a host of diverse situations.[68] But Type C is another matter. Alongside the undeniable moment of intimacy, earnestness, and heightened emotional state stands the verb *enenipen* ("he/she reproached"), which adds another layer to the traditional signal by imputing shameful conduct to the addressee. Thus, for example, Hektor upbraids Melanippos, his childhood comrade in Priam's house, for not fighting harder (*Il.* 15.552f.); and Penelope rebukes her longtime suitor Antinoos for planning to kill Telemachos, courting her, and despoiling their household (*Od.* 16.417f.). There are eight instances of **Emotional speaker** that all bear this double implication of close, earnest communication and outright castigation.[69] The traditional sign engages a finely drawn recipe for reception of the speech that immediately follows, framing a variety of interactions in a familiar context.

4. Rhetorical fulcrum. Many Homeric speeches fall into two major segments, with each section treating a different (though usually related) subject and the two-part structure divided by and balanced on a "word" that serves as a rhetorical fulcrum.

4a. **Command**. Far the most common such divider and balance-point is the small phrase "But come . . ." (ἀλλ᾽ ἄγε[τε] . . .), which always occurs at the opening of the hexameter line, where it begins a new sentence as well as a new thought and speech-section by introducing an order or command.[70] Incomplete in itself, "But come . . ." requires another verb, customarily an imperative or a hortatory subjunctive, to round out its function as a traditional signal. This is what an audience expects. Thus Achilleus uses this phrase to urge Agamemnon to consult a seer who can explain Apollo's anger (*Il.* 1.62), while late in the final book the best of the Achaeans employs the same signal to urge old man Priam to break his fast and share a meal of reconciliation (24.618). In each case the **Command** *sêma* initiates a call to action, urging a dramatic change in the present direction of the narrative. In each case Achilleus leaves one topic—in Book 1 the question of whether to depart from Troy and in Book 24 the expatiation on Niobe's remembering to eat despite the catastrophic loss of her children—in order to embark on a separate but related topic. For an audience or readership fluent in the Homeric register, this modest-sized phrase has appreciable rhetorical impact, creating a traditional frame within which even the most singular events can be resonantly perceived.

Indeed, as a generalized signal, "But come . . ." is applicable to an especially wide variety of narrative situations—fully 154 separate situations in the epics and hymns. A central reason for this flexibility, and a quality that distinguishes ἀλλ᾽ ἄγε[τε] . . . from signals like "green fear," is its open-endedness in meaning. Except for the rhetorical implications of division, balance, and mandated action, this "word" is virtually context-free. This is not to say that "But come . . ." is weaker or less important than some other traditional signs; it is merely to recognize a natural difference in function, parallel to the differences among the various signals for **Traditional punctuation** discussed above. For example, at *Odyssey* 1.224 the disguised Athena partitions her speech to Telemachos via **Command**, moving from a brief compliment on the young man's lineage to challenging and critical questions about the suitors' raucous behavior. Much later, Penelope illustrates the concurrent transitional and unifying force of the signal when she turns from a rebuttal of the stranger's criticism of her stubbornness to ordering Eurykleia to do the impossible—to make up their bed outside the bedchamber (23.171). In the terms developed in Chapter 5, the "But come . . ." sign helps to create a pathway from Penelope's life-preserving indeterminacy to the riddle that will key the final recognition and achievement of the *telos*.

4b. **Righting a wrong.** Another, much less frequent rhetorical fulcrum consists of the equally short phrase "But come along . . ." (ἀλλ᾽ ἕπευ . . .).[71] Like the **Command** sign, this initatory marker signals a change in direction and in mode within a speech, leading to a command. But ἀλλ᾽ ἕπευ also carries the idiomatic implication that the action prescribed will right a present wrong, as when Hektor calls for Aineias to stand by the corpse of Alkathoos, just killed by Idomeneus (*Il.* 13.465), or when Hektor scolds Melanippos and orders him to advance against the Greeks (*Il.* 15.556).[72] This *sêma* occurs in the *Odyssey* as well, contextualizing Telemachos' granting of sanctuary to Theoklymenos by admitting the fugitive seer to his ship's company (15.281), and buttressing Eurykleia's plea as she encourages the recalcitrant Penelope to join Odysseus and end the twenty-year deprivation (23.52, 78). In all cases, **Righting a wrong** actually does lead to the realization of the action being urged by the speaker: as a speech-act this phrase cannot fail.[73]

5. Practical impossibility. When Homer wishes to gloss an action or potential development as inherently unlikely, he can use an impersonal phrase with the adjective *chalepon* (literally, "difficult, hard"). Thus the construction "It is/would be hard . . ." slots the activity in question as something impractical or impossible under normal circumstances, despite the fact that the action may be inherently well-meaning or courageous. Contexts include the limitations of humans as compared with the much greater powers of gods and goddesses (*Il.* 21.184; *Od.* 10.305, 11.156, 23.81, 23.184); a disproportionate numerical weakness in force (*Il.* 16.620; *Od.* 20.313); and other situations.[74] It is important to note that the traditional morphology of this sign allows for considerable variability: the core of the impersonal sentence, *chalepon*, can occur in a number of different positions in the hexameter line, and the overall structure requires only an infinitive to complete its basic structure.[75] Within that flexible structure **Practical impossibility** can accommodate a great many different situations. As compared, for example, with the fixed noun-epithet formulas of **Dramatis personae**, it helps to illustrate how traditional phraseology cannot be reduced to a single formulaic definition. Taken together, all of these "words" show how oral tradition works like a language, only more so.

Of particular interest for our purposes is the traditional referentiality of the phrase as applied to two dramatic moments in *Odyssey* 23. At line 81 Penelope employs **Practical impossibility** to hold Eurykleia at arm's length and prolong the process of recognition, claiming with the full proverbial force of this signal that "it is hard" for Eurykleia or anyone else to comprehend the gods' plans. Not just the fact but the form of her resistance resonates with idiomatic connotations, as do the other instances of this phrase deployed elsewhere in the epics and hymns. About one hundred lines later Odysseus uses the same "word" to express how difficult it would be for any mortal to move his bed (23.184). By referring these two potentialities to the category of **Practical impossibility**, by slotting the immediate in a traditional category, Penelope and Odysseus harness the expressive power of the register, emphasizing their observations in a unique and inimitable fashion.

6. "You should know better!" Eight times in the epics one character responds to another with the following signal: ποῖόν σε ἔπος φύγεν ἕρκος ὀδόντων, "What sort of word escaped your teeth's barrier?" Literally, this phrase stands as a startled exclamation and question, expressing surprise and perhaps outrage over the preceding speech. But the traditional referentiality of the sign goes deeper than that. In all cases an older or more experienced figure is chiding a younger or less experienced previous speaker for the rashness of his or her foregoing remarks, and the idiomatic content of the *sêma* amounts to "you should know better!" Unlike **Practical im-**

possibility, this phrase does not vary in the least: all eight instances are identical and occupy the same section of the hexameter verse.[76] Its traditional morphology is thus quite narrow, leaving only the first colon of the line, where the addressee is named, open for variation.

Examples of how Homer applies **"You should know better!"** include the exchange between Zeus and Athena early in Book 1 of the *Odyssey*. Odysseus' patron is questioning her father's apparent indifference toward the plight of the long-lost Ithakan hero, and eventually secures his promise to bring Poseidon into line. But Zeus begins his response to Athena's special pleading and implicit criticism by chiding her for thinking he could forget Odysseus. Even within the divine realm, the older and more experienced figure is reprimanding the younger and less experienced speaker for her rashness, indicating that she should not have made what is demonstrably a false assumption.[77] Likewise, at *Odyssey* 21.168 the suitor Leodes, who disapproves of his comrades and their conduct, is the first to try and fail to string Odysseus' bow. After giving it his best effort, he puts the bow aside, offering his opinion that the rest of them will also fail and that they should therefore give up the courting of Penelope and turn elsewhere. This honorable initiative is met with a harsh rebuke by Antinoos, leader and most outrageous of the suitors, who begins his criticism of Leodes with the **"You should know better!"** sign.[78] In this instance traditional referentiality sharpens the irony of the imbalanced situation: the older and more experienced Antinoos (usurping king of Ithaka) chides the younger and less experienced Leodes (far more worthy than his "superior") for the rashness of his remarks (although the younger man is the only suitor who takes an honorable position in the courting procedure). To have Antinoos tell his comrade "You should know better!" is to intensify the irony of his "correction" of Leodes' speech, and to do so through the agency of traditional referentiality.

7. Long-term goal. The phrase "with enduring heart" (τετληότι θυμῷ), which occurs nine times and only in the *Odyssey*, signals the necessity and fact of enduring an unpleasant present reality in order to reach an eventual goal. Such present discomfort conventionally lasts an appreciable period of time, long enough for the fainthearted or even those of average courage and stamina to give up, choose the easier route, and thus fail in their attempt at a very worthy but also very difficult achievement. The traditional morphology of **Long-term goal** calls for exact recurrence of the key phrase—"with enduring heart"—at the end of the line.[79] Apart from the two exactly repeated clusters of lines,[80] there is no larger, overarching pattern for deployment of this signal.

The implications of the *sêma* are, however, indexical, providing a traditional context for each of the nine instances. Thus Menelaos and his men must spend the morning wrapped in sealskins in order to trick Proteus and have a chance to capture him (4.447); they must retain their grip on the Old Man of the Sea as he shifts shapes in order to subdue him and gain crucial information about returning home (4.459); and Odysseus must hold on to the underside of his ram all night in order to escape Polyphemos' cave (9.435). At 11.181 Antikleia uses this idiomatic signal to warn her son that Penelope has been enduring too long, a sentiment that meshes well with other signs that Penelope's ability to maintain her fidelity—and precarious indeterminacy—is ever threatened; and Eumaios conveys the very same thing in the very same terms at 16.37 (11.181–83 = 16.37–39):

> "All too much *with enduring heart* she does wait for you
> there in your own palace, and always with her the wretched
> nights and the days also waste her away with weeping."

In addition to two other straightforward instances,[81] the **Long-term goal** signals at 23.100 and 23.168 are highly resonant. First Telemachos and then Odysseus wonder at Penelope's obstinacy (100–102 = 168–70):

> "No other woman would keep back *with enduring heart*
> as you are doing from her husband who, after much suffering,
> came at last in the twentieth year back to his own country."

Neither Telemachos nor Odysseus can fathom why she will not go ahead and acknowledge the man before her as her returned husband. **Long-term goal**, indexing as it does the endurance of an unpleasant present reality in favor of a longer-range and more difficult achievement, amplifies their logical query. Why has she not admitted that the goal has been reached? Why does she persist in her suffering? These are reasonable questions; the answer to both is that, as Homer and the Return Song *sêma* warrant, she is the heroine of the epic. She must persist.[82]

8. Weak in the knees. When Homer wishes to index a given situation as not only a moment of supreme helplessness but also a matter of life or death and a turning point in the narrative, he can use a key "word" that recurs nine times in the epics: "[someone's] knees and dear heart were loosened" (. . . λύτο γούνατα καὶ φίλον ἦτορ).[83] While the literal force of the phrase is memorably visceral in its portrayal of a character's temporary unraveling, the implications go substantially further: as a *sêma* it marks a life-threatening or life-affirming moment. Moreover, it is fluid and highly adaptable in structure and application. The traditional morphology of **Weak in the knees** is malleable enough to "slot" the diverse experiences of any character or group—human or divinity, male or female, singular or plural. As is common in ancient Greek epic phraseology, the adjustment made in order to name the particular individual(s) consists of combining variable elements with the basic "word," as illustrated below:[84]

τοῦ/τῆς/τῶν δ' αὐτοῦ
and here his/her/their

                λύτο γούνατα καὶ φί)ν ἦτορ
                knees and dear hea₁ (were loosened

καὶ τότ' Ὀδυσσῆος
and then Odysseus'

With the first half of the hexameter line variable and the latter half invariable, this sign adheres to the classic Homeric principle of right justification. To pursue our analogy of traditional phrase to "word," this Homeric sign, like so many others, accommodates change in its opening "syllables" and secures its referentiality and traditional structure in the ending "syllables." In this sense poet and tradition think from right to left.[85]

To gain a sense of the ways in which **Weak in the knees** serves as a linchpin, contributing traditional implications to each local instance, consider its range of applications. At *Odyssey* 4.703, for example, the news that the suitors are planning an ambush for Telemachos understandably unhinges his mother, Penelope. Odysseus experiences the same overwhelming feeling of life and death hanging in the balance when he discovers that the traitorous servant Melanthios is arming the heretofore defenseless suitors during the slaughter (22.147). In the *Iliad* this *sêma* marks Aphrodite's reaction as she reels under Athena's attack (21.425). Like other traditional signs, **Weak in the knees** can be used to "slot" even a divine reaction— not literally, of course, since Aphrodite is certainly in no danger of dying, but figuratively: the signal creates a familiar context and networks the divine instance with the other, mortal instances.[86] Finally, this powerful "word" harmonizes with the climactic moments of recognition by Penelope (23.205) and Laertes (24.345), who are momentarily undone by their discoveries. Especially in these last two cases, but also throughout the seven other occurrences, the *sêma* both glosses the significance of the present realization and identifies a major turning point in the overall narrative. Much hangs in the balance when a character's knees and dear heart are loosened, and traditional referentiality warrants that things will never again be the same from that juncture onward.

9. Sleep: Sweet release and vulnerability

ἀλλ' οὐ γάρ πως ἔστιν ἄϋπνους ἔμμεναι αἰὲν
ἀνθρώπους·

But it is not possible for people to be sleepless forever.
(*Odyssey* 19.591–92)

With these words Penelope tells the stranger that she could sit beside him and be entertained all night, but that no one can forestall the onset of sleep indefinitely. Whatever else she may be doing at this point, she is asserting a powerful truth central not only to human physiology but also to Homeric poetics. Sleep is inevitable, and so are its well-defined traditional implications. When characters give themselves over to *hupnos* ("sleep") in the epics, they are opening a double possibility: sweet release and vulnerability. While sleep promises a much-needed escape from daytime, earthly woes and a physical refreshment that can be gained in no other way, it just as certainly harbors the threat of danger, loss of control, or even death.[87] What is more, that trademark vulnerability remains very near the surface of every episode that involves *hupnos*. Which one of the two possibilities will it be—peaceful rest or danger? Which way will the narrative turn? Homer's sign doesn't say: rather, it encodes a fork in the road and, as do so many traditional *sêmata*, leaves the resolution of the quandary to the immediate situation. As with story-pattern and typical scene, the sign meshes with its local surroundings—the implications with the instance— to produce the rich chemistry of Homeric art.

And of what does the *hupnos* sign consist? In contrast to *sêmata* that take one form only, examples of which we have discussed above, the traditional idea of *hupnos* can be expressed via a variety of "words." Its morphology is thus very broad and comparatively open-ended. First, sleep can appear entirely unadorned as the noun *hupnos* alone, or combine with an epithet or appositive, or even give way to a substitute noun. Unmodified *hupnos* is the simplest form of the sign, but no less potent for that simplicity.[88] Among various "inflections" of the sign, sleep is quite often described as in some way "sweet," with nearly synonymous adjectives such as *glukus*, *glukeros*, *nêdumos*, and *hêdus*, along with *meliêdês* ("honey-sweet") and *meliphrôn* ("honey-hearted"). At other times it is *malakos* ("soft, gentle"), *ambrosios* ("ambrosial"), or *apêmona te liaron te* ("harmless and warm"). But although it is accorded the distinction of being a gift (*hupnou dôron*), sleep is also explicitly named *pandamatôr* ("all-conqueror") and identified as the brother of Death. Each of these inflected forms of the sleep sign is sometimes the primary feature of *hupnos*, but none of them is always and everywhere an accurate portrayal of sleep if we take its usage only literally. In the terms we have developed to describe Homeric language and art, each amounts to or contributes to a traditional "word" for sleep. Collectively, then, the many different phrases, including some that are not formulaically or even lexically related, mark multiple equivalent pathways to the same ambient reality. In its broad traditional morphology, the sleep *sêma* thus allows for both compositional flexibility and idiomatic precision. It proves extremely useful for composition and reception alike.

In an attempt to evaluate the contribution this *sêma* makes to various moments in the *Iliad* and *Odyssey*, let us examine a few of its alternate forms and some actual instances of each.

Glukus hupnos. The most common shape of the sleep "word" consists of *glukus hupnos* ("sweet sleep") embedded in a longer phrase that fills the second half-line or hemistich of the hexameter.[89] Within this pattern alone one finds appreciable and functional variation within limits, with two opposite applications, falling asleep and waking up—

ὅτε τὸν γλυκὺς ὕπνος ἱκάνοι (*Od.* 9.333)
when sweet sleep might reach him
ἐμὲ δὲ γλυκὺς ὕπνος ἀνῆκεν (*Il.* 2.71)
and sweet sleep released me

—accommodating a range of characters and other small changes.[90] While *glukus hupnos* (nominative case) seldom occurs outside these hemistich sequences, the accusative *glukun hupnon* opens up a wide range of possibilities.[91] Taken together, this evidence points toward a close partnership between *glukus* and *hupnos*, whatever the phraseological context. That is, it points toward "sweet sleep" as an expressive whole, on the model of several noun-epithet *sêmata* discussed above, such as "green fear" and "wine-dark sea." Like any "word," of course, it can also participate in larger patterns of diction.[92] This is the first clue that we cannot expect the quality of sweetness to match any one particular narrative context; instead, like "green" and "wine-dark" in the phrases just cited, *glukus* amounts to a traditional inflection of *hupnos*. As a unit they work within the epic register to index the double reality of sleep as both welcome release and problematic vulnerability. Notwithstanding the superficial semantics, such is the idiomatic meaning behind the sign.

A closer look at *Odyssey* 9.333 shows just how idiomatic such traditional implications can be, and how they can play an important role in the overall poetics of Homeric verse. At this juncture Odysseus is recapitulating his and his comrades' blinding of the Kyklops, telling how they planned to take advantage of his vulnerability "when sweet sleep might reach him."[93] Read outside the register and without attention to the poetics of traditional signs, this passage seems distinctly and harshly ironic: Polyphemos' wine-induced sleep may indeed prove sweet for his adversaries, but it is anything but *glukus* for him. Of course, this literal reading of *glukus hupnos* as two words rather than a single "word" ignores the compositional and referential logic of Homeric epic, deflecting reception by paying attention to the wrong register. Reading the passage in this fashion may be acceptable to us, presuming as it does that the cognitive units of Homer's language are always and everywhere the same as those of our modern literary texts. But this unexamined interpretation, and the textual kind of irony it suggests, is an illusion. It focuses on the sign at the expense of what lies behind it.[94]

If, on the other hand, we take *glukus hupnos* on its own terms as one of the approved traditional pathways leading toward the idiomatic double meaning of sleep in Homer, then we can successfully read not just one but all of its occurrences and still retain the irony at *Odyssey* 9.333. Because the phrase refers as a whole to the twin possibilities of release and vulnerability, only the latter of which eventuates here, its usage is both predictive and ironic—but *at a traditional level*. That is, "sweet sleep" keys a double expectation, one half of which is fulfilled and the other half of which is controverted: the wine-induced slumber releases Polyphemos from practical concerns, to be sure, but it also costs him dearly. His "rest" is hardly restorative, since it renders him vulnerable to Odysseus' and his companions' attack. To put it another way, what happens to Polyphemos echoes not against "sweet" but against the traditional implications of "sweet sleep" as a whole, as an indexical "word." The line is certainly ironic, but because of what lies behind the sign and not because of the sign's constituent parts.

The gift of sleep.   The sleep sign can assume many other shapes as well, even as the implications of release and vulnerability remain the referent. For example, the hemistich phrase καὶ ὕπνου δῶρον ἕλοντο ("and they accepted the gift of sleep") occurs twice in the *Odyssey*, both times at the closure of a feast, and twice in the *Iliad*, again following feasts and libations.[95] Here the endemic tension between release and vulnerability interacts with a recurring local context: as discussed in Chapter 6, the Feast pattern always culminates with some kind of Mediation, and in these cases that predictable result solves the inherent ambiguity of sleep, certifying that in these four cases the potential threat encoded in the sign as one of the two expectable possibilities will not materialize. Mediation will without doubt win out over any contingent danger, the narrative pattern warrants. A twofold implication meshes with instance, as two traditional signs—Feast and sleep—combine to provide a resonant and idiomatic context for the reader's or listener's reception of these four different moments.

All-conqueror.   Often enough in the *Iliad* and *Odyssey*, those who pursue the "gift of sleep"—by whatever pathway—are granted it. But sometimes characters are denied, either briefly or for a longer period, the state to which human physiology, diurnal rhythm, and the poetic tradition entitle them. Thus, for example, on more than one occasion Penelope tosses and turns before sleep takes her, and Achilleus spends much of the *Iliad* with-

out the refuge and refreshment of *hupnos*.[96] These interludes run counter
to expectation, signaling something decidedly and radically wrong, and
present temporary challenges to Penelope's proverbial-sounding remark
that served as the epigraph to this section of the chapter: "it is not possible
for people to be sleepless forever."[97]

The *pandamatôr* ("All-conqueror") phraseology that occurs twice in Ho-
mer puts the alternatives into relief. Soon after the "Nobody" exchange, a
disabling sleep overcomes Polyphemos, just as Odysseus and his men had
plotted (9.371–74):

Ἦ καὶ ἀνακλινθεὶς πέσεν ὕπτιος, αὐτὰρ ἔπειτα
κεῖτ᾽ ἀποδοχμώσας παχὺν αὐχένα, κὰδ δέ μιν ὕπνος
ἥρει πανδαμάτωρ· φάρυγος δ᾽ ἐξέσσυτο οἶνος
ψωμοί τ᾽ ἀνδρόμεοι· ὁ δ᾽ ἐρεύγετο οἰνοβαρείων.

He spoke and slumped away and fell on his back, and lay there
with his thick neck crooked over on one side, and All-conqueror
sleep captured him. The wine gurgled up from his gullet
with gobs of human meat. This was his drunken vomiting.

Although on the surface this may look quite different from other versions
of the sleep *sêma*, it performs a cognate function. *Hupnos* the *pandamatôr*
renders even the fearsome Kyklops vulnerable, indeed defenseless, and
Odysseus and his comrades will not miss the opportunity. Polyphemos
will pay for his "sweet" release[98]—so carefully engineered by his human
antagonists—with his sight and effectively with his way of life. Reading
behind the sign helps us to understand the imminent danger of sleep, a
danger always implied traditionally and here so graphically realized.

But even the usually overpowering advance of the All-conqueror can
be resisted for an extensive period of time under extraordinary circum-
stances, as when Achilleus, unstrung by his grief for Patroklos, cannot find
rest. Early in Book 24 his arhythmic relationship to the rest of society man-
ifests itself via the sleep sign (2–6):

τοὶ μὲν δόρποιο μέδοντο
ὕπνου τε γλυκεροῦ ταρπήμεναι· αὐτὰρ Ἀχιλλεὺς
κλαῖε φίλου ἑτάρου μεμνημένος, οὐδέ μιν ὕπνος
ἥρει πανδαμάτωρ, ἀλλ᾽ ἐστρέφετ᾽ ἔνθα καὶ ἔνθα,
Πατρόκλου ποθέων ἀνδροτῆτά τε καὶ μένος ἠΰ,[99] . . .

and the rest of them took thought of their dinner
and of sweet sleep and its enjoyment; only Achilleus
wept still as he remembered his beloved companion, nor did
the All-conqueror sleep capture him, but he tossed from one side to the other
in longing for Patroklos, for his manhood and his great strength.

How deep and unrelenting is Achilleus' unstaunched sadness over the loss of his friend? Sufficient to forestall sleep, Homer answers traditionally as well as literally; sufficient to preclude the release that would lessen his suffering, if only for a time.[100] Even the All-conqueror, subduer of the man-eating monster Polyphemos and of Zeus himself, cannot ease his manic grief.

The unnatural quality of Achilleus' insomnia is emphasized by contrast to his fellow Achaeans' expectable, idiomatic actions. After the Funeral Games they go off in search of a feast, which leads dependably to the mediation supplied by *hupnos*. For them all is as it should be; keyed by the sequence associated with feasting, their rest must be a sweet release devoid of threat. But how opposite for Achilleus, left behind by his comrades (and by the traditional pattern), still fasting, sleepless, and manifestly out of rhythm with the world he must now inhabit without Patroklos. That is how overwhelming his grief really is, and we feel it the more keenly when we read behind the signs of sleep and Feast.

The power to control sleep. Three times in the epics Hermes is dispatched for a special errand that he among all the gods seems best equipped to accomplish: to guide Priam to Achilleus' hut in *Iliad* 24, to bear Zeus' message to Kalypso in *Odyssey* 5, and to lead the suitors' shades down to Hades in *Odyssey* 24. In each instance he is carrying his trademark *hrabdos*, the magic wand "with which he charms the eyes of men when he wishes, / and then again wakes the sleepers."[101] That is, whether he actually uses it or not, Hermes possesses the power to override the natural, inevitable rhythm of waking and sleeping, to control the *pandamatôr* that otherwise overcomes everyone.[102] Hermes' power—imaged in the *hrabdos*—is in effect a traditional attribute in its own right (not unlike an epithet) as well as another inflection of the sleep *sêma*. Although it bears no formulaic relationship to the other inflections, and although no epithet accompanies the sleepers themselves (*hupnôontas*), this two-line phrase belongs to the family of diction that implies the double meaning of release and vulnerability. Only here it is no longer a question of the natural diurnal rhythm: Hermes' wand is simply so powerful that it supervenes a defining human characteristic. While reading only the surface of this sign will not denature the poem, reading behind it deepens our understanding of both Hermes' signal attribute and each of the three passages in question. Zeus' messenger can suspend much more than sleep, it appears; he can also control its traditional implications.

Penelope reads behind the sign. To this point we have been relying on what can be gleaned from collating the various "inflections" of the sleep *sêma* in the *Iliad* and *Odyssey*. According to the method employed throughout this volume, we have been inquiring what is implied—as well as lexically stated—by the use of these key "words." We have been attempting to read behind as well as between the signs.

As a final perspective on *hupnos* and its idiomatic associations, and in keeping with her role as a truly major figure in the Return pattern that undergirds the *Odyssey*, let us give Penelope herself both the last word and the last "word." Near the beginning of Book 20 both Odysseus and Penelope grow uneasy with the emerging events, Odysseus questioning Athena about the practicality of their upcoming battle against the suitors, who greatly outnumber them, and Penelope so distraught that she awakens and prays to Artemis for a merciful death—another kind of release.[103] Athena quickly and firmly banishes Odysseus' misgivings, and he falls into a limb-relaxing (*lusimelês*) sleep.[104] Just at the moment of her husband's release, Penelope starts from her own slumber, unable to rest, and grieves that she would rather be dead, since meeting Odysseus "even under the hateful earth" (81) would be far superior to accepting one of the suitors. She then goes on effectively to explicate the sleep *sêma* in Homer (83–90):

"ἀλλὰ τὸ μὲν καὶ ἀνεκτὸν ἔχει κακόν, ὁππότε κέν τις
ἤματα μὲν κλαίῃ, πυκινῶς ἀκαχήμενος ἦτορ,
νύκτας δ' ὕπνος ἔχῃσιν - ὁ γάρ τ' ἐπέλησεν ἁπάντων,
ἐσθλῶν ἠδὲ κακῶν, ἐπεὶ ἆρ βλέφαρ' ἀμφικαλύψῃ -
αὐτὰρ ἐμοὶ καὶ ὀνείρατ' ἐπέσσευεν κακὰ δαίμων.
τῇδε γὰρ αὖ μοι νυκτὶ παρέδραθεν εἴκελος αὐτῷ,
τοῖος ἐὼν οἷος ἦεν ἅμα στρατῷ· αὐτὰρ ἐμὸν κῆρ
χαῖρ', ἐπεὶ οὐκ ἐφάμην ὄναρ ἔμμεναι, ἀλλ' ὕπαρ ἤδη."

"Yet the evil is endurable, when one
cries through the days, with heart constantly troubled, yet still
is taken by sleep in the nights; for sleep is the oblivion of all
things, both good and evil, when it has shrouded the eyelids.
But now the god has sent evil dreams thronging upon me.
For on this very night there was one who lay by me, like him
as he was when he went with the army, so that my own heart
was happy. I thought it was no dream, but a waking vision."

With the stubborn refusal to yield to circumstances we expect of the Return Song heroine, Penelope begins by affirming that, everything else being equal, her present lot has been endurable. Although her days may be laced with trouble and despair, by night all-conquering sleep gives her regular respite. This is the voice of the woman who weaves and unweaves, whose greatest strength—both personally and as a member of the sisterhood of Return Song heroines—is her unfailing ability to suspend closure. But everything else is no longer equal. Now, she says, she can no longer

count on sleep's sweet release, for an evil *daimôn* has interrupted her re-
storative reverie with a dream-rendering of Odysseus. Her last few lines
press home the cruelty of what she takes as some god's hoax: the vision so
resembled her long-lost husband that not only was she enervated by the
loss of *hupnos*, but she actually believed the dream to be a waking reality.
In effect, Penelope was convinced that Odysseus' wanderings and her
struggle were over. For the audience, reading behind the signs, this would
mean that the song was virtually over as well.

Here Homer's and his tradition's brilliance shines through. Unlike any
other Return Song in my experience, in this passage the *Odyssey* manages
not only to forecast its own *telos* but to do so through the words of a hero-
ine who does not yet realize the full implications of the *sêmata* that sur-
round her.[105] Or perhaps it would be more appropriate to say that Penel-
ope cannot yet *afford* to fully recognize the very signs she is reading. It is
simply too early.

From inside the traditional code, the dream reunites hero and heroine
in a facsimile Wedding element, foreshortening the Return Song sequence
and bypassing Odysseus' vengeance. Under the spell of *hupnos*, Penelope
sees into the future toward the *telos* of the story she has kept alive through
her obstinate refusal to resolve the most taxing ambiguities. Sleep, which
could provide either release or vulnerability, brings her not an evil or cruel
dream, as she suggests, but what is in one sense the most profoundly re-
storative preview she could hope for. That is, what she interprets as a false
image, presumably one that has passed through the gates of ivory, is actu-
ally a true vision, the issue of the gates of horn.[106]

In addition to the fact that dreams as portrayed in Homeric epic almost
always come true, this reading gains support from the traditional referen-
tiality of the sleep *sêma*. As the fluent audience knows, the dream-vision
Penelope cannot accept is real and benign, a product of *hupnos* in its posi-
tive, restorative aspect. Although she may see things otherwise, under-
standing the incursion of the dream as negative and threatening—also a
possible implication of "sweet sleep," as we have seen—she happens to be
wrong. To put it another way, it is too early in the idiomatic progress of the
Return Song for her to see things any other way.[107] By taking referential ad-
vantage of the double meaning of the sleep sign, Homer manages to keep
Penelope in a heroic state of indeterminacy even while signaling his audi-
ence that the *telos* is in sight. This is the genius of his and his tradition's art:
allowing the audience to read both between and behind the signs.

It is to encourage just this kind of *sêma*-reading that I have presented
these examples of "words" at the level of phraseology in this chapter.
Whether the particular phrases in question index very simple and gen-
eral meanings, such as **Traditional punctuation** or **Rhetorical fulcrum**, or
much more specific notions, such as **You should know better!** or **Weak in**

the knees, the basic principle is the same: even the smallest-scale *sêmata* work like language, only more so. Because of the referential advantage offered by such "words," Homer and his tradition can convey a great deal with remarkable expressive economy. Does the poet wish to characterize Achilleus in all his complexity—half-divine, driven by honor but out of touch with human society for much of the *Iliad*? Then let him use the **Dramatis personae** function. It does far more than simply solve a compositional problem; as a shorthand way to summon a figure center stage, it serves as a key for unlocking a traditional, mythic personality. Does the bard wish to slot a given moment in the narrative as one of those instances motivated by supernaturally inspired fear, whether the character realizes the source or not? Then **Stock emotions,** in the form of "green fear," can do the job. Does Homer wish to key a change of direction in a speech and forecast either a command to follow or a righting of some wrong? **Rhetorical fulcrum** provides traditional signs applicable to myriad different situations. These and many more signs—most fundamentally the fact of the diction as a whole, with its recognizable rhythm and rules for combining words into "words"—provide the poet and the audience or reader a special medium for communication. By reading both behind and between such signs, we can more deeply grasp Homer's traditional art.

In the following chapter I will turn to a rereading of a short passage from Book 23 of the *Odyssey* in which many of the *sêmata* discussed individually in the chapters on story-pattern (5), typical scene or theme (6), and phraseology (7) come into play together, as an integrated signifying system. As a companion to this rereading, I will append not an *apparatus criticus*, which directs interpretation by reference to other texts, but what I call an *apparatus fabulosus*, a story-based apparatus that refers primarily to the poetic tradition and the implications it harbors.[108] At all points, the core question driving the inquiry will continue to be, What difference do a work's roots in oral tradition make to its understanding as verbal art?

PART IV

HOMERIC SIGNS AND *ODYSSEY* 23

8

REREADING *ODYSSEY* 23

Ταῦτ' ἄρ' ἀοιδὸς ἄειδε περικλυτός·
So the renowned singer sang these things.
—*Odyssey* 8.521

For this volume, and presumably for a great many other inquiries as well, the most important question posed by studies in oral tradition must remain "So what?" Given the fact of the traditional register, discussed here in terms of story-pattern (Chapter 5), typical scene or theme (Chapter 6), and phraseology (Chapter 7), as well as the core concept of *sêma* (Chapter 1) and the comparison with South Slavic oral epic (Chapters 2–4), what do we make of that register's implications? How does Homer's specialized way of speaking affect our reading of the *Iliad* and *Odyssey*? What and how does it mean? How do we read behind as well as between the signs?

Over the preceding seven chapters I have focused in one way or another on Homer's traditional art, on the referential advantage offered by the ancient Greek epic register. Instead of emphasizing the structural usefulness of Homeric "words" as pieces in a compositional jigsaw puzzle, I have stressed their idiomatic force. Whatever the particular unit of expression, and whatever the particular narrative situations in which it appears, our major concern has been its more than literal meaning, the extent to which it functions not *metri causa* ("for the sake of meter") but *artis causa* ("for the sake of art"). We have been interested in how oral tradition works like language, only more so.

In an attempt to illustrate these principles cumulatively and in a convenient and easily apprehendable fashion, I now turn to a rereading of the penultimate book of the *Odyssey*, in many ways the climax of the epic. What I propose to do—in extremely brief compass—is to make explicit some of the most important implications of the *sêmata* that constitute its traditional sign-language. Thus we will be considering the context provided by "words" at all three levels: the Return Song story-pattern, the typical scene of Bath, and a succession of smaller phraseological cues.[1] Adopting once again the double perspective advocated throughout this volume, we will employ a twofold strategy. We will of course be reading *behind* the signs, bringing their traditional referentiality into play; but at the same time we will not be neglecting to read *between* the signs, to weigh the particular local context of the given *sêma*. The object of the exercise is to strike flint against steel, to mesh instance and implication, to understand the uniquely powerful combination of the immediate and the traditional.

Story-Pattern as *Sêma*

As Book 23 opens, Eurykleia is joyously reporting to Penelope the news that they have both awaited for many years: Odysseus is home and the usurping suitors are dead by his hand. In terms of the Return pattern studied in Chapter 5, the story-map prescribes an immanent fulfillment or *telos* (though not necessarily an end) in the reunion of the hero and the heroine. All the structural and idiomatic preliminaries have taken place: Odysseus has found his way from Absence and Devastation (Kalypso's island through the Phaeacian episode) to Return (in the mandated disguise) and on to Retribution; Penelope has done her equally heroic part in defending herself and Ithaka and making the whole story possible. Moreover, most of the principal characters have recognized the returning hero at various prior points in the narrative, with two important exceptions—Laertes and Penelope.[2] In short, the stage is set for the final act of the epic drama. All that remains is the fulfillment of the tale's trajectory in the Wedding element.

So much for reading *behind* the signs, whose traditional implications establish the horizons of expectation within which the story-specific actions will take place. We know, at least in general terms, what to anticipate; in fact, if we are a fluent audience we are now waiting for Penelope to shed her cloak of obstinate unbelieving and for Odysseus to manifest himself through some strategy that only he and Penelope can understand. This much is inscribed behind the *sêma* of story-pattern.

But against that background and that certainty—that is, *between* the signs—Homer and his tradition create actions and relationships peculiar to these characters, this place, this singular story. It is after all a tale not only of the Return hero and heroine in general but also of that inimitable pair, Odysseus and Penelope. Thus Eurykleia's ostensibly welcome news falls on deaf ears; her mistress simply will not credit the reality of return and retribution without incontrovertible proof, rock-solid evidence that she herself will elicit via sign-language. We can trace part of her stubbornness to the fundamental indeterminacy of the Return heroine as a traditional figure, but another part must be ascribed to Penelope herself. She is generically that traditional figure, of course, but she is also specifically Penelope—the woman who weaves and unweaves, who perseveres without apparent hope, who eschews the expedience of remarriage in favor of keeping the Ithakan household (and the Homeric story) together. The brilliance of Homer's art stems in an important way from the doubled, complementary sources of Penelope's heroic behavior.

We are still waiting for the curtain to rise on the final act when Telemachos impatiently intervenes to castigate his mother for failing to admit that the stranger truly is Odysseus, to accept the fact that their long separation has finally come to an end. She responds by claiming that she knows of "signs" that are "hidden" from others, transparent only to her and her husband, and the stranger, smiling, goes along with her dismissal of their indignant young son in favor of a more intimate interview to come. We can cogently read this sequence as husband and wife sending the child off to his room in order to have some privacy, and on one level this is certainly what is happening. But we read this moment better if we remember that the final recognition always involves a trick known only to the two partners, and that Penelope is here pointing toward the ultimate sign that keys the *telos*. Even the family dynamics with Telemachos and his parents, then, draws from both local realities and traditional context.

More minor events also occur between the signs. Although the chief concern of any audience or reader aware of the implications of the Return pattern must be the immanent climax of the Wedding element, these smaller local details productively forestall the momentum of the story, delaying its dénouement and heightening our expectation. At the same time, they point beyond the *telos* to that part of the *Odyssey* in which the potentially unending cycle of revenge is halted once and for all by the Peace of Athena. One of these between-the-signs events is the pretended wedding celebration, constructed by the ever-vigilant Odysseus to delay discovery of the slaughter and consequent vengeance by the suitors' relatives. This ruse, which just precedes the Bath or Anointment theme to be treated below, retards the narrative's progress toward climax; by the same token, it also creates a pathway leading toward the post-*telos* confrontation between the house of Laertes and the suitors' kin. We can observe another between-the-signs gambit in Odysseus' retelling of Teiresias' prophecy to Penelope. This interlude, which occurs after the Bath-Anointment and Penelope's final recognition, is perhaps even more preemptive, since it postpones a truly immediate *telos* for which every last preliminary has now been completed and refers to activities well beyond the story of the *Odyssey* as we know it.[3] But such is the nature of Homer's style and art: although the signs are unequivocal, the transit between them is ever unpredictable, situational, and contingent. However we understand the meaning of the parable of the winnowing shovel,[4] it and all of the rest of the *Odyssey*'s fine detail emerge in the act of its telling—varying within limits, foreground against background, durable signs in an ever-changing context.

Typical Scene as *Sêma*

Just as we simultaneously process many levels of signals during a conversation or the reading of a novel, so Homer and his tradition use many levels of "words" to encode and transmit their *Odyssey*. The Return pattern is one of those "words" in the traditional vocabulary; what we have identified in Chapter 6 as the theme or typical scene is another. Without positing any necessarily hierarchical relationship among different units of expression,[5] let us consider the *sêma* of Bath-Anointment at 23.153–64:

> Now the housekeeper Eurynome bathed great-hearted
> Odysseus in his own house, and anointed him with olive oil,
> and threw a beautiful mantle and a tunic about him; 155
> and over his head Athena suffused great beauty, to make him
> taller to behold and thicker, and on his head she arranged
> the curling locks that hung down like hyacinthine petals.
> And as when a master craftsman overlays gold on silver,
> and he is one who was taught by Hephaistos and Pallas Athena 160
> in art complete, and grace is on every work he finishes;
> so Athena gilded with grace his head and his shoulders.
> Then, looking like an immortal, he strode forth from the bath,
> and came back then and sat on the chair from which he had risen.

As demonstrated elsewhere, these grouped actions of bathing, anointing with olive oil, and donning new clothes constitute a typical scene that appears seven times in the *Odyssey*, taking a similar shape with certain regular features in each occurrence.[6] More to the point for our present discussion, however, this modest-seeming "stock" description is also rife with traditional implications. Without fail in Books 3, 4, 8, 10, 17, and 24 the Bath-Anointment theme forecasts a consequent feast. Although the dinner may not be grand and surroundings less than palatial (the immediate con-

text varies from Nestor's palace to Laertes' humble farm), the linkage be-
tween the two events is secure: one sign directly implies the next in six of
the seven situations. Even the less than full-blown Bath scenes conven-
tionally lead to a meal of some sort, as when Athena's beautification of the
recently shipwrecked Odysseus—keyed as here by washing and anoint-
ment—precede the food and drink offered him by Nausikaa in Book 6.

This is the expectation with which the fluent audience then encoun-
ters the passage quoted above from Book 23. Reading behind the Bath-
Anointment sign, we posit an immanent feast, a breaking of bread that
in turn implies a third sign—a mediation to come.[7] Indeed, if anything,
this particular instance of the typical scene implies these two consequent
events more strongly than many other instances. In addition to the famil-
iar phraseology associated with washing and anointing, this scene echoes
the transfiguration of Book 6 (23.157–62 = 6.230–35 almost exactly), even
including the same amplifying simile of the metalsmith. Moreover, it
closes with the one telltale detail that most dependably cues a following
feast: the seating of the guest (164). Of course, no actual meal occurs, but
the compositional and referential logic runs deeper than that. Although
the Bath theme in *Odyssey* 23 seems at first to be the single exception to an
otherwise idiomatic rule, it is in fact nothing of the sort. Instead of the rit-
ual of sharing food and drink, the narrative turns toward the "feast" of
Penelope's and Odysseus' reunion and the profound mediation that will
result as they reclaim their abdicated identities and rebuild the ruptured
Ithakan community.

Reading *between* the signs, we certainly sense a logical connection be-
tween Odysseus' divinely managed beautification and the *telos* that fol-
lows at 23.296. One event leads into the other quite effectively without as-
sistance from traditional *sêmata*, and on its own the overall movement
toward the olive-tree bed is without doubt memorable and resonant. But
reading *behind* the signs adds a traditional context, deepens our expecta-
tions, and slots what is of course an absolutely unique outcome in what
is just as certainly a familiar sequence of events. Understanding the Bath-
Anointment in Book 23 as both a singular, inimitable moment and as a
sêma with idiomatic implications does justice to both individual craft and
traditional referentiality. It avoids shortchanging ancient Greek epic on ei-
ther score, and shows how another of Homer's "words" works like lan-
guage, only more so.

Phrase as *Sêma*

In turning to the smallest-scale signs in the Homer register, let us first re-
call the general role of the traditional phraseology as a communicative me-

dium. Whether in Book 23 or elsewhere in the epics and Hymns, far the most prominent *sêma* at this level is the specialized language as a whole, as an expressive instrument whose dedicated function is to enable composition and reception. For Homer and his tradition this instrument derives from a symbiosis of prosody and diction, a steady background against which each individual phrase or line takes shape.[8] However much it may vary from phrase to phrase and line to line, in one fundamental respect Homeric phraseology never changes: with every increment or "word," this marked way of speaking designates and redesignates the special communicative channel. With every verse or verse-part it alerts us to the range and scope of the transaction between poet and audience, creating a familiar stage for the presentation of the drama, a familiar performance arena. When we go on below to single out this or that phrase as particularly clear examples of traditional referentiality, then, let us not forget what makes them possible: the rules that govern Homeric verse-making and verse-receiving, the backbone that gives shape to the pliable musculature of phraseology. To put the matter simply, Homeric phraseology is itself a traditional sign, behind which we are asked to read.

But reading behind that sign is not enough. Because Homeric poetics is in all its dimensions a rich mixture of foreground and background, of local and traditional contexts, we must also read between the recurrences of this most general of *sêmata*. Ideally, this second responsibility means an appreciation of how formulaic phraseology permits and even fosters difference—of how Achilleus speaks like no one else, or of how Trojans and Achaeans do not really speak the "same language," for example.[9] More broadly, we should avoid conceiving of traditional phraseology as limiting a poet's or audience's horizons and grant Homer the ability to express and convey whatever he and his tradition wish to express and convey, in as complex a manner as may be necessary to their purpose. Indeed, the burden of this entire volume has been to show that the dual expressive mode of traditional signs and what lies between them makes possible a kind of verbal art that neither medium alone could foster.

To illustrate the role of *sêmata* in the overall poetics of the *Odyssey* and more widely, I now propose a close rereading of a brief passage from Book 23 (69–103) at the level of specific phrases. Toward that end, in the quotation below I have highlighted some of the phrases that appear to provide poet and audience with a referential advantage, with a key to idiomatic usage. That is, they augment or amplify the particular, local details of the scene by implying larger, traditional meanings, by slotting the immediate moment in familiar, resonant traditional categories. Let me be clear that in doing so I make no pretense of fully analyzing the passage for every last implication, some of which must naturally remain beyond the scope of any investigation limited to the surviving sample of ancient Greek epic.

Furthermore, I have selected the particular examples highlighted below because they can be explained relatively briefly and because they offer a fair sense of how signs interact with one another and with what lies between them.

As the exchange opens, then, Eurykleia is pleading with Penelope to abandon her intransigence and recognize her husband. The signs to be emphasized are underlined; their traditional meanings are glossed in **boldface** underneath each underlined phrase:

> The beloved nurse Eurykleia then said to her in answer:
> **Dramatis personae**   **Traditional punctuation**
> "My child, what sort of word escaped your teeth's barrier?   70
> **You should know better!**
> Though your husband is here beside the hearth, you would never
> say he would come home. Your heart was always mistrustful.
> **You are wrong**
> But come, let me tell you another sign that is very clear.
> **Fulcrum: command**   **Sêma**
> That scar, which once the boar with his white teeth inflicted.
> **Key: boar story**
> I recognized it while I was washing his feet, and I wanted   75
> to tell you about it, but he stopped my mouth with his hand, would not
> let me speak, for his mind sought every advantage.
> Come then, follow me, and I will hazard my life upon it.
> **Fulcrum: righting a wrong**
> Kill me by the most pitiful death, if I am deceiving you."
> Circumspect Penelope said to her in answer: 80
> **Dramatis personae**   **Traditional punctuation**
> "Dear nurse, it is difficult for you to comprehend the purposes
> **Practical impossibility**
> of the everlasting gods, though you are very clever.
> **Dramatis personae**
> Still, I will go to see my son, so that I can look on
> these men who courted me lying dead, and the man who killed them."
> She spoke, and came down from the chamber, her heart much   85
> pondering, whether to keep away and question her dear husband,
> **Quandary: fork A**
> or to go up to him and kiss his head, taking his hands.
> **Quandary: fork B**
> But then, when she came in and stepped over the stone threshold,
> she sat across from him in the firelight, facing Odysseus,
> by the opposite wall, while he was seated by the tall pillar,   90
> **Guest of honor**
> looking downward, and waiting to find out if his majestic
> wife would have anything to say to him, now that she saw him.
> She sat a long time in silence, and her heart was wondering.
> Sometimes she would look at him, with her eyes full upon him,
> and again would fail to know him in the foul clothing he wore.   95
> **Clothing and status: beggar**

Telemachos spoke to her and called her by name and scolded her:
> **Emotional speaker: hostile**
"My mother, my harsh mother with the hard heart inside you,
why do you withdraw so from my father, and do not
sit beside him and ask him questions and find out about him?
> **Doubly question**
No other woman, with enduring heart, would keep back   100
> **Long-term goal**
as you are doing from her husband who, after suffering much,
> **Fruits of labor**
came at last in the twentieth year back to his own country.
But always you have a heart that is harder than stone within you."

Most of these *sêmata* have already been singled out for analysis in Chapter 7, so a relatively brief treatment should be sufficient to illustrate their contribution to the overall poetics of this passage. In addition to offering the discussion below, I make reference to fuller accounts of their structure and implications in the *Apparatus Fabulosus* located at the end of this chapter.[10]

The passage begins in a vein familiar to any reader of Homer. Eurykleia enters the scene via one of her traditional formulaic names, which serves not merely to fill a structural need but more importantly to bring her entire character center stage (**Dramatis personae**). The initial line also uses one of the homely, generic signs of **Traditional punctuation**, no more or less functional than in its other sixty-eight occurrences in the epics, to introduce her speech. From this point on, however, the rhetorical implications of the signs are more focused, reacting more strongly and resonantly with what lies between them. With her very first "word"—**You should know better!**—the old woman sets the traditional context for her speech, assuming the indexed role of "an older or more experienced figure chiding a younger or less experienced previous speaker for the rashness of his or her foregoing remarks." This is the sign with which Zeus affectionately chastises Athena for her impatience on two different occasions, for example, a signal that carries with it sincere disappointment mollified by the equivalent of a pat on the head. Reinforced by the intimacy of addressing Penelope as "my child,"[11] **You should know better!** situates the exchange between Eurykleia and her mistress in a recognizable frame. That much lies behind the sign.

But we must also read between the signs, giving the particular situation its due. To what is the referential advantage of this "word" applied in the nurse's speech? Here the play of *sêma* and local context becomes vital to Homer's art. For Eurykleia, after all, there can be no doubt whatsoever about Odysseus' identity and the defeat of the suitors. She has discovered his scar, seen the slaughter, rejoiced in his victory. If she is upset with circumspect Penelope, it is at least in part because, unlike her mistress, she is effectively "reading ahead" in the story-pattern of the *Odyssey*. Like her peers in the well-informed audience, she knows that Return and Retribution have in fact already taken place, and she thus awaits only the climactic resolution of *telos* and Wedding. But Penelope lags behind in her own reading, since as heroine of the Return Song she cannot do anything else. Her particular relationship with Eurykleia—the instance—thus meshes richly with the traditional referentiality of the **You should know better!** sign—the implication. Reading between the signs, we locate the nurse's impatience in the discrepancy between her knowledge and Penelope's lack of knowledge; reading behind the sign, we understand the nurse's criticism as direct and real but also tenderly imparted. Penelope should indeed know better, but Homer and his tradition understand why she does not.

After lodging her specific complaint—that Penelope would not acknowledge her husband before her by the hearth—and backing up her criticism with the **You are wrong** sign in line 72, Eurykleia signals a rhetorical pivot in her speech with the "But come . . ." phrase in the next line. Using this *sêma* of **Fulcrum: command**, she accomplishes two purposes at once, both of which we can appreciate by reading behind the sign. First, by convention she exits the first part of her exposition, marking a shift in topic by the use of a frequent rhetorical strategy. Concurrently, the audience or reader fluent in the idiom is primed to expect a command, an adamant urging to action if not an outright order. Homer fulfills that expectation with Eurykleia's insistence that Penelope pay attention to "another *sêma* that is very clear." Sign follows sign, as the old nurse then goes on to explicate the unmistakable *sêma* and proof, Odysseus' telltale scar, which is itself glossed by **Key: boar story**. Any reader or audience conversant with Homeric sign-language gleans a great deal from this succession of phraseological cues.

But how do these cues mesh with the immediate proceedings? How do the traditional signs complement what lies between and among them? As we have discovered, they slot the inimitable, unique reality by placing it within a recurring, idiomatic frame, and this passage is no exception. Eurykleia's objection to Penelope's intransigence is a singular moment, to be sure, and we should not lose sight of the poignancy it achieves because of its singularity. That poignancy is what lies between the signs. But the old woman's dismay also meshes with the **You are wrong** signal, used twice by the disguised Odysseus to criticize Eumaios for believing his master dead.[12] Likewise, the *sêma* of **Fulcrum: command** offers another example of the framing function of traditional phrases, as Eurykleia taps into the expressive power only Homeric signs can muster in shifting her speech from gentle chastisement to what she takes as incontrovertible proof of what Penelope does not (and cannot yet afford to) see. If we understand the register, we also understand the simple but overwhelming force of her language at this point: she commands her mistress to listen to a *sêma*—to whose meaning, in this instance or any other, there can be no appeal. Only Odysseus' immediate and unqualified injunction against explicating that sign has kept Eurykleia from reading it openly for others. She now reads it for Penelope, whose self-preserving, poem-preserving indeterminacy must thereby be tested against the irresistible momentum of traditional referentiality. With this burden and the nurse's pledge to die if she is not telling the truth, underlined by the **Fulcrum: righting a wrong** signal, one begins to wonder just how long Penelope can maintain her stolid refusal to believe in Odysseus' return. Whether behind the signs or between them, everything points toward the *telos*, and does so urgently.

What can Penelope possibly say to counter such a forceful argument and demonstration? How can even this most stubborn and resolute of women maintain her incredulity in the face of such explicit and implicit evidence? She attempts to invalidate Eurykleia's news and proof—the slaughter and the scar—as divinely wrought fictions, as the gods' bafflement of the old woman. What is more, Homer slots her reinterpretation of the *sêma* with yet another sign. That is, her contention that the gods have fooled Eurykleia gains support from the referential advantage of the **Practical impossibility** signal, a phrase that throughout its eleven occurrences in the *Iliad* and *Odyssey* consistently marks the action in question as impractical or impossible under normal conditions. Although the particular narrative proposition may be otherwise brave or reasonable, the sign certifies categorically that it is not to be achieved. Of course, in this case the necessary implication runs diametrically against what we know to be true. Once again, we join Eurykleia in reading behind a sign that Penelope refuses to read. But although the women disagree fundamentally, the way in which they express themselves is the same: idiomatic meaning meshes resonantly with the uniqueness of what lies between the signs.

Penelope agrees to accompany Eurykleia and examine the aftermath of battle, ostensibly as much to see her son as to lay eyes on the dead suitors or the still unnameable "man who killed them" (84). Once descended from her chamber into the hall, she finds herself on the horns of a dilemma, as she ponders whether to keep her distance and question the "stranger" or to kiss his head and take his hands—essentially whether to recognize him openly or not. The same characteristic ambiguity echoes through the next few lines, as she seems to know and yet not to know the man before her. Reading between the signs, we sense Penelope losing her grip on her own indeterminacy, perhaps approaching the end of her heroic struggle but still not quite able to push through her uncertainties once and for all. She cannot quite accept a returned Odysseus, a restored Ithakan community, or for that matter an unambiguous Penelope. That much lies between the signs.

Two additional *sêmata* deepen the reader's impression of her oscillating perspective. One of these is **Clothing and status: beggar** (95), which traditionally cues one of the two identities with which Penelope is wrestling. Like the noun-epithet formulas, this phrase automatically designates the unknown stranger, the "other side" of Odysseus whom at this point in the story only she can see, and then only part of the time.[13] Of course, we look at the same *sêma* from our vantage point and see Odysseus himself—and therein lies a familiar tension, induced again by sign-language. The other cue is **Quandary: narrative fork** (86–87), which occurs twenty-five times in the Homeric poems in a very wide range of individual situations. Consisting of a verb meaning "ponder, consider" (*hormainô* or *mermêrizdô*) plus the "either . . . or" construction, this signal marks a bifurcation in the narrative, a frozen moment in time before one of two competing alternatives wins out. For example, a version of **Quandary: narrative fork** also slots Odysseus' painful self-examination before he confronts the woebegone Laertes in Book 24 (235–38). The dilemma there—and dilemmas like this one present frequent problems for the Return Song hero across different songs and traditions[14]—is whether the son should immediately embrace his father or delay his revelation until he tests the old man, and we know what Odysseus decides. Both quandaries, and many others throughout the epics, are sharpened by slotting them according to this *sêma*, by indexing them according to a cognitive category enshrined in the traditional idiom. Reading behind the signs only enriches our appreciation of all of these moments.

For Telemachos, however, his mother's quandary is unacceptable and inexplicable. On the face of it, she has resisted what is patently obvious to him; at the level of implication, they have simply read the same signs differently. Even Telemachos' line of speech-introduction is uncharacteristically aggressive and critical, one of eight instances of **Emotional speaker: hostile**, the negative version of a common phrase that occurs a total of forty-five times in the epics and hymns. Overall this sign carries with it either a positive and intimate or a sharply negative valence; in either case it always establishes the speaker's earnestness and a heightened emotional tension while leading to a question, command, or prayer. Here, of course, the signal takes the form that slots the exchange to follow as uncompromisingly hostile, forecasting that Telemachos' words will ring with a familiar challenge—the same challenge issued by Hektor to his comrade Melanippos, for example, at *Iliad* 15.552–58:

> Hektor spoke to him and called him by name and scolded him:
> "Shall we give way so, Melanippos? Does it mean nothing
> even to you in the inward heart that your cousin is fallen?
> Do you not see how they are busied over the armor of Dolops?
> Come then; no longer can we stand far off and fight with
> the Argives. Sooner we must kill them, or else sheer Ilion
> be stormed utterly by them, and her citizens be killed."

Hektor's speech draws from the traditional resources of at least two signs: **Emotional speaker: hostile**[15] and **Fulcrum: righting a wrong** ("Come then . . ."). It is with this kind of harsh criticism and the clear implication that his mother is going against all applicable logic that Telemachos begins his speech to Penelope.

Nor does the sign-language end there. **Emotional speaker: hostile** alerts the audience or reader to expect not only a certain tone in what follows, but also one or more questions. We are not disappointed, as Telemachos demands to know why his mother withdraws from Odysseus and why she does not "ask him questions and find out about him" (99). Moreover, this second part of his query is itself another idiomatic sign, **Doubly question**, that harbors its own complementary implications. When the two nearly synonymous verbs *eiromai* and *metallaô*, both of which mean "ask, inquire," occur together in one of three related formulaic configurations, they project a recurrent traditional context: they signal a deep probing for some important fact, with a tight-lipped addressee being called upon to divulge a secret of some sort.[16] Significantly, in none of its fifteen appearances in the epics does **Doubly question** foreshadow either success or failure in the inquiry; rather it focuses on the special nature of the information and the reluctance of the addressee to divulge it. Thus Zeus warns Hera not to **Doubly question** him about Thetis' visit (*Il.* 1.550), while the *sêma* also frames Telemachos' painful and ignominious account of his household's condition after pseudo-Mentes prods him to explain (*Od.* 1.231). In the case before us from Book 23, the young man is urging his mother to relinquish her distance and get to the bottom of the long-standing mystery. The traditional sign slots this particular inquiry—unique in itself—as one that will if successful divulge some precious information. Both the immediate context and the *sêma* argue that, as far as Telemachos is concerned, the burden now rests with his mother and the answer she must seek is precious indeed.

Two final signs amplify Telemachos' criticism. The first of them, **Long-term goal** (100), indexes a resolution earned only after much anguish; as discussed in Chapter 7, it encodes a discomfort protracted enough to discourage any but the bravest or most strong-willed, followed by some sort of remarkable achievement. By citing this *sêma* Telemachos is saying that his mother's refusal to credit his father's presence goes beyond even this maximum level of forbearance, that any other woman would acknowledge that the wait and the suffering were over. In a real sense he is criticizing her for acting unidiomatically, for transgressing beyond the referentiality of **Long-term goal**. In the very next line the phrase "after suffering much" (101) echoes the same idea even on a literal, textual level; as the sign **Fruits of labor** it also bears the traditional implication of a positive achievement or reward after much prior toil. Thus the two signals harmonize in focusing Telemachos' complaint to Penelope, bringing to bear traditional patterns and expectations that categorize her behavior as even less explicable to him.

Soon, beyond the scope of the passage we have examined here, Penelope will reply to her understandably impatient son. She will assure him that

she and Odysseus share "secret signs" (*sêmath'* . . . *kekrummena*, 110) deci-
pherable only by the two of them. One of these signs is of course the olive-
tree bed that only she, her husband, and a serving-maid can "read" behind
and which, once read, will fully confirm both of their identities. With the
advent of certainty their disguises can be dropped; the *nostos* itself will be
complete. From the point of view of the overall story, the bed *sêma* thus
removes the last barrier separating wife and husband—not to mention
poet, audience, and readership—from the fulfillment of the *telos*. Indeed,
Homer, his tradition, and the fluent audience or reader also share "secret
signs" decipherable only by those who speak the register, implications
that move the entire epic—phrase by phrase and pattern by pattern—
toward its own *telos* as a work of traditional verbal art. We have only to
learn how to read both behind and between those signs.

A Sign-Language Companion: Traditionally Glossed Text with *Apparatus Fabulosus*

Reading behind the signs amounts to glossing the immediate, between-
the-signs course of the narrative by reference to implied traditional mean-
ing. The text below is an original-language version of the glossed text
(*Odyssey* 23.69–103) that appeared earlier in this chapter, with traditional
signs identified in italics to the right of the passage. Appended to the text
is an *Apparatus Fabulosus* that further documents the idiomatic meaning
and textual distribution of each *sêma*. In this way the textual presentation
mimics the fluent audience's reception, opening up the Homeric "way of
speaking" to the modern reader of texts. By juxtaposing the actual passage
with the *sêmata* through which it is told, this format will support concur-
rent attention to the situation-specific action at hand and its traditional
referentiality. It will also allow the reader to glimpse the ongoing nego-
tiation of traditional meaning, always a tension between instance and
implication.

A few introductory remarks are appropriate. We concentrate here on the
smallest-scale Homeric *sêmata*, the traditional phrases that help to index
idiomatic meanings that complement the immediate moments and scenes
of the narrative (see espec. Chapter 7 above). Many of them have already
been summarized as part of the rereading of *Odyssey* 23 in the earlier part
of the chapter. Discussion of signs at the level of story-pattern and typical
scene in Book 23 is also available there. Finally, although the emphasis
here is on individual phrases and their contribution to the chemistry of in-
stance and implication, let me repeat that the most important *sêma* at this
microlevel is the phraseology as a whole, as a specialized register with its
own rules for composition and therefore for reception.

Traditionally Glossed Text: *Odyssey* 23.69–103

[Register: Traditional Phraseology]

Τὴν δ' ἠμείβετ' ἔπειτα // φίλη τροφὸς Εὐρύκλεια·
"τέκνον ἐμόν, **ποῖόν σε ἔπος φύγεν ἕρκος ὀδόντων,**
ἥ πόσιν ἔνδον ἐόντα παρ' ἐσχάρῃ οὔ ποτ' ἔφησθα
οἴκαδ' ἐλεύσεσθαι· **θυμὸς δέ τοι αἰὲν ἄπιστος.**
ἀλλ' ἄγε τοι καὶ **σῆμα** ἀριφραδὲς ἄλλο τι εἴπω·
οὐλήν, τήν ποτέ μιν σῦς ἤλασε λευκῷ ὀδόντι,
τὴν ἀπονίζουσα φρασάμην, ἔθελον δὲ σοὶ αὐτῇ
εἰπέμεν· ἀλλά με χεῖνος ἑλὼν ἐπὶ μάστακα χερσὶν
οὐκ ἔα εἰπέμεναι πολυκερδείῃσι νόοιο.
ἀλλ' ἕπευ· αὐτὰρ ἐγὼν ἐμέθεν περιδώσομαι αὐτῆς,
αἴ κέν σ' ἐξαπάφω, κτεῖναί μ' οἰκτίστῳ ὀλέθρῳ."

Τὴν δ' ἠμείβετ' ἔπειτα // περίφρων Πηνελόπεια·
"μαῖα φίλη, **χαλεπόν σε θεῶν αἰειγενετάων**
δήνεα εἴρυσθαι, μάλα περ πολυΐδριν ἐοῦσαν·
ἀλλ' ἔμπης ἴομεν μετὰ παῖδ' ἐμόν, ὄφρα ἴδωμαι
ἄνδρας μνηστῆρας τεθνηότας, ἠδ' ὅς ἔπεφνεν."

70

75

80

Traditional referentiality
Traditional punctuation // Dramatis personae
You should know better!

You are wrong.
Fulcrum: command // Sêma
Key: boar story

Fulcrum: righting a wrong

Traditional punctuation // Dramatis personae
Practical impossibility // Dramatis personae

Ὣς φαμένη κατέβαιν' ὑπερώϊα· πολλὰ δέ οἱ κῆρ
ὅρμαιν', ἢ ἀπάνευθε φίλον πόσιν ἐξερέοιτο,
ἦ παρστᾶσα κύσειε κάρη καὶ χεῖρε λαβοῦσα.
ἡ δ' ἐπεὶ εἰσῆλθεν καὶ ὑπέρβη λάϊνον οὐδόν,
ἕζετ' ἔπειτ' Ὀδυσῆος ἐναντίη, ἐν πυρὸς αὐγῇ,
τοίχου τοῦ ἑτέρου· ὁ δ' ἄρα **πρὸς κίονα μακρὴν**
ἧστο κάτω ὁρόων, ποτιδέγμενος εἴ τί μιν εἴποι
ἰφθίμη παράκοιτις, ἐπεὶ ἴδεν ὀφθαλμοῖσιν.
ἡ δ' ἄνεω δὴν ἧστο, τάφος δέ οἱ ἦτορ ἵκανεν·
ὄψει δ' ἄλλοτε μέν μιν ἐνωπαδίως ἐσίδεσκεν,
ἄλλοτε δ' ἀγνώσασκε **κακὰ χροΐ εἵματ' ἔχοντα.**
Τηλέμαχος δ' **ἐνένιπεν ἔπος τ' ἔφατ' ἔκ τ' ὀνόμαζε·**
"**μῆτερ ἐμή, δύσμητερ,** ἀπηνέα θυμὸν ἔχουσα,
τίφθ' οὕτω πατρὸς νοσφίζεαι, οὐδὲ παρ' αὐτὸν
ἑζομένη μύθοισιν **ἀνείρεαι οὐδὲ μεταλλᾷς;**
οὐ μέν κ' ἄλλη γ' ὧδε γυνὴ **τετληότι θυμῷ**
ἀνδρὸς ἀφεσταίη, ὅς οἱ κακὰ **πολλὰ μογήσας**
ἔλθοι ἐεικοστῷ ἔτει ἐς πατρίδα γαῖαν
σοὶ δ' αἰεὶ κραδίη στερεωτέρη ἐστὶ λίθοιο."

85

90

95

100

Quandary: fork A
Quandary: fork B

Guest of honor

Clothing and status: beggar
Emotional speaker: hostile

Doubly question
Long-term goal
Fruits of labor

Apparatus Fabulosus

Line 69: Traditional punctuation. This standard speech introduction (τὴν δ' ἠμείβετ' ἔπειτα, "And then [he/she] answered her") is a generic introductory "word" that occurs sixty-nine times in the epics and twice in the *Hymn to Aphrodite*, combining with twenty-nine different noun-epithet phrases and identifying twenty-five different characters. As is the case with other such generic patterns, this half-line has little or no special implication beyond its introductory function. **Dramatis personae.** This noun-epithet phrase indexes Eurykleia via one of her institutionalized names, bringing the entire character to center stage by invocation of the traditional semantic code. This second part of the line (φίλη τροφὸς Εὐρύκλεια, "beloved nurse Eurykleia") is the most common way of naming the old woman (nine occurrences [occs.]), others including the whole-line phrase Εὐρύκλει᾽, ῏Ωπος θυγάτηρ Πεισηνορίδαο ("Eurykleia, daughter of Ops the son of Peisenor") and the half-line phrase περίφρων Εὐρύκλεια ("wise Eurykleia"), which has the same metrical extent as her most common name. See also the discussion of δῖα γυναικῶν in Chapter 7.

Line 70: You should know better! Via this phrase an older or more experienced figure indicates to the previous speaker that his or her statement was rash, and chides him/her; the referential content amounts to "you should know better!" The whole-line pattern occurs six times in the *Odyssey* (1.64, 3.230, 5.22, 19.492, 21.168, 23.70) and twice in the *Iliad* (4.350, 14.83), each time introducing a harsh criticism of what immediately preceded. The fact that the simplex ἕρκος ὀδόντων ("barrier of the teeth"; *Il.* 9.409; *Od.* 10.328) has no such overtone illustrates the indivisibility of this *sêma*.

Line 72: You are wrong. More specific than many other *sêmata*, this phrase or a slight variant is used three times in the *Odyssey*: once in this form by the disguised Odysseus to criticize Eumaios for believing Odysseus dead (14.150), again by the disguised Odysseus in a variant form (θυμὸς ἐνὶ στήθεσσιν ἄπιστος, 14.391) for the same purpose, and here in Book 23, with Eurykleia criticizing Penelope for the same belief. Note that the word *apistos* appears only four times in Homer, and its only occurrence outside this phrase is the phraseologically unrelated usage at *Iliad* 24.63. For the force of the scar as *sêma*, see Chapter 1.

Line 73: Fulcrum: command. This extremely general sign marks (*a*) a change in direction within a speech and (*b*) a change in mode by introducing a command in the form "Come do something" or "Come let us do something." The phrase appears a total of 154 instances in Homer (sixty-five in *Iliad*, eighty-four in *Odyssey*, five in Hymns). It compares in breadth of function to **Traditional punctuation** and is at the opposite end of the spectrum from the rarer and more narrowly focused **You are wrong**. All signs are not equivalent in semantic resonance, just as they are not equivalent in structure.

Line 74: **Key: boar story**. At 19.392–466 the implicit story of Odysseus' wounding by the boar is made explicit. Two additional traditional features are important: (1) the episode is framed via ring-composition (393/465), and (2) the recurrence of 393 and 466 as contiguous lines at 21.219–20 further illustrates the expandability of the keying phrase. The Oxford *Odyssey Commentary* takes this correspondence as a possible indication of spuriousness, citing the absence of the two lines from two manuscripts, but I interpret the same data as evidence of traditional composition and grounds for traditional reception. The one-line version at 23.74 is thus a *sêma* for the inset story, just as Eurykleia effectively says. See also 24.331–33, which performs the same function with slightly different phraseology.

Line 78: **Fulcrum: righting a wrong**. Like ἀλλ᾽ ἄγε (**Fulcrum: command**), this phrase signals a change in direction and in mode within a speech, leading to a command. But ἀλλ᾽ ἔπευ is more focused: it also carries the implication that the action prescribed will right a present wrong, as when Hektor calls for Aineias to stand by Alkathoos, just killed by Idomeneus (*Il.* 13.465). Total of five instances; the three others are at *Iliad* 15.556; *Odyssey* 15.281, 23.52.

Line 80: **Traditional punctuation** (see note to line 69 above). **Dramatis personae**. This noun-epithet phrase indexes Penelope via one of her institutionalized names, invoking the entire character via the traditional semantic code. Penelope has three epithetic names: περίφρων Πηνελόπεια ("wise Penelope," used a total of fifty-one times in the nominative, dative, and vocative cases, with thirty of these linked to one of two phrases, κούρη/-η Ἰκαρίοιο ["daughter of Ikarios"] and τὴν/τὸν δ᾽ αὖτε προσέειπε, **Traditional punctuation**); ἐχέφρων Πηνελόπεια ("discreet Penelope," used a total of seven times in the nominative, dative, and accusative cases); and the unique usage ἀμύμονι Πηνελοπείη ("blameless Penelope," 24.194; cf. ἀμύμονι Βουκολίωνι ["blameless Boukolion"] at *Il.* 6.22 and ἀμύμονι Πουλυδάμαντι ["blameless Poulydamas"] at *Il.* 12.88, 14.469). Her name occurs twenty-four times without an epithet (all cases except the vocative). The metrically equivalent epithets *periphrôn* and *echephrôn*, also very close in lexical meaning ("wise, sage" and "sensible, discreet," respectively), vary in their phonological properties and reveal thrift in their systemic arrangement: the consonant that begins *periphrôn* avoids short-vowel hiatus after a first hemistich that ends in a vowel (all fifty-one of its instances follow a hemistich-ending vowel), while the vowel that begins *echephrôn* avoids overlengthening at the same juncture (all three hemistichs that end in a consonant are matched with *echephrôn* [16.130, 24.198, 24.294]; there are also four cases in which *echephrôn* follows a diphthong, and all seven of the lines involved have no formulaic relatives in the epics or hymns). This system of naming is thus based not on lexical distinction among epithets but on the traditional structure of the entire *sêma*: in each case it is the noun-epithet phrase as a whole—in whatever form—that is the focal point for **Dramatis personae**.

Line 81: **Practical impossibility**. The impersonal phrases involving χαλε-πόν ("hard, difficult") mark the action in question as impractical or impossible under normal circumstances, despite the fact that the action may be inherently brave or reasonable. Contexts include the limitations of humans as compared with the powers of gods (*Il.* 21.184; *Od.* 10.305, 11.156, 23.81, 23.184), a disproportionate numerical weakness in force (*Il.* 16.620, *Od.* 20.313), and other situations (*Il.* 19.80, *Od.* 4.651, 13.141; *HHer* 205). **Dramatis personae**. A widespread phrase (three times in Hesiod's *Theogony*, five times in *Iliad*, twice in *Odyssey*, three times in Hymns) that has no discernible expressive force beyond its function as traditional characterization. Also occurs in dative plural, θεοῖς αἰειγενέτῃσι(ν), six times in Hesiod and Homer with the same generalized function.

Lines 86–87: **Quandary: forks A and B**. The phraseology associated with *hormainô* (and with *mermêrizdô*) describes an as yet unsolved quandary. In simplest form, the verbs convey a process of pondering the meaning or outcome of a present dilemma. With the ἤ . . . ἤ (either . . . or) extension, the quandary becomes a narrative fork, with two competing alternatives set out for possible action; resolution takes place by choice, by intercession of a god, or simply by circumstance. What the phraseology signals is a frozen moment of indecision or uncertainty, and it slots those situations to which it is applied into this familiar category. The ἤ . . . ἤ extension thus deepens whatever moment it frames and prescribes alternative pathways for the progress of the song. Compare *Odyssey* 24.235–38, where Odysseus faces the same dilemma of whether to kiss and embrace Laertes or to question and test him further; here **Quandary** is expressed with *mermêrizdô* plus the ἤ . . . ἤ structure (in part understood) and narrative fork. There are twenty-five clear instances (nine with *hormainô* and sixteen with *mermêrizdô*) that use the extension, but in many instances lacking the ἤ . . . ἤ extension a dual choice is still implied, and/or precedes rather than follows the verb.

Line 90: **Guest of honor**. With the phrase πρὸς κίονα μακρὴν (lit., "against the tall pillar") Homer regularly keys an immediately subsequent seating and feast. It is employed four additional times in the epics, always in the *Odyssey*: see further its indexical function at 1.127 (pseudo-Mentes' spear is leaned against a pillar in the Ithakan palace), 8.66 and 8.473 (Demodokos' chair is placed against a pillar in the Phaeacian palace), and 17.29 (Telemachos leans his spear against a pillar in the Ithakan palace). While its superficial sense has no link to seating and feast, the role of this phrase as a *sêma* is clear. This is yet another traditional indication that the *telos* of the poem is being interpreted as a feast that in turn implies mediation (see the discussion of typical scenes in Chapters 6 and 7).

Line 95: **Clothing and status: beggar**. The donning of *heimata* (clothes) marks a reinforcement or change of status. For mortals this often means movement in one of two directions: either toward one's true, or restored, identity or its opposite—the lowest rung on the social ladder, a beggar (see espec. Odysseus' own understanding of the polar opposites at 16.209–10). For gods and goddesses, donning *heimata* marks a positive transformation, as in the case of the moon Selene (*HSel* 7–8), who after bathing in Ocean puts on "far-shining clothes" for her trip across the sky. This same enabling function is mirrored in Hebe's furnishing "pleasing clothes" as part of Ares' healing process (*Il.* 5.905) and in Zeus' instructions to Apollo to care for Sarpedon by putting "ambrosial clothes" on the corpse (*Il.* 16.670). A similar function applies to humans through the promised or actual conferral of a "mantle and tunic" that empowers an action or signals status; so Nausikaa gives Odysseus these formulaic *heimata* and starts him on the road to being a guest-friend (φᾶρός τε χιτῶνά τε εἵματ᾽ ἔθηκαν [*Od.* 6.214]; cf. also 7.234, 238), Kirke puts these same *heimata* on Odysseus before he sets out on the trip to Hades (χλαῖνάν τε χιτῶνά τε εἵματα ἕσσεν [*Od.* 10.542]), and, tellingly, Penelope promises the beggar a mantle and tunic should he string the bow (χλαῖνάν τε χιτῶνά τε, εἵματα καλά [*Od.* 21.339]). This implied meaning explains Eurykleia's otherwise curious insistence at 22.487–89 that Odysseus, having just slaughtered the suitors and thereby restored himself, immediately change into a fresh mantle and tunic; she admonishes him not to stand there in the hall with his broad shoulders covered with (beggar's) rags, for νεμεσσητὸν δέ κεν εἴη ("that would be scandalous [worthy of indignation, shame, or disgrace]"). It would also be untraditional. On the other hand, the phrase at line 95 and its relatives describe the donning of *kaka* or *lugra heimata* ("foul or wretched clothes"), thus keying the beggar identity, which also coincides by convention with the portrait of the Return hero (caught as he is in an ambiguous and duplicitous mode of becoming, before the final and empowering triumph over his foes and restoration of his family and personal identity).

This phrase or one of its relatives is used ten times of Odysseus and once of Laertes, whom Antikleia describes in the same way during her report to her son in Hades (*Od.* 11.191); in effect, the devastation that has reduced Odysseus to mendicant status has done the same to his father. The implication of the **Clothing and status: beggar** signal is never more obvious than in the passage under consideration, wherein Penelope vacillates between recognition of her husband and seeing the stranger as a mere beggar (note the balanced syntax with *allote . . . allote* and matched iterative aorist verbs). See also *Odyssey* 23.115.

Line 96: **Emotional speaker (hostile), with question to follow**. This is one of the series of "spoke a word and called him/her by name" instances (forty-five total in epics and hymns) that index (1) the relationship between speaker and addressee as either very positive and intimate or very negative and hostile; (2) the speaker's earnestness; (3) a heightened emotional tension; and (4) a subsequent question, command, request, or prayer. The question may be an actual interrogative or a speech-act that implies a framing question ("Do you know that . . . ?"). Here the phrase glosses an exchange between Telemachos and Penelope that is both intimate (as son to mother) and hostile (because she refuses to recognize his father). It emphasizes his earnestness and a heightened emotional tension, and creates a traditional expectation fulfilled by his challenging question ("Why do you so withdraw from my father, and do not sit beside him and ask him questions and find out about him?" [98–99]). In addition to *Odyssey* 23.96, the negative form of this sign occurs at *Iliad* 15.552 (Hektor scolds Melanippos for not fighting harder) and at *Odyssey* 16.417 (Penelope reproaches Antinoos for his actions toward Telemachos and herself), 18.78 (Antinoos threatens the beggar Iros over his upcoming boxing match with the disguised Odysseus), 19.90 (Penelope scolds Melantho for speaking sharply to the disguised Odysseus), 21.84 (Antinoos accuses Eumaios and Philoitios of troubling Penelope and for saying that none of the suitors will be able to string the bow), 21.167 (Antinoos castigates Leodes for his prophecy concerning the bow), and 21.287 (Antinoos scolds the disguised Odysseus for asking to try the bow).

Line 99: **Doubly question**. When some form of *eiromai* (prefixed or not) and of *metallaô* co-occur, the implication is as follows: (1) a deep probing and/or divulging of (2) some factual information heretofore hidden or unknown, with (3) the inquiry justified or unjustified but always very demanding, followed by (4) some subsequent revelation certified as true. This apparent lexical redundancy well illustrates the arbitrary sign-meaning relationship. The three phrases used are *dieireo/-ai (m)êde metalla(is)* ("[you] do not ask or inquire," two occs.), *aneireai êde metallais* ("you ask and inquire," seven occs.), and *metallêsai kai eresthai* ("to inquire and ask," five occs.), plus the instance at *Iliad* 1.553.

Line 100: **Long-term goal.** This phrase, which occurs only in the *Odyssey*, literally means "with enduring heart" and signals the necessity and fact of enduring an unpleasant present reality in order to reach an eventual goal. The present discomfort lasts an appreciable period of time, long enough for the faint hearted to give up, choose the easier route, and fail in their attempt at a worthy but very difficult achievement. Thus Menelaos and his men must spend the morning wrapped in sealskins in order to trick Proteus and have a chance to capture him (4.447); they must retain their grip on Proteus as he shifts shapes in order to subdue him and gain crucial information about returning home (4.459); and Odysseus must hold on to the underside of his ram all night in order to escape Polyphemos' cave (9.435). At 11.181 Antikleia uses the same signal to tell her son that Penelope has been enduring perhaps "too long" (λίην), a sentiment that meshes well with other indications that Penelope's ability to maintain her fidelity is threatened; and Eumaios tells the newly returned Telemachos the very same thing in the very same terms at 16.37 (11.181–83 = 16.37–39). Two other straightforward instances are also of interest. At 18.135 Odysseus lectures the minor suitor Amphinomos on life's vicissitudes: when the gods bring wretched times, then a man must endure in his heart, though it may be against his will. At 24.163 Amphimedon's ghost describes how the disguised Odysseus endured the suitors' throwing things at him and generally reproaching him, all for the sake of the later plan of vengeance (as implied by the *sêma* of the Return pattern). Against this idiomatic background, the **Long-term goal** signals at lines 23.100 and 168 (100–102 = 168–70) are particularly resonant, underlining the between-the-signs reality that neither Telemachos (in the former) nor Odysseus (in the latter) can understand why Penelope will not at this point officially recognize the man before her as her returned husband. The phrase τετληότι θυμῷ—indexing as it does the endurance of an unpleasant present reality in favor of an eventual goal—deepens the resonance of their critical disbelief: even the traditional referentiality of the phrase, which implies a resolution after much anguish, seems compromised by her intransigence. This is an example of how traditional referentiality cooperates with and enriches the narrative, lending it an indexical force that it would otherwise lack. As for its traditional morphology, **Long-term goal** calls for exact recurrence of the key phrase—τετληότι θυμῷ (a C1+ fourth colon).

Line 101: **Fruits of labor.** Rather than simply "toiling" or "suffering," this phrase (with variation in inflection and position) implies the outcome or end result of suffering: a goal that is always positive, earned, long-term, and as permanent as any human achievement can be in the Homeric world. For example, Achilleus earns his prize, Briseis, through heroic combat (see *Il.* 1.162, 2.690); Agamemnon's appropriation is thus the more galling because it controverts a traditional expectation. Other demanding activities that lead to parallel goals, and are glossed by the πολλὰ μογήσας signal, include child rearing (Phoinix of Achilleus, *Il.* 9.492), another case of heroic combat (Antilochos and his family, *Il.* 23.607), Eumaios' survival of a desperate earlier life (*Od.* 15.489), an old man's longing for his absent son (*Od.* 16.19, in a simile), Laertes' cultivation of his land (*Od.* 24.207), and, most significant for present purposes, Odysseus' arduous wandering during the process of his return (twelve instances in the *Od.*). Notice that the difficulty of the return is further emphasized by citing its extent in the following line when Odysseus is negotiating his identity with those closest to him (Eurykleia, 19.483; Eumaios and Melanthios, 21.207; Penelope [via Telemachos], 23.101; and Penelope [in his own voice], 23.169): ἔλθοι (or ἤλυθον) ἐεικοστῷ ἔτεϊ ἐς πατρίδα γαῖαν ("might come/came in the twentieth year back to his fatherland"). **Fruits of labor** also harmonizes with the preceding signal, **Long-term goal**, in harboring the implication that some positive outcome will stem from a period of misfortune or difficulty. Each signal, of course, appears elsewhere by itself, and each has its own idiomatic meaning. Given their joint associative thrust, however, Telemachos' and Odysseus' complaints to Penelope only gather more force: in effect, she is being asked how she can go against traditional expectation.

AFTERWORD
"Deor" and Anglo-Saxon *Sêmata*

Homer and the South Slavic *guslar* have delivered their testimony. For a third witness to the importance of traditional signs and their referential advantage, I now turn to a brief interview with the Anglo-Saxon *scop*, the early medieval English poet who practiced his craft on the cusp of oral tradition and texts.[1] Specifically, we will be considering the small, elegiac poem "Deor," which survives in a single version in the Exeter Book manuscript, thus dating from before the end of the tenth century C.E. Although far removed from Homeric epic in genre as well as in language, time, and place, this composite lyric illustrates in brief compass the operation of traditional referentiality in verbal art. The poem contends that Deor himself was its singer, and that may be true, but for our purposes the most important feature of the presentation is the deeply traditional language in which it has taken shape. As with the ancient Greek materials, the Old English poems are difficult if not impossible to place accurately in their historical and cultural contexts. Much remains unknown, and the traditional nature of the poetry resists the usual matrix imposed by conventional types of literary history. But one thing is certain: whoever composed "Deor" could speak the poetic register fluently. Whoever was responsible for the poem as it stands could deploy Anglo-Saxon *sêmata* idiomatically and in full awareness that Old English sign-language (even when textualized) works like a language, only more so.

Here is the poem in its entirety in modern English translation. I have marked certain phrases for subsequent discussion with italics and included the Anglo-Saxon original for those phrases to the right of the translation.[2]

By his sword Welund *had knowledge of exile;*		wræces cunnade
single-minded warrior, he suffered hardships,		
had as his companions sorrow and longing,		
winter-cold exile. He often discovered woe		wintercealde wræce
after Nithhad laid fetters on him,	5	
supple sinew-bonds on the excellent man.		
That passed away, so may this.		[Refrain]
To Beaduhild her brothers' death was not		
so painful in her mind as her own predicament,		
once she had readily perceived	10	
that she was with child; never could		
she boldly think what had to come of that.		
That passed away, so may this.		[Refrain]
We heard that Maethhild's lamentations,		We . . . gefrugnon
the Geat's lady's moans, became numberless,	15	
that love-sorrow robbed her of all sleep.		
That passed away, so may this.		[Refrain]
For thirty winters Theodric ruled		
the Maerings' stronghold; that was known to		
many.		
That passed away, so may this.	20	
We came to learn Eormanric's		
wolfish thought; he ruled widely over the		
people		
of the Ostrogoths' kingdom; *that was a savage*		
king.		þæt wæs grim cyning
Many a man sat bound in sorrows,		
expecting woes, constantly wished	25	
that his rule would be overcome.		
That passed away, so may this.		[Refrain]
The sorrowful one sits, *deprived of joys,*		sælum bidæled
gloomy of mind; it seems to him		
that his share of hardships is endless.	30	
Then he may think that throughout this world		
wise God moves constantly;		
He grants honor to many a man,		

certain renown; to certain others a share of woes.
I wish to tell this about myself,   35   secgan wille
that I was the singer of the Heodenings for a
    time,
dear to my lord. My name was Deor.
For many winters I had a good position,
a gracious lord, until now Heorrenda,
a song-skilled man, took over the land-right   40
that the protector of warriors formerly gave me.
That passed away, so may this.   [Refrain]

The implications we have learned to locate behind traditional *sêmata* are everywhere in this forty-two-line poem.[3] At the most general level, we can observe that Deor tells his tale by induction, depending directly on the implications of often cryptic cues, each one ending with what is apparently the earliest recorded refrain in English verse—"That passed away, so may this" (lines 7, 13, 17, 20, 27, and 42). As it stands, cut off from its traditional background, "Deor" makes little sense. Precisely because it depends so crucially on traditional referentiality, it may seem like an unconnected, incomplete pastiche of scattered characters and their actions. Once the audience or reader is aware of the referential advantage offered by the poetic tradition, however, the episodes bloom into fullness, their interrelationships become apparent, and a network of implication cogently glosses Deor's own sad fate. Proceeding through a series of disappointing or unfortunate episodes drawn from the wealth of early Germanic mythology, the poet leads up to an account of his own difficult situation: he has been displaced as court bard by another singer, named Heorrenda.[4] Each analogous mythic episode is summoned by a thumbnail description of fewer than ten poetic lines, so the audience or reader has an important role to play in filling in the expressive blanks. Whether by drawing on cultural knowledge or, as in our day, resorting to a critical apparatus that documents and summarizes the implied stories, the hearer or reader must get behind the signs, expanding the lyric abbreviations to their full narrative complexity.

    The first two sections of the poem, through the refrain at line 13, refer to the widely attested misery and vengeance associated with Welund, the famous Germanic smith, and Beaduhild, daughter to Nithhad. As the implied story goes, Nithhad captures Welund, who rapes Beaduhild and eventually escapes. In some versions Welund is hamstrung and forced to serve as the royal smith during his captivity; this may be the source of the "fetters" and "sinew-bonds" (5–6) in the Old English poem. But however we decide to piece together the details, the "Deor" poet is relying upon our ability to summon at least the broad outlines of the affair involving the smith, the violated Beaduhild, and her father Nithhad. Welund is captured and suffers exile, the worst fate that can befall anyone in Germanic tradition; his lonely isolation from his normal social context mirrors Deor's own loss of identity, while Welund's revenge holds forth at least some promise for possible amelioration of the singer's situation. Likewise, Beaduhild's unwanted pregnancy and the stigma that accompanies it also reflect Deor's expulsion from society; only the reality—here left entirely as implication—that she ends up bearing an estimable hero, Widia, offers Deor any hope of improving his own lot.

The story of Maethhild in the third section (14–17) is if anything more telegraphic than the first episode, and more rarely attested. A Norwegian and an Icelandic analogue both tell the tale of a woman who tearfully informs her mate on or soon after their wedding night that she is irremediably fated to drown in a river.[5] His protestations notwithstanding, her prediction comes only too true; unable to halt the process, he responds by playing his poet's harp and through its magic power bringing her to the surface. In the Icelandic source all he can do is to raise her body, but in the Norwegian ballad he manages to save her life. It is arguably this latter "happy ending" to which the "Deor" poet is alluding, aligning his own downfall and hoped-for reemergence with Maethhild's death and magical resuscitation.

Scholars more or less agree that the fourth episode, the briefest of all at merely two lines plus the refrain (18–20), refers to Theodric's exile. Although there is no explicit information to guide us, his rule over the Maerings seems to represent a period during which he was separated from his original, proper kingdom. We are on firmer ground with the fifth and final mythic excerpt about Eormanric (21–27), which treats not just the unjust and savage king himself but also the woebegone subjects who must suffer under his cruelty. As the poet points toward possible betterment of his own lot, then, he is thinking not of Eormanric, who showed no intention of abandoning his evil ways, but rather of the warriors who could be released from their misery only by his death.

With these examples in mind, the "Deor" poet then indulges in a moment of existential reverie before turning to his own problem. While each of the preceding sections represents a complex episode keyed by traditional signs, this interlude (28–34) has no direct recourse to any implied Germanic story. Nonetheless, it shares the earlier sections' focus on the joyless state of exile and points toward a possible—though hardly certain—change in the present state of affairs. Things are always in flux and God is constantly moving throughout the world, the poet explains; in the fact of such mutability some hope can be found. That grim awareness and measured expectation are all he has as comfort for his own exile, his dislodging as court poet, once "dear to [his] lord" (37a), in favor of a competitor. With the refrain, "That passed away, so may this," Deor aligns his own fate with the destinies of the celebrated figures whose *sêmata* occupy the first 27 lines of his poem. Like Welund and Beaduhild, like Maethhild, Theodric, and Eormanric's beleaguered subjects, he languishes in abject despair; on their model, he hopes for relief from his current despondency.

The entire structure of "Deor" thus depends on traditional referentiality for its intelligibility and for its art. Without a knowledge of the implied background, without the ability to expand sign into story, this collection of Germanic vignettes must seem more an exercise for a philologist than a poem. Reading behind the signs, however, makes the work come alive: a bard laments his fate by reference to the story-hoard that is both his possession and his benefactor. Drawing subtly and poignantly on tales that flesh out the tragic present and potential future of his own situation, he uses traditional referentiality in a powerfully indexical way.

But the poet's artistry does not end with this most general level of sign-language. Like Homer and the South Slavic epic poets, Deor also deftly uses the referential advantage of the typical scene or theme, in this case the ubiquitous and immediately recognizable Exile pattern.[6] Briefly stated, this theme portrays the ultimate cultural nightmare in Anglo-Saxon society and poetry: enforced, long-term separation from family and social unit, with a consequent loss of identity. As a traditional signal or "word" it consists of what Stanley Greenfield (1955) identified as four constituent elements: status, deprivation, state of mind, and movement in or into exile. That is, the scene normally includes a character's stipulation of his or her current status as disattached from the customary kin-group or social unit, as well as pictures him or her consciously experiencing a state of deprivation. Commentary on what the separation feels like also contributes to this pattern, as does some historical account of how it came about. Clearly, all of these elements are readily found in the forty-two lines of "Deor," some of them secured by phrases that, as we shall see below, traditionally cue the poetic reality of Exile.

Before we consider the first of those phrases let me point out, as I did with both the Homeric poems and the South Slavic epics, that the most important *sêma* at the level of verse lines is the phraseology as a whole. More than any single phrase, the overall way of speaking (and listening and reading) prescribes a channel for expression and reception, and it does so by following traditional rules for the construction and maintenance of phraseology. Of course, these traditional rules are different for Old English verse than for the other two poetries we have examined in this book. Indeed, as we saw in Chapter 3, Homer and the *guslar* speak in similar but hardly identical poetic dialects. Since each way of speaking is after all a language, each one has its own *modus operandi*: some poetic languages count syllables, some count stresses, some depend upon musical accompaniment, and so forth.[7] Despite this variation, however, the principle remains the same. Traditional registers govern the poetic exchange; they prescribe performance arenas and foster highly economical communication. The chief phraseological sign is the language or register itself.

Within this register we can highlight a few phrases or "words" that key particular meanings, signs bearing idiomatic implications that harmonize tellingly with the genre and expressive program of "Deor" as a lament. Two of these *sêmata* occur within the first few lines, as the poet seeks to establish the Exile pattern as a traditional context for each of the Germanic episodes and, not least, for his own position as an outcast. In the opening line we hear that Welund "had knowledge of exile" (*wræces cunnade*, 1b), a phrase that sounds the knell for this typical scene by using diction customarily associated with it.[8] More metaphorically indicative is the mention of cold weather accompanying this state of separation and deprivation—Welund's "winter-cold exile" (*wintercealde wræce*, 4a). Throughout Old English poetry, imagery associated with winter, ice, storm, and the like is employed as a traditional sign for the condition of exile.[9] Merely the bare mention of such a telltale detail confers upon the local situation all of the trappings of the typical scene, as when Saint Andrew, confined in a Mermedonian prison overnight, is effectively slotted as an exile by invocation of the customary meteorological images. Because the phraseology works like a language, only more so, Andrew can be swiftly and precisely categorized by reference to the traditional network of implication.[10] Just so with Welund, and, by extension, with Deor himself.

Traditional signs not linked directly to a narrative pattern can also prove useful for the poet composing an Anglo-Saxon poem, as well as uniquely resonant for its audience or readership. After finishing the two-section tale of Welund and Beaduhild, for example, Deor begins the Maethhild passage with "We heard . . ." (*We . . . gefrugnon*, 14), the same traditional sign that opens poems like *Beowulf* and *Andreas*. Here it provides a signal that the subject is changing, that some new topic is now under way; in this initiatory function it mirrors the "But come . . ." rhetoric employed so frequently by Homer.[11] It also stipulates—rhetorically or not—that the information to follow was gleaned from oral tradition, an attribution that carries a singular authority. A similar kind of signal, "I wish to tell . . ." (*secgan wille*, 35b), will help to introduce the final section of the poem, when the poet turns at last to the subject for which he has so carefully and idiomatically prepared: his personal history.[12]

Within the fifth small vignette two signs help reenforce the poet's presentation of Eormanric's unfortunate rule and his subjects' unfortunate fate. At line 23 we hear a kind of summation of his reign: "that was a savage king" (*þæt wæs grim cyning*). While on the surface it may seem a redundant or superfluous annotation, this phrase has deep poetic resonance in Old English verse. Syntactically independent of what surrounds it and virtually proverbial in its structure and meaning, the customary and positive version—"that was an excellent king" (*þæt wæs god cyning*)—certifies the person to whom it is applied as an effective leader who fulfills the Anglo-Saxon ideal of reciprocity toward faithful subjects. Along with variations like "that was a wise/true/noble/peerless king," it slots figures as diverse as Scyld Scefing and Hrothgar (in *Beowulf*), Beowulf himself, Guthhere (in *Widsith*), and the Christian God in the classic profile of staunch defender and wise provider.[13] Imagine how ironically this *sêma* functions when all of the cherished values associated with the ideal king, epitomized in the proverbial phrase, are summarily overturned in an excoriation of Eormanric's malfeasance. Not unlike the reversal of the "satisfaction" marker during Polyphemos' perverse feast,[14] the statement is that much more damning because we read behind the sign.

As noted above, the section that follows Eormanric's violation of custom and office lacks the specific focus of the episodes that precede it. But it does not lack traditional referentiality. In support of the Exile theme that has been so important an expressive strategy throughout the earlier descriptions, and which has real bearing on Deor's own status as a displaced person, the phrase "deprived of joys" (*sælum bidæled*, 28b) foregrounds important implications in the sixth section of the poem. As Greenfield established, this "word" and its variants are strongly linked to the element of deprivation in the tradition-wide typical scene. Along with a selection of abstract nouns meaning "comfort, joy," this signal consists of a past participle meaning "deprived." In concert with rules for the formation and maintenance of phraseology in Anglo-Saxon poetry, a number of different combinations can and do answer this expressive need, but the syntax and traditional meaning of the composite "word" remain the same throughout. By using the *sêma* "deprived of joys," the "Deor" poet evokes the idea of exile just as surely as if he mentioned the key word *wræc* or added the idiomatic imagery of winter, ice, and storm to his description. "Deprived of joys" indexes the exile pattern and helps guide the audience's or reader's reception of the sixth section in particular and the entire lament in general.

I have reserved commentary on the much-discussed refrain—"That passed away, so may this" (*þæs ofereode, þisses swa mæg*)—until after we treated some examples of sign-language at all levels of the poem.[15] As proverbial as this tightly knit line may sound, we cannot prove it to be traditional except in the sense of following traditional rules for structure; there is nothing in the Anglo-Saxon poetic corpus that matches it at all closely in any formulaic way. Strictly speaking, then, the refrain does not belong with the other phrases we have studied here, and we can make no case for its traditional referentiality. But what we can point out is its analogous function as an indexical signal—not across the poetic tradition but within the single poem "Deor." Although on available evidence it bears no idiomatic meaning from outside, "That passed away, so may this" imitates sign-language by helping to unify the different sections within the lament. Just as some *sêmata* slotted an episode within the category of exile or emphasized Eormanric's cruelty by reference to the ideal of Anglo-Saxon kingship, so the refrain acts as a touchstone that both divides the episodes one from the next and emphasizes their similarity and pertinence to Deor's present situation. Like true traditional signs in Homer and elsewhere, the refrain is effectively a *sêma*-shot through the axeheads, only in this case the separate contexts are limited to the same poem. Even if the proverbial phrase was the creation of an individual poet, even if it was molded for use in this poem alone, the analogy with traditional signs will hold. The refrain creates and activates a network of implication that slots disparate episodes and events. It helps to make "Deor" both a singular and a singularly traditional poem.

What this third witness testifies, then, is that the composition and reception of Anglo-Saxon poetry depends upon reading behind as well as between the signs. The special register that serves as the vehicle for poetic communication demands a good deal of the audience or reader as well as of the poet, but the rewards for a fluent transaction are great. At the level of the poem as a whole, the excerpts from Germanic myth act as signs to be expanded in the process of interpretation, so that the figures so briefly mentioned over the first five vignettes come to life as recognizable characters with stories germane to Deor's own bitter experience. That process of filling in the blanks is necessary to the poem's intelligibility, and necessary to the poet's traditional art of implication. Likewise, the typical scene or theme of Exile serves as a *sêma* behind which we must read, an idiomatic pattern that helps to focus and align the five stories on an axis that also includes the exiled singer's recent history. Finally, particular phrases act as cues that slot or index individual moments as well as the entire lament by referring them to familiar traditional categories. Although "Deor" consists of a series of freestanding episodes, it is also a unified poem; perhaps we can now see that its unity is due in no small part to its traditional register, which works like language, only more so.

Feasting in the *Odyssey*

Locus	Host/Guest	Seating	Actions	Satisfaction	Mediation
1.113f.	Telemachos/Mentes	130	Core: 136–42	149–50	Instilling courage in Telemachos
3.31f.	Nestor/Tel., Mentor	37	Libation	67	Nestor's news and memories of Odysseus
3.404f.	Nestor/Tel.	416	Sacrifice	473	Telemachos' departure with Peisistratos
4.47f.	Menelaos/Tel., Peis.	51	Core: 52–58	67–68	Menelaos' news and memories of Odysseus
5.85f.	Kalypso/Hermes	86	Divine	94–95	Negotiating Odysseus' release (K. and H.)
5.192f.	Kalypso/Od.	195	Divine/mortal	200–201	Negotiating Odysseus' release (K. and O.)
6.96f.	Nausikaa & maids	(elided)	Brief	99	Game of ball and discovery of Odysseus
7.155f.	Alkinoos/Od.	162–63, 169	Core: 172–76	228	Od.'s recent history and sleep for all
8.1f.	Alkinoos/Od.	6	Sacrifice	71–72	Demodokos' song, Od.'s rx., athletic games
8.449f.	Alkinoos/Od.	469	Brief	484–85	Dem.'s song; Od. identifies self, begins Books 9–12
9.250f.	Polyphemos/Od. +	(none)	*Perverse	288, 296–97	*Sleep and blinding of Polyphemos
10.348f.	Kirke/Od. +	366	Core: 368–72	467–70	K.'s advice concerning Hades and Teiresias
12.16f.	Kirke/Od. +	30	Brief	31	K.'s advice on challenges ahead
12.291f.	[Kirke]/Od. +	(elided)	Brief	308	Mourning lost companions and sleep

Locus	Host/Guest	Seating	Actions	Satisfaction	Mediation
12.339f.	Hyperion/Od.'s men	(elided)	*Perverse	397–400	*Zeus' vengeance; companions lose *nostos*
13.23f.	Phaeacians/Od.	(elided)	Brief	28–30	Farewell, departure, sleep
14.45f.	Eumaios/stranger	49	Modest	111	Od. tests Eum. (lying tale); loyalty
14.413f.	Eumaios/stranger	(elided)	Sacrifice	453–54	Od. tests Eum. (Troy tale); loyalty and sleep
15.92f.	Menelaos/Tel.	134	Core: 135–39	142–43	Farewell, omen, departure, sleep
15.301f.	Eumaios/stranger	(elided)	Brief	303	Od. tests Eum. (begging plan); loyalty
15.499f.	Tel. and comrades	(elided)	Brief	501	Plans and good omen (interp. by Theoklymenos)
16.41f.	Eum./Tel. and stranger	44–48	Brief	54–55	Od. tests Tel. and reveals himself to Tel.
16.452f.	Eum./Tel. and stranger	(elided)	Brief	480	Sleep; then Tel. to Pen. and stranger to megaron
17.84f.	Tel./stranger	90	Core: 91–95	98–99	Theoklymenos says Od. already in Ithaka
17.328f.	Tel./Eum. and stranger	334	Brief	359/603	Agonistic exchange w/ suitors; Eum. departs
18.418f.	[Variant: Suitors' libation > Satisfaction (427) > Sleep]				
19.317f.	Pen./stranger	321–22	Future	(none)	Eurykleia recognizes Od. via scar
19.413f.	Autolykos/Od.	(elided)	Alternate	424–26	Sleep (embedded in story by narrator)
20.244f.	Suitors and Tel./stranger	249, 257	Alternate	[256]	Never really ends; prefig. blood-feast
21.263f.	[Variant: Suitors' libation > Satisfaction (273) > Stranger asks for bow]				
23.153f.	Pen./stranger	295–96 (*telos*)	Lovemaking	300	Her story, his story, sleep
24.356f.	Laertes/Od. +	385, 394, 408–11	Brief	489	Battle w. suitors and Peace of Athena

Feasting in the *Iliad*

Locus	Host/Guest	Seating	Actions	Satisfaction	Mediation
9.89f.	Agam./Ach. leaders	(elided)	Brief	91–92	Formulation of Embassy to Achilleus
9.199f.	Achilleus/Embassy	200	Alternate	221–22	Od. begins offer to Ach. (to be refused)
24.515f.	Ach./Priam, Hektor	522, 553	Alternate	627–28	Coming to terms and sleep

GENERAL NOTE: Line numbers marking *Locus* are approximate, designating only where feasting activities may be understood to commence; each scene has its own shape and process. *Seating* customarily involves the verbs *hêmai, hezdomai, hidruô,* and their prefixed forms. *Actions* constitute either the "core" sequence illustrated by 1.136–40 (or –42) or some variant, often libation or sacrifice; this component can also be briefly presented in a few summary lines. *Satisfaction* is signaled most regularly by the verses "They put their hands to the good things that lay ready before them. / But when they had cast off their desire for eating and drinking," or just the latter of these two; other equivalent phrases may occasionally take their place.

APPENDIX II: "DEOR"

Welund him be wurman   *wræces cunnade*,   had knowledge of exile
anhydig eorl,   earfoþa dreag,
hæfde him to gesiþþe   sorge ond longaþ,
wintercealde wræce,   wean oft onfond   winter-cold exile
siþþan hine Niðhad   on nede legde,   5
swoncre seonobende,   on syllan monn.
    Þæs ofereode;   þisses swa mæg.   [Refrain]
Beadohilde ne wæs   hyre broþra deaþ
on sefan swa sar   swa hyre sylfre þing,
þæt heo gearolice   ongieten hæfde   10
þæt heo eacen wæs;   æfre ne meahte
þriste geþencan   hu ymb þæt sceolde.
    Þæs ofereode;   þisses swa mæg.   [Refrain]
We þæt Mæðhilde   mone gefrugnon   We . . . heard
wurdon grundlease   Geates frige,   15
þæt hi seo sorglufu   slæp ealle binom.
    Þæs ofereode;   þisses swa mæg.   [Refrain]
Ðeodric ahte   þritig wintra
Mæringa burg;   þæt wæs monegum cuþ.
    Þæs ofereode;   þisses swa mæg.   20   [Refrain]
We geascodan   Eormanrices
wylfenne geþoht;   ahte wide folc
Gotena rices;   *þæt wæs grim cyning.*   that was a savage king
Sæt secg monig   sorgum gebunden,
wean on wenan,   wyscte geneahhe   25
þæt þæs cynerices   ofercumen wære.
    Þæs ofereode;   þisses swa mæg.   [Refrain]
Siteð sorgcearig,   *sælum bidæled,*   deprived of joys
on sefan sweorceð,   sylfum þinceð
þæt sy endeleas   earfoða dæl,   30
mæg þonne geþencan   þæt geond þas woruld
witig Dryhten   wendeþ geneahhe,
eorle monegum   are gesceawað,
wislicne blæd,   sumum weana dæl.
Þæt ic be me sylfum   *secgan wille,*   35   I wish to tell
þæt ic hwile wæs   Heodeninga scop,
dryhtne dyre;   me wæs Deor noma.
Ahte ic fela wintra   folgað tilne,
holdne hlaford,   oþ þæt Heorrenda nu,
leoðcræftig monn,   londryht geþah   40
þæt me eorla hleo   ær gesealde.
    Þæs ofereode;   þisses swa mæg.   [Refrain]

NOTES

Preface

1. For a survey of anticipations of and influences on Parry and Lord, see Foley 1988: 1–18.

Introduction

1. While there is certainly no consensus on exactly how the received texts of the *Iliad* and *Odyssey* relate to oral tradition, very few doubt that a relationship exists; see further M. Edwards 1986, 1988, 1992. G. S. Kirk (1990: 181) calls the episode in *Iliad* 6 "the only definite reference in Homer to writing."

2. Powell (1991: 199–200) cites numerous parallels to the story and concludes: "Homer, then, has received an Eastern story in an Eastern form. The 'fatal letter' has come with the story." I find the parallels persuasive and the hypothesis of an Eastern origin for the tale quite attractive, but also caution that we must take account of the specific terms in which Homer describes this new technology.

3. Kirk (1990: 181) comments that the episode is "generally taken as a memory of Mycenaean Linear B (or Hittite hieroglyphs or Cypriot syllabary) rather than a reference to the new alphabetic script—which, however, must have seemed no less mysterious on its first introduction to the Greek world, probably in the late 9th cent. B.C." He further contends (*idem*) that "the present allusion is vague and indirect, perhaps intentionally so rather than through progressive misunderstanding in the poetical tradition." As indicated below, I suggest a third alternative to intentional vagueness and progressive misunderstanding: namely, a clear interpretation of the mysterious inscription as composed of Homeric *sêmata*. For more on Homer and writing, see Heubeck 1979: 126–46, W. Harris 1989: espec. 48–49, and H.-J. Martin 1994: espec. 46–48. Powell (1991: 199–200) argues that "no specific script is meant in his tale of Bellerophon. . . . On Homer's own evidence σήματα [*sêmata*] refer to semasiographic, not lexigraphic signs." See further Shear 1998.

4. For a sense of the variety of interactions within a single culture, see Lord 1986b on the "merging of two worlds" in the former Yugoslavia. For an example of a highly literate individual (a university professor) who nonetheless has assumed a full role in the oral traditional performance of Jack tales in North Carolina, see McCarthy, Oxford, and Sobol 1994.

5. *Pace* Bellamy 1989, based on a revision of the history of writing and some unusual conclusions about phonology, meter, and phraseology. On the persistence of oral traditional language into texts, see espec. Chapter 1 below and Foley 1995a: ch. 3. For solid work on the interactive quality of oral traditions and texts, see espec. Thomas 1989 on ancient Greek and Stock 1983, 1990 on medieval English; of related interest is Pratt 1995 on the seal of Theognis as marking the textualization of oral poetry. For cross-cultural perspectives on the processing of texts, see Boyarin 1993.

6. Interestingly, even the ancient commentators warn against understanding *sêmata* as "written letters." See espec. the scholion to *Il.* 6.168 (a) that identifies *sêmata* as *eidôla* ("images, phantoms"; used in Homer for dream-images and the shades of the dead); also Erbse 1969–83: 2.160–61, 260–62; Wolf 1985: 97–102; Jeffery 1967: 161; and espec. Saussy 1996: 305, 330 n. 36. An important corollary of the durability of such signs is the comparative brittleness of the tablet: taken as the language it is, traditional representation via *sêmata* is naturally more persistent than any of its derivative textualized instances.

7. See further "The Rhetorical Persistence of Traditional Forms," Foley 1995a: ch. 3.

8. Cf. espec. Foley 1991, 1995a. We cannot afford to overestimate the accuracy with which we can gauge Homer's proximity to an oral-traditional performance. Likewise, we cannot afford to underestimate the implications of that oral-traditional background for Homer's art.

9. Let me emphasize once again that these six proverbs focus on oral-connected traditional art, but make no claim to categorically distinguish that body of expression (itself heterogeneous) from verbal art in written, textual media. To some extent, reading behind as well as between the signs, to take one example, is a universal mandate for all poetry and prose, or even all verbal communication in any medium. Such a maxim becomes especially important for understanding traditional poetic language, but it is not restricted to that arena. I cite and employ all of these proverbs in this volume in the hope that they will assist us in the culturally challenging task of learning to speak Homer's traditional language.

Chapter 1.   Homeric Signs and Traditional Referentiality

1. *Tradition* is of course a notoriously difficult concept that has received many definitions; see espec. Dan Ben-Amos' comments on the "seven strands" of tradition (1984). I use the term throughout this book to refer to at least two of his seven possible (and interlocking) senses—as process and as *langue*—and I stress the referential advantage offered by tradition. For further specification, see Foley 1991, 1992a, 1995a.

2. For a thorough discussion of traditional referentiality, see Foley 1991: espec. chs. 1, 2, 5 and 1995a: chs. 1–2; clearly distinguished from literary allusion in Bradbury 1998; cf. also McDowell 1995. Let me explicitly acknowledge four recent studies of *sêmata* that have been of assistance in my own thinking about this resonant poetic term. The first (Nagy 1990a) focuses on showing that "the semantics of *sêma* are indeed connected with the semantics of thinking" (202), while the second (Ford 1992: 131–71) concentrates on the fixity of signs, especially in the *Iliad*, but also notes very helpfully that "the oral tradition is the necessary supplement to the durable, provocative, but unreadable sign" (144). The third (Prier 1989) points out that Homeric *sêmata* designate "phenomena of affective signification" (111, italics deleted; see also Prier 1976, 1978), and the fourth (Holmberg 1997) argues generally that "the *Odyssey* is interested in the relationship between the sign and the signified" (30) and comments specifically on the role of *mêtis* ("cunning intelligence") and its linkage with traditional signs. Also of interest is Saussy 1996 on the "theme of writing" and the role of *sêmata* in the *Odyssey*, as well as Svenbro (1993: 53), who observes that "in the case of the Homeric *sêma*, there is no writing." See further Lang (1982), whose definition of the Aristotelian *sêmeion*, or fallible sign—"a material access to something immaterial which would otherwise remain unavailable to us" (350)—closely mirrors the understanding of Homeric signs advocated throughout this volume; cp. *Poetics* 16 (Halliwell 1995: 83) on Aristotle's notion of recognition "through tokens" (*dia tôn sêmeiôn*).

3. Cf. R. Martin 1989: espec. 12–18 on the distinction between *muthos* and *epos*, native poetic terms that identify speech-acts according to their illocutionary force; also cf. Kahane 1997 on the traditional semantics of *oios* and *mounos*. As remarked in the Preface, and as illustrated

throughout this volume, I see no necessary conflict between traditional referentiality and other approaches, *pace* Ledbetter 1996: 490 n. 20.

4. For a history and annotated bibliography of this rediscovery, see respectively Foley 1988 and 1985 (with updates in the journal *Oral Tradition*: 1 [1986]: 767–808; 3 [1988]: 191–228; and 12 [1997], also available electronically at http://www.missouri.edu/~csottime); on ancient Greek in particular, see M. Edwards 1986, 1988, 1992; and Foley 1997.

5. See espec. Murko 1929 (trans. 1990) and 1951; Radlov 1885 (trans. 1990).

6. Of particular importance here is Lord's later work (espec. 1991, 1995), which continued to evolve and to extend his and Parry's "theory." As Nagy points out (1992: 28), what Parry and Lord studied was not so much a theory as the empirical fact of oral poetry, ascertained by fieldwork in the former Yugoslavia.

7. Story-patterns are exemplified in Lord 1960 (espec. 99–123 and 242–65); defined and described explicitly in Lord 1969, Coote 1981. See also Foley 1990: 359–87 and 1991: 64– 68, 100–106, 118–20; and Chapter 5 below. Cf. Oesterreicher's (1997) distinction between *Wiedergebrauchs-Rede* ("reusable discourse"), to which category the units of Oral Theory would belong, and *Verbrauchs-Rede* ("self-consuming discourse").

8. On the pedagogical importance of studies in oral tradition (both the Parry-Lord approach and other approaches), with special reference to classroom strategies in a variety of areas and disciplines, see *Teaching Oral Traditions* (Foley 1998a).

9. Thus, in speaking of the effect of studies in oral tradition on Homeric scholarship, Jasper Griffin (1980: xiii) registers "disappointment at the lack of light it has shed on the poems themselves"; see also iv. Cf. the welcome problematization of reading, writing, and texts in ancient Greece apparent in Bakker 1993a, b; and Thomas 1989; more generally in Boyarin 1993. Also of note is Rose's Marxist view of the politics of form in traditional language (1992: 43–91).

10. Perhaps the strongest version of this quantitative, categorical approach is that of Duggan (1973), who established a percentage threshold for the orality or literacy of various Old French *chansons de geste*.

11. But see Lord 1986a (espec. 478–81), in which he accepts the notion of the "transitional text" and modifies the concept of "formulaic density." In 1986b he describes three quite different encounters between oral tradition and literacy in the former Yugoslavia.

12. See Foley 1990: 11–15, and espec. Ch. 3 below on what South Slavic epic can—and cannot—tell us about Homer.

13. See, e.g., Foley 1983, 1991: ch. 4 on Christian epic; 1995a: ch. 4 on magical charms.

14. Scholarship on Old English verbal art has been particularly forward-looking in this regard; see espec. O'Brien O'Keeffe 1990 and Doane 1991, 1994. Also of importance for the understanding of "vocality" in medieval vernacular texts are Zumthor 1990 and, particularly, Schaefer 1992; see further Schaefer 1997 on how vocality links narrator and audience in a joint context of meaning. The ongoing discussion between Dell Hymes and Dennis Tedlock on oral traditions and textuality in Native American languages (summary in Foley 1995a: ch. 3) is also very instructive in this regard, as is the history of how oral traditions have been editorially memorialized as texts (see espec. Fine 1984; Foley 1995b; also McCarthy 1995).

15. "Way of speaking" is a term and concept developed by Hymes (see espec. 1989; also 1981, 1994). Cf. R. Martin (1993: 227), who describes practitioners of a living oral tradition as "bilingual, fluent in their natural language but also in the *Kunstsprache* of their local verbal art forms." On an interesting parallel in Indonesian ritual speech, see Kuipers 1990, 1998.

16. Cf. Foley 1990 on the rules that govern traditional epic idioms in ancient Greek (ch. 4), South Slavic (ch. 5), and Anglo-Saxon (ch. 6); also Nagy 1974: espec. 140–49 and 1990b: espec. 4–5, 50–51 on the symbiosis of meter and phraseology. For illustration of idiolect and dialect within a living oral tradition, see the discussions of South Slavic phraseology (Foley 1990: ch. 5) and narrative patterning (ch. 8). These many levels of traditional language offer

one reason to agree with Ruth Scodel (1997) that the audience, while certainly aware of traditional allusions as a part of the poet's technique, hardly had "to understand every poetic trick" (217). This perspective does not seem in conflict with R. Martin's helpful formulation that "we can consider Homer a master poet *without* abandoning our belief that he works *within* a traditional performance medium" (1993: 227), or with Minchin's cognitive model of poet and audience (1992a: espec. 232–37). See also Donlan 1993: espec. 158–59.

17. For the structure of typical scenes (also called "themes"), see Foley 1990: ch. 7 (ancient Greek), ch. 8 (South Slavic), and ch. 9 (Old English); on story-patterns, see note 7 above. M. Edwards (1992) provides an excellent summary of research on typical scenes in Homer. Cf. Foley 1991 on the traditional referentiality of narrative units in South Slavic (chs. 3–4), ancient Greek (ch. 5), and Old English (ch. 6).

18. As a suggestion of the reported diversity worldwide, see Finnegan 1977; also the cumulative contents of the journal *Oral Tradition* (1986–). A great deal of the evidence on variety has come from African traditions (see espec. Finnegan 1970; Okpewho 1992); see also the applications to biblical studies (e.g., Balch 1991, Niditch 1995 and espec. 1997 on "oral register," Kelber 1997: espec. xix–xxxi). Interesting and highly instructive examples from other sources in the ancient world include Maurizio's (1997) treatment of Delphic oracles as oral-derived texts and Gagarin's (1999) discussion of the orality of Greek oratory. Another perspective on the complexity of oral traditions and texts is available in Saenger's (1997) magisterial account of the role of spaces between words in the trajectory from reading aloud to silent reading.

19. On the traditional poetics of Middle English texts, relatively far removed from actual oral tradition, see espec. Parks 1986 and Amodio 1994.

20. See Foley 1991: espec. chs. 1–2. Cf. the complementary findings of Kahane 1994 and Russo 1994, as well as Biebuyck (1971: 14) on African epic, F. Andersen 1985 on European balladry, and DuBois (1994: 177) on Finnish oral poetry. Bakker (1997b) demonstrates how within Homeric narrative the grammatical signal of tense inherently involves the "cumulative mass of the tradition" in what he calls an act of "commemoration." Scodel (1997) offers a useful reminder that tradition and innovation should not always and everywhere be simply counterposed; as she puts it, "By taking so much for granted, the poet invites his audience to reconfirm his authority" (219). See espec. Sale's brilliant explanation (1999) of Virgil's formulaic language as implying a heritage that, notwithstanding its origins in the craft of the individual poet, provides his poem an artistic and political ballast that normally stem only from an actual, ongoing oral poetic tradition.

21. For a full account of this and parallel examples, see Foley 1994b. In the field of Anglo-Scottish balladry, the collector William Motherwell observed (Brown 1995: 10) that "the expressions of *wiping on the sleeve*, *drying on grass*, and *slating owre the strae* always occur in such ballads as indicate a dubious and protracted and somewhat equal combat." Pronouncing such phrases a "brachigraphy" or "short hand way of saying something," he noted that they provided for the ballad-singer "a kind of ground-work on which the poem could be raised," to "rapidly model any event which came under his cognizance into song." Motherwell is describing a traditional idiom of *sêmata*.

22. For me one of the most striking illustrations of the power of a traditional idiom is the preservation of apparently illogical conventions, first developed in puppet theater, in present-day Chinese opera (see Werle-Burger 1996). Identifiable hand gestures to index crying, a particularly stiff-legged gait to denote marching, and numerous other nominal features owe their origins to the physical limitations of puppet figures but are carried on into opera and employed by human actors as idiomatic signs. More naturalistic signals—e.g., crying actual tears, marching less awkwardly—are of course quite possible in the opera, where the physical limitations of puppets are no barrier, but such nonidiomatic signals would lack traditional referentiality. One could observe that the stage-register of Chinese opera works like a language, only more so.

23. Foley 1991: 155; cf. R. Martin 1989: 38.

24. For further discussion and examples, see further Foley 1991: 168–74; cf. Alexiou 1974: 33.

25. See note 7. The enormous spread of this story through time and space illustrates how stories—and the traditions they embody—don't so much begin and end as *continue*.

26. Simple lines of introduction do their homely job in signaling a speech, but it is a different kind of job than that allotted by convention to the phrases *pukinon epos* and *hupodra idôn* mentioned above; see further Chapters 7–8 below. On *word-power*, see espec. Foley 1992a; 1995a: 27–28, 56–59.

27. For a comparison of this web of linked sites to the modern Internet, see Foley 1998b.

28. Cp. this meshing of instance and implication with O. Andersen's notion of the interdependency of "tradition" and "occasion" in the oral-derived *Iliad* (1990: espec. 41–45). Further, *pace* Kullmann 1984, there exists a significant and defining difference between the perspective from traditional referentiality (as an extension of oral poetry theory) and that from Neoanalysis, the latter of which always posits another singular and *textual* situation as the referent for any shared feature in the source work. For an excellent historical survey of Neoanalysis, including an attempt to see overlaps with oral-formulaic theory, see Willcock 1997; of related interest is M. Edwards 1990: espec. 316–21.

29. Cf. Rubin 1995: espec. chs. 8–9 on cognitive processes, memory, and oral tradition.

30. Cf. Foley 1995a: 28: "Empowerment of the communicative act results from the keying of performance—whether in the first instance by an actual experienced event or in the textual instance by its rhetorical vestige—and from the shared immersion in traditional context that is the performer's and audience's experiential heritage." Cf. also Bakker 1993b, 1997a on speech, performance, and text; also Minchin 1992b. On a cognate kind of performance—the role of discipleship and embodiment of the Torah text—see Jaffee 1997: espec. 541–43; also Jaffee 1992, 1994, and the forthcoming cluster of essays in *Oral Tradition*: E. Alexander 1999, Elman 1999, Fraade 1999, and Jaffee 1999; cf. Culley 1993 on the biblical Psalms. For a magisterial review of Jewish folklore, cf. Ben-Amos 1999a and 1999b.

31. On the approach through performance studies, see espec. Bauman 1986; Bauman and Briggs 1990. Of related interest is Nagy 1996a. See also Bender 1996 on Chinese *tanci* storytelling for an interesting example of the array of performance cues available to performer and audience; as well as Dauenhauer and Dauenhauer 1995 on the ways in which oral literatures (and their study) are "embodied."

32. For a full discussion of these aspects, see Foley 1995a: performance arena (47–49, 79–82, 108–10); register (49–53, 82–92, 110–15); communicative economy (53–56, 93–95). On the role of register and communicative economy in Chinese *pinghua* storytelling, see Blader 1996.

33. This "way of speaking" was of course the thrust of Parry 1932, which took the crucial step of showing how Homer's language was a highly refined, multidialectal linguistic instrument. Thus Minchin observes, from the perspective of cognitive research, that "like any language the metrical poetic language of traditional epic has its own vocabulary and its own rules of combination and production" (1992a: 236 n. 33); see also Sherratt 1990 on the correspondence of the (achronological) Homeric language and the contemporary archaeological record. Likewise, Boerdahl (1997: 7) observes of the Yangzhou *pinghua* oral storytelling tradition that "the language of the storytellers carries a long historical tradition with special characteristics different from the language of the ordinary townsfolk." Cf. Niditch 1995 and espec. 1997 for a direct application to biblical poetics. Many more examples of this phenomenon from different periods and places are available in Foley 1995a: 49–53. See Chapter 3 below for a comparison of the Homeric *koinê* with the South Slavic epic language as specialized dictions.

34. Horrocks (1997: 213) makes the case that "Ionic provides the predominant dialect base and that the Aeolic forms appear routinely only where they offer an alternative metrical

shape to their Ionic equivalents." For a sample of Homeric vocabulary items discovered on the Linear B tablets, see Horrocks 1997: 197.

35. See espec. Foley 1995a: ch. 4; and cf. Feld 1990 on Kaluli weeping.

36. This is to say nothing of the "transitional reading" well documented for the Old English period, wherein, as O'Brien O'Keeffe (1990: 41) puts it, "reception . . . , conditioned by formulaic conventions, produces variants which are metrically, syntactically, and semantically appropriate. In such a process, reading and copying have actually become conflated with composing." Also of paramount importance are the limitations imposed by the nascent technology of writing in the ancient and medieval worlds (see espec. Thomas 1989 and W. Harris 1989; as well as Stock 1983, 1990), which should not be anachronistically assimilated to the technology and readership that support the modern scenario of mass-market paperbacks.

37. See Foley 1990: chs. 5–6.

38. See further the *apparatus fabulosus* for *Odyssey* 23.69–103 in Chapter 8. Cp. the method advocated by R. Martin (1993: 228) of constucting a "dictionary" of traditional meaning, as well as Honko (1984) on what he calls "transformal meaning." Just how established an expressive idiom the Homeric register became can be glimpsed in the earliest inscriptions, so many of them hexametric. Even though the particular lines and partial lines in question are not found in the ancient poetic corpus, being usually more personalized or locally focused (see espec. the Mantiklos inscription, in Powell 1991: 167–69), still they closely follow the *traditional rules* for poetic structure (on which, see Foley 1990: chs. 3–4) that rationalize the apparent difference between formulaic and nonformulaic language (Finkelberg 1989).

39. Let me again acknowledge the work of Nagy (1990a), who remarks that "the Greek poem is a *sêma* that requires the *nóēsis* of those who hear it" (222), and Ford (1992), who concentrates on the Iliadic instances and the issues of fixity and text.

40. Burial mounds, like noun-epithet signs such as "swift-footed Achilleus," mark a heroic identity via a traditional sign. As do other *sêmata*, burial mounds symbolically open onto a reality beyond the present time and place of the narrative. It is as if the character's traditional identity were "interred" in the *sêma*, in the sense of both burial mound and sign. The paradigm case may be the grave of Elpenor (*Od.* 11.75), which acquires an immanent significance: Elpenor cannot rest without establishment of this *sêma* and all that it implies. Cf. the *sêma* prescribed by Hektor for the Achaean champion he may vanquish (*Il.* 7.89) and Hektor's own properly constituted burial mound (24.799, 801) only a few lines from the culminating funeral feast that closes the *Iliad* (on the latter, see Foley 1991: 174–89).

41. On which, see espec. Hansen 1977, 1990 and Nagy 1990a: 214.

42. Slatkin 1991: xv. Cf. S. West 1981, Reece 1994, and Slatkin 1996 on implied alternative versions of the Odyssey tale.

43. Cf. the Serbian magical charms (see Foley 1995a: ch. 4) for an example of an extremely densely coded—and superficially opaque—medium.

44. On Eurykleia's "reading" of the "letter" of the scar, cp. Saussy 1996: 302–5. On the linkage between Odysseus' identifying feature and the scar that identifies Orestes in Euripides' *Elektra*, see Tarkow 1981, Goff 1991.

45. See Chapter 5 below on special objects as triggers for recognition in the Return Song at large.

46. See Chapter 8 for a rereading of *Odyssey* 23.69–103 at a number of different levels.

47. Cf. the similar conclusions of Lateiner (1989: 20) and R. Griffith 1995. For other nonverbal signals, see Levine 1984 and espec. Lateiner 1995.

48. Note also the two uses of this phrase in the *Iliad*, in both of which Odysseus, well recognized for his wisdom and cunning, chides the impulsive Agamemnon. In one case (4.350) Odysseus is responding to the Achaean leader's wrongfully accusing him and Peteos of cow-

ardice or slackness in battle; in the other (14.83) he seeks to contest Agamemnon's retreat from Troy. In both cases, the traditional sign cues the context for the incident: the Greek commander should indeed know better, and his rashness certainly does cry out for remedy.

49. Indeed, this feature of the leg wound also identifies the disguised hero in some South Slavic return songs, where it is called a *beleg* ("sign, mark").

50. Cf. Felson-Rubin 1994: 63: "Two intersubjective symbols, the marriage-bed and the engraved clasp, illuminate the courtship dance of Penelope and Odysseus. Both are objects the couples share: Odysseus built the bed for his wife; she gave him the pin. This makes them ideal signs (*sêmata*) for mutual recognition." Cf. also Zeitlin 1995: 137 and Holmberg 1997: 19–21.

51. Cf. Katz (1991), who speaks of "the trick of the bed, which constitutes the final stage in the transformation of the *xeinos* into Odysseus" (177) and observes that "the narrative of the bed and its construction . . . is a complex figuration for the moment in the poem when the marriage of Penelope and Odysseus is reconstituted" (182). See further Chapter 5 below. On the primacy of the metonymic over the literal in South Slavic and Native American (Zuni) narrative, cf. Foley 1995a: 30–41; cp. Muellner's differing sense of metonymic in his reconstruction of *mênis* in the *Iliad* and the *Theogony* (1996: espec. 52–93).

52. In addition to *Od.* 23.205, this signal also glosses passages in which Lykaon realizes his death at Achilleus' hands is imminent (*Il.* 21.114), Aphrodite is struck down by Athena (21.425), Penelope learns of the suitors' intended ambush of Telemachos (*Od.* 4.703), Odysseus fears the life-threatening storm stirred up by Poseidon (5.297), the exhausted Odysseus can find no landing spot on Scheria (5.406), Eurymachos realizes his death at the hands of Odysseus is imminent (22.68), Odysseus learns the suitors are being covertly armed by Melanthios (22.147), and Laertes—in a close parallel to Penelope a book earlier—reads the *sêma* of the scar and recognizes his son (24.345).

53. Cf. R. Martin 1989 on the speech-act called *muthos*, which "always implies 'public speech,' and involves a performance before an audience" (37) and "is the name that the poet gives to actual genres of discourse which are also poetic genres, and which we find embedded in the speeches of the *Iliad*" (42). On speech-acts as collocations of word (*epos*) and deed (*ergon*), see Roochnik 1990.

54. On the importance of these signs as *sêmata* and the irrelevance of the oral/written dichotomy for Bellerophon's tablet, see the Introduction above. Cf. also Holmberg (1997: 29 n. 104), who observes that "nowhere in ancient Greek does *sêma* refer to the spoken or written word."

55. See further Foley 1991: 174–89 and Chapter 6 below.

56. This seems to be similar to what Morrell (1996) attempts to demonstrate by applying chaos theory to oral tradition and the *Iliad*.

57. Cf. Foley 1995c; I translate the phrase in question with intentional redundancy to mark its idiomatic character: "And they were struck silently to silence" (οἱ δ᾽ ἄρα πάντες ἀκὴν ἐγένοντο σιωπῇ, *Il.* 3.95 etc.). The sign conventionally marks a paradigm wherein an initial speech proposing or reporting a radical, unexpected action [that entails either winning or losing *kleos*] will give way to stunned silence and some sort of reversal. Cf. Person (1995), who uses the principles of conversation analysis to arrive at similar conclusions for the same phrase.

58. To summon a parable, one could compare Odysseus' successful shot through the twelve individual axeheads in Book 21 to the poet's alignment of disparate episodes (and in the case of living oral epic traditions, even different performances) along the same axis of traditional referentiality. This analogy is drawn out further in Chapter 5 below. On the mix of tradition and "innovation," cf. Nagy (1992: 30): "Granted, to the extent that the performer controls or 'owns' the performance in conjunction with the audience, the opportunity for innovation is there. Such innovation, however, takes place within the tradition, not beyond it."

Thus, even the kind of special formulaic echo that appears to link the deaths of Patroklos and Hektor (*Il.* 16.856–57 and 22.362–63, respectively) amounts to, as M. Edwards puts it (1990: 323), an "individual and innovative use of traditional material."

Chapter 2.   Homer and the South Slavic *Guslar*: The Analogy and the Singers

1. Given present political conditions, I prefer to call the epics (and their singers and language) "South Slavic," rather than "Serbian," "Croatian," "Bosnian," or "Serbo-Croatian." Although "South Slavic" is employed by linguists to denote the language family that also includes Bulgarian, Slovenian, and Macedonian, it seems better to err on the side of inclusiveness rather than parochialism or segregation. Moreover, many of the songs, characters, and situations referred to below also populate the unprinted "pages" of other South Slavic oral traditions.

2. For a history of the so-called Oral Theory and its spread, see Foley 1988; for an annotated bibliography, Foley 1985, with updates in the journal *Oral Tradition*, now available electronically at http://www.missouri.edu/~csottime. With specific reference to Homer, see M. Edwards 1986, 1988, 1992; Steinrueck 1997. For a recent and wide-ranging sample of Homeric scholarship inspired by Parry's work, see Létoublon 1997.

3. For example, consider the concerns of Keith Stanley (1993) about what he understands as the necessary connection between Homer's complexity, especially as reflected in ring-composition, and literacy.

4. See Foley 1990: 158–200, 278–328.

5. The unpublished Moslem songs cited or analyzed herein were all recorded in the region of Stolac in 1934–35. They include four performances by Mujo Kukuruzović of the *Captivity of Ograšćić Alija / Alagić Alija* (Parry Collection nos. *6617* [sung, 2,180 lines], *6618* [sung, 1,422 lines], *1287a* [dictated, 1,288 lines], and *1868* [dictated, 2,152 lines]); three performances by Ibro Bašić of the *Alagić Alija and Velagić Selim* (*291b* [sung, 1,360 lines], *6597* [sung, 1,558 lines], and *1283* [dictated, 1,403 lines]); two performances by Halil Bajgorić (*The Wedding of Mustajbeg's Son Bećirbeg*, *6699*, sung, 1,030 lines; *Halil Rescues Bojičić Alija*, *6703*, dictated, 637 lines); and a single performance by Salko Morić (*Hrnjičić Omer Rescues His Father and Uncle*, *892*, sung, 727 lines). This amounts to a total of 13,473 decasyllabic lines, with all but Bajgorić's and Morić's narratives belonging to the Return Song subgenre (essentially the story of the *Odyssey*; see Chapter 5 below). The examples from Karadžić's collection of Christian epic (1841–62) are drawn from volume 2: Tešan Podrugović's performance of *Marko Kraljević Recognizes His Father's Sword* (no. 56, 141 lines); the same song by an unknown singer (no. 57, 114 lines); and *The Death of Kraljević Marko* (no. 73, 166 lines). I will quote and cite lines from both sources according to performance or text numbers, with the heretofore unpublished material presented precisely as it was acoustically recorded or taken in dictation, without normalizing the morphology. Translations from South Slavic are my own (with the historical present tense rendered in the usual fashion as a simple past).

6. For a full account of scholarship that anticipated or influenced the Parry-Lord Oral Theory, see Foley 1988: 1–18.

7. *Contra Apionem* 1.11–12, in Thackeray 1926: 167. Cf. Nagy (1992: 28), who points out that the term *Oral Theory* obscures the tangible fact of Parry's and Lord's empirical fieldwork.

8. See espec. Murko 1929/1990; his posthumous magnum opus (1951) was published too late for consultation by Parry. Cf. Parry's own acknowledgment (1933–35: 439): "It was the writings of Professor Murko more than those of any other which in the following years led me to the study of oral poetry in itself and to the heroic poems of the South Slavs."

9. On the then-current textcentrist models of Analysis and Unitarianism against which Parry was reacting, see Foley 1988: 4–6. Cf. Parry 1925 for an early version of the critical program developed in Parry 1928a, b; and later.

10. Early scholarship on Old English poetry was especially doctrinaire in this regard; for a survey of the application of the Oral Theory to this area, see Olsen 1986, 1988. For a more recent perspective, see also O'Brien O'Keeffe 1997.

11. See the extended critique of the Oral Theory in Finnegan 1977: espec. 52–87.

12. A relatively recent example of the former is Hugh Lloyd-Jones (1992: 55), who asserts of South Slavic that "the epics in question are hardly as distinguished as, say, Sir Walter Scott's long poems, *Marmion, The Lady of the Lake, The Lay of the Last Minstrel*. It seems clear enough that they cannot be compared with Homer."

13. As a basis for his assertion quoted above, Lloyd-Jones seems to have read only example passages from Lord's *The Singer of Tales*, which he quotes with numerous misspellings, and a German translation of eighty-four lines total in Dirlmeier 1971: 34–39. Or cf. Oliver Taplin (1992), who speaks without quotation or reference of "the relatively small-scale and second-rate south-Slavic bards" (36). Yet more seriously misleading is Taplin's remonstration against "one unacceptable notion of Parry's . . . that the *Iliad* as we have it *must* have been the product of a one-off improvised delivery" (35). Parry's entire research program was aimed at illuminating the *traditional* nature of the Homeric poems, just the opposite of "one-off improvisation." Equally problematic are the remarks of Finkelberg (1990), who constructs a comparative view of Homer's and the South Slavic bards' "creativity"; she confuses ethnographic with poetic portraits, imposes modern and highly textual categories and criteria, and works with the South Slavic material only through English translation and secondhand reports. Cp. Sale 1996b on the importance of consulting both sides of the comparison in the original language.

14. Compare the apparently much shorter poems of the Epic Cycle as reported in Proclus (cf. Davies 1988); and note Nagy (1990b: 70–71): "Because we are dealing with a relative concept, we may speak of the poetry of the *Iliad* and the *Odyssey* as more Panhellenic than the poetry of the Epic Cycle."

15. Published in *SCHS*, vols. 3–4 and 6, respectively.

16. For Indian oral epics, see Blackburn and Flueckiger (1989: 11), who give examples of "immensely long epic stories, which would take hundreds of hours to sing if performed in one sitting." For Turkic oral epics, cf. Reichl's (1992: 71–72) account of an Uzbek bard: "Of exceptional size was the repertory of the singer Polkan-šâir (1874–1941), who knew about seventy *dastans*, the longest among them (*Qirân-xân*) comprising no less than 20,000 verse lines"; cf. Reichl 1996. Mongolian epics of more than fifty thousand lines are not rare, and recently a performance of approximately 230,000 lines was recorded (Chao Gejin, personal communication). Cf. Finkelberg's unfortunate comments on length as a measure of creativity (1990: espec. 296, 298).

17. A related question concerns the supposed "artificiality" of the Parry-Lord songs, which some have seen as unnaturally induced performances that, except for the interfering encouragement of the fieldworker, would never have reached such size. In part this misapprehension stems from a misunderstanding of the different subgenres of epic in South Slavic (the significantly longer Moslem as opposed to the shorter, better known Christian poems), and in part from Parry's own preference for the Moslem songs on the grounds that their relative length and complexity made them a better match for the Homeric poems (cf. Lord 1953b: 16). On the appropriateness of this fieldwork procedure, see Foley 1990: 1–19 and 1991: 62–63. For another perspective on the advantages and disadvantages of the recording process, see also John D. Niles' useful concept of the "oral poetry act," which he understands as "a staged event that aims to generate a readable text of an oral poem for the benefit of a textual community" (1993: 131).

18. Cf. Daniel Biebuyck's report on his recording of the "whole" of the *Mwindo Epic* (1971: 14): "The interesting point is that the narrator would never recite the entire story in immediate sequence, but would intermittently perform various select passages of it. Mr. Rureke . . . repeatedly asserted that never before had he performed the whole story within a continuous span of days." Such is also the case with Gopala Naika, the Tulu epic singer recorded and studied by Lauri Honko (1998a and 1998b). See further Foley 1991: 10–13.

19. Respectively, lines 6481–7108, 7691–9309.

20. On the Wedding Song as a story-type, see Bynum 1980: xi–xii. For synopses of sung and dictated versions of the *Ženidba Vlahinjić Alije* (*The Wedding of Alija Vlahinjić*) by Avdo Medjedović, another Wedding Song, cf. Bynum 1980: xi–xxxi. An even more common story-pattern, the Return Song, will be discussed below in Chapter 5.

21. Cf. Scodel 1997: 217: "Controversy about invention and tradition has persisted in an unhelpful way because scholars needlessly identify invention with creativity or imagine that a poet who invents a detail is somehow less fully traditional." Indeed, as shown by the figure of the legendary singer studied later in this chapter, the bards who constitute an oral epic tradition imagine that tradition as an individual.

22. Speaking of Homer's status and influence only within the sphere of literature and then strictly in English translation, George Steiner remarks (1996: xx): "The empathies of vision and revision lie deep. The light from Achilles' helmet, from the eyes of the 'cat-like Penelope' (T. E. Lawrence's epithet), 'screams . . . across three thousand years.' That dizzying phrase is out of Christopher Logue's transmutation of the *Patrocleia*. It 'screams' in English as it does in no other language after Greek. From the beginnings of our literature to the present, to tomorrow. Whatever the underlying causes, this crowded vitality and constancy of echo offer a wealth of implications." Add Virgil, Dante, and so many other Western authors to the mix, and the volume only rises.

23. On this understudied poet and his poems, see espec. Lord 1991: 57–71 and 1995: 203–11; also Sale 1996b, an elegant appraisal of the poetic qualities of Medjedović's performance on its own terms, within its linguistic domain, and against other epic poetry. For a complementary perspective on the art of the Stolac *guslari*, see Foley 1991: 61–95.

24. On the trickster Tale as a test case for the importance of implied meaning, see Foley 1995a: 32–41.

25. Cf. note 18 above on the very common circumstance worldwide in which, as noted above, an epic singer performs only a "part" of the "whole," with traditional implication providing the necessary, though unspoken, background. See further Clover 1986: espec. 23–37.

26. Examples of the importance of traditional referentiality for South Slavic epic will be adduced in Chapter 4 below. For the application of this principle to Homer, see Foley 1991: 135–89, 1995a: 136–80, and espec. Chapters 5–7 below. Throughout this volume I refer to the South Slavic *guslar* with the masculine pronouns because I know of no modern female singers. For mention of the extremely rare female *guslari* from the early 1900s, see Murko 1951.

27. Of course, I speak here exclusively of the Parry-Lord method. Folklorists and anthropologists had long explored the nature of (chiefly living) oral traditions from perspectives that harmonize in interesting ways with the Oral Theory. See the discussion of the Ethnography of Speaking, Ethnopoetics, and Oral Theory in Foley 1995a: espec. ch. 1.

28. Cf. the case of the Anglo-Scottish ballad, a traditional oral genre to which many literate practitioners have contributed (e.g., McCarthy 1990: 26).

29. On the trajectory from performance to text in archaic Greece, see Buxton 1994: 45–52, as well as Foley 1995a: ch. 3 and Nagy 1996b. Cf. Finnegan 1988: 110–22 and espec. Finnegan and Orbell 1995 on the complex weave of oral and literate influences typical of various cultures in the South Pacific region.

30. In premodern times, before and after the Turkish conquests, there seems to have been a place for the singer in various courtly contexts; see further Lord 1960: 16; and 1972.

31. See espec. Lord 1960; also 1991, 1995, and the bibliography of his writings in Foley 1992b (61–65). Of special pertinence are the conversations with *guslari*, selectively published

in *SCHS*. On the little-studied musical dimension of South Slavic epic singing, see espec. Erdely 1995; also Bartók 1953–54, Herzog 1951, and Bynum 1980. Although much of Erdely's presentation transfers directly to the Stolac songs that are our major emphasis here (see espec. his remarks on "melodic formula" [e.g., 10–11] and the conclusion on 631–32), it should be noted that the Bihać tradition he examines utilizes the plucked *tambura* rather than the bowed *gusle*, and that some musical differences do exist between these two regional varieties of South Slavic epic performance.

32. Cf. the possibly initiatory function of the shorter Homeric Hymns, which since Thucydides and Pindar have been understood by some as *prooimia*, lyrical preludes to the main event of long epic. See further Foley 1995a: 144–45. For a survey of internal poetic evidence on the role of singers in the *Iliad* and *Odyssey*, see espec. Walsh 1984: 3–21, Segal 1994, and Doherty 1995; on the related issue of song and storytelling, Mackie 1997. For a history of scholarly conceptions of ancient Greek epic poets and their audiences, see Dalby 1995, who argues that the *Iliad* and *Odyssey* reflect the worldview not of aristocrats but of "quite humble people" (279). Cf. also Minchin 1995a on the proems as metanarrational devices.

33. The designation "start #2" acknowledges Parry's habit of asking singers to restart their performances after approximately 20–50 lines. Labeled *probe* ("tests") in the dictated texts and Vujnović's transcriptions, these multiple beginnings were apparently intended to measure the stability of a given song from one singing to another. In the first line of the following quotation and elsewhere among singers from various regions, *djeca* (collective of *djete*, n., "child") is treated as a feminine singular noun. Its vocative pl. then takes the form *djeco* and the modifying adjectives are inflected accordingly. Cf. also *braćo* in the next quoted passage.

34. For additional published evidence of this understood collectivity as well as echoes of the Moslem epic's historical placement in the coffeehouse during and before the period of Parry and Lord's research trips, see, e.g., the proems by the Bihać singer Mujo Velić to his *Ženidba Ograšović Ale* (*The Wedding of Ograšović Ali*; *SCHS*, vol. 14: lines 1–7), and by the Novi Pazar singer Salih Ugljanin in his *Pjesma od Bagdata* (*The Song of Baghdad*; *SCHS*, vol. 2: lines 1–10).

35. Cf. the distinctions drawn among story, performance, and event in Bauman 1986.

36. The verb *računati* ("to calculate, count, figure") is also used to describe incremental composition in performance. See Chapter 3 for a discussion of *reči* ("words"), conceived of by the singers themselves as colonic, linear, and scenic units, as well as enjambement. Two of the earliest and most influential statements on parataxis or "adding style" in oral poetry were Notopoulos 1949 and Lord 1960: 54–56. Cf. Thornton 1985 on repetition and appositional style in Maori oral narrative, which she compares to recurrence and parataxis in Homer.

37. Cp. the Anglo-Saxon poem "Widsith," wherein the traditional poet of the same name describes a performance by him and his lyre Scilling (Malone 1962: 26, lines 103–5): "Ðonne wit Scilling sciran reorde / for uncrum sigedryhtne song ahofan, / hlude bi hearpan hleoþor swinsade" ("Then we two, Scilling and I, with a shining voice / raised up a song before our victory-lord, / the sound rang loudly on the lyre"). See further note 69 below.

38. For another sort of parallel, consider the following *pripjev* for continuation, used by the Stolac *guslar* Mujo Kukuruzović to restart his song-performance after a break for rest: "Dje li bismo? Dje li ostavismo? / Dje malešnu pjesmu prekidosmo?" ["Where were we? Where did we leave it? / Where did we interrupt our little song?" (6617.660–61)]. It is typical of this highly traditional couplet that all three verbs should be conjugated in the aorist tense, an archaic feature of the poetic language (see Chapter 3 below).

39. *Hakati* literally means to yell "ha!" while *dekati* means to shout "de!"; both exclamations are meant to urge a recalcitrant animal to action.

40. Vocal performance of South Slavic epic is a rigorous, physically demanding undertaking, as one element of the proprietary terminology for performance clearly indicates: in many *pripjevi*, the singers describe their feat of narration with the verb *turati* (lit., "to drive out"; cf. Anglo-Saxon *wrecan*, "to expel, drive out," used for the same descriptive purpose and signaling a similar physical activity, as in *The Seafarer*, line 1b or *Beowulf*, line 873a).

41. Cf. Bauman 1977: 21–22 on "disclaimer of performance" as in fact a key to performance.

42. Cf. Nagy 1996b: 89–90, 111–12.

43. In many lectures, as well as in a videotaped presentation recorded in 1987, Lord used this phrase to refer to the enormous collection of traditional oral epic that he and Parry made in the years 1933–35, much of it encoded on aluminum disks. For a description of the fieldwork expeditions, see Lord 1953b; Foley 1988: 31–35. For a full index of the 1933–35 collections, see Kay 1995.

44. As noted above, Parry was especially interested in Moslem songs because they were generally much longer and more ornate than the relatively brief songs from the Christian tradition, and therefore more like Homeric epic. For brief biographies of these three singers from Stolac, see Foley 1990: 42–51.

45. What follows is drawn from unpublished conversations with the three singers: Parry nos. *6598* (Bašić), *6698* (Bajgorić), and *6619* (Kukuruzović). All translations from South Slavic are mine. On the nature of the "word" (*reč*) in an epic performance, as opposed to the lexical item featured in texts, see Chapter 3 in this volume. On the theory of oral dictated texts, see Lord 1953a.

46. One internal indication of the performative and symbolic importance of the instrument is a common proem that begins: "O my *gusle*, maplewood *gusle*, / Speak now and ever, / Speak softly, loudly, / The *gusle* is mine and it's played for you" (version by Bajgorić, Parry no. 6703.1–4); cf. also the *pripjev* sung by Morić, as quoted above. Note that performance without the *gusle* was not unknown in the parallel Christian tradition of epic: Tešan Podrugović, one of the most celebrated of the oral poets collected by Vuk Karadžić (see Koljević 1980: 118–23, 311–14), always performed a cappella.

47. Bajgorić first says that he does not know how his father, who taught him, learned to sing; he later changes his story, citing Hasan Ćoso as his father's teacher. Kukuruzović claims that Isak taught Huso Tarahija, who in turn taught him. Bašić's claim is at once less personal and more expansive: according to him, Isak, who died some seventy years before and "was not even my father's father," taught all of the singers in the Stolac region.

48. See Foley 1998c for treatment of the legendary singer Ćor Huso Husović, the source of the titles given to Parry's field notes ("Ćor Huso," 1933–35) and Lord's early series of articles on "Homer and Huso" (1936, 1938, 1948a, 1948b), who was reputed to have performed before the court of Emperor Franz Jozef in Vienna. Husović's exploits are recounted by the singer Salih Ugljanin (*SCHS*, vol. 1, p. 61) and the fieldworker-scholar Alois Schmaus (1938).

49. Parry and Lord found that the ecology of South Slavic oral epic was basically regional, with distinctive styles and repertoires developing in modest-sized areas or districts as a result of both learning and performance patterns. Both their fieldwork and their publication plans reflect this analysis (see Lord 1953b: 16–17; also 1960: ch. 2). Of course, this does not mean that idiosyncratic and multiregional levels of language and narrative organization did not exist as well; see Foley 1990: chs. 5, 8.

50. The phrase used here is *baciti gusle* (lit. "throw [down]," better "cast aside" the *gusle*); it signals the end of a continuous performance session.

51. Parry estimates the average length of a performance session at twenty–forty minutes, citing a single stretch of two hours (about 1,300 lines) by Ćamil Kulenović in Kulen Vakuf as "quite unique in my own knowledge, and I have never heard nor read of anything which approaches it" (1933–35: 458). My own experience with recordings of epic singers from the Parry Collection, and on a much more limited basis with actual *guslari* in Serbia, corroborates this estimate.

52. We may wonder whether Bašić's own part-time occupation as a *kahvedžija* made this story especially attractive or meaningful to him.

53. Cf. Avdo Medjedović's remarkable 12,311-line version of this song, published in *SCHS*, vols. 3–4.

54. See Chapter 1 above.

55. Cf. Parry 1933–35: 446–47.

56. In response to a brief presentation of these ideas at the 1996 American Folklore Society, Margaret Mills suggested that the legendary singer amounted to a kind of emic or internal "theory" generated by singers and parallel to the etic or external theories imposed upon the tradition by scholars and fieldworkers. Correspondingly, Aaron Tate (1998) has observed that the portrayal of the rhapsode in Plato's *Ion* may amount to Plato's misreading of a Homeric epic tradition he wished to dismiss from his ideal state.

57. See espec. Lamberton 1997; also Davison 1963, Turner 1997, Wilamowitz-Moellendorff 1982.

58. Allen 1969: 11–41. See especially the comparative chart between 32 and 33, from which these examples are drawn. Allen's sources are the Herodotean life, accounts by Plutarch and Proclus, the *Certamen Homeri et Hesiodi* (*Contest of Homer and Hesiod*), Suidas' tripartite chapter, and four anonymous lives.

59. Cf. Nagy 1979: 296–300 on an etymology yielding "he who fits [the song] together." The *Hymn to Apollo* (172–73; see Allen 1946: 27–28) seems to campaign for authorship by the master bard Homer when it claims as its composer "a blind man, and he lives on rocky Chios, / and all his songs are the best now and forever" (τυφλὸς ἀνήρ, οἰκεῖ δὲ Χίῳ ἔνι παιπαλοέσσῃ, / τοῦ πᾶσαι μετόπισθεν ἀριστεύουσιν ἀοιδαί).

60. For a dependable edition of all relevant evidence (fragments, descriptions, and authorial attributions), see Davies 1988, from which the following remarks are derived. Possible reconstructions of content and context are available in Davies 1989.

61. Cf. the shorthand summary in Hammond and Scullard 1977: *s.v.* Epic Cycle. Reports of *nostos* (return) poems are especially intriguing given the widespread occurrence of Return songs that very closely approximate the narrative pattern of the *Odyssey* throughout the former Yugoslavia, Albania, Bulgaria, Turkey, and elsewhere. See further Foley 1990: Chapter 10, and espec. Chapter 5 in this volume.

62. See Allen, Halliday, and Sikes 1980: lxxxiii–lxxxviii for what is known about these and other poets as possible hymnists; also Clay 1989: 5–16, 270, H. Foley 1994: 28–30, and Shelmerdine 1995: 1–10. Cf. Foley 1995a: 136–80 on traditional referentiality in the *Homeric Hymn to Demeter*.

63. I take approximately the same position as Lamberton, viewing the Cycle as a critical construction that conveniently names some of the epic songs that constituted the Homeric poetic tradition, and thus do not see the poems as existing in a truly intertextual relationship wherein one could influence another *as texts* (cf. the similar, textless model suggested by Davies [1989: 4–5]). As Holmberg puts it in relation to apparent variations among the Epic Cycle poems, "a more fruitful approach to these inconsistencies might be to understand them as remnants of the living oral tradition, and to accept the inherent multiplicity, rather than insisting upon determining the one true version" (1999: forthcoming). Cf. Burgess, who argues that "the Cyclic epics, even in their ultimate fixed condition as texts, were independent in content and even form from the Homeric poems" (1996: 78). For other views, stressing the uniqueness of Homer and the presumed textuality of the Cycle poems from a Neoanalytic perspective, see Huxley 1969, Griffin 1977, and Willcock 1997.

64. See further Nagy 1990b: 55, 80; 1992: 29; 1996a: 76. Cf. also R. Martin 1992 on the *persona*-like figure of Hesiod.

65. On the specialized poetic languages of the *guslar* and *aoidos*, see Chapter 3 below.

66. Foley 1991, 1995a; espec. Chapter 4 below.

67. For a discussion of these traditional signs, see Foley 1990: 191–92 (phrases for a period of time); 288–327 ("Shouting in Prison" pattern).

68. See Hansen 1990: 246–49.

69. To these candidates for the position of legendary singer may be added the Old English bard named Widsith (literally, "Wide-journey"), who would have had to travel across the face of Europe for two centuries or more in order to visit the courts in which he claims to have

performed (see Malone 1962: 105–10 and Creed 1975; also note 37 above). Similarly, the Anglo-Saxon bard Deor claims at the end of his litany of woes that his own perilous situation results from having been displaced by a rival, one Heorrenda, who happens to have had a "real" existence as "the most famous minstrel of Old-Germanic story" (Malone 1966:16). Both Widsith and Heorrenda thus fit the mold of the larger-than-life figure who stands as a *sêma* for the poetic tradition. See further the discussion of the poem "Deor" in the Afterword below. From another perspective, Roberta Frank's eloquent survey (1993) of the enigmatic search for the Anglo-Saxon oral poet shows how difficult it can be to reduce the multiformity of a legendary singer to everyday, human reality—just as impossible, I would argue, as reducing the poetic tradition to any single text.

70. Let me express my sincere gratitude to Professors Chao Gejin and Zhalgaa of the Institute of Literature of National Minorities at the Chinese Academy of Social Sciences in Beijing, who arranged the fieldwork trip and served as translator and liaison, respectively; and to the bard Losor, who patiently answered all of our questions as well as performed for our group. Thanks are also due to all those colleagues in Tong Liao and Zharut Banner, especially Sampulnorbu, who welcomed us into their midst and joined in the series of performances and interviews. For general sources on Mongolian epic, see Chao Gejin 1997, Heissig 1987; on the contiguous epic traditions of the central Asiatic Turkic peoples, which share some tales, heroes, and performance characteristics with Mongolian epic, see Reichl 1992.

71. These two last details set Choibang apart from all contemporary singers, who practice an art that, although widely respected as a cultural institution, is also relatively unremunerative and of low social status. For such a noble and wealthy individual as Choibang to have assumed the position of bard thus constitutes a complete reversal of (at least contemporary) expectation.

72. See Schmaus (1938), who attempted without success to precipitate a historical figure from this legend, and the discussion in Foley 1998c.

73. Sampulnorbu (1990: 213–16) lists a primary Zharut Banner "family tree" of forty-six epic singers, twenty-seven of whom were still alive in 1990. Choibang's dates are given as 1836–1928, a life span of ninety-two years. He is shown as one of the two protégés of Dansannima, the "first" bard, whose dates are set at 1836–1889. Of course, the Mongolian epic tradition goes back far beyond the mid-nineteenth century, but singers trace their lineage only as far as Dansannima and Choibang, who epitomize the collective inheritance. Losor's account, and the stories told by others from this region, vary both among themselves and in comparison with the published "historical biography" in Sampulnorbu 1990.

Chapter 3.　Homer and the South Slavic *Guslar*: Traditional Register

1. Hymes 1989: 440. On "register" see Chapter 1 above and Foley 1995a: 49–53.

2. We should also note those important related areas that lie beyond the scope of our present focus: the two histories of transmission and the various media of preservation (on which, cf. Janko 1990, Powell 1991, Nagy 1996b, and Haslam 1997) and the levels of idiolect, regional dialect, and pantraditional language within the epic idiom (on which, cf. Foley 1990: chs. 5, 8 on South Slavic and Brockington 1996 on Sanskrit). Cf. Peabody's five "tests" for oral tradition (1975: 3–5) and their application to Hesiod's *Works and Days* (*passim*).

3. To the question of priority of meter or formula I plead agnosticism, recognizing the persuasive arguments from diachronic analysis (espec. Nagy 1990b: 48–51). All that is necessary for the present comparison is to recognize that formulaic phraseology and meter are inextricably linked in both Homeric and South Slavic epic. For the sources of the South Slavic quotations, see Chapter 2, n. 5. In order to emphasize their traditional nature, I avoid restricting

formulaic phrases from Greek or South Slavic by assigning them any single (textual) citation. For an example of formulaic analysis of South Slavic epic phraseology, see Goldman 1990; and cp. Foley 1990: 158–200 on the priority of traditional rules (the process) over phraseological units (the products).

4. On colonic meter and encapsulated phraseology in the two poetries, see further Foley 1990: chs. 4–5.

5. On speech-acts in Homer, see R. Martin 1989: espec. 1–42 and Bakker 1997a: espec. 54–85; in Arabic oral poetry, Reynolds 1995: espec. 207–12.

6. I employ the convention of "word"—in quotation marks—to distinguish the South Slavic singers' *reč*, a unit of utterance, from our own morpheme- and typography-based concept of a word. With this distinction in mind, we should note that the singers' frequent claim that they composed a given song "word for word" (*rečima po rečima*, pl. in original) is fully justified. *Pace* Kirk (1960: 100), e.g., they did in fact proceed on each occasion one traditional unit of utterance after the next, moving along a story-pattern via deployment of typical scenes and formulaic phraseology and expressing themselves through an idiomatic way of speaking. The fact that a textual transcription of any two performances reveals discrepancies based on our own very different sense of word-for-word literality is irrelevant to the dynamics of the traditional register.

7. Parry no. *6619*. For similar remarks by the Stolac *guslar* Ibro Bašić, see Foley 1990: 44–45.

8. Parry no. *6612*.

9. Cf. also the opening *reči* (dialect equivalent = *riječi*) in Avdo Medjedović's 1935 performance of *The Wedding of Smailagić Meho* (*SCHS*, vol. 4, lines 1–2): "Prva riječ: 'Bože, nam pomozi!' / Evo druga: 'Hoće, ako Bog da'" ["The first *reč*: 'O God, help us!' / And the next [*reč*]: 'It will be as God grants'"].

10. On metrical structure in the decasyllable, see Foley 1990: 94–106; on hypersyllabism and hyposyllabism, 88–94, 104. Some metrists indicate a "secondary caesura" between syllables 8 and 9, but this segmentation is not at all regular and, when it does occur, seems to be a function of the zeugma at syllables 9–10 rather than an institutionalized tendency toward word-break at 8–9 (cf. Foley 1990: 95–96).

11. On colonic structure in the hexameter (theories from Fränkel 1926 onward), see Foley 1990: 73–84, with the twelve cola diagrammed on 84. To these should be added the overview by M. West (1997) and the suggestive work by Devine and Stephens (1984, 1994). It should be emphasized that the decasyllable reveals other, compensating kinds of complexities not a part of Homeric prosody (Foley 1990: 85–106), and that it would therefore be reductive to describe the South Slavic line as generally "less demanding" than the hexameter.

12. For more details on the differing roles of the two cola, see Foley 1990: 94–103, 176–96.

13. On the extent of Parryan economy, cf. Shive 1987.

14. *Pace* Lord (1960: 52–53), I do not find "acoustical context" a consistent basis for thrift in South Slavic epic. Note that acoustic patterning in the decasyllabic diction is an occasional and optional aspect of prosody rather than, like colonic structure, a fundamental and defining feature of every line.

15. The differences in colonic structure—at the level of *product*—are traceable to a difference in the rule-governed *processes* that underlie the two registers. On the traditional rules for ancient Greek epic phraseology, see Foley 1990: ch. 4; for South Slavic epic phraseology, ch. 5. In lieu of explaining formulaic elements as a systemic inventory of items (espec. Lord 1960: ch. 3), as "flexible" structures (Hainsworth 1968, e.g.), or as quantitatively significant combinations (Sale 1989, 1993, 1996a), I advocate understanding such structures *as a rule-governed language*, as a true mathematics rather than simply a collection of integers. For a focused comparison of noun-epithet names for heroes in ancient Greek and South Slavic epic, see Danek 1991.

16. On syllabic definition, see Question III below; on the "quantitative close," see Jakobson 1952: 25, Foley 1990: 95–96.

17. Summarized in Foley 1990: 163–64.

18. See espec. Higbie 1990: 82, Table 3.1. More generally, see her ch. 1 for a helpful history of enjambement studies.

19. Herzog 1951. On musical dimensions, see espec. Erdely 1995; also Bartók 1953–54, Lord 1960: 37–41, and Bynum 1979: 14–43.

20. See Higbie 1990: espec. chs. 2 and 5 for an excellent analysis of the various types of enjambement and their interplay with other aspects of Homeric diction. On other poems and traditions, cf. the sources cited by Higbie (1990: 14); on Old English, Foley 1990: 204. For a cognitive perspective on enjambement in oral as opposed to literate poetry, see Bakker 1990.

21. Although the South Slavic epic uses pleonasm more frequently than the Homeric, it is of course not unknown in the *Iliad* and *Odyssey* (cf. Higbie 1990: 34–35). Note that in these examples and elsewhere the relationship between successive lines in South Slavic epic is not always well symbolized by conventional punctuation, which is after all intended for textual signaling. This amounts to an interesting problem in ethnopoetics, according to which the transcription of oral narratives must be tailored to represent the nontextual reality of oral performances. Cf. Tedlock 1983; Foley 1995a: espec. 17–27.

22. I would distinguish this phenomenon of slotting from conventional anaphora and epiphora, which privilege the correspondence of individual instances over the resonance of traditional referentiality. See further Foley 1991: 9–10.

23. For a supplementary view of metrical irregularities in Homer, see Finkelberg 1988.

24. The only other metrical irregularities encountered with any frequency at all are hypersyllabism and hyposyllabism of the line as a whole. But these are still extremely rare: within the Stolac songs examined, eleven- or twelve-syllable lines amount to 1.2 percent of sung performances and 0.13 percent of oral-dictated texts, while eight- and nine-syllable lines account for only about 0.5 percent in both categories. See further Foley 1990: 88–94. On the theory of oral-dictated texts, see Lord 1953a.

25. Bajgorić employed an unusual variety of consonants (*h, v, j, m*, and *n*) as hiatus bridges. The repertoire of actual sounds, though not the placement or frequency of their deployment, varies considerably even within the group of Stolac *guslari*.

26. Not all of the Stolac *guslari* employ interlinear bridges, presumably because the vocal rest after the ten-syllable line (an instrumental interlude usually equivalent to two syllables in duration) provides enough of a break that hiatus is not sensed as acutely. See further Bartók's transcription (1953–54).

27. The publications of the Milman Parry Collection (*SCHS*), committed to representing epic performances as they actually occurred, are the exception to this rule; the editors regularly include performatives in the published texts. Interestingly, Nikola Vujnović, Parry and Lord's native assistant who first transcribed many of the sung performances and took down most of the dictated texts in 1933–35, omitted many of these non-lexical elements. Such omissions are the more intriguing in view of the fact that Vujnović was himself a *guslar*. For an engaging discussion of the challenges of textual representation in the hybrid tradition of European ballad, see F. Andersen 1994. Cf. the evidence garnered by Miller (1996) on the discrepancy between acoustic recordings of Japanese storytelling and transcriptions of those same performances, a discrepancy that reveals "a native tendency to omit overt oral components during transcription" (313 n. 16).

28. Although evidence exists of the Alexandrians' interest in metrical structure and editing principles, it is impossible to say precisely how that interest affected the actual transmission of the text that has reached us (see further Foley 1990: 20–31, Janko 1992b, Nagy 1996b: 65–112 and 1997, Haslam 1997). For that reason I refrain from attempting to estimate the contribution of editorial manipulation to the metrical structure of the received Homeric text. Two lines from the *Iliad* illustrate the range of metrical irregularity beyond vowel hiatus (cf. also Parry 1928b) and its solution by ancient and modern critics: 3.172, where ἑκυρέ repre-

sents an original σϝεκυϱός (the aspiration deriving from a geminated digamma and initial sigma [Kirk 1985: 289] and thus makes position for the preceding φίλε; and 9.394, with Aristarchus' widely adopted emendation from γαμέσσεται to γε μάσσεται, which occurs in none of the manuscripts but avoids compromising Hermann's Bridge (the emendation made more justifiable by the collocation of γυναῖκά plus enclitic [γε/τε] at four additional sites [Il. 3.72, 3.93, 24.58; Od. 14.123; cf. γυναῖκα μὲν at Il. 7.362] and that combination's colonic form u–u u at position 8 in the hexameter, a 95.6 percent word-type localization by O'Neill's figures [1942: 143; cf. Foley 1990: chs. 3–4]). Cf. the role of the (transcribed) nu-moveable and the (untranscribed) digamma; see espec. Horrocks 1997: 204–6.

29. Among the genres of oral tradition studied by our research team in central Serbia were epic, lyric, folktale, charm, graveside lament, and genealogy (see further Foley 1982); each of these has its own expressive register within the male (decasyllabic) versus female (octosyllabic) synergy.

30. Especially in the late 1990s, with fragmentation of the former Yugoslavia on an unprecedented scale, the notion of an "unmarked conversational standard" must be understood as no more than a convenient generalization that allows us to highlight certain unusual aspects of specifically poetic registers. This is the logic behind measuring the *guslari's* epic language against their own conversational registers instead of against a (mythical) regional or national standard.

31. For an elegant presentation of the major features of Homer's dialect, see Horrocks 1997. I owe the following perspective on artificiality to a question posed by Kurt Raaflaub during a paper session at the 1995 meeting of the American Philological Association. Cf. also Wyatt (1988:28), who observes that "Homeric Greek is the ordinary language of Greek epic; and that in no way, save in the need of dactylic shape, does it differ *in principle* from any other language spoken by man."

32. For another example, cf. the specialized idiom employed in performing Serbian charms, which depend on "nonsense language" as well as multiple dialects, archaisms, and lexical borrowings. See further Foley 1995a: 110–15; also Radenković 1982, 1996.

33. Cf. Bakker 1993b: 8–9: "Homeric diction, then, is strictly speaking not a *Kunstsprache* in the sense of a man-made, 'unnatural' vehicle for poetic expression; what *Kunst* there is, is a regularization of what is most natural in speech, and essential for its comprehension."

34. Witness the Homeric-Mycenaean correspondences discussed by Horrocks (1997: 196–97). Speaking of tmesis in Homer (the metrically governed separation of a prefix from the verb to which it is conventionally attached outside epic usage), Horrocks had earlier observed (1980: 5): "It can now be demonstrated that the preservation of these archaic rules of syntax in the language of the Epic is due entirely to the fact that they are absolutely fundamental to the art of oral composition of dactylic verse."

35. Braun 1961: 49. See further note 31 above.

36. Horrocks 1997: 212–17; also, more generally, Wyatt 1970. On Ionic and Aeolic forms, and the various theoretical models for explaining their sequence and deployment, see Horrocks 1997: 212–17.

37. Magner (1972: 245) furnishes this basic breakdown of geographical dialects in South Slavic: "In general, ekavski is spoken in Serbia, while ijekavski (also referred to as jekavski) is spoken in Montenegro, Herzegovina, Bosnia, Croatia, Southern Dalmatia and Lika; ikavski dialects are spoken in Western Bosnia, in Slavonia (Posavina), in northwestern Dalmatia and in the archipelago north of Pelješac." The ikavski dialect does not enter the picture to any appreciable extent with the Moslem epic collected by Parry and Lord, our major focus here. See further Braun's similar remarks on the general South Slavic "epic dialect" (1961: 47–49).

38. On this phonological contrast and its history, see espec. Vuković 1974: 66–85.

39. There are of course other contrasts between these two dialects, and between Serbian and Croatian at large—in accent, noun gender, word formation, syntax, meaning, alphabet,

and other phonological features (see Magner 1972: 247–50)—but none of these seems to have any systemic effect upon the constitution of the epic diction. Differences in lexicon, which do have such an effect, are treated below in IVb.

40. For the history of interpretation, see Chadwick 1958; Palmer 1962: 99, 108; Janko 1982: 50–53; Horrocks 1997: 207–8.

41. *Il.* 1.34, 2.209, 6.347, 9.182, 13.798, 23.59; *Od.* 13.85, 13.220; *Hymn to Hermes* 341; *Hymn to Aphrodite* (vi) 4; cf. also Hesiod, *Works and Days* 648. The combination of θαλάσσης with *πολυφλοίσβου would make this hemistich phrase unmetrical and dissolve its identity and usefulness as a formulaic element.

42. For further examples of Aeolicisms, see Horrocks 1997: 213.

43. As explained below (this section), the vocative often serves as a bi-form for the nominative in order to eke out a colonic length.

44. The usual combinations would be *ovčjem mlēkom* and *tvojem mlēkom*, both of which would yield hypometric lines.

45. Strictly speaking, one could argue that *ovčijem* and *tvojijem* represent formations by analogy with ijekavski inflection, rather than examples of that inflection itself. But the point remains, and is perhaps even strengthened: the poetic language provides metrical bi-forms as necessary, and within the poetic register there is no absolute dividing line between "naturally" occurring and analogous forms.

46. See, e.g., Briggs 1988.

47. Thus Braun observes (1961: 48) "dass Sänger, die an sich eine andere Mundart sprechen, beim Liedvortrag diesen 'epischen Dialekt' nachzuahmen suchen"; cf. Palmer (1962: 98), who understands the Homeric register as "the product of a long tradition of oral poetry." This was of course Parry's basic argument (1932) about the Homeric language as the language of an oral poetry. Cf. also Horrocks 1980: 4–5; 1997.

48. These are synchronic adjustments used by the Stolac *guslari* and can be distinguished, in theory if not in practice, from the dialect-based alternative forms discussed immediately above. Given the uncertainty of the editorial history of the Homeric texts, it would be difficult if not impossible to locate unambiguous examples of the same (performance-based) phenomenon in our *Iliad* and *Odyssey*. Note, however, G. Edwards, who observes that "Hesiod is not averse to eking out a word artificially with an extra syllable" (1971: 104).

49. Of course, this descriptive convenience privileges the unmarked language, viewing the epic register as somehow aberrant—wanting in regularity, unstable, and so forth. As noted above, the present chapter aims at a more democratic view of registers and speech-acts.

50. Other frequent reductions of this type include *išao/iš'o* ("[he] went]") and *dao/d'o* ("[he] gave"). In South Slavic epic the past participle is very often used without the copular auxiliary typical of the standard language to express a simple past action. This is another feature of the epic *koinê*; cf. the Homeric practice of selectively deleting augment.

51. For example, the genitive singular of the second-person pronoun can be *tebe*, the enclitic *te*, or the elided enclitic *t'*; this last possibility is effectively zero syllables long, since it must co-occur with a following vowel to yield even a single syllable.

52. This operation of analogy is yet another indication that the traditional register is first and foremost a living language and not a collection of parts.

53. Another way in which the Parry-Lord singers from the Stolac region eke out Mustajbeg's name into a six-syllable form is by repeating the *beg* morph contained in his simplex name and reversing the order of the other elements: thus, *beg Mustajbeg lički*, an apparently redundant phrase that nonetheless proves more popular than the vocative expansion in our sample of Stolac performances (forty-six versus eighteen occurrences). Note that the vocative inflection is customarily attached at the end of the colon, that is, the end of the "word." Kraljeviću Marko seems to be an exception to this rule, perhaps because of the easy reversibility of its constituent parts (Marko Kraljeviću as often as Kraljeviću Marko).

54. In addition to lexicon and morphology, the decasyllabic prosody itself has been shown to be of considerable antiquity; see Jakobson 1952, Vigorita 1976, Foley 1990: 94–98. On the Homeric side, see espec. Sherratt 1990 on the achronological nature of the epics and their correspondence with the archaeological record.

55. Turkicisms are numerous enough in the South Slavic epic songs to require a special lexicon (Škaljić 1979; see further Lord 1972). In the Stolac songs many of the Turkicisms are lodged in a second-colon formula, "X *učiniti*," where X = the borrowed Turkish word. Frozen within this general-purpose phrase, which means "to do or perform X," they take on the identity of a larger "word" and resist internal change; see further Foley 1990: 192–94. Cf. Skendi 1953 on the influence of Albanian language and epic phraseology on South Slavic epic nearer the Albanian border. On the bilingual (Albanian and South Slavic) singer, see Kolsti 1968, 1990, 1997.

56. Either with the proper name *Alija* (6) or another Turkicism, *jabandžija* ("foreigner, stranger"; 1). Thus *gazija* is fossilized either by "word"-making (*careva gazija*) or by rhyme.

57. Note that of 69 total instances of *buljubaša* (in various cases) in the Stolac sample, 58 are involved in this same noun-epithet formula, *Mujo buljubaša*, or its metathesized equivalent *buljubaša Mujo*; cp. the cognate formulas *buljubaša Tale* (3) and *buljubaša Ibro* (1). On the morphological rhyme in 556, cf. *6699*.582: "Buljubaša, turski selambaša," which amounts to the same line with the (inessential) copula deleted and replaced by the adjective "Turkish."

58. See Benson (1980: 774). Magner (1972: 322) observes that "the aorist is sometimes used in speech, but its usage is usually limited to storytelling," and that "aorist forms of a verb indicate that the verbal action or situation took place in the past and . . . was terminated, though perhaps not completed, at a definite time in the past." Other South Slavic folk genres employ the aorist with some regularity, such as the metrical charms, or *bajanje*; cf. Foley 1995a: 118, lines 26–28 (version A3), 25–27 (version B1). On usage in proverbs, see below the discussion of proverbial expressions in the epic. Also pertinent is the fact that the literate Montenegrin poet and archbishop Petar II Petrović Njegoš (1813–51), composing his poems pen in hand but also very much in the traditional register of South Slavic epic, makes frequent use of "words" involving the aorist tense and other archaic features. See further Lord 1986b: espec. 30–34 and Haymes 1980.

59. The historical present forms would be, respectively, *padnu* (imperfective aspect *padaju* unlikely), *stanu*, and *mole*, all being two rather than three syllables in length. The simple past inflection would yield, respectively, *su pali*, *su stali*, and *su molili*. While the first two of these latter verbs are three-syllable forms, the fact is that the auxiliary *su* is often deleted in the epic register, causing a diminution of one syllable; even if it were not deleted, the auxiliary is enclitic and would cause a revision of order among the constituents of the phrase. In short, modifying the verb from aorist to either historical present or simple past means a major, usually unacceptable revision of the phrase.

60. See further Foley 1994b: 85–86.

61. Examples include "Pa je Pero rano podranijo" ("Then [General] Pero arose early," 1868.1642, etc.) and "Pa banica rano podranila" ("Then the banica arose early," 1287a.23, etc.). A similar observation may be made of the line examined just above: the only other uses of *klanjati* ("to pray") are the two occurrences of the following line, with a historical present tense: "Pred džamijom dje klanjaju Turci" ("Before the mosque where the Turks prayed," 1287a.866, *6617*.1770).

62. But note Gesemann's earlier notion of the *Kompositionsschema*, a kind of narrative architecture that resembles the theme or story-pattern (1926: espec. 66–69); further discussion in Foley 1988: 14–15. For additional thematic analysis of South Slavic epic narrative, see Fisher 1990 (focusing on Christian songs from Hercegovina) and Clark 1995 (comparing narrative patterns in *Beowulf*).

63. Cf. Lord 1951, 1960: 68–98, 1995: 203–11. See espec. M. Edwards 1992 for a survey of

scholarship on typical scenes in Homer; cf. also Minchin 1995a on the Homeric proem and Foley 1991: 68–74 on the proem in South Slavic epic.

64. Cf. Foley 1990: 288–327 for a full analysis of this typical scene in the Stolac songs.

65. Cf. Foley 1992c for a description of bloodsisterhood/-brotherhood in actual practice and as a motif in the epic songs.

66. Logically speaking, we would expect the most obvious variation at those levels of the unit that are most dependent on individual language characteristics. Since the latticework of ideas—as opposed to their expression—is not language-dependent, the lack of variance on this score is understandable. Cf. the case of Anglo-Saxon narrative, whose typical scenes, when compared to South Slavic and ancient Greek narrative, show similar idea-patterning alongside dramatically different patterns of phraseology; see further Foley 1990: ch. 9.

67. This dimension of the typical scene has caused considerable critical disagreement in the field of Anglo-Saxon poetry, for example. See, e.g., Foley 1990: 333–36.

68. We will take up this precise problem in Chapter 4.

69. See espec. Coote 1980, Foley 1990: ch. 8.

70. See espec. M. Edwards 1992.

71. Lord 1969: 18. To Lord's "composition and transmission" I would add their role in the *reception* of traditional oral art; see further Answer 2 and espec. Chapter 5 below. See also Lord 1960: 158–85, 1965, 1971.

72. See Coote 1981, Foley 1990: ch. 10, with references in both; also Arant 1973 on Russian and Badalkhan 1994 on Balochi. Cf. the Return Song pattern in the *Homeric Hymn to Demeter*, as described in M. Lord 1967 and Foley 1995a: 175–80.

73. Lord 1969.

74. Much more will be said along the same lines in Chapter 5, where the issue of story-pattern as *sêma* is taken up at length.

Chapter 4.   Homer and the South Slavic *Guslar*: Traditional Referentiality

1. On the morphology of the musical dimension of South Slavic epic, see espec. Erdely 1995.

2. When textualization takes place, it is only too easy to assimilate oral traditional events to the kind of communication prompted exclusively by graphic signals on a page. Once the keys to performance are camouflaged in this way, traditional referentiality may be submerged almost entirely. See further "The Rhetorical Persistence of Traditional Forms" (Foley 1995a: ch. 3); also Fine 1984 and Foley 1995b on editing oral traditional works.

3. For further discussion of traditional art in South Slavic epic, see espec. Foley 1991: chs. 3–4, R. Alexander 1995, and Koljević 1994; cf. Butler 1993.

4. The Return Song, very briefly treated here, is the subject of Chapter 5 below, which includes specific comparisons with the *Odyssey* and the consideration of three major Odyssean cruces: narrative sequence, the role of Penelope, and closure.

5. Exempting, of course, the optional proem (*pripjev*) that begins many performances. On the traditional referentiality of the initiatory *sêma* of the *pripjev*, see Foley 1991: 68–75.

6. Note that this is the same combination of tradition and individuality that we observed in the anthropomorphic figure of the legendary singer in Chapter 2 above. What the story-pattern and the legendary singer share is the quality and function of *sêmata*.

7. For more examples from Moslem South Slavic epic, see Foley 1991: 68–75 (proem or *pripjev*); 75–82 (negative comparison).

8. For bibliography, see espec. M. Edwards 1992: section 2.4 on ancient Greek; Olsen 1986: 577–88 on Old English.

9. Espec. Lord 1960: 68–98, Foley 1990: ch. 8, Clark 1995.

10. On the sequence of arming, boast, monster's approach, death of a substitute, and battle in *Beowulf*, cf. Foley 1991: 231–42; also Amodio 1995.

11. Bloodbrother- and bloodsisterhood are important relationships in both real life and epic tradition among the South Slavs (cf. Foley 1992c). Here as elsewhere this type of synthetic kinship bridges a gap between two people who are otherwise ineligible to form an alliance (other situations involve a Christian female captor and a Moslem male prisoner, a young Moslem woman and a Christian warrior, etc.). Informants who have experience with the real-life situation indicate that once a relationship of synthetic kinship has been established, it persists indefinitely, thus proscribing intermarriage among descendants, for example.

12. Here Bašić refers to a type of headdress worn into battle by Turkish heroes. Škaljić (1979) glosses *čelenka* as "a type of plume, made of gold or silver in the shape of linked feathers, sometimes adorned with precious gems. It is placed on the front side of a cap or turban. It also serves as a decoration for bravery."

13. "Taking off and putting on," *6699*.52 and 6703.372 [also 1283.976; cf. *6617*.1834, 1841, where Mujo is given a disguise]; feathered headgear, *6699*.66, 92 and 6703.406; pistols, *6699*.72–73 and 6703.393–94; encirclement, *6699*.67 and 6703.389; belt of arms, *6699*.70; long steel dagger, *6699*.74; four chains, *6699*.75; golden coins, *6699*.97; sharp saber, e.g. *6617*.1161.

14. On this narrative strategy of "negative comparison," see further Foley 1991: 75–83 (for Moslem epic) and 111–15 (for Christian epic).

15. Cf. the series of questions posed by Odysseus (11.171–79) to his mother Antikleia's ghost (11.181–203), examined in detail below in Chapter 5.

16. On the initiatory function of the *pripjev*, a powerful *sêma* but much more generic than the "Shouting in Prison" opening in that it does not signal what kind of epic tale will follow, see Foley 1991: 67–75.

17. The next line then closes a small figure of ring-composition with the repetition of *cmili* (lines 1 and 6). This pattern, often in the form of a capsule, is common in South Slavic Moslem and Christian narrative as well as other oral-connected traditional poems; see Lord 1986b: 53–64 on Moslem epic and cp. Stanley 1993 on Homer, Niles 1983: 152–62 on *Beowulf*, and Parks 1988 on both ancient Greek and Old English.

18. Cf. the *topoi* studied by Curtius (1953).

19. Note that Halil is also named with whole-line systems within the Stolac sample: ". . . Halile, mijo pobratime" ("Halil, my bloodbrother") and ". . . Halila, nesretnoga sina" ("Halil, unfortunate son"), both of which amount to composites, in that their second-colon elements are extensively used with other characters.

20. Karadžić 1852/1975: *s.v. kukavica*. The attribute of blackness may also stem from the anatomical fact of the bird's color (its beak), the common metaphorical association of lamentation and the color black, or the specific negative connotation of a cuckoo in a black forest as an omen for evil (as opposed to the same bird appearing in a green forest, a harbinger of good luck; cf. Karadžić 1852). Whatever the case, the important point is that the cuckoo's blackness is now part of a single, indissoluble "word" that must be perceived according to its overall traditional referentiality.

21. Unlike the wife or fiancée, the hero's mother normally recognizes her son—or credits his recognition by another person—without a period of indeterminacy. See further Chapter 5 below.

22. Such usages may shed light on the infamous "winged words" (*epea pteroenta*) phrases in Homer.

23. Cf. the *Rhetorical fulcrum: command* phrases in the Homeric poems, as analyzed in Chapter 7 below.

24. "Pa da vidiš lijepe djevojke." This and all other specific citations from the Stolac sample are provided as convenient examples; in reality, all such phrases are ubiquitous throughout the recorded tradition, so that (textual) citation is in fact misleading.

25. "A upade u šikli odaju" (6597.1079).
26. Kukuruzović uses this phrase twenty-five times over three song-performances (Parry nos. 1287a, 1868, and 6617). As discussed in Chapter 3, the frequent use of the aorist tense is an identifying, constitutive feature of the specialized epic language of the *guslar*.
27. Notice the in-line rhyme and syntactic balance of this stable pattern.
28. On this day, which apparently served as a recurrent annual marker well before the advent of Christianity, young Serbian villagers of marriageable age used to go into the fields, throwing themselves into the wheat in a celebration of fecundity. Cf. Kulišić et al. 1970: 119; Halpern and Kerewsky-Halpern 1972: 117.
29. Equated by Karadžić (1852: *s.v. vjerenica ljuba*). This pair of expressions, one four and one six syllables long (equivalent to the first and second cola of the line, respectively), provides an example of metrical accommodation within the traditional register. Although the unmarked meaning of *vjerenik/-ica* seems to be fiancé(e) (cf. Benson 1980: *s.v. vjerenik*), the traditional register reveals no such special discrimination. As with the speech introductions, the deflection in meaning from unmarked to epic register here translates to a suppression of semantic specificity.
30. In the original, "A od tala na noge skočijo." For a full discussion, see Foley 1991: 83–87.
31. On this central figure, see espec. Popović 1988.
32. 6698, ms. p. 13.
33. 6698, ms. pp. 13–14.

Chapter 5.   Story-Pattern as *Sêma*: The *Odyssey* as a Return Song

1. In this regard compare the process of elucidating traditional referentiality in the well-collected Moslem South Slavic epic, where multiple versions of songs are commonplace; see further Chapter 4 above and Foley 1991: espec. 61–95.
2. On this widely distributed pattern, which informs at least ancient Greek, South Slavic, Russian, Bulgarian, Albanian, Anglo-Saxon, Middle English, Turkic (central Asian), and Balochi narrative poetry, see espec. Lord 1960: 112–23, 242–59; 1969; 1991: 64–68, 87–91; Arant 1973; Coote 1981; Parks 1983; Foley 1990: 359–87; 1991: 64–68, 87–91; 1995a: 175–79; Badalkhan 1994; Slatkin 1996; and Feldman 1997. For another perspective on Return Songs, see Malkin 1998.
3. On the Agamemnon references, see Olson 1990. I also refer to the scattered accounts and fragmentary remains of the Epic Cycle (see espec. Davies 1988, 1989), conceiving of those lost poems not as fixed texts that influence the *Iliad* and *Odyssey* according to a literary model but as other poems within the larger constellation of ancient Greek oral epic tradition (cf. Kannicht 1982; Burgess 1996; Nagy 1996b: 22, 38, 41; Burgess 1997: espec. 2 n. 3; and Holmberg 1999). See below the discussion of the implications of Agamemnon's ghost's typology of Return Songs at *Odyssey* 24.192–202.
4. Cf. Nagler (1974: 131–66; based on Lord 1960: 186–97), who posits a pattern of Withdrawal-Devastation-Return, apparently not nearly so widely distributed as the *nostos* story. On comparability across genres, note the Return pattern in the *Hymn to Demeter* (cf. Foley 1995a: 175–79; also Crane 1988:18–20); on possible intertextual relations, see Pucci 1987. For a review of the various theories of the performance structure of the *Iliad*, see Heiden 1996: espec. 6–16 (though the South Slavic analogy is inadequately treated; cf. Foley 1990: 284–88 on singers' pauses and thematic structure); of related interest is Murnaghan 1997. On the pattern of the *Iliad* from a perspective involving the "second self," see Van Nortwick 1992: chs. 2–3.
5. Even the Christian epic tradition, which consists of poems and performances customarily much shorter than those characteristic of the Moslem tradition, occasionally features

the Return story-pattern; see further Foley 1986. On the potential of the comparative method in general, see espec. Hansen 1990: 241–42 and *passim*.

6. See M. West 1988 for suggestions on the prehistory of ancient Greek epic that acknowledges Indo-European roots, a Mycenaean to Ionic development, and the stimulus provided by Near Eastern influence.

7. For a digest of various opinions on the *telos* or *peras* of the poem at this point, with a vote decidedly in favor of the "continuation" as an important and organic part of the *Odyssey*, see Russo et al. 1992: 342–45.

8. The following general summary is based primarily on the Return Songs recorded by Parry and Lord in the years 1933–35 in the central Hercegovinian region of Stolac; within that sample special prominence is given to songs performed by the *guslari* Halil Bajgorić, Ibrahim Bašić, Mujo Kukuruzović, and Salko Morić. Basic data on these singers and their (unpublished) repertoires are available in Kay 1995; further descriptive information drawn from conversations with the singers may be found in Foley 1990: 42–51, and in Chapter 2 above. It is noteworthy that the morphology sketched below also follows Aristotle's summary of the *Odyssey* (*Poetics* 17; in Halliwell 1995: 91), with the telling exception that Aristotle focuses entirely on Odysseus the hero and not at all on his heroic counterpart Penelope.

9. On synthetic kinship in social life and in the epic, see further Foley 1992c.

10. Our aim is analogous to Ann Bergren's goal of "narratological competence" (1983: 39), but might better be termed an "idiomatic competence" based on fluency in the traditional register. I am well aware that other comparative contexts could be invoked (cf. Kakridis' invocation of a modern Greek ballad as parallel, as recounted in Katz 1991: 181–82), but choose to focus on the South Slavic Moslem epic because of the uniquely rich and closely analogous traditional morphology it offers.

11. On closure in ancient works, see Roberts et al. 1997; in specific reference to the *Iliad*, Murnaghan 1997.

12. Parry no. 665: original, *SCHS*, vol. 2, no. 32, pp. 316–23; English translation, *SCHS*, vol. 1, pp. 314–22.

13. On the *pripjev* as a traditional form, see Foley 1991: 68–75.

14. Within the Stolac epic tradition, this *sêma* marks "a monumental (if not necessarily heroic) death . . . , a demise that somehow involves tragedy or shame and that, all other things being equal, should not have happened" (Foley 1991: 95).

15. Lord notes that Milutin is forgotten for the moment, since "he is not organic to this theme of recognition" (*SCHS*, vol. 1, 431 n. 18). Here the generic story-pattern temporarily overrides the details of the particular story. For another example of this kind of generic override, cf. Foley 1990: 369–87.

16. The *sêma* "truelove" (*vjerna ljuba* or *vjerenica ljuba*) identifies the pivotal female figure in the Return Song (see Chapter 4 above), just as the *sêma* "unlucky captive" identifies the disguised Odysseus figure. In the original language this latter phrase, *sužanj nevoljniče*, seems redundant, since captives are always "unlucky," but once again the semantic force of the constituent parts are subordinated to the function of the entire "word." The phrase means as a whole, as a unitary *reč* or speech-act, rather than part by part. See further Foley 1991: 20–21, 75–76.

17. I have reedited this performance from the records and Vujnović's transcription. The other two are no. *291b*, sung, 1,360 lines, recorded on 15 July; and no. 1283, dictated, 1,403 lines, taken down on 18 February. For further information on the singer Bašić, see Foley 1990: 42–45 and Chapter 2 above; for analysis of these three song-performances, see Foley 1990: 50–51, 284–88.

18. To an audience lacking fluency in the traditional register, the act of "asking after each other's heroic health" will seem pointless or even ludicrous: the prisoners do not exactly find themselves in a promising situation, after all. But this verbal sign traditionally indexes the meeting of Turkish heroes, regardless of their present situation, and "link[s] an unpromising

present to the promise always implicit in the timeless heroic continuum of Return" (Foley 1991: 78). On the traditional character of the question-and-answer series, both its content and its rhetorical form, see Foley 1991: 75–83.

19. On the motif of "grinding the bones," see Foley 1990: 298–302 and Chapter 3 above.

20. See further Chapter 8 on the stranger's rags as his disguise (and *sêma*).

21. Like all major figures in South Slavic epic, Mustajbey has a traditional presence that goes far beyond his appearance in any one situation or poem. On his particular brand of imperiousness and treachery, implied in every one of his appearances, see Foley 1991: 18–19. Cf. the trickster-hero Tale of Orašac (Foley 1991: 19–20 and espec. 1995a: 32–41), whose famously ambiguous reputation likewise accompanies all of his appearances.

22. See Chapter 4 above for a discussion of the traditional sign of the *kukavica crna*.

23. Like other written messages in South Slavic epic, this amounts to a long-distance face-to-face conversation, with the message "read aloud" by the narrator or one of the principals at both ends of the transmission. Cf. the discussion of Bellerophon's tablet in the Introduction above.

24. As a *sêma* or traditional sign, "decorated letter" identifies "the kind of letter sent by one important personage to another in order to convey a message of some significance (summons to war, invitation to a wedding, intelligence about the enemy, and so on)" (Foley 1995a: 114 n. 47). Likewise, as explained in the preceding chapter, when a person "jumps from the ground to his or her feet," the physical act is less important than its traditional signification: it indicates "a heroic or honorable response to an unexpected or threatening turn of events that demands the principal's immediate attention" (Foley 1991: 84).

25. See Chapter 4 on the typical scene of Arming the Hero as applied to this female stand-in.

26. On the role of female intermediaries such as this one, see Foley 1991: 91–94.

27. Note again that Muminaga's change of heart takes place offstage. This apparent discrepancy parallels Homeric instances in which implicit information fills a "gap" (cf. Foley 1991: 159–63, e.g.). Neither Bašić nor Homer is "nodding"; both are depending on the (nontextual) strategy of traditional referentiality.

28. It may go without saying that audience expectation exists at the level of passive expectation; knowing the idiom means fluent awareness of the sequence without conscious deliberation, just as one "expects" subjects to agree with verbs or prepositions to take a particular case. In yet another way, then, the traditional register works like language, only more so.

29. For background information on the *guslar* Mujo Kukuruzovíc, see Foley 1990: 48–51; for analysis of this group of songs, see Foley 1990: 50–51, 288–312, and espec. 359–87.

30. As with Bašić's *Alagić Alija and Velagić Selim*, I have reedited this performance.

31. Were Mustajbey to expatiate at any length here, and Alibegovica to respond in kind, the ambiguity of the truelove figure would be diminished if not dissolved. The overall story-pattern demands that the exposure of her real nature be delayed until later in the narrative. This is not to preclude the possibility that an audience familiar with the story of *this particular hero* might balance that generic uncertainty with specific knowledge of what happened to Ograšćić Alija; it is merely to affirm what lies behind the sign.

32. Within the South Slavic epic tradition no relationship is closer or more permanent than that between a hero and his horse. Even the cleverest hero may relinquish control of an expedition to his faithful mount, who typically will not submit to being ridden by anyone else. In the Christian songs Kraljević Marko regularly converses with his horse Šarac, and even shares the ritual sustenance of wine at certain points with his lifelong companion. Thus, in setting the contest as she does, the truelove has chosen the absent hero's single most characteristic possession as the *sêma* that will identify her mate—although that choice will yield a much different outcome than she at this point imagines.

33. On this typical scene, see Chapter 4 above.

34. In the other versions (see note 29), Alija first severs Alibegovica's hands and then dis-

patches her altogether. This is not an uncommon sequence of events in the Return Songs from Stolac and more widely, and something like it would be traditionally implied by the story-pattern whether the particular actions are stipulated or not.

35. For detailed analysis of this sequence, see Foley 1990: 377–85.

36. Cf. the *sêma* of the bow in the *Odyssey*, as Odysseus reveals himself to the suitors by successfully stringing it and then testing the tautness by plucking the string and sounding a musical note (21.410–11): "Then plucking it in his right hand he tested the bowstring, / and it gave him back an excellent sound like the voice of a swallow" (δεξιτερῇ δ' ἄρα χειρὶ λαβὼν πειρήσατο νευρῆς· / ἡ δ' ὑπὸ καλὸν ἄεισε, χελιδόνι εἰκέλη αὐδήν). See further the discussion of the bow-shot below.

37. But cf. the *Nostoi* from the Epic Cycle, which Proclus describes as closing with a double *nostos*, one essentially positive (Menelaos and Helen) and the other unquestionably negative (Agamemnon and Klytemnestra); see further Davies 1988: 67.

38. That is, we have ample evidence that Kukuruzović sang this song as both a single unit and as two separate tales; see Foley 1990: 359–87, espec. 376–79.

39. Traditional "citations" of the Agamemnon-Klytemnestra-Orestes parallel, essentially the equivalent of the first part of Kukuruzović's *Captivity of Ograšćić Alija*, are frequent and widely distributed in the *Odyssey*: 1.29f., 298–300; 3.193f.; 4.90–92, 512f., 584; 11.387–466; 13.383–85; 24.24f., 192–202. On these embedded, telegraphic references, see also Olson 1990, espec. 57: "The poet uses the tales of Agamemnon . . . to hint repeatedly to his audience that this *Odyssey* may end in a way they know it should not." Likewise, Slatkin contends that "the *Odyssey* acknowledges the Agamemnon story not just as a parallel series of events but precisely as an *alternative narrative model*" (1996: 227, her italics); cf. S. West 1981.

40. Note the traditional implications of *kouridios* ("wedded"), which is linked with the idea of the hero's return home (or its lack) in seventeen of its eighteen epic occurrences and two of three instances in the Hymns. Even within the compass of Odysseus' lying tale to Penelope at 19.266, this word enters the picture as an index of *nostos*—in this case his admission that mourning is natural for a woman whose *andr'. . . kouridion* ("wedded husband") has lost his return home.

41. Exactly how the woman manages to hold off her suitors is, like many other moments, treated in somewhat more detail in the *Odyssey* than in the typical South Slavic Return Song. See Penelope's account of the weaving/unweaving trick for the disguised "stranger" (19.137–56) and Antinoos' chagrin-filled rehearsal of the same chain of events for Telemachos (2.88–110).

42. The South Slavic song devotes about 13 percent of its narrative to the flashback, the Greek epic about 17 percent. On the (idiomatic) flashback as motivated locally by Odysseus' telling his name and thus rehearsing his *kleos*, see Webber 1989; cf. Most 1989 on the narrative economy of the episode and its rhetorical force of "Let me go home now" (30), both a local and large-scale logic entirely consonant with the overall momentum of the Return Song.

43. See below for discussion of the ring-composition underlying Odysseus' questions and Antikleia's ghost's answers.

44. The only two members of his household to see through his disguise almost from the start are Eurykleia, when she notices his scar (as *sêma*; see Chapter 1), and his old dog Argos (17.291f.). On the beggar's rags that serve as a *sêma* marking the stranger's (as opposed to Odysseus') identity, see further Chapters 7–8.

45. Several of these recognitions will be treated individually below. For the record, they are seven: by Telemachos (16.187f.), Argos (17.291f.), Eurykleia (19.392f.), Eumaios and Phi-loitios (21.205f.), the suitors en masse (22.34f.), Penelope (stipulated at 23.205f.), and Laertes (24.320f.).

46. The term *xeinos* designates the "stranger" who by custom must be treated honorably as a "guest" even before his true identity is revealed; see further Reece 1993: espec. 5–46.

47. Like the South Slavic heroes whose special musical ability or style identify them

acoustically to family and community, Odysseus plucks the string of his bow and sounds a musical note just before the slaughter begins (see note 36 above).

48. Just as Homer's specialized language as a whole is no more artificial than any unmarked everyday variety of ancient Greek; see further Chapter 2 above.

49. Thus, while (to my knowledge) Reece (1993: 159) is correct that the extent of the Telemacheia and the centrality of the vengeance theme are unique to our *Odyssey* (though each finds briefer analogues in the South Slavic tradition), his contention that "the complex narrative structure resulting from the elaborate hysteron-proteron of Odysseus' tales in books 9–12" is similarly innovative cannot pass muster. This elaborate and complex order is in fact the trademark, idiomatic order of the Return Song. On a smaller scale, cf. Louden's (1993) proposal of a thrice-repeated multiform pattern involving the hero's arrival, a powerful female, and a band of young male rivals within the *Odyssey*; this internal pattern and the overall Return sequence could coexist quite peacefully. Likewise, viewing the *Odyssey* as a Return Song does not conflict in any fashion with Cook's (1995) proposal that the poem took something akin to its present form in the context of Athenian ritual. Cf. the delineation of the hero's return in Olson 1995: 140–60; also Thalmann 1992: 95–123.

50. Cf. Felson-Rubin's suggestive discussion in her chapter titled "Weaving" (1994: 15–42).

51. Katz 1991: 193; also Katz 1994 on the convergence of *nostos* and *xenia* (hospitality). See further McDonald (1997), who observes that "as we pass into the final action of the Odyssey, we retain this suspension of final solutions, a suspension of belief that constitutes poetic truth" (21). Cf. Gregory (1996), who sees Penelope's confirmation of Odysseus' story as "the manufacture of a 'truth' out of multiple versions of reality" (4).

52. See espec. Foley 1991: chaps. 1–2, with applications to the *Iliad* in chap. 5; also Katz 1991.

53. As Ingrid Holmberg (1997) construes it, Penelope is deeply involved with *mêtis*, "cunning intelligence"; as she further observes, "Odysseus is the most prominent male representative of acceptable male μῆτις [*mêtis*]" (13). This quality dovetails importantly with his ability to manage reality via traditional signs; cf. Chapter 1 above with Holmberg's contention that "Odysseus is also a remarkable encoder and decoder of σήματα [*sêmata*]"](13–14).

54. "Sing in me, Muse, the man *of many devices* . . ." (Ἄνδρα μοι ἔννεπε, Μοῦσα, πολύτροπον . . .).

55. Cf. Schein (1995: 23), who observes that "Penelope . . . becomes a virtually equal, second hero of the poem, along with Odysseus." On Odysseus' polytropism, see Pucci 1987; on his "evasiveness," Scodel 1999.

56. These characteristics are drawn from or reflected in Return Songs other than the three summarized above, especially from the unpublished Stolac epics sung or dictated by Bašić, Kukuruzović, Halil Bajgorić, and Salko Morić (on which, see Kay 1995).

57. Cf. Penelope's complaint along these lines late in the poem (23.209–12).

58. This is parallel to the necessity Penelope faces after her strategy of weaving and unweaving has been discovered; see Amphimedon's ghost's account (24.125–46).

59. It is the latter reaction that prompts Alibegovica, wife to Ograšćić Alija, to laugh out loud.

60. Although it does not happen in the three songs summarized above, the hero's tamboura-playing can also signal the wife/fiancée's fidelity as she rejoices over the unmistakable sound-*sêma*.

61. We should note that "the horse that can be ridden only by its true owner" is a common motif in South Slavic tradition, perhaps epitomized by the relationship between Kraljević Marko and his mount Šarac (see Foley 1995a: 36 n. 14; and, more generally, Lord 1991: 222–24). The fact that Fata is (unexpectedly) able to equip and manage Alija's horse as she embarks on her errand as substitute champion should be measured against the traditional referentiality of this motif; see further Chapter 4.

62. The *guslari* from whom Parry and Lord collected South Slavic epic had no titles for

the songs they sang, since such textual paraphernalia were irrelevant to their experience of performance. Rather they referred to them with phrases like "When [character X] went to [town Y] and did [action Z]," designations that identified some of the principal (male) characters and major (explicit) actions.

63. On the proxemic nature of Penelope's powerful indeterminacy, see Lateiner 1992: 150–54.

64. As Ahl and Roisman adroitly put it (1996: 205): "Her role is that of the waiting wife, suspended in time for the twenty years Odysseus has been away. Since her indecision controls many other people, however, she controls time rather than being controlled by time, and she defines the situation in which she exists rather than being defined by it." On the role of similes in the dynamics of Odysseus' *nostos* and the *telos* of the *Odyssey*, see R. Friedrich 1981: 133–37.

65. See Odysseus' quoted directions at 18.259–70 and Penelope's realistic assessment of her situation as made in the stranger's presence at 19.157–61. Roisman (1987) argues that her "indignation" shows through in the speech that occurs immediately after she finally accepts his return (23.209–30); cf. Murnaghan 1994.

66. See note 39 above. Of additional relevance is Fredricksmeyer's (1997) demonstration of Penelope's duality as expressed in her comments about Helen, and particularly his argument that Homer "builds suspense by alluding to an epichoric tradition that generates uncertainty about Penelope's loyalty" (495).

67. These paired possibilities may both have been illustrated in the now-lost *Nostoi* (*Returns*) from the Epic Cycle, a poem or poems said to end with (1) Agamemnon's murder and the subsequent story of revenge undertaken by Orestes and Pylades and (2) Menelaos' safe return home and reunion with Helen. See further Davies 1988: 66–70; 1989: 80–86.

68. Cf. Nestor's citation of Zeus ordaining a *lugron . . . noston* for the Acheans at 3.132. At 3.130f. Nestor will report on what he knows of the various Achaeans' *nostoi*: among the eventual safe returns are Diomedes to Argos, himself to Pylos, Neoptolemos to Phthia, Philoktetes to his home, and Idomeneus to Crete; he also cites Agamemnon's fate at 3.193f. At Book 4.492f. Menelaos relates to Telemachos what he learned from Teiresias about those who attempted to return from Troy: he notes that Agamemnon and Aias perished, the former on arrival and the latter en route, while Odysseus was stalled on Kalypso's island.

69. As when, for example, the *vjerna ljuba* insists on honoring her husband's memory by monetarily rewarding the person reporting his death and burial (who is, of course, the Return hero in disguise).

70. See further the discussion of this and related traditional phrases in Chapter 7 below.

71. The second hemistich of the latter line (κακὸν δ' ἀνεμώλια βάζειν) has some traditional resonance in the *Odyssey* and *Iliad* as an index of the limitations of knowledge that are part of a character's makeup or situation; rhetorically it forecloses quickly and absolutely on an unproductive avenue of discussion. Compare Odysseus' deflection of Agamemnon's inquiry about whether his son Orestes still lives (*Od.* 11.464) and Odysseus' rebuke of Agamemnon's claim of Achaean cowardice (*Il.* 4.355).

72. Even the rhetoric of the question-and-answer series is strikingly similar to the traditional form of exchange in the South Slavic Moslem epics; cf. Foley 1991: 75–83.

73. Also cf. 16.30–39, where Telemachos also asks Eumaios about whether his mother is still waiting for Odysseus and receives precisely the same answer (16.37–39 = 11.181–83).

74. Cf. Frame's (1978) contention that a linguistic kinship between *nostos* and *noos* ("mind") also links Odysseus' return to the trickery and wiles for which he is well known. I see no reason why Penelope's carefully managed indeterminacy—which Agamemnon's ghost's words certify has entered the tradition as *kleos*—would not qualify as another aspect of that *nostos/noos* linkage. On the centrality and activity of Penelope's ambiguity, cf. also Holmberg 1995.

75. Within the Return story-pattern, the truelove's expressed wish to question a (dis-

guised) stranger amounts to a traditional sign. From this point, whether the wish is immediately fulfilled or not, the prepared audience or reader is awaiting their predictable exchange. Thus a kind of traditionally generated suspense results.

76. Cf. Forsyth (1979), who contends that this appearance before the suitors is an instance of the typical scene of "allurement," and Pedrick (1994), who examines Eurynome's advice in the context of the role of female confidantes.

77. For an analysis of Odysseus' lying tales as *kata kosmon* ("proper," "fitting"), see Pratt 1993: 55–94.

78. As will be explained in Chapter 7 and illustrated in Chapter 8, this small phrase "But come" is a powerful traditional signal not only for a rhetorical shift but also for a command about to be issued by the speaker.

79. On Penelope's indeterminacy as expressed in her reaction to the dream, see Pratt 1994: espec. 152.

80. Nobody, that is, outside of the charmed circle to whom the stranger's identity is already secretly known (Telemachos, Eumaios, Philoitios, and Eurykleia—and Argos!), none of whom is eligible to participate in the contest. On the analogy between Penelope and the poet, both of whom strategically hold certainty in abeyance, see Peradotto 1990: espec. 83–85; cf. also Morrison 1992 on the poet's strategic use of misdirection.

81. On the timing of the contest of the bow and the ethical dimensions of Penelope's actions, see H. Foley 1995: 102–4. On her "stout hand" (*cheiri pacheiêi*) as a *sêma* of this heroic act, see Chapter 7 below.

82. Note that this same equivocation precedes Penelope's initial discussion of the contest with the stranger (19.577–81 = 21.75–79).

83. As Nagler emphasizes (1990), the bow-shot leads to Odysseus' cryptic remark that he will now shoot at a mark that "no other man has yet hit" (22.6), a veiled reference to the bridge from contest to slaughter, from ritual battle to actual, life-or-death battle. This same link is implied in the Return Song pattern at large.

84. See the evenhanded discussion of *telos* and *peras* in Russo et al. 1992: 342–45. On the *ends* of the *Odyssey*, as he puts it, see Peradotto 1990: 59–93; for an emphasis on closure and the poetics of old age, Falkner 1995: espec. 48–51.

85. On various theories of recording and transmission, see Janko 1990, 1992b (following Lord 1953a); Powell 1991: espec. 221–37; Nagy 1996b: espec. 39–44, 1997; and Haslam 1997.

86. On the further question of the "aftermath" following the actual end of the *Odyssey* narrative, see Roberts 1997: espec. 252–54.

87. Cf. "the impossibility of canon" in oral tradition, as described in Foley 1998b. I thus agree with the Oxford *Commentary*'s statement on assessing the later scenes of the poem, at least as far as it goes (Russo et al. 1992: 345): "The deciding factor must be how well the linguistic and stylistic features of the passage under question, as well as its subject matter, fit into the framework of the poem as established up to xxiii 296, and whether the conclusion (xxiii 297–xxiv 548) fulfills a necessary and important function in the structure of the poem as a whole." As shown below, however, we must go beyond a literary, textual definition of the poem's subject matter and framework.

88. On other Return Song epics, see note 2 above.

89. The *Nostoi* in the Epic Cycle would serve as one example. On available evidence, neither the homecoming experienced by Agamemnon—parallel in its outcome to the South Slavic tale of Ograšćić Alija—nor that involving Menelaos could have led to final episodes equivalent to the post-*telos* section of the *Odyssey*.

90. In a sense Odysseus epitomizes this shared characteristic when he identifies himself as *Outis* (No one) to Kylops Polyphemos. Only by resisting the certainty of names and (apparent) commitments do Odysseus and Penelope manage to survive.

91. On the resonant traditional phraseology associated with pondering alternatives, often involving μερμήριζε ("deliberated"), see further Chapter 8 below.

92. Let me reemphasize that the "necessary" aspect of structure also confers a referential advantage. Because poet and audience communicate in this specialized register, following this pathway is not limiting but rather explosively connotative. For these reasons I cannot agree with Pratt's (1993: 94) judgment that this last of Odysseus' lying tales is *ou kata kosmon* ("not proper," "not fitting").

93. Note also Laertes' reaction to his son's revelation (24.345–46): Ὣς φάτο, τοῦ δ' αὐτοῦ λύτο γούνατα καὶ φίλον ἦτορ, / σήματ' ἀναγνόντος τά οἱ ἔμπεδα πέφραδ' Ὀδυσσεύς· ("He spoke, and Laertes' knees and the heart within him went slack, / as he recognized the clear proofs that Odysseus had given"). These are the same two traditional signs with which Homer marks Penelope's final recognition of Odysseus (23.205–6); see further Chapter 1. For bibliography on the recognition by Laertes, see Scodel 1998: 9–11.

94. On Athena's role toward the end of the *Odyssey*, cf. Murnaghan 1995: espec. 77–78.

95. Foley 1991: 186. For analysis of this pattern in the *Iliad*, see 174–89; enumeration of instances in the *Odyssey* at 186. Cf. Chapter 6 and Appendix I below on the morphology of the feast itself.

Chapter 6.   Typical Scenes of Feast and Lament

1. For a useful digest of pertinent research to date, see M. Edwards 1992. See Mackay 1996: espec. 44–45 for a suggestive analogy between Homeric typical scenes and what she calls "scene patterns" in Attic black-figure vase-painting; also Mackay 1993, 1995.

2. Many other examples could have been chosen. My selection of the Feast and Lament is based on three criteria: (1) the general prominence and artistic importance of these scenes in Homer; (2) available prior analysis of their structure (Foley 1990: 265–76 and M. Edwards 1992: 306–7 [Feast] and Foley 1991: 168–74 [Lament]; and (3) the wide spectrum of ways in which they mesh instance and implication in the *Odyssey* and *Iliad*. On traditional themes as cognitive scripts shared by poet and audience, see Minchin 1992a: espec. 234–35; and cf. Minchin 1999 on patterns that underlie descriptions of objects. On the variability of typical scenes and the issue of "truth" in representation, see M. Edwards 1990: 322–23.

3. The six principal laments are: Briseis for Patroklos (19.287–300), Hekabe for Hektor (22.431–36), Andromache for Hektor (22.477–514), Andromache for Hektor again (24.725–45), Hekabe for Hektor again (24.748–59), and Helen for Hektor (24.762–75).

4. Of course, these passages vary widely in length and complexity, from highly developed and elaborate presentations (see espec. those instances analyzed in Foley 1990: 265–77) to telegraphic portrayals that, I maintain, still serve as *sêmata*. To put it simply, the spectrum of Feast scenes reflects the inherent plasticity of the traditional register, as well as of language in general. A full inventory of the thirty-five passages is available in Appendix I.

5. On the political dimensions of Homeric feasting, see Rundin 1996: 181–205.

6. The phraseology here is interesting: all three verbs can appear as simplex or prefixed, depending on the metrical value of the particular inflected form and accommodation to traditional rules of word-placement in the hexameter (on which, see Foley 1990: ch. 4).

7. See further Foley 1991: 182–83.

8. *Od.* 1.136–40, 4.52–56, 7.172–76, 10.368–72, 15.135–39, 17.91–95. Note that two additional lines may also join the four-line cluster (1.141–42 = 4.57–58): δαιτρὸς δὲ κρειῶν πίνακας παρέθηκεν ἀείρας / παντοίων, παρὰ δέ σφι τίθει χρύσεια κύπελλα ("while a carver lifted platters of all kinds of meat and set them / in front of them, and placed beside them the golden goblets").

9. See the complete digest of Feast scenes in the *Odyssey* and *Iliad* in Appendix I.

10. Both lines at *Od.* 1.149–50, 4.67–68, 8.71–72, 8.484–85, 14.453–54, 15.142–43, 16.54–55, 17.98–99, and *Il.* 9.91–92, 9.221–22, 24.627–28; second line only at *Od.* 3.67, 3.473, 15.303,

15.501, 16.480. Virtually all of the remaining Feast instances close with an equivalent either of both lines or of the latter one alone; see further Appendix I. On the antiquity of the second line, see M. West 1988: 164 (based on Durante 1971: 55ff.); the survival of such an archaic verse implies both the traditional structure and the traditional referentiality of this signal from an early stage in ancient Greek epic.

11. For a full discussion of this sequence, with special reference to *Iliad* 24, see Foley 1991: 174–89. On the version of this sequence that ends the *Odyssey*, see Chapter 5 above. We should add that the two possibilities for the first stage in this sequence, assembly or mourning, amount structurally to the same thing: people gather, under rules prescribed by society, in an attempt to deal with a serious threat to the community.

12. See Chapter 7 for a discussion of these and other *sêmata* at the level of traditional phraseology.

13. As when Athena (as pseudo-Mentes) establishes a relationship with Telemachos on the basis of "his" imputed history of hereditary guest-friendship with Odysseus (see *Od.* 1.187–88).

14. It is only fair to stipulate here that I have chosen these nine examples (over eight different books) not at random but precisely because of the wide variety of ways in which they mesh instance and implication. Not covered in the following survey is the feast at *Od.* 8.449ff. that leads to the mediation of Odysseus' tale-within-a-tale in Books 9–12, which Webber (1989) sees as locally stimulated by the hero's telling his name and therefore his *kleos*. Cf. Griffin 1980: 15–17 on the feast's implications. See further the complete digest of Homeric feasts in Appendix I.

15. See Chapter 8 for an *apparatus fabulosus* intended as a companion to *Odyssey* 23.69–103.

16. Cf. Reece's careful discussion of the guest-friendship pattern as applied to this scene (1993: 47–57). Note that the traditional phrase *anathêmata daitos* ("accompaniments to the feast," *Od.* 1.152, referring to music and dance) glosses this qualified feast ironically, as it does just before the suitors' final feast turns into slaughter (21.430).

17. It is well to emphasize that this is not the "first" Feast in Homer's or his audience's experience. Like any other such typical scene in the epics, it is an instance of a familiar expressive sign. Each occurrence echoes not against prior or later occurrences in the given poem that has reached us, but against the tradition at large. As readers of linear texts, we must make an effort to simulate this fluency.

18. On the traditional structure and implication of the delivery of divine messages, see Foley 1991: espec. 183.

19. Espec. *Od.* 5.215–20, where he acknowledges Kalypso's superiority to Penelope but adds (219–20): ἀλλὰ καὶ ὣς ἐθέλω καὶ ἐέλδομαι ἤματα πάντα / οἴκαδέ τ' ἐλθέμεναι καὶ νόστιμον ἦμαρ ἰδέσθαι ("But even so, what I want and all my days I pine for / is to go back to my house and see my day of homecoming"). That day of homecoming, or *telos*, is the poet's and the poem's goal as well; see further Chapter 5.

20. See Chapter 5 on the analogous actions of the banica, wife to the hero's Christian captor in the South Slavic Return Song, who negotiates the hero's release.

21. Specifically labeled as such at *Od.* 9.106, 189, 428. Cf. the application of the same term to the suitors generally (17.363 and indirectly at 18.141) and particularly to Ktesippos, who throws an ox hoof at the disguised Odysseus (20.287).

22. Note the resonance of the phraseology, which combines aural allusions to seating and satisfaction at the same time that it compromises the signal by halting the progress of the feast (*Od.* 10.375–76): Κίρκη δ' ὡς ἐνόησεν ἔμ' ἥμενον οὐδ' ἐπὶ σίτῳ / χεῖρας ἰάλλοντα, κρατερὸν δέ με πένθος ἔχοντα . . . ("When Kirke noticed me sitting there and not /putting my hands to the food, and having strong sorrow upon me . . .").

23. See Chapter 7 for a full discussion of sleep phraseology, collectively a *sêma* that betokens both release and vulnerability.

24. Correspondences as follows: *Od.* 12:354, νεὸς κυανοπρῴροιο: *Od.* 9.482, 9.539, 10.127,

11.6, 12.100, 12.148, 14.311, 22.465; 355, καλαὶ βόες εὐρυμέτωποι: *Od.* 12.262, cf. 11.289; 357, δρυὸς ὑψικόμοιο: cf. *Od.* 14.328, 19.297; 358, κρῖ λευκὸν: *Od.* 4.41, 4.604, *H. Cer.* 309, *H. Cer.* 452; 358, ἐϋσσέλμου ἐπὶ νηός: *Od.* 17.160, 19.243; 360, κατά τε κνίσῃ ἐκάλυψαν: *Od.* 3.457; 361, δίπτυχα ποιήσαντες, ἐπ' αὐτῶν δ' ὠμοθέτησαν: *Od.* 3.458; 364, αὐτὰρ ἐπεὶ κατὰ μῆρε κάη καὶ σπλάγχνα πάσαντο: *Od.* 3.461; 365, μίστυλλόν τ' ἄρα τἆλλα καὶ ἀμφ' ὀβελοῖσιν ἔπειραν: *Od.* 3.462, 14.430. On irony at the level of typical scene, see also Dickson 1992.

25. Of course, all of these lines and part-lines follow the generalized traditional rules for structure (see Foley 1990: ch. 4), the rules that govern the *process* of composition. Some of the *products* are demonstrably formulaic, recurring elsewhere in the epics, and some are not.

26. Cf. 12.419: θεὸς δ' ἀποαίνυτο νόστον ("and the god took away their return").

27. Thus the connections stressed by Nagler (1990: 339–42) among this feast and the suitors' depradations in Books 1 and 20 are also supported by a common traditional context that in all three cases contradicts the mediation that one normally expects as a result of a feast.

28. See further the discussion of disguise and the Return Song hero in Chapter 5.

29. Cf. 20.244f., with seating at 249, 257; preparation and serving at 250–55; and satisfaction at 256. On the unusual nature of this feast, see further Foley 1987; on the correlation of feasting and slaughter here and in Book 22, see Clay 1994.

30. On Penelope's enduring and heroic indeterminacy, see Chapter 5.

31. Foley 1990: 248–57.

32. See also Chapter 5 in this volume.

33. We could well imagine this extraordinary deployment of traditional materials as the feat of a superb individual poet working brilliantly and within his tradition, perhaps on the model of Filip Višnjic's *The Death of Kraljević Marko*, which puts familiar patterns to absolutely unparalleled uses (cf. Foley 1991: 118–33). Note also the other instances of smaller parts of the scene: 23.157–62 = *Od.* 6.230–35, a suggestive parallel in which Athena transfigures Odysseus just before he meets (and visibly impresses) Nausikaa; and 154–55 ≅ *Od.* 24.366–67, where *Euronomê tamiê* ("housekeeper Eurynome") is replaced by *amphipolos Sikelê* ("maidservant Sikele"), who washes and anoints Laertes in preparation for the feast (see the discussion below). Contrast the implications of the **Clothing and status: beggar** sign (Chapter 8, discussion of 23.96).

34. In this respect the act of seating modulates into the approach to the olive-tree bed (23.295–96), and any explicit description of the feast of lovemaking is elided (while the poet describes Telemachos, Eumaios, and Philoitios joining the dance and then going off to bed).

35. On the sleep phraseology and its implications, see Chapter 7.

36. See Chapter 7 for a discussion of this sign, which announces a supernaturally inspired fear.

37. This is not to ignore the many cases in which Athena intercedes on Odysseus' behalf throughout the *Odyssey*, but simply to underline the uniqueness of the Peace of Athena.

38. Taken together, Feast and Lament illustrate how the morphology of a typical scene can vary even within the same tradition. For a larger comparative context, see Foley 1990: chs. 7–9.

39. See further Foley 1991: 168–74.

40. Conventionally in Homer, a person who is in some way defiled, whether by battle gore or by some socially unacceptable action, must be purified through washing and anointment before taking part in a feast or libation ritual. Often these occurrences are associated with the term *lôbê* ("defilement") or its reflexes (cf. espec. *Il.* 9.387, where it becomes clear that Achilleus' main complaint is over the *thumalgea lôbên* ["heartrending defilement"] caused by Agamemnon's brutish behavior). At 6.266–68 Hektor says as much, refusing the libation because of the "blood and gore" (*haimati kai luthrôi*, 268) that mark his heroic participation in battle even as they disqualify him from an active role within Trojan domestic society.

41. See the discussion of seating and the Feast above.

42. Cf. Paris' arming for battle at *Il.* 3.328–38, a version of the same typical scene and *sêma*

that describes similar activities undertaken by Agamemnon (11.15f.), Patroklos (16.130f.), and Achilleus (19.364f.); see also the smaller correspondences with the arming of Teukros (15.478f.) and Odysseus (*Od.* 22.122f.). In addition to describing Paris' arming in straight-forward heroic terms, this scene indexes Paris along with the other, more accomplished heroes, allowing for specific detail to be inserted to balance implication with instance and producing irony at a traditional level. The discrepancy between Paris' cowardly distaste for battle and the usual heroic implications of this traditional sign are starkly evident.

43. γοόωσά τε μυρομένη τε. Cf. the housekeeper's description of Andromache's anxious flight to the wall—"like a woman gone mad" (μαινομένη ἐϊκυῖα, 6.389)—after hearing that the tide was turning against the Trojans. These actions correlate with the mourning ritual, in which the participants defile themselves; cf. further Foley 1991: 158, 1995a: 165–66. On violent enjambement, intonation groups, and what I call the proto-lament see Bakker 1999.

44. See Chapter 7 for a full discussion of the *Emotional speaker* signal. On narrative conventions involving prayers, see Morrison 1991.

45. On the function of the lament within the larger pattern leading through (funeral) feast to mediation in *Iliad* 24, see Foley 1991: 174–89.

46. Cf. Penelope, who is theoretically able to go back to her father's household, from which she could be remarried.

47. Cf. Kirk's reading of this sign as "affectionate remonstrance" (1985: 111). On the important issue of verbal dueling in general, particularly its ritual and poetic implications, see Parks 1990.

48. See espec. Stanley 1993, Minchin 1995b; for South Slavic epic, Lord 1986b: 53–64; for analogical patterns in Athenian black-figure vase-painting, Mackay, Harrison, and Masters 1999.

49. Andromache's later laments naturally do not begin with the metonymic key *daimonie*, since Hektor has died and the "Strange one" salutation can apparently be applied only to conventional, face-to-face exchanges wherein direct debate is possible. Note the salutations used in the other laments: Briseis: "Patroklos, far most pleasing to my heart in its sorrows" (19.287); Hekabe: "Child" (22.431); Andromache: "Hektor" (22.477); Andromache: "Husband" (24.725); Hekabe: "Hektor, of all my sons the dearest by far to my spirit" (24.748); Helen: "Hektor, of all my lord's brothers dearest by far to my spirit" (24.762).

50. Cf. the "pivotal contrafactuals" described by de Jong 1987: 68–81 and Louden 1996.

51. Note also the indexical force of *pukinon epos* ("intimate word") itself, which connotes "a message or communication of great importance, one that if properly delivered and received would change the present course of events profoundly" (Foley 1991: 155; cf. more generally 154–56, 173–74).

52. "But come" (*all' age / ageth' / agete*) signals a change in direction and in mode within a speech by introducing a command in the form "Come do something" or "Come let us do something." See further Chapter 7.

53. See further Newton 1998 on the resonance of traditional implication in the Thoas story in *Odyssey* 14.

Chapter 7. Word, Idiom, Speech-Act: The Traditional Phrase as *Sêma*

1. For background, see especially M. Edwards 1986, 1988; of particular importance recently are Bakker 1997a and the essays in Bakker and Kahane 1997. On the characteristics of the Homeric register (the system of signs itself), see Chapter 3 above and Foley 1990: chs. 3–4; on traditional referentiality in South Slavic epic, Chapter 4 above.

2. Recall that the Homeric poems themselves do not provide adequate material for an investigation of story-pattern, since they include only one Return Song (but cf. the Return pattern in the *Hymn to Demeter*; see Foley 1995a: 175–79). On the other hand, the available textual sample permits collation of instances of many typical scenes; see further Foley 1990: ch. 7 and Chapter 6 in this volume.

3. On traditional rules for Homeric phraseology, see Foley 1990: ch. 4. On repetition versus re-creation, see Foley 1991: 56–58.

4. For two further examples from much different sources, see Hymes's discussion of the various levels of cues in Northwest Coast Native American tales (espec. 1981, 1989, 1994) and Foley 1995a: ch. 4 on structural signals in South Slavic magical charms.

5. On the rationalizing nature of traditional rules, which certify *every line* of Homer as traditional whether or not we can locate a repetition or analog within the extant epics, see Foley 1990: espec. 137–55. On register, performance arena, and communicative economy, see Foley 1995a and Chapter 1 above.

6. For an analysis of the traditional rules informing the epic phraseologies of South Slavic and Anglo-Saxon, see Foley 1990: chs. 5 and 6, respectively. It is well to remember that similar nonverbal strategies (e.g., musical accompaniment) were no doubt importantly at play in Homeric epic as well, but have been lost in the history of textualization. On Rajasthani epic performance, see Smith 1991; on the aesthetic dimensions of the *Kalevala*, DuBois 1995.

7. On "green fear," see below; on "looking darkly," Holoka 1983; on "silently to silence," Foley 1995c. Of related interest is Kahane 1992 on the special meaning of *andra* ("man"; but marked as "Odysseus") in the language of the *Odyssey*.

8. In addition to Foley 1990: ch. 4, see espec. Hainsworth 1968, Sale 1996a on the mutability of formulaic phrases.

9. Cf. espec. Parry 1930: 276: "The thrift of a system lies in the degree in which it is free of phrases which, having the same metrical value and expressing the same idea, could replace one another."

10. This kind of network also goes beyond the phonic relationships suggested by Nagler (1974: 1–63) and Peabody (1975: 176–215). Cf. Pazdernik 1995 on the morphology and formulaic resonance associated with *ollumi* phrases.

11. Importantly, this view, under which single lexical items can participate in the traditional network of phraseology and signs, supports rewarding investigations that focus on key terms in Homeric speech (espec. Nagy 1979, 1990b on numerous such items; R. Martin 1989: espec. 12f. on *muthos* versus *epos*; and Lincoln 1997 on *logos* and *muthos*).

12. For an evenhanded review of much recent scholarship in this area, see Sale 1996a. Bakker (1997a: 156–83, espec. 159–62) offers an understanding of the noun-epithet formulas that has much in common with what follows below. See Mackay 1996: espec. 43 on the analogy (in both structure and implication) between noun-epithet formulas and the iconography of Attic black-figure vase-painters; also Mackay 1993, 1995.

13. Parry 1928a: 22.

14. Throughout his work Parry acknowledges his debt to German linguists such as Karl Witte, who had illuminated the metrical governance of Homeric diction in prior studies. See further Foley 1988: 6–10.

15. On the singers' idea of a *reč* or "word" as a unit of expression, see Chapter 2 above.

16. As Bakker puts it (1997a: 161): "Instead of ascribing a property to an absent referent, noun-epithet formulas make this absent referent present, conjuring it, in its most characteristic form, to the here and now of the performance, as an essential part of the universe of discourse shared between the performer and his audience." Cf. Calame 1995: ch. 7. On the many dimensions of naming Homeric heroes, see also Higbie 1995: espec. 129–35 and 169–74 on Penelope.

17. As Vivante puts it (1982: 111) in relation to another of his names, "Say ποδάρκης and

the very word evokes Achilles." I would modify this statement only slightly by insisting on citing the whole *sêma*: "Say ποδάρκης δῖος Ἀχιλλεύς and the very 'word' evokes Achilles." He also speaks of a "broad inevitable appropriateness" (1980: 172) that is not unlike the concept of traditional referentiality advocated throughout this volume. On the interplay of Achilleus' development and the metonymic force of this formulaic name, see Dunkle 1997.

18. See Foley 1995a: 150–60 on *kratus Argeïphontês* in the *Hymn to Hermes*; cf. Haft 1996 (espec. 43) on Hermes' precociousness as an etiological justification for present-day animal thievery in Crete.

19. See further notes 9 and 20. I speak here strictly of *metrical* thrift, Parry's sense of the term, and not of the selection of phraseology according to the demands of narrative pattern.

20. See Shive 1987 on exceptions to Homeric thrift and Foley 1990: 65–66, 128, 163–64, 354 on the lack of thrift in other oral epic poetries.

21. As explained in Chapter 3 above, South Slavic oral epic furnishes a clear and telling comparison here. Virtually all of the noun-epithet formulas in that register are six syllables in length, exactly fitting the second colon in the decasyllable. Even those noun-epithet combinations that would yield a five-syllable combination are eked out by attaching a vocative ending to the second element in the pair (an aspect of traditional morphology within the South Slavic epic language; on which, see Foley 1990: ch. 5). Under such conditions, where all formulas are metrically identical, thrift is of course impossible.

22. See Chapter 5 on the story-pattern of Return and its alternative climaxes.

23. On the gruesome history of family cannibalism associated with Thyestes, brother to the Atreus who fathered Agamemnon, see espec. Gantz 1993: 545–50. The epithet *analkis* is applied to the suitors in the *Odyssey* (4.334, 17.125); in the *Iliad* it marks the antithesis of heroic behavior, as when Diomedes mocks Paris for his cowardly arrow-shot (11.390) or when Aphrodite is characterized as an unwarlike goddess who is out of place among fighting men (5.331, 349). There can be little doubt that *dolomêtis* is also highly negative. Within the *Odyssey* Aigisthos is called *dolomêtis* four times; the only other figure so named is Klytemnestra. The single usage of the term in the *Iliad* (1.540) appears in Hera's harsh attack on Zeus for his secret conference with Thetis. The epithetic system as a whole exhibits a characteristic traditional morphology, with thrift governing the deployment of its constituents: *amumonos* is a genitive combining with *Aigisthoio* to make a "word" that extends from the B2 midline caesura to line-end; *analkidos* adds the same *Aigisthoio* plus an initial *kai* to form another genitive "word," but this time from the B1 midline caesura to line-end; *Thuestiadês* combines with *Aigisthos* to make a nominative "word" from B2 to line-end; and *dolomêtis/-n* can join with *Aigisthos/-n* to yield a nominative or accusative "word" that extends from line-beginning to the B2 caesura.

24. See further Chapter 5, note 39.

25. Amory Parry 1973: espec. 165, 167; Heubeck, West, and Hainsworth 1988: 77. Cf. Vivante 1982: 107–8, espec. 131.

26. The differences between this approach and the collation of *sêmata* advocated throughout this volume are many, beginning with the question of focusing on the proper unit and mapping its traditional morphology. The largest difference, however, lies in the kind of semantics one is attempting to establish: a generalized, "blanket" coverage of all individual instances or a traditional referentiality that is neither generalized nor situation-specific but rather context-complementary.

27. See espec. Janko 1992a: 125, who contests Amory Parry's redefinition and summarizes relevant scholarship.

28. To be exact, from the B2 or feminine midline caesura to the end of the line. As throughout this chapter, I restrict the sample of diction in order to maintain a focused and principle-driven presentation that all readers can follow readily, without sacrificing accuracy or representative analysis. Consider also the genitive singular combinations that occur between the

A2 and C2 caesurae: *Odusêos amumonos* (eight times in the *Od.*), *Achilêos amumonos* (*Il.* 16.854, 17.186, 22.113), *Nêlêos amumonos* (*Il.* 11.692), and *Pêlêos amumonos* (*Il.* 20.206).

29. Antilochos (*Il.* 23.522; *Od.* 4.187, 11.468, 24.16), Alkinoos (*Od.* 8.118, 419), Anchises (*Il.* 5.247), Achilleus (*Il.* 16.140, 854), Eumolpos (*HDem* 154).

30. See H. Foley 1994: 41, 44.

31. Cf. the application of the phrase "mighty slayer of Argos" to the newborn Hermes, long before he accomplishes that feat (see note 18 above).

32. Deriving *dios* from the oblique cases of Zeus (*Di-*). Cf. Vivante 1982: 129.

33. In the first and second instances the usage is directly traceable to the etymon *Διϝγος, to which Mycenaean *di-u-ja, di-wi-ja* are compared; in the third instance *dios* is seen as "preserving, even if indirectly, the force of the root **dei-*" (Heubeck, West, and Hainsworth 1988: 256). Cf. also Hainsworth 1993: 133, 319–20; and Janko 1992a: 158.

34. On the tendency of this part of the line, called the adonean clausula, to host noun-epithet formulas and other fixed phrases, see Foley 1990: 80–84.

35. Note that both of the combinations can, however, be expanded; according to traditional rules (Foley 1990: ch. 4), *podarkês* ("swift of foot") and *polutlas* ("much-suffering") can precede *dios Achilleus* and *dios Odusseus*, respectively, to eke out hemistich-length (as opposed to colonic) forms of the two heroes' names. This amounts to a compositional flexibility that offers alternate "words," and neither "word"-length—colon or hemistich—can be meaningfully subdivided.

36. In decreasing frequency, the others are Epeios (*Il.* 23.689, 838, 839), Orestes (*Od.* 1.298, 11.461), Alastor (*Il.* 8.333, 13.422), Agenor (*Il.* 14.425, 15.340), Epeigeus (*Il.* 16.571), and Echephron (*Od.* 3.439). The same epithet is applied to other characters but in different positions in the hexameter verse: Alexandros (*Il.* 3.329, 7.355, 8.82), Menestheus (*Il.* 13.195), and the river god Skamandros (*Il.* 12.21, a troubled instance; cf. Hainsworth 1993: 319–20).

37. Plus an additional five occurrences of the accusative form, *dion huphorbon*, four of which occupy the same position at the end of the hexameter line. In the interest of a brief and focused presentation, I leave aside the other oblique-case usages, but remark in passing that far the most commonly named character in the accusative is Hektor (*Hektora dion*, fully twenty-six times), who is never assigned this epithet in the nominative case. Again the combination depends not on the definition of *dios* but on the metrical and idiomatic identity of *Hektora dion* (positioned at either line-end or line-beginning).

38. See the weighing of alternatives by Ahl and Roisman (1996: 185–88). I would not rule out the possiblity of a traditional irony, mirroring the discrepancy between Eumaios' possibly royal beginnings and his present reduced state. We may choose to credit the story of his former status, much as we may choose to credit Aigisthos with being "blameless" earlier in his life (see above). But once again this is not the core issue in the use and understanding of the larger sign.

39. That is, either a short syllable followed by two long syllables (u– –) or a short syllable followed by a long plus a short syllable (u–u). Since the final syllable of the hexameter can be long or short (*brevis in longo*), these two metrical patterns are functionally identical when they occur in final position.

40. Cf. *Od.* 8.74, 481; 22.347.

41. In the *Odyssey* all ten additional occurrences of *dia gunaikôn* are applied to Penelope and Helen; in the *Iliad* Helen is so named three times and Alkestis once. Note also that Eumaios and Eurykleia share an association with the word *êpios*, conventionally translated "kindly, gentle"; but see Edmunds 1990: 18–22 on a traditional network of meaning.

42. Note that *podas ôkea* is used of the goddess Iris in the same part of the hexameter line (ten times in the *Odyssey*; cf. *podênemos ôkea Iris* ["wind-swift Iris," a hemistich alternative] employed another ten times over the two epics), but that its gender and internal metrics, not to mention its application to an immortal, help to distinguish it from *podas ôkus*. Also relevant

is the alternate expression for "swift-footed," the adjective *podarkês*, used only in combination with *dios Achilleus* to make up a second-hemistich formula (21 times in the *Iliad*).

43. On the surface these two kinds of epithets mirror Parry's distinction between "particularized" and "ornamental" epithets (see espec. Parry 1928a: 119–65). But in both cases I am discounting the lexical meaning of the epithet taken alone and directing attention toward the expressive force of the composite. The difference between Parry's and my understanding is most basically that he concentrated on tectonic function as an end in itself, while I see tectonic function as a characteristic of the sign that must be read against the poetic tradition. The difference is a theory of *metri causa* versus a theory of *artis causa*.

44. Cf. the view of "significant objects" advocated by Griffin (1980: 1–49).

45. Here are the instances and traditional morphology of this "word":

> *Il.* 7.479: σμερδαλέα κτυπέων· τοὺς δὲ χλωρὸν δέος ᾕρει·   B1+
>
> *Il.* 8.77: θάμβησαν, καὶ πάντας ὑπὸ χλωρὸν δέος εἷλεν.   A2+
>
> *Il.* 17.67: ἀντίον ἐλθέμεναι· μάλα γὰρ χλωρὸν δέος αἱρεῖ·   B1+
>
> *Od.* 11.43: θεσπεσίη ἰαχῇ· ἐμὲ δὲ χλωρὸν δέος ᾕρει.   B1+
>
> *Od.* 11.633: ἠχῇ θεσπεσίη· ἐμὲ δὲ χλωρὸν δέος ᾕρει,   B1+
>
> *Od.* 12.243: ψάμμῳ κυανέη· τοὺς δὲ χλωρὸν δέος ᾕρει.   B1+
>
> *Od.* 22.42: Ὣς φάτο, τοὺς δ' ἄρα πάντας ὑπὸ χλωρὸν δέος εἷλε·   A1+
>
> *Od.* 24.450: Ὣς φάτο, τοὺς δ' ἄρα πάντας ὑπὸ χλωρὸν δέος ᾕρει.   A1+
>
> *Od.* 24.533: Ὣς φάτ' Ἀθηναίη, τοὺς δὲ χλωρὸν δέος εἷλε·   B1+
>
> *HDem* 190: τὴν δ' αἰδώς τε σέβας τε ἰδὲ χλωρὸν δέος εἷλεν·   B2+

46. Note that of the fifteen additional occurrences of *deos* ("fear") in the epics and hymns, only one identifies a supernaturally inspired fear, and that occurrence is likely more a function of the narrative context of the hymn (and its genre) than anything else (*HAp* 447; *HAphr* 194 may be construed similarly). Clearly, the smallest unit of utterance is the entire phrase: *green fear seized them/her/him*. Cf. also the alternate "word" for the same purpose, χλωροὶ/-ὸς ὑπαὶ δείους ("green with fear"), used twice in the *Iliad* to indicate a fear that stems directly from divine action: 15.4, where the Trojans retreat in fear after Poseidon has turned the tide of battle; and 10.376, where Dolon shakes with fear over his impending slaughter by Diomedes, whose footspeed Athena has just increased to accord him the honor of the kill. This alternate "word" is not used in the *Odyssey*, and may thus be an idiolectal or dialectal expression. We can dismiss the possibility that "green" is the sole source of the traditional meaning, since it is employed in other, unrelated ways as well; once again, the whole unit stands as the sign and cannot be dismembered. Cf. also Vivante 1982: 125.

47. Accusative: *Il.* 2.613, 5.771, 7.88, 23.143; *Od.* 1.183, 2.421, 3.286, 4.474, 5.349, 6.170; *HDio* 7. Dative: *Il.* 23.316; *Od.* 5.132, 5.221, 7.250, 12.388, 19.172, 19.274; *HApo* 391. Only the first *Odyssey* occurrence is not situated at line-end. The regularity and especially the positioning of the phrase bespeak traditional structure (cf. Foley 1990: 129–55 on right justification).

48. Vivante (1982: 122) associates *oinops* with "that heaping movement and turbulence which is also expressed in πορφύρεος." While I see no particular reason to derive that motion from either adjective, I agree with what I take as Vivante's underlying conception—that the epithets cooperate in formulating timeless, recurrent ideas with an identifiable poetic resonance. Cf. Rutherfurd-Dyer (1983), who links this phrase to the sunset-red color often associated with departing ships. Cp. the half-line formula *diipeteos potamoio*, usually interpreted as "fallen from Zeus" and therefore swollen by rain, which R. Griffith (1997) renders as "celestial river"; indexically, this sign marks an interlude in which one or more heroes in dire straits fight for their survival (*Il.* 17.263, the Achaeans versus the onrushing Trojans; 21.268 and 326, Achilleus versus Skamandros and Simoeis; *Od.* 4.477 and 581, Menelaos must go back to the Egyptian river to secure his *nostos*; 7.284, Odysseus exits the Scherian river that has provided him safety—even the odd occurrence at *Il.* 16.174 during the Catalogue of the Myrmidons closely follows Patroklos' donning of Achilleus' armor).

49. That is, it always constitutes the adonean clausula, or the last two feet or metra in the

line. The traditional morphology associated with "stout hand" is interesting in itself, in that three half-line or hemistich patterns account for eight of the nineteen occurrences of *cheiri pacheiêi*: "he/she caught up [X] in his/her stout hand" ([X] εἵλετο χειρὶ παχείῃ, *Il.* 7.264, 10.31, 21.403, and *Od.* 22.326, where X = a stone, a spear, or a sword); "and he leaned on his stout hand" (καὶ ἐρείσατο χειρὶ παχείῃ, *Il.* 5.309, 11.355); and "holding in his stout hand" (ἔχων ἐν χειρὶ παχείῃ, *Il.* 8.221, 14.385). As is so often the case in the Homeric register, there are thus many levels of "words," all of them obeying traditional rules of right justification and word-type placement (the first two half-line patterns begin at the B1 midline caesura, the third at the B2 caesura; see further Foley 1990: ch. 4).

50. See below the discussion of the traditional phraseology associated with *hupnos*, "sleep."

51. See section 8 below for discussion of the **Weak in the knees** sign that immediately follows at 21.425.

52. For a full discussion of this attribution, see Foley 1995a: 166–68. Let me add to this group of three divine applications the single nonepic usage of *cheiri pacheiêi* in the *Homeric Hymn to Apollo* (340), in which Hera petitions the other gods for a child conceived without Zeus and strikes the ground with her stout hand to emphasize her demand. This usage seems not to be related to the traditional sense of the phrase in the *Iliad* and *Odyssey*, and may reflect a difference in traditional dialect (on which, see Foley 1995a: ch. 5; also 1990: chs. 5, 8).

53. On the importance of this action, cf. the perspective offered by Goff (1991: 262–63).

54. In fact, Odysseus' words to Leodes, spoken just prior, are transparent on this score (22.321–25): "If you boast to be the diviner among these people, / then many times you must have prayed in my halls / for the *telos* of my sweet *nostos* to be far away from me, / and that my beloved wife would follow you and bear you children. / For this you must not escape woeful death."

55. For a history of critical commentary on this crux, see Russo, Fernández-Galiano, and Heubeck 1992: 148–49, to which should now be added Lowenstam 1993: 26–32 (strong hand), Nagler 1993: 255–56 (male hand), Reece 1993: 118–19 ("uncomfortably applied," "ineptly adapted"), and Roller and Roller 1994 (hand of the weaver).

56. τόξον μνηστήρεσσι θέμεν πολιόν τε σίδηρον / ἐν μεγάροις Ὀδυσῆος, ἀέθλια καὶ φόνου ἀρχήν.

57. See Chapter 5 for a full discussion of this question in the context of the traditional pattern of Return.

58. One can of course argue that this is not as much of a gamble as it seems, that only Odysseus could string the bow and that Penelope knows as much. But the Return Song pattern always holds open the possibility (seldom fulfilled though it may be) that a rival may defeat or displace the disguised or absent hero, whatever the nature of the competition. See further Chapter 5.

59. On what amount to more abstract stage props, the "threshold of old age" (*gêraos oudon/-ôi*) and the "measure of youth" (*hêbês metron*), see Létoublon 1990.

60. See Mackay 1996: espec. 44 on the analogy between stock speech introductions and what she terms the "figure-patterns" of Attic black-figure vase-painting; also Mackay 1993.

61. Interestingly, this predicate does not appear with nu-moveable in the *Odyssey*. We could interpret the difference between the two epics as one of idiolect or dialect, or more likely as the result of the poet's not having had to accommodate noun-epithet formulas of this length that begin with a vowel. Note that the nu-moveable form is used in the Homeric Hymns to match the king far-worker Apollo (ἄναξ ἑκάεργος Ἀπόλλων, *HHer* 333) and fair-crowned Demeter (ἐϋστέφανος Δημήτηρ, *HDem* 224). On the role of the initial digamma in this process, e.g., with (ϝ)ἄναξ ([w]anax), see Parry 1934: espec. 394–96 and Horrocks 1997: 204–6.

62. Cf. the same muting effect in South Slavic epic phraseology, which uses verbs such as *besjediti* ("to orate, deliver a sermon") simply to mean "say" when initiating a conversation

or a response within the poetic register. Benson (1980) indicates that such a generalized us-
age is "obsolete" (a frequent dictionary gloss for traditional epic meanings of words). In all
of the lexicons to which I have access, *besjediti* is accorded a much more focused and formal
meaning as an isolated word than it appears to have as a constituent of a "word" in the epic
register.

63. Cf. Aristotle, *Poetics* 25 (Halliwell 1995: 132–33), who in discussing the challenge of
Homer's specialized language observes that "some people adopt an unreasonable premise,
base inferences on their prejudgment, and, if something contradicts their opinion, blame the
poet as though he had said what they merely suppose."

64. Note that this second example of "answering" predicates is never used with female
subjects, either mortal women or goddesses (perhaps to avoid overlengthening), but can ac-
commodate a neuter noun-epithet subject: *eidôlon amauron* ("faint image," *Od.* 4.824, 835).
Other small variations within the traditional morphology include *prosephônee* for *prosephê* to
promote combination with shorter noun-epithet phrases (e.g., *Od.* 14.401, with *dios huphorbos*,
on which see 1c above) and the narrator's direct address of Eumaios with the second-person
singular form *prosephês* (e.g., *Od.* 14.55).

65. More specifically, the first is located between line-beginning and the B2 (or feminine)
caesura, the second between line-beginning and the C1 caesura. See further Foley 1990: ch. 4.

66. Parry's concept of utility is in such simplest cases hardly distinguishable from tradi-
tional referentiality. For a suggestive structural analysis of lines involving **traditional punc-
tuation**, see Riggsby 1992, in response to Visser 1987, 1988.

67. For ease of presentation, I choose to represent a female speaker and male addressee in
the translations here, but also note explicitly that this sign can and does preface exchanges in-
volving all possible combinations of genders. Cf. Parry 1937 on this phrase, which he main-
tains is used "for purely grammatical reasons" (416)—a claim made in response to Calhoun's
contention that the phrase connotes "earnestness or affection" (1935: 225).

68. One could argue, in fact, that A and B constitute a single type, with two of the
hemistich variations having taken their place in the register as whole-line "words."

69. *Il.* 15.552; *Od.* 16.417, 18.78, 19.90, 21.84, 21.167, 21.287, 23.96.

70. In the singular (*age*) or elided plural inflection before a rough breathing (*ageth'*), this
signal occupies the first colon ending with the A1 caesura; in the unelided plural (*agete*), it is
localized in the first colon extending to the A2 caesura. Thus all three forms are colonic.

71. Once again the phrase fills the first colon in the hexameter, always ending at the A1
caesura. One other formal feature of the traditional morphology is the necessity for the next
word to begin with a vowel, so that the last syllable of the traditional phrase is rendered met-
rically short as the final element in the opening dactyl. More focused than **Command**, the
Righting a wrong sign occurs a total of five times in the epics.

72. See the discussion of *Il.* 15.552 in the context of another traditional sign, **Emotional
speaker: hostile**, that helps to shape Hektor's scolding speech (Chapter 8 below, *Apparatus
fabulosus*).

73. Cf. Garner 1996 on the traditional implications of successful supplication associated
with the simple phrase *ei pote . . .* ("if ever . . ."). Other superficially simple signals include the
particles *dê/de* and *ara* (see Bakker 1993b: 11–23).

74. The remainder of the eleven instances cover a variety of contexts (see *Il.* 19.80;
Od. 4.651, 13.141; *HHer* 205).

75. To be specific, the sentence may start at the beginning of the line, or at the A1, A2,
B1, or C1 caesura, and *chalepon* may either begin the phrase or occur at a caesural boundary
within it. This scenario promotes a wide range of variant realizations of **Practical impossi-
bility**, an extremely broad traditional morphology (see further the discussion of the "sleep"
sign below in section 9).

76. From the A2 caesura through the end of the line. The instances are *Il.* 4.350, 14.83;
Od. 1.64, 3.230, 5.22, 19.492, 21.168, and 23.70.

77. Cf. the similar exchange between Zeus and Athena at 5.22, where this *sêma* once again frames her complaint and his reaction.

78. Antinoos' speech to Leodes is introduced by the sign **Emotional speaker: hostile** (21.167), occurring immediately before **You should know better!** See further the summary of related usages in Chapter 8, *Apparatus fabulosus*, note to 23.96.

79. τετληότι θυμῷ occupies the fourth colon between the C1 caesura and the end of the line. Immediately preceding participles and adverbs indicate a possible structural pattern, but the more important consideration is the organization of the line according to the traditional rules of the register.

80. *Od.* 11.181–83 = 16.37–39; 23.100 = 23.168.

81. At 18.135 Odysseus instructs the minor suitor Amphinomos on life's vicissitudes: when the gods bring wretched times, then a man must face the challenge *with enduring heart*. At 24.163 Amphimedon's ghost describes how the disguised Odysseus persisted *with enduring heart* while the suitors reproached him and threw things at him.

82. On Penelope's heroism, see Chapter 5 above.

83. *Il.* 21.114, 21.425; *Od.* 4.703, 5.297, 5.406, 22.68, 22.147, 23.205, 24.345.

84. In the first case, five of six examples begin with *hôs phato* ("thus he/she spoke"), an extremely common phrase in its own right; the exception is *Il.* 21.425.

85. On this quality of "right justification," see Foley 1990: espec. 96–106, 129–55, 178–96.

86. Cf. the application of the **Refusal of nourishment** sign to the immortal Demeter (*HDem* 47–50, 200–201, 206–9). While the goddess is of course in no danger of starvation, the traditional implications of the *sêma* slot her in a category of mourners that includes the bereaved Achilleus and Andromache.

87. Just how pervasive this traditional meaning of sleep really is can be seen in the extended drama in *Iliad* 14 (espec. 153–362), wherein Hera persuades Sleep to assist in subduing Zeus—via the sweetness of love and rest together with the vulnerability sleep can confer—so that Poseidon can continue to aid the Achaeans' cause unrestrained by Zeus. This scene is virtually an allegory of the traditional implications of the *hupnos* sign. In view of the following discussion, note particularly lines 14.164, 231, 242, and 354 (the last two *nêdumos Hupnos*, "sweet Sleep"). Lacore (1997: 40) focuses on a related quality of sleep—"non la douceur mais la profondeur de l'inconscience," arguably the foundation for the two opposite possibilities inherent in the Homeric idea of sleep.

88. See note 11 above.

89. Specifically, the segment from the midline caesura (B1 or B2) to line-end in the metrical shape (u) u—u u—u u——, a primary tectonic form (Foley 1990: ch. 4). In addition to the instances cited just below, this hemistich "word" occurs at *Il.* 23.232, *Od.* 7.289, and *HAphr* 170.

90. Cf. *Il.* 1.610 and *Od.* 19.49 for variations of the first version, *Il.* 2.71 for variation of the second version.

91. For other deployments of *glukus hupnos*, see *Od.* 10.31 (= 13.282) and *HHer* 8. On the more diverse usages of the accusative *glukun hupnon*, see *Od.* 8.445, 10.548, 12.338, 18.188.

92. Even themes or typical scenes exist in commonly used sequences, and whole storypatterns are part of a singer's or tradition's larger repertoire. The individual singer as *sêma* may analogously be construed as one "sign" in the larger "song" that is his ongoing tradition; see further Chapter 2 in this volume.

93. My thanks to two incarnations of the Homer Seminar at the University of Missouri–Columbia for posing the challenging questions that led to the following discussion.

94. The problem glimpsed here runs deep in Homeric poetics. If *glukus* were active as a freestanding element in this passage, engendering irony as Odysseus constructs his plan, then why is it apparently inactive (or oblique) in other instances? How can it be chosen with such supposed deftness on one occasion and merely stumbled into as a compositional expedient on other occasions? Either Homer is "in control" or he is not: context-appropriateness should be either universal or entirely lacking (*pace* Mahacek [1994], whose argument for the

"occasional contextual appropriateness of formulaic diction" seems both linguistically un-tenable and, from the point of view of living oral traditions, simply unparalleled; cf. the lim-ited situational relevance championed by Cosset [1983a, b]). From the perspective of tradi-tional referentiality, all such usages are *context-complementary*.

95. Note also that three of the four instances (*Od*. 16.481; *Il*. 7.482, 9.713) end their respec-tive books in the received texts of the epics (of course the book divisions are notoriously prob-lematic, so we claim nothing more monumental than rhetorical force here). Even the excep-tion (*Od*. 19.427) marks an important juncture in the narrative's reconstrual of how Odysseus received the famous *sêma* of the scar.

96. Penelope mourns for Odysseus "until bright-eyed Athena cast sweet sleep on her eye-lids" (ὄφρα οἱ ὕπνον / ἡδὺν ἐπὶ βλεφάροισι βάλε γλαυκῶπις Ἀθήνη at *Od*. 1.363–64, 16.450–51, 19.603–4, and 21.357–58). This is another form of the sleep *sêma*, here with "sweet sleep" (*hupnon hêdun*) configured as an enjambed phrase over two lines. The implications are, how-ever, the same, with Athena's merciful act dissolving the ambiguity: Penelope will sleep, free of danger, and for a while forget her woes. On Achilleus' epic-long lack of a true sleep until he and Priam come to terms with each other and themselves, see the discussion below and Foley 1991: 174–89.

97. All four of the other instances of the adjective *aüpnos* ("sleepless") in the epics also mark occasions in which a person is or has been deprived of the natural release of sleep, with something dysfunctional or at least abnormal implied: *Il*. 9.325 (Achilleus' complaint to Odysseus and the embassy); *Od*. 9.404 (the Kyklopes' complaint to Polyphemos); 10.84 (the unusual diurnal situation in the land of the Laistrygonians); and 19.340 (the stranger's com-plaint to Penelope).

98. See the discussion of 9.333 above. *Glukus hupnos* and *pandamatôr* represent alternative pathways to the same traditional reality.

99. In line 3 note another version of the sleep sign, again literally meaning "sweet sleep" (*hupnou . . . glukerou*). It provides another inflection of the *sêma*, useful because it fills needs that are both grammatical (genitive sing.) and metrical (first hemistich to the B1 caesura). Such fluidity in the surface morphology empowers the *sêma* compositionally but in no way lessens its idiomatic impact.

100. Throughout the latter part of the *Iliad* Achilleus fasts and forgoes sleep. Even those few occasions on which his sleeplessness seems to abate (23.62, 232) are quickly reversed, and he is abruptly awakened and brought back to his misery. On the forestalling of natural rhythms in the *Iliad*, see Foley 1991: 174–89.

101. *Od*. 5.47–48 = 24.3–4 = *Il*. 24.343–44: εἵλετο δὲ ῥάβδον, τῇ τ' ἀνδρῶν ὄμματα θέλγει / ὧν ἐθέλει, τοὺς δ' αὖτε καὶ ὑπνώοντας ἐγείρει.

102. Another proverbial-sounding phrase encapsulates the basic human rhythm tersely: as the flagging storyteller Odysseus tells Alkinoos at *Od*. 11.379, "there is a season for many words and also a season for sleep" (ὥρη μὲν πολέων μύθων, ὥρη δὲ καὶ ὕπνου).

103. Here and elsewhere it is well to keep in mind the fraternal relationship between Sleep and Death in ancient Greek mythology, especially the fact that both of them provide a release from temporal woes at a certain unnegotiable price.

104. For a cognate sense, see another inflection of the sleep sign: λύων/ἔχων μελεδήματα θυμῷ/οῦ ("loosening/having cares in/of the heart") at *Il*. 23.62, *Od*. 4.650, and *Od*. 23.343, the last two of which co-occur with *lusimelês*. Cf. also *Od*. 15.7–8, where *glukus hupnos* will not hold Telemachos, and the cares (*meledêmata*) associated with his father keep him awake all night.

105. Note that many Return Song heroines in South Slavic epic fail to recognize signs im-mediately, especially those who prove unfaithful, but—to my knowledge—none of them forecasts the *telos* of the tale while denying the implications of those signs.

106. Cf. *Od*. 19.562–67; also Amory Parry 1966.

107. Thus also Penelope's insistence that the dream of the eagle slaughtering the geese, which the stranger himself interprets as Odysseus' vengeance on the suitors, must be false. From her perspective as the Return Song heroine, Penelope simply cannot credit such a preview at this point in the story's development.

108. I thank my colleague Barbara Wallach for coining the metapoetic term, *apparatus fabulosus*. This term and the apparatus it names refer to the meaning resident *behind* the signs. Although some might criticize the concentration on idiomatic associations, perhaps even citing the apparatus itself as overly "fabulous" on that account, I would insist that it is inattention to traditional referentiality that condemns interpretation to a truly "fabulous" or fictive presentation.

Chapter 8.   Rereading *Odyssey* 23

1. In order to keep the presentation as "user-friendly" as possible for the greatest number and variety of readers, the examples in the first part of this chapter will be treated in English translation only. See the *Apparatus Fabulosus* in the second part of the chapter for the same passage (*Od.* 23.69–103) in ancient Greek, with all traditional signs marked exactly as in the English translation. Many of these same "words" have been treated at more length in Chapters 1 and 5–7.

2. As discussed in Chapter 5, Laertes' recognition takes place in that section of the *Odyssey* (paralleled in many South Slavic Return Songs) between the *telos* and the actual close of the narrative. It should be added that the hero's confrontation with his aged and decrepit mother (see again Chapter 5 above), another common feature of this story-pattern, has also occurred in the form of Odysseus' conversation with the shade of his mother (who died mourning for him) in Hades in Book 11.

3. On the importance of implied mythic backgrounds, see espec. Slatkin 1991 on Thetis in the *Iliad*.

4. As a final peace with Poseidon, for example, or as a double-sign for Odysseus' apprehension of cultural variance; see espec. Hansen 1990 and Nagy 1990a: 212–14.

5. For at least two reasons it seems safest not to prescribe any lockstep relationship among the various levels of *sêmata*: first because such a hierarchy more often than not fails to describe the various signs' activity and complexity, and second because language simply does not work in so one-dimensional a fashion.

6. On the traditional morphology of this sign, see Chapter 6 above, and espec. Foley 1990: 248–57.

7. See Foley 1991: 174–89 and espec. Chapter 6 above. On the rest of the thirty-two major or minor feasts in the *Odyssey* and the three such scenes in the *Iliad*, together with their structural profiles (seating, satisfaction, mediation), see Appendix I.

8. On the colonic meter, system of word-boundaries, and metrical word-placement that define Homeric phraseology, see espec. Chapter 3 above and Foley 1990: chs. 3–4.

9. On Achilleus' language, see the seminal article by Adam Parry (1956), responses to which include Donlan 1971, Reeve 1973, Claus 1975, Cramer 1976, Hogan 1976, Friedrich and Redfield 1978 and 1981, Duban 1981, Messing 1981, Scully 1984, and Nimis 1986. On Trojan versus Achaean language, see Mackie 1996.

10. While some may feel that "filling in the blanks" with traditional referentiality is "fabulous" in the sense of "imaginary" or "fanciful," I would argue that limiting interpretation to reading only between the signs is the fanciful endeavor. Unless we are willing to speak Homer's language on its own terms, reading behind as well as between the signs, we cannot aspire to the kind of interpretation that Homeric traditional art deserves.

11. "My child" (*teknon emon*) begins four of the six instances of **You should know better!** (1.64, Zeus to Athena; 5.22, Zeus to Athena; 19.492, Eurykleia to Odysseus; and the present instance at 23.70, Eurykleia to Penelope); two of these situations involve true kinship and the other two entail foster kinship. The same brief address also begins three other lines in the *Odyssey*—11.155, Antikleia's ghost to Odysseus; 23.105, Penelope to Telemachos; and 24.478, Zeus to Athena—and is directed each time to a blood relative. The remaining two instances of **You should know better!** involve Athena (pseudo-Mentor) speaking to Telemachos (3.230) and Antinoos to Leodes (21.168), with neither pair sharing either true or foster kinship. In short, the evidence indicates that **You should know better!** can be deployed with or without "my child," and applied to a wide range of relationships from father-daughter through comrades or acquaintances.

12. *Od.* 14.150, 391.

13. Let me note in passing that the nearby **Guest of honor** sign (90) regularly keys the onset of a feast, preceded as convention warrants by the seating of the honored guest (see Chapter 6). As if to mirror the ambiguity of Penelope's perception, this *sêma* counterbalances **Clothing and status: beggar**. On the linkage between beggar's clothing, lies, testing, and recognition, see espec. Block 1985.

14. See Chapter 5 above.

15. See the *Apparatus Fabulosus* below for the remaining six instances.

16. On the face of it, this construction may seem redundant, mechanical, or just highly stylized. But reading behind the sign reveals that **Doubly question** makes an indexical contribution in whatever instance it appears. Cf. the apparently redundant nature of the "silently to silence" line (Foley 1995c).

Afterword: "Deor" and Anglo-Saxon *Sêmata*

1. On the relationship of Anglo-Saxon poetry to oral tradition, see espec. Olsen 1986, 1988; Jager 1990; O'Brien O'Keeffe 1990; Doane 1991, 1994; Pasternack 1991; Schaefer 1992, 1997; and Foley 1990: chs. 6, 9; 1991: ch. 6; and 1995a: ch. 6 (on "indexed translation"). O'Brien O'Keeffe's demonstration that Old English scribes were reading and copying formulaically (espec. 23–46) is another indication that the traditional idiom persists into texts, acting like a language even after successive commissions to writing. As one measure of the role of oral tradition behind surviving Old English texts, see Saenger 1997: 97 on the correlation between oral traditional provenance and less rigorous word separation in Anglo-Saxon vernacular (as opposed to Latin) manuscripts. I am especially grateful to Lori Peterson and Denise Stodola, whose shared discussion of "Deor" in an informal seminar led to the remarks that follow.

2. For a full text of "Deor" in the original Anglo-Saxon (after Malone 1966), see Appendix II.

3. What follows is intended as a brief and illustrative presentation. It therefore aims not at inclusiveness on any level, but rather at showing how the *sêma* principle functions in a third poetic environment.

4. Most commentators treat this competition as fictitious, but more important for our present purposes is the fact that the author characterizing himself as "Deor" has chosen as his rival nothing less than "the most famous minstrel of Old-Germanic story" (Malone 1966: 16). What better way to boost his own prowess and renown—and in the process to signal the depths to which he now has fallen—than to speak of an epochal contest against this paragon? Cp. Chapter 2 above for the interpretation of such figures (Homer; the South Slavic bards Isak, Hasan Ćoso, and Ćor Huso; and the Mongolian epic singer Choibang) as legendary singers and *sêmata* for their poetic traditions.

5. For summaries of the sources, see Malone 1966: 8–9; for background on prior approaches, Klinck 1992: 43–46.

6. For a digest of scholarship and relevant bibliography, see Foley 1990: 331–32; also 1995a: 186–87. Of special importance are Greenfield 1955, Rissanen 1969, and Renoir 1981, 1988. For a discussion of the equally ubiquitous Beasts of Battle theme, with consideration of both its traditional morphology and its rhetorical implications, see M. Griffith 1993.

7. On the variety of traditional registers, see Foley 1990: chs. 4 (ancient Greek), 5 (South Slavic), and 6 (Old English). For a list of the generally accepted abbreviations for individual poems used herein, see Bessinger and Smith 1978: xiii–xv.

8. The *wræc* (exile) word would be enough to accomplish this by itself, especially given the focus on individual words in Anglo-Saxon poetics (cf. Foley 1990: ch. 6), but see also *WfL* 38b and *Wds* 50–53, e.g. Cf. the special force of the word "to laugh" (*hliehhan*) and its derivatives in the Old English poetic corpus, which Soon-Ai (1997) has shown to convey a combination of fear and inner joy (although it may be the formulaic phrase, or larger "word," which is the true vehicle for traditional referentiality in this case).

9. Of the myriad possible examples, see espec. the exile figure in "The Wanderer," who "wod *winter*cearig ofer waþema gebind" ("traveled *winter*-sorrowful over the binding of the waves," 24), and the parallel figure in "The Seafarer," who tells "hu ic earmcearig iscealdne sæ / *winter* wunade" ("how I, wretched and sorrowful, dwelled the *winter* on the ice-cold sea," 14–15a).

10. For a full explanation and comparison with the likely source of the Old English poem, see Foley 1995a: 186–87.

11. On the Old English initiatory marker, see Foley 1991: 214–23; on "But come" (*"all' age[te]"*), see Chapter 7 above.

12. Among the many parallel phrases, cf. espec. the opening line of "The Dream of the Rood": "Hwæt! Ic swefna cyst secgan wylle" ("Lo! I wish to tell the best of dreams"); also *HbM* 1, *Bwf* 1818, *Sfr* 1, and the lengthier analogue at *WfL* 1–4.

13. See further Foley 1991: 210–14.

14. See the discussion of Homeric feast scenes in Chapter 6 above.

15. On the refrain, see espec. J. Harris (1987), who conducts a comparative examination of this possible proverb, and Klinck (1992: 43), who looks at repetition in Old English folk poetry, especially charms, as a precedent for the refrain; also Malone 1966: 17, Mandel 1977.

MASTER BIBLIOGRAPHY

Ahl, Frederick, and Hanna M. Roisman. 1996. *The Odyssey Re-Formed*. Ithaca: Cornell University Press.

Alexander, Elizabeth Shanks. 1999. "The Fixing of the Oral Mishnah and the Displacement of Meaning." *Oral Tradition* 14. Forthcoming.

Alexander, Ronelle. 1995. "The 'Tension of Essences' in South Slavic Epic." In *O Rus! Studia litteraria slavica in honorem Hugh McLean*, ed. Simon Karlinsky, James L. Rice, and Barry P. Scherr. Berkeley: Berkeley Slavic Specialties, 153–65.

Alexiou, Margaret. 1974. *The Ritual Lament in Greek Tradition*. Cambridge: Cambridge University Press.

Allen, Thomas W., ed. 1946. *Homeri Opera*. Vol. 5. Oxford: Clarendon Press.

———. 1969. *Homer: The Origins and the Transmission*. Rpt. of 1924 ed. Oxford: Clarendon Press.

Allen, Thomas W., W. R. Halliday, and E. E. Sikes, eds. 1980. *The Homeric Hymns*. Rpt. of 1936 ed. Amsterdam: Adolf M. Hakkert.

Amodio, Mark C., ed. 1994. *Oral Poetics in Middle English Poetry*. New York: Garland.

———. 1995. "Affective Criticism, Oral Poetics, and Beowulf's Fight with the Dragon." *Oral Tradition* 10: 54–90.

Amory Parry, Anne. 1966. "The Gates of Horn and Ivory." *Yale Classical Studies* 20: 3–57.

———. 1973. *Blameless Aegisthus: A Study of AMYMΩN and Other Homeric Epithets*. Leiden: E. J. Brill.

Andersen, Flemming G. 1985. *Commonplace and Creativity*. Odense: Odense University Press.

———. 1994. "'All There Is . . . As It Is': On the Development of Textual Criticism in Ballad Studies." *Jahrbuch für Volksliedforschung* 39: 28–40.

Andersen, Oeivind. 1990. "The Making of the Past in the *Iliad*." *Harvard Studies in Classical Philology* 93: 25–45.

Arant, Patricia. 1973. "The Persistence of Narrative Patterns: Variants of 'Dobrynja and Vasilij Kazimirov' and Homer's *Odyssey*." In *American Contributions to the Seventh International Congress of Slavists, Warsaw, August 21–27, 1973*, vol. 2: *Literature and Folklore*, ed. Victor Terras. The Hague: Mouton, 9–21.

Badalkhan, Sabir. 1994. "Poesia epica e tradizioni orali balochi: I menestrelli *Pahlawân* del Makran." Ph.D. diss. (University of Naples).

Bakker, Egbert J. 1990. "Homeric Discourse and Enjambement: A Cognitive Approach." *Transactions of the American Philological Association* 120: 1–21.

———. 1993a. "Activation and Preservation: The Interdependence of Text and Performance in an Oral Tradition." *Oral Tradition* 8: 5–20.

———. 1993b. "Discourse and Performance: Involvement, Visualization, and 'Presence' in Homeric Poetry." *Classical Antiquity* 12: 1–29.

————. 1997a. *Poetry in Speech: Orality and Homeric Discourse.* Ithaca: Cornell University Press.

————. 1997b. "Storytelling in the Future: Truth, Time, and Tense in Homeric Epic." In Bakker and Kahane 1997: 11–36, 233–36.

————. 1999. "How Oral Is Oral Composition?" In Mackay 1999: 29–48.

Bakker, Egbert J., and Ahuvia Kahane, eds. 1997. *Written Voices, Spoken Signs: Tradition, Performance, and the Epic Text.* Cambridge: Harvard University Press.

Balch, David L. 1991. "The Canon: Adaptable and Stable, Oral and Written. Critical Questions for Kelber and Riesner." *Foundations & Facets Forum* 7: 183–205.

Bartók, Béla. 1953–54. "[Musical Transcription of] No. 4. The Captivity of Djulić Ibrahim." In *SCHS*, vol. 1: 438–67.

Bauman, Richard. 1977. *Verbal Art as Performance.* Prospect Heights: Waveland Press.

————. 1986. *Story, Performance, and Event: Contextual Studies of Oral Narrative.* Cambridge: Cambridge University Press.

Bauman, Richard, and Charles L. Briggs. 1990. "Poetics and Performance as Critical Perspectives on Language and Social Life." *Annual Review of Anthropology* 19: 59–88.

Bellamy, Rufus. 1989. "Bellerophon's Tablet." *Classical Journal* 84: 289–307.

Ben-Amos, Dan. 1984. "The Seven Strands of *Tradition*: Varieties in Its Meaning in American Folklore Studies." *Journal of Folklore Research* 21: 97–131.

————. 1999a. "Jewish Folk Literature: I." *Oral Tradition* 14. Forthcoming.

————. 1999b. "Jewish Folk Literature: II." *Oral Tradition* 14. Forthcoming.

Bender, Mark. 1996. "Shifting and Performance in Suzhou Chantefable." Paper given at the International Workshop on Oral Literature in China, Nordic Institute for Asian Studies, Copenhagen, Denmark, 30 August.

Benson, Morton. 1980. *Srpskohrvatsko-engleski rečnik.* Belgrade: Prosveta.

Bergren, Ann L. T. 1983. "Odyssean Temporality: Many (Re)Turns." In *Approaches to Homer*, ed. C. A. Rubino and C. W. Shelmerdine. Austin: University of Texas Press, 38–73.

Bessinger, Jess B., ed. 1978. *A Concordance to the Anglo-Saxon Poetic Records.* Programmed by Philip H. Smith. Ithaca: Cornell University Press.

Biebuyck, Daniel, ed. and trans. 1971. *The Mwindo Epic from the Banyanga.* Berkeley and Los Angeles: University of California Press.

Blackburn, Stuart H., et al., eds. 1989. *Oral Epics in India.* Berkeley and Los Angeles: University of California Press.

Blackburn, Stuart H., and Joyce Burkhalter Flueckiger. 1989. Introduction to Blackburn et al. 1989: 1–11.

Blader, Susan. 1996. "Oral Narrative and Its Transformation into Print: *Bai Yutang* by Jin Shengbo?" Paper given at the International Workshop on Oral Literature in China, Nordic Institute for Asian Studies, Copenhagen, Denmark, 30 August.

Block, Elizabeth. 1985. "Clothing Makes the Man: A Pattern in the *Odyssey*." *Transactions of the American Philological Association* 115: 1–11.

Boerdahl, Vibeke. 1997. "Professional Storytelling in Modern China: A Case Study of the *Yangzhou Pinghua* Tradition." *Asian Folklore Studies* 56: 7–32.

Boyarin, Jonathan, ed. 1993. *The Ethnography of Reading.* Berkeley and Los Angeles: University of California Press.

Bradbury, Nancy Mason. 1998. "'Traditional Referentiality': The Aesthetic Power of Oral Traditional Structures." In Foley 1998a: 136–45.

Braun, Maximilian. 1961. *Das serbokroatische Heldenlied.* Göttingen: Vandenhoeck and Ruprecht.

Briggs, Charles L. 1988. *Competence in Performance: The Creativity of Tradition in Mexicano Verbal Art.* Philadelphia: University of Pennsylvania Press.

Brockington, John. 1996. "The Textualization of the Sanskrit Epics." Paper given at the Conference on Textualization and Oral Epics, Turku University, Finland, 28 June.

Brown, Mary Ellen. 1995. "Authenticity, Musicality, Oral-Formulaic Composition: A Re-examination of William Motherwell's Ballad Theory." Paper given at the Twenty-Fifth Meeting of the Ballad Commission, Mellac, France, 15 May.

Burgess, Jonathan S. 1996. "The Non-Homeric *Cypria.*" *Transactions of the American Philological Association* 126: 77–99.

———. 1997. "Beyond Neo-Analysis: Problems with the Vengeance Theory." *American Journal of Philology* 118: 1–19.

Butler, Thomas. 1993. "Muslim Singers of Tales in the Balkans: The Clue to Homer." *Cross Currents* 12: 166–71.

Buxton, Richard. 1994. *Imaginary Greece: The Contexts of Mythology.* Cambridge: Cambridge University Press.

Bynum, David E., ed. 1979. *Bihaćka krajina: Epics from Bihać, Cazin, and Kulen Vakuf.* *SCHS,* vol. 14.

———. 1980. "Prolegomena." In *SCHS,* vol. 6: ix–il.

Calame, Claude. 1995. *The Craft of Poetic Speech in Ancient Greece.* Ithaca: Cornell University Press.

Calhoun, George M. 1935. "The Art of Formula in Homer—ΕΠΕΑ ΠΤΕΡΟΕΝΤΑ." *Classical Philology* 30: 215–27.

Chadwick, John. 1958. "Mycenaean Elements in the Homeric Dialect." In *Minoica: Festschrift for J. Sundwall,* ed. E. Grumach. Berlin: Akademie-Verlag, 116–22.

Chao Gejin. 1997. "Mongolian Oral Epic: An Overview." *Oral Tradition* 12: 354–68.

Clark, Francelia Mason. 1995. *Theme in Oral Epic and in Beowulf.* New York: Garland.

Claus, David B. 1975. "*Aidôs* in the Language of Achilles." *Transactions of the American Philological Association* 105: 13–28.

Clay, Jenny Strauss. 1989. *The Politics of Olympus: Form and Meaning in the Major Homeric Hymns.* Princeton: Princeton University Press.

———. 1994. "The Dais of Death." *Transactions of the American Philological Association* 124: 35–40.

Clover, Carol J. 1986. "The Long Prose Form." *Arkiv för nordisk filologi* 101: 10–39.

Cohen, Beth, ed. 1995. *The Distaff Side: Representing the Female in Homer's Odyssey.* New York: Oxford University Press.

Cook, Erwin F. 1995. *The Odyssey in Athens: Myths of Cultural Origins.* Ithaca: Cornell University Press.

Coote, Mary P. 1980. "The Singer's Themes in Serbocroatian Heroic Song." *California Slavic Studies* 11: 201–35.

———. 1981. "Lying in Passages." *Canadian-American Slavic Studies* 15: 5–23.

Cosset, Evelyne. 1983a. "Choix formulaire ou choix sémantique? La désignation d'Ulysse et de la lance (ἔγχος) dans l'*Iliade.*" *Revue des études anciennes* 85: 191–98.

———. 1983b. "Tradition formulaire et originalité Homérique: Réflexions sur trois épithètes de l'*Iliade.*" *Revue des études grecques* 96: 269–74.

Cramer, Owen C. 1976. "Speech and Silence in the *Iliad.*" *Classical Journal* 71: 300–304.

Crane, Gregory. 1988. *Calypso: Backgrounds and Conventions of the* Odyssey. Frankfurt am Main: Athenäum.

Creed, Robert P. 1975. "Widsith's Journey Through Germanic Tradition." In *Anglo-Saxon Poetry: Essays in Appreciation for John C. McGalliard*, ed. Lewis E. Nicholson and Dolores Warwick Frese. Notre Dame: University of Notre Dame Press, 376–87.

Culley, Robert C. 1993. "Psalm 102: A Complaint with a Difference." *Semeia* 62: 19–35.

Cunliffe, Richard John. 1963. *A Lexicon of the Homeric Dialect*. Norman: University of Oklahoma Press. Rpt. of 1924 ed.

Curtius, Ernst Robert. 1953. *European Literature and the Latin Middle Ages*. Princeton: Princeton University Press.

Dalby, Andrew. 1995. "The *Iliad*, the *Odyssey*, and Their Audiences." *Classical Quarterly* 45: 269–79.

Danek, Georg. 1991. "Πολύμητις 'Οδυσσεύς und *Tale budalina*: Namensformeln bei Homer und im serbokroatischen Epos." *Wiener Studien: Zeitschrift für klassische Philologie und Patristik* 104: 23–47.

Dauenhauer, Richard, and Nora Marks Dauenhauer. 1995. "Oral Literature Embodied and Disembodied." In *Aspects of Oral Communication*, ed. Uta M. Quasthoff. Berlin: de Gruyter, 91–111.

Davies, Malcolm, ed. 1988. *Epicorum Graecorum Fragmenta*. Göttingen: Vandenhoeck & Ruprecht.

———. 1989. *The Epic Cycle*. Bristol: Bristol Classical Press.

Davison, J. A. 1963. "The Homeric Question." In *A Companion to Homer*, ed. Alan J. B. Wace and Frank H. Stubbings. New York: Macmillan, 234–68.

de Jong, Irene J. F. 1987. *Narrators and Focalizers: The Presentation of the Story in the* Iliad. Amsterdam: Grüner.

Devine, A. M., and L. D. Stephens. 1984. *Language and Metre: Resolution, Porson's Bridge, and Their Prosodic Basis*. Chico, Calif.: Scholars Press.

———. 1994. *The Prosody of Greek Speech*. Oxford: Oxford University Press.

Dickson, Keith. 1992. "Kalkhas and Nestor: Two Narrative Strategies in *Iliad* 1." *Arethusa* 25: 327–58.

Dirlmeier, Franz. 1971. *Das serbokroatische Heldenlied und Homer*. Heidelberg: Carl Winter.

Doane, A. N. 1991. "Oral Texts, Intertexts, and Intratexts: Editing Old English." In *Influence and Intertextuality in Literary History*, ed. Jay Clayton and Eric Rothstein. Madison: University of Wisconsin Press, 75–113.

———. 1994. "Performance as a Constitutive Category in the Editing of Anglo-Saxon Poetic Texts." *Oral Tradition* 9: 420–39.

Doherty, Lillian E. 1995. *Siren Songs: Gender, Audiences, and Narrators in the Odyssey*. Ann Arbor: University of Michigan Press.

Donlan, Walter. 1971. "Homer's Agamemnon." *Classical World* 65: 109–15.

———. 1993. "Duelling with Gifts in the *Iliad*: As the Audience Saw It." In Roisman and Roisman 1993: 155–72.

Duban, Jeffrey M. 1981. "Les Duels majeurs de l'Iliade et le langage d'Hector." *Les Etudes classiques* 49: 97–124.

DuBois, Thomas. 1994. "An Ethnopoetic Approach to Finnish Folk Poetry: Arhippa Perttunen's *Nativity*." In *Songs Beyond the Kalevala: Transformations of Oral Poetry*, ed. Anna-Leena Siikala and Sinikka Vakimo. Studia Fennica, Folkloristica, 2. Helsinki: Suomalaisen Kirjallisuuden Seura, 138–79.

———. 1995. *Finnish Folk Poetry and the* Kalevala. New York: Garland.

Duggan, Joseph J. 1973. *The Song of Roland: Formulaic Style and Poetic Craft.* Berkeley and Los Angeles: University of California Press.

Dunkle, Roger. 1997. "Swift-Footed Achilles." *Classical World* 90: 227–34.

Durante, Marcello. 1971. *Sulla preistoria della tradizione poetica greca. I. Continuità della tradizione poetica dall'età micenea ai primi documenti.* Rome: Edizioni dell' Ateneo.

Edmunds, Susan T. 1990. *Homeric Nêpios.* New York: Garland.

Edwards, G. Patrick. 1971. *The Language of Hesiod in Its Traditional Context.* Oxford: Basil Blackwell.

Edwards, Mark W. 1986. "Homer and Oral Tradition: The Formula, Part I." *Oral Tradition* 1: 171–230.

———. 1988. "Homer and Oral Tradition: The Formula, Part II." *Oral Tradition* 3: 11–60.

———. 1990. "Neoanalysis and Beyond." *Classical Antiquity* 9: 311–25.

———. 1992. "Homer and Oral Tradition: The Type-Scene." *Oral Tradition* 7: 284–330.

Elman, Yaakov. 1999. "Orality and the Redaction of the Babylonian Talmud." *Oral Tradition* 14. Forthcoming.

Erbse, Hartmut, ed. 1969–83. *Scholia Graeca in Homeri Iliadem (scholia vetera).* Berlin: de Gruyter.

Erdely, Stephen. 1995. *Music of Southslavic Epics from the Bihać Region of Bosnia.* New York: Garland.

Falkner, Thomas M. 1995. "On the Threshold: Homeric Heroism, Old Age, and the End of the *Odyssey.*" In his *The Poetics of Old Age in Greek Epic, Lyric, and Tragedy.* Norman: University of Oklahoma Press, 3–51.

Feld, Stephen. 1990. *Sound and Sentiment: Weeping, Poetics, and Song in Kaluli Expression.* 2d ed. Philadelphia: University of Pennsylvania Press.

Feldman, Walter. 1997. "Two Performances of the 'Return of Alpamiş': Current Performance-Practice in the Uzbek Oral Epic of the Sherabad School." *Oral Tradition* 12: 323–53.

Felson-Rubin, Nancy. 1994. *Regarding Penelope: From Character to Poetics.* Princeton: Princeton University Press.

Fine, Elizabeth C. 1984. *The Folklore Text: From Performance to Print.* Bloomington: Indiana University Press.

Finkelberg, Margalit. 1988. "A Note on Some Metrical Irregularities in Homer." *Classical Philology* 83: 206–11.

———. 1989. "Formulaic and Nonformulaic Elements in Homer." *Classical Philology* 84: 179–97.

———. 1990. "A Creative Oral Poet and the Muse." *American Journal of Philology* 111: 293–303.

Finnegan, Ruth. 1970. *Oral Literature in Africa.* Oxford: Clarendon Press.

———. 1977. *Oral Poetry: Its Nature, Significance, and Social Context.* Cambridge: Cambridge University Press.

———. 1988. *Literacy and Orality: Studies in the Technology of Communication.* Oxford: Basil Blackwell.

Finnegan, Ruth, and Margaret Orbell, eds. 1995. *South Pacific Oral Traditions.* Voices in Performance and Text. Bloomington: Indiana University Press.

Fisher, Laura Gordon. 1990. *Marko Songs from Hercegovina a Century After Karadžić.* New York: Garland.

Foley, Helene P., ed. 1994. *The Homeric Hymn to Demeter.* Princeton: Princeton University Press.

———. 1995. "Penelope as Moral Agent." In Cohen 1995: 93–115.

Foley, John Miles. 1982. "Field Research on Oral Literature and Culture in Serbia." *Pacific Quarterly Moana* 7(2): 47–59.

———. 1983. "Literary Art and Oral Tradition in Old English and Serbian Poetry." *Anglo-Saxon England* 12: 183–214.

———. 1985. *Oral-Formulaic Theory and Research: An Introduction and Annotated Bibliography.* New York: Garland. Rpt. 1988, 1992.

———. 1986. "Tradition and the Collective Talent: Oral Epic, Textual Meaning, and Receptionalist Theory." *Cultural Anthropology* 1: 202–22.

———. 1987. "Reading the Oral Traditional Text: Aesthetics of Creation and Response." In *Comparative Research on Oral Traditions: A Memorial for Milman Parry,* ed. John Miles Foley. Columbus, Ohio: Slavica, 185–212.

———. 1988. *The Theory of Oral Composition: History and Methodology.* Bloomington: Indiana University Press. Rpt. 1992.

———. 1990. *Traditional Oral Epic: The* Odyssey, Beowulf, *and the Serbo-Croatian Return Song.* Berkeley and Los Angeles: University of California Press. Rpt. 1993.

———. 1991. *Immanent Art: From Structure to Meaning in Traditional Oral Epic.* Bloomington: Indiana University Press.

———. 1992a. "Word-Power, Performance, and Tradition." *Journal of American Folklore* 105: 275–301.

———. 1992b. "Obituary: Albert Bates Lord (1912–1991)." *Journal of American Folklore* 105: 57–65.

———. 1992c. "Synthetic Kinship in Serbo-Croatian Epic." In *De Gustibus: Essays for Alain Renoir,* ed. John Miles Foley. New York: Garland, 201–15.

———, ed. 1994a. "Oral Literature Today." In *The HarperCollins World Reader,* ed. Mary Ann Caws and Christopher Prendergast. New York: HarperCollins, 2590–2655.

———. 1994b. "Proverbs and Proverbial Function in South Slavic and Comparative Epic." *Proverbium* 11: 77–92.

———. 1995a. *The Singer of Tales in Performance.* Bloomington: Indiana University Press.

———. 1995b. "Folk Literature." In *Scholarly Editing: A Guide to Research,* ed. David C. Greetham. New York: Modern Language Association, 600–26.

———. 1995c. "Sixteen Moments of Silence in Homer." *Quaderni Urbinati di cultura classica,* n.s., 50: 7–26.

———. 1997. "Oral Tradition and Its Implications." In Morris and Powell 1997: 146–73.

———, ed. 1998a. *Teaching Oral Traditions.* New York: Modern Language Association.

———. 1998b. "The Impossibility of Canon." In Foley 1998a: 13–33.

———. 1998c. "Individual Poet and Epic Tradition: The Legendary Singer." *Arethusa* 31: 149–78.

Ford, Andrew. 1992. *Homer: The Poetry of the Past.* Ithaca: Cornell University Press.

Forsyth, Neil. 1979. "The Allurement Scene: A Typical Pattern in Greek Oral Epic." *California Studies in Classical Antiquity* 13: 107–20.

Fraade, Steven. 1999. "Literary Composition and Oral Performance in Early Midrashim." *Oral Tradition* 14. Forthcoming.

Frame, Douglas. 1978. *The Myth of Return in Early Greek Epic*. New Haven: Yale University Press.

Frank, Roberta. 1993. "The Search for the Anglo-Saxon Oral Poet." *Bulletin of the John Rylands University Library of Manchester* 75: 11–36.

Fränkel, Hermann. 1926. "Der kallimachische und der homerische Hexameter." *Nachrichten von der Gesellschaft der Wissenschaften zu Göttingen* [*phil.-hist. Klasse*]: 197–229.

Fredricksmeyer, Hardy C. 1997. "Penelope *Polutropos*: The Crux at *Odyssey* 23.218–24." *American Journal of Philology* 118: 487–97.

Friedrich, Paul, and James Redfield. 1978. "Speech as Personality Symbol: The Case of Achilles." *Language* 54: 263–88.

———. 1981. "Contra Messing." *Language* 57: 901–3.

Friedrich, Rainer. 1981. "On the Compositional Use of Similes in the *Odyssey*." *American Journal of Philology* 102: 120–37.

Gagarin, Michael. 1999. "The Orality of Greek Oratory." In Mackay 1999: 163–80.

Gantz, Timothy. 1993. *Early Greek Myth: A Guide to Literary and Artistic Sources*. Baltimore: Johns Hopkins University Press.

Garner, R. Scott. 1996. "*Ei Pote*: A Note on Homeric Phraseology." *Oral Tradition* 11: 363–73.

Gesemann, Gerhard. 1926. *Studien zur südslavischen Volksepik*. Reichenberg: Verlag Gebrüder Stiepel.

Goff, Barbara E. 1991. "The Sign of the Fall: The Scars of Orestes and Odysseus." *Classical Antiquity* 10: 259–67.

Goldman, Kenneth A. 1990. *Formulaic Analysis of Serbocroatian Oral Epic Song: Songs of Avdo Avdić*. New York: Garland.

Greenfield, Stanley B. 1955. "The Formulaic Expression of the Theme of 'Exile' in Anglo-Saxon Poetry." *Speculum* 30: 200–206.

Gregory, Elizabeth. 1996. "Unravelling Penelope: The Construction of the Faithful Wife in Homer's Heroines." *Helios* 23: 3–20.

Griffin, Jasper. 1977. "The Epic Cycle and the Uniqueness of Homer." *Journal of Hellenic Studies* 97: 39–53.

———. 1980. *Homer on Life and Death*. Oxford: Clarendon Press.

Griffith, M. S. 1993. "Convention and Originality in the Old English 'Beasts of Battle' Typescene." *Anglo-Saxon England* 22: 179–99.

Griffith, R. Drew. 1995. "A Homeric Metaphor Cluster Describing Teeth, Tongue, and Words." *American Journal of Philology* 116: 1–5.

———. 1997. "Homeric ΔΙΙΠΕΤΕΟΣ ΠΟΤΑΜΟΙΟ and the Celestial Nile." *American Journal of Philology* 118: 353–62.

Haft, Adele. 1996. "'The Mercurial Significance of Raiding': Baby Hermes and Animal Theft in Contemporary Crete." *Arion* 3: 27–48.

Hainsworth, J. B. 1968. *The Flexibility of the Homeric Formula*. Oxford: Clarendon Press.

———, ed. 1993. *The Iliad: A Commentary*. Vol. 3: Bks. 9–12. Cambridge: Cambridge University Press.

Halliwell, Stephen, ed. and trans. 1995. *Aristotle, The Poetics*. In W. Hamilton Fyfe and W. Rhys Roberts, eds., *Aristotle, The Poetics; Longinus, On the Sublime; Demetrius, On Style*. Loeb Classical Library, vol. 199. Cambridge: Harvard University Press, 1–141.

Halpern, Joel, and Barbara Kerewsky-Halpern. 1972. *A Serbian Village in Historical Perspective*. New York: Holt, Rinehart and Winston.

Hammond, N. G. L., and H. H. Scullard, eds. 1977. *The Oxford Classical Dictionary.* 2d ed. Rpt. of 1970 ed. Oxford: Clarendon Press.

Hansen, William F. 1977. "Odysseus' Last Journey." *Quaderni Urbinati di cultura classica* 24: 27–48.

———. 1990. "Odysseus and the Oar: A Folkloric Approach." In *Approaches to Greek Myth,* ed. Lowell Edmunds. Baltimore: Johns Hopkins University Press, 241–72.

Harris, Joseph. 1987. "'Deor' and Its Refrain: Preliminaries to an Interpretation." *Traditio* 43: 23–53.

Harris, William V. 1989. *Ancient Literacy.* Cambridge: Harvard University Press.

Haslam, Michael. 1997. "Homeric Papyri and Transmission of the Text." In Morris and Powell 1997: 55–100.

Haymes, Edward R. 1980. "Formulaic Density and Bishop Njegoš." *Comparative Literature* 32: 390–401.

Heiden, Bruce. 1996. "The Three Movements of the *Iliad.*" *Greek, Roman, and Byzantine Studies* 37: 5–22.

Heissig, Walther, ed. 1987. *Fragen der mongolischen Heldendichtung.* Wiesbaden: Otto Harrassowitz.

Herzog, George. 1951. "The Music of Yugoslav Heroic Epic Folk Poetry." *International Folk Music Journal* 3: 62–64.

Heubeck, Alfred. 1979. *Schrift.* Archaeologica Homerica, vol. 3, chap. 10. Göttingen: Vandenhoeck and Ruprecht.

Heubeck, Alfred, Stephanie West, and J. B. Hainsworth, eds. 1988. *A Commentary on Homer's Odyssey.* Vol. 1: Bks. 1–8. Oxford: Clarendon Press.

Higbie, Carolyn. 1990. *Measure and Music: Enjambement and Sentence Structure in the* Iliad. Oxford: Oxford University Press.

———. 1995. *Heroes' Names, Homeric Identities.* New York: Garland.

Hogan, James C. 1976. "Double πρίν and the Language of Achilles." *Classical Journal* 71: 305–10.

Holmberg, Ingrid E. 1995. "The *Odyssey* and Female Subjectivity." *Helios* 22: 103–22.

———. 1997. "The Sign of ΜΗΤΙΣ." *Arethusa* 30: 1–33.

———. 1999. "Homer and the Beginning of the Sequel." *Oral Tradition* 14. Forthcoming.

Holoka, James P. 1983. "'Looking Darkly' (ΥΠΟΔΡΑ ΙΔΩΝ): Reflections on Status and Decorum in Homer." *Transactions of the American Philological Association* 113: 1–16.

Honko, Lauri. 1984. "Empty Texts, Full Meanings: On Transformal Meaning in Folklore." *Arv: Scandinavian Yearbook of Folklore* 40: 95–125.

———. 1998a. *Textualising the Siri Epic.* Folklore Fellows Communications, vol. 264. Helsinki: Academia Scientiarum Fennica.

———, ed. 1998b. In collaboration with Chinnappa Gowda, Anneli Honko, and Viveka Rai. *The Siri Epic as Performed by Gopala Naika.* 2 vols. Folklore Fellows Communications, vols. 265–66. Helsinki: Academia Scientiarum Fennica.

Horrocks, Geoffrey C. 1980. "The Antiquity of the Greek Epic Tradition: Some New Evidence." *Proceedings of the Cambridge Philological Society,* n.s., 26: 1–11.

———. 1997. "Homer's Dialect." In Morris and Powell 1997: 193–217.

Huxley, G. L. 1969. *Greek Epic Poetry: From Eumelos to Panyassis.* Cambridge: Harvard University Press.

Hymes, Dell. 1981. *"In Vain I Tried to Tell You": Essays in Native American Ethnopoetics.* Philadelphia: University of Pennsylvania Press.

————. 1989. "Ways of Speaking." In *Explorations in the Ethnography of Speaking*, ed. Richard Bauman and Joel Sherzer. 2d ed. Cambridge: Cambridge University Press, 433–51, 473–74.

————. 1994. "Ethnopoetics, Oral-Formulaic Theory, and Editing Texts." *Oral Tradition* 9: 330–70.

Jaffee, Martin S. 1992. "How Much 'Orality' in Oral Torah? New Perspectives on the Composition and Transmission of Early Rabbinic Tradition." *Shofar* 10: 53–72.

————. 1994. "Writing and Rabbinic Oral Tradition: On Mishnaic Narrative, Lists and Mnemonics." *Journal of Jewish Thought and Philosophy* 4: 123–46.

————. 1997. "A Rabbinic Ontology of the Written and Spoken Word: On Discipleship, Transformative Knowledge, and the Living Texts of Oral Torah." *Journal of the American Academy of Religion* 65: 525–49.

————. 1999. "Oral Tradition in the Writings of Rabbinic Oral Torah: On Theorizing Rabbinic Orality." *Oral Tradition* 14. Forthcoming.

Jager, Eric. 1990. "Speech and the Chest in Old English Poetry: Orality or Pectorality?" *Speculum* 65: 845–59.

Jakobson, Roman. 1952. "Studies in Comparative Slavic Metrics." *Oxford Slavonic Papers* 3: 21–66.

Janko, Richard. 1982. *Homer, Hesiod, and the Hymns: Diachronic Development in Epic Diction*. Cambridge: Cambridge University Press.

————. 1990. "The *Iliad* and Its Editors: Dictation and Redaction." *Classical Antiquity* 9: 326–34.

————, ed. 1992a. *The Iliad: A Commentary*. Vol. 4: Bks. 13–16. Cambridge: Cambridge University Press.

————. 1992b. "The Text and Transmission of the *Iliad*." In Janko 1992a: 20–38.

Jeffery, Lilian H. 1967. "ΑΡΧΑΙΑ ΓΡΑΜΜΑΤΑ: Some Ancient Greek Views." In *Europa: Studien zur Geschichte und Epigraphik der frühen Aegaeis: Festschrift für Ernst Grumach*, ed. William C. Brice. Berlin: de Gruyter, 152–66.

Kahane, Ahuvia. 1992. "The First Word of the *Odyssey*." *Transactions of the American Philological Association* 122: 115–31.

————. 1994. *The Interpretation of Order: A Study in the Poetics of Homeric Repetition*. Oxford: Clarendon Press.

————. 1997. "Hexameter Progression and the Homeric Hero's Solitary State." In *Written Voices, Spoken Signs: Tradition, Performance, and the Epic Text*, ed. Egbert Bakker and Ahuvia Kahane. Cambridge: Harvard University Press, 110–37, 244–49.

Kannicht, Richard. 1982. "Poetry and Art: Homer and the Monuments Afresh." *Classical Antiquity* 1: 70–86.

Karadžić, Vuk Stefanović, ed. 1841–62. *Srpske narodne pjesme*. Beč. Rpt. Belgrade: Nolit, 1975.

————. 1849. *Srpske narodne poslovice*. Beč. Rpt. Belgrade: Nolit, 1975.

————. 1852. *Srpski rječnik*. Beč. Rpt. Belgrade: Nolit, 1975.

Katz, Marilyn A. 1991. *Penelope's Renown: Meaning and Indeterminacy in the Odyssey*. Princeton: Princeton University Press.

————. 1994. "Homecoming and Hospitality: Recognition and the Construction of Identity in the *Odyssey*." In Oberhelman, Kelly, and Golsan 1994: 49–75.

Kay, Matthew. 1995. *The Index of the Milman Parry Collection 1933–1935: Heroic Songs, Conversations, and Stories*. New York: Garland.

Kelber, Werner H. 1997. *The Oral and the Written Gospel: The Hermeneutics of Speak-

ing and Writing in the Synoptic Tradition, Mark, Paul, and Q. With a new introduction. Bloomington: Indiana University Press.

Kirk, G. S. 1960. *The Songs of Homer*. Cambridge: Cambridge University Press.

———, ed. 1985. *The Iliad: A Commentary*. Vol. 1: Bks. 1–4. Cambridge: Cambridge University Press.

———, ed. 1990. *The Iliad: A Commentary*. Vol. 2: Bks. 5–8. Cambridge: Cambridge University Press.

Klinck, Anne, ed. 1992. *The Old English Elegies: A Critical Edition and Genre Study*. Montreal: McGill-Queen's University Press.

Koljević, Svetozar. 1980. *The Epic in the Making*. Oxford: Clarendon Press.

———. 1994. "Vuk Karadžić and the Achievement of His Singers." In *The Uses of Tradition: A Comparative Enquiry into the Nature, Uses, and Functions of Oral Poetry in the Balkans, the Baltic, and Africa*, ed. Michael Branch and Celia Hawkesworth. London: School of Slavonic and East European Studies and Helsinki: Finnish Literature Society, 23–36.

Kolsti, John S. 1968. "Albanian Oral Epic Poetry." In *Studies Presented to Professor Roman Jakobson by His Students*, ed. Charles E. Gribble. Cambridge, Mass.: Slavica, 165–67.

———. 1990. *The Bilingual Singer: A Study in Albanian and Serbo-Croatian Oral Epic Poetry*. New York: Garland.

———. 1997. "Albert Lord in Albania." In *Usna epika: Epnični tradiciji ta vikonavstvo*, ed. O. Bricina and G. Dovženok. Kiev: Institut mistedtvoznavstva, folkloristiki ta etnologiji, vol. 2: 137–40.

Krapp, George Philip, and E. V. K. Dobbie, eds. 1931–53. *The Anglo-Saxon Poetic Records*. 6 vols. New York: Columbia University Press.

Kuipers, Joel C. 1990. *Power in Performance: The Creation of Textual Authority in Weyewa Ritual Speech*. Philadelphia: University of Pennsylvania Press.

———. 1998. *Language, Identity, and Marginality in Indonesia: The Changing Nature of Ritual Speech on the Island of Sumba*. Cambridge: Cambridge University Press.

Kulišić, Š., P. Ž. Petrović, and N. Pantelić, eds. 1970. *Srpski mitološki rečnik*. Belgrade: Nolit.

Kullmann, Wolfgang. 1984. "Oral Poetry Theory and Neoanalysis in Homeric Research." *Greek, Roman, and Byzantine Studies* 25: 307–23.

Lacore, Michelle. 1997. "Νήδυμος ὕπνος." *Gaia: Revue interdisciplinaire sur la Grèce ancienne* 1–2: 13–40.

Lamberton, Robert. 1997. "Homer in Antiquity." In Morris and Powell 1997: 33–54.

Lang, Helen S. 1982. "An Homeric Echo in Aristotle." *Philological Quarterly* 56: 329–39.

Lateiner, Donald. 1989. "Teeth in Homer." *Liverpool Classical Monthly* 14: 18–23.

———. 1992. "Heroic Proxemics: Social Space and Distance in the *Odyssey*." *Transactions of the American Philological Association* 122: 133–63.

———. 1995. *Sardonic Smile: Nonverbal Behavior in Homeric Epic*. Ann Arbor: University of Michigan Press.

Lattimore, Richmond, trans. 1951. *The Iliad of Homer*. Chicago: University of Chicago Press.

———, trans. 1965. *The Odyssey of Homer*. New York: Harper.

Ledbetter, Grace M. 1996. "Achilles' Self-Address: *Iliad* 16.7–19." *American Journal of Philology* 117: 481–91.

Létoublon, Françoise. 1990. "De la syntaxe à la poétique générative, ou Grammaire et mesure." In *La Langue et les textes en grec ancien: Actes du Colloque Pierre Chantraine (Grenoble—5–8 septembre 1989)*, ed. Françoise Létoublon. Amsterdam: J. C. Gieben, 93–104.

———, ed. 1997. *Hommage à Milman Parry: Le Style formulaire de l'épopée homérique et la théorie de l'oralité poétique.* Amsterdam: J. C. Gieben.

Levine, Daniel B. 1984. "Odysseus' Smiles: *Odyssey* 20.301, 22.371, 23.111." *Transactions of the American Philological Association* 114: 1–9.

Liddell, Henry George, and Robert Scott. 1968. *A Greek-English Lexicon.* Rev. Henry Stuart Jones with the assistance of Roderick McKenzie. With a supplement. Oxford: Clarendon Press.

Lincoln, Bruce. 1997. "Competing Discourses: Rethinking the Prehistory of *Mythos* and *Logos.*" *Arethusa* 30: 341–67.

Lloyd-Jones, Hugh. 1992. "Becoming Homer." *New York Review of Books* 39 (5 March): 52–57.

Lord, Albert Bates. 1936. "Homer and Huso I: The Singer's Rests in Greek and South Slavic Heroic Song." *Transactions of the American Philological Association* 67: 106–13.

———. 1938. "Homer and Huso II: Narrative Inconsistencies in Homer and Oral Poetry." *Transactions of the American Philological Association* 69: 439–45.

———. 1948a. "Homer and Huso III: Enjambement in Greek and Southslavic Heroic Song." *Transactions of the American Philological Association* 79: 113–24.

———. 1948b. "Homer, Parry, and Huso." *American Journal of Archaeology* 52: 34–44. Rpt. in M. Parry 1971: 465–78.

———. 1951. "Composition by Theme in Homer and Southslavic Epos." *Transactions of the American Philological Association* 82: 71–80.

———. 1953a. "Homer's Originality: Oral Dictated Texts." *Transactions of the American Philological Association* 84: 124–34.

———. 1953b. "General Introduction." In *SCHS*, vol. 1: 3–20.

———. 1960. *The Singer of Tales.* Cambridge: Harvard University Press. Rpt. New York: Atheneum, 1968 et seq.

———. 1965. "Beowulf and Odysseus." In *Franciplegius: Medieval and Linguistic Studies in Honor of Francis Peabody Magoun, Jr.*, ed. Jess B. Bessinger and Robert P. Creed. New York: New York University Press, 86–91.

———. 1969. "The Theme of the Withdrawn Hero in Serbo-Croatian Oral Epic." *Prilozi za književnost, jezik, istoriju i folklor* 35: 18–30.

———. 1971. "An Example of Homeric Qualities of Repetition in Medjedović's 'Smailagić Meho.'" In *Serta Slavica In Memoriam Aloisii Schmaus: Gedenkschrift für Alois Schmaus*, ed. Wolfgang Gesemann et al. Munich: Rudolf Trofenik, 458–64.

———. 1972. "The Effect of the Turkish Conquest on Balkan Epic Tradition." In *Aspects of the Balkans: Continuity and Change*, ed. Henrik Birnbaum and Speros Vryonis, Jr. The Hague and Paris: Mouton, 298–318.

———. 1986a. "Perspectives on Recent Work on the Oral Traditional Formula." *Oral Tradition* 1: 467–503.

———. 1986b. "The Merging of Two Worlds: Oral and Written Poetry as Carriers of Ancient Values." In *Oral Tradition in Literature: Interpretation in Context*, ed. J. M. Foley. Columbia: University of Missouri Press, 19–64.

———. 1991. *Epic Singers and Oral Tradition.* Ithaca: Cornell University Press.

———. 1995. *The Singer Resumes the Tale.* Ithaca: Cornell University Press.

The Albert Bates Lord Studies in Oral Tradition. 1987–. 17 vols. Ed. John Miles Foley. New York: Garland.

Lord, Mary Louise. 1967. "Withdrawal and Return: An Epic Story Pattern in the Homeric Hymn to Demeter and in the Homeric Poems." *Classical Journal* 62: 241–48.

Louden, Bruce. 1993. "An Extended Narrative Pattern in the *Odyssey.*" *Greek, Roman, and Byzantine Studies* 34: 5–33.

———. 1996. "A Narrative Technique in *Beowulf* and Homeric Epic." *Oral Tradition* 11: 346–62.

Lowenstam, Steven. 1993. *The Scepter and the Spear: Studies on Forms of Repetition in the Homeric Poems.* Lanham, Md.: Rowman and Littlefield.

McCarthy, William B. 1990. *The Ballad Matrix: Personality, Milieu, and the Oral Tradition.* Bloomington: Indiana University Press.

———. 1995. "Transcribing Märchen for the Eye and for the Ear: Theory and Practice in the United States." *Yearbook of English Studies* 25: 80–102.

McCarthy, William B., Cheryl Oxford, and Joseph D. Sobol, eds. 1994. *Jack in Two Worlds: Contemporary North American Tales and Their Tellers.* Chapel Hill: University of North Carolina Press.

McDonald, W. E. 1997. "On Hearing the Silent Voice: Penelope and the Daughters of Pandareus." *Helios* 24: 3–22.

McDowell, John H. 1995. "Immanence and Immanent Truth." *Oral Tradition* 10: 235–62.

Mackay, E. A. 1993. "The Oral Shaping of Culture." *Scholia: Natal Studies in Classical Antiquity,* n.s., 2: 97–116.

———. 1995. "Narrative Tradition in Early Greek Oral Poetry and Vase Painting." *Oral Tradition* 10: 282–303.

———. 1996. "Time and Timelessness in the Traditions of Early Greek Oral Poetry and Archaic Vase-Painting." In *Voice into Text: Orality and Literacy in Ancient Greece,* ed. Ian Worthington. Leiden: Brill, 43–58.

———, ed. 1999. *Signs of Orality: The Oral Tradition and Its Influence in the Greek and Roman World.* Leiden: Brill.

Mackay, E. A., D. A. Harrison, and S. Masters. 1999. "The Bystander at the Ringside: Ring-Composition in Early Greek Poetry and Athenian Black-Figure Vase-Painting." In Mackay 1999: 115–42.

Mackie, Hilary. 1996. *Talking Trojan: Speech and Community in the* Iliad. Lanham, Md.: Rowman and Littlefield.

———. 1997. "Song and Storytelling: An Odyssean Perspective." *Transactions of the American Philological Association* 127: 77–95.

Magner, Thomas F. 1972. *Introduction to the Croatian and Serbian Language.* State College, Pa.: Singidunum Press. Rev. ed. University Park: Pennsylvania State University Press, 1991.

Mahacek, Gregory. 1994. "The Occasional Contextual Appropriateness of Formulaic Diction in the Homeric Poems." *American Journal of Philology* 115: 321–35.

Malkin, Irad. 1998. *The Returns of Odysseus: Colonization and Ethnicity.* Berkeley and Los Angeles: University of California Press.

Malone, Kemp, ed. 1962. *Widsith.* Rev. ed. Copenhagen: Rosenkilde and Bagger. Original ed. 1936.

———, ed. 1966. *Deor.* New York: Appleton-Century-Crofts.

Mandel, Jerome. 1977. "Exemplum and Refrain: The Meaning of 'Deor.'" *Year's Work in English Studies* 7: 1–9.

Martin, Henri-Jean. 1994. *The History and Power of Writing*. Trans. Lydia G. Cochrane. Chicago: University of Chicago Press.

Martin, Richard P. 1989. *The Language of Heroes: Speech and Performance in the* Iliad. Ithaca: Cornell University Press.

———. 1992. "Hesiod's Metanastic Poetics." *Ramus* 22: 11–33.

———. 1993. "Telemachos and the Last Hero Song." In Roisman and Roisman 1993: 222–40.

Maurizio, Lisa. 1997. "Delphic Oracles as Oral Performances: Authenticity and Historical Evidence." *Classical Antiquity* 16: 308–34.

Messing, Gordon M. 1981. "On Weighing Achilles' Winged Words." *Language* 57: 888–900.

Miller, J. Scott. 1996. "Early Voice Recordings of Japanese Storytelling." *Oral Tradition* 11: 301–19.

Minchin, Elizabeth. 1992a. "Scripts and Themes: Cognitive Research and the Homeric Epic." *Classical Antiquity* 11: 229–41.

———. 1992b. "Homer Springs a Surprise: Eumaios' Tale at *Od*. o 403–484." *Hermes* 120: 259–66.

———. 1995a. "The Poet Appeals to His Muse: Homeric Invocations in the Context of Epic Performance." *Classical Journal* 91: 25–33.

———. 1995b. "Ring-Patterns and Ring-Composition: Some Observations on the Framing of Stories in Homer." *Helios* 22: 23–36.

———. 1999. "Describing and Narrating in Homer's *Iliad*." In Mackay 1999: 49–64.

Monro, David B., and Thomas W. Allen, eds. 1969. *Homeri opera*. 3d ed. 4 vols. Oxford: Clarendon Press.

Morrell, Kenneth Scott. 1996. "Chaos Theory and the Oral Tradition: Nonlinearity and Bifurcation in the *Iliad*." *Helios* 23: 107–34.

Morris, Ian, and Barry B. Powell, eds. 1997. *A New Companion to Homer*. Leiden: Brill.

Morrison, James V. 1991. "The Function and Content of Homeric Prayers: A Narrative Perspective." *Hermes* 119: 145–57.

———. 1992. *Homeric Misdirection: False Predictions in the Iliad*. Ann Arbor: University of Michigan Press.

Most, Glenn W. 1989. "The Structure and Function of Odysseus' *Apologoi*." *Transactions of the American Philological Association* 119: 15–30.

Muellner, Leonard. 1996. *The Anger of Achilles: Mênis in Greek Epic*. Ithaca: Cornell University Press.

Murko, Matija. 1929. *La Poésie populaire épique en Yougoslavie au début du XXe siècle*. Paris: Librairie Ancienne Honoré Champion. Part 1 trans. by J. M. Foley, *Oral Tradition* 5 (1990): 107–30.

———. 1951. *Tragom srpsko-hrvatske narodne epike: Putovanja u godinama 1930–32*. 2 vols. Zagreb: Jugoslavenska Akademija Znanosti i Umjetnosti.

Murnaghan, Sheila. 1994. "Reading Penelope." In Oberhelman, Kelly, and Golsan 1994: 76–96.

———. 1995. "The Plan of Athena." In Cohen 1995: 61–80.

———. 1997. "Equal Honor and Future Glory: The Plan of Zeus in the *Iliad*." In Roberts, Dunn, and Fowler 1997: 23–42.

Nagler, Michael N. 1974. *Spontaneity and Tradition: A Study in the Oral Art of Homer*. Berkeley and Los Angeles: University of California Press.

———. 1990. "Odysseus: The Proem and the Problem." *Classical Antiquity* 9: 335–56.

———. 1993. "Penelope's Male Hand: Gender and Violence in the *Odyssey*." In Roisman and Roisman 1993: 241–57.

Nagy, Gregory. 1974. *Comparative Studies in Greek and Indic Meter*. Cambridge: Harvard University Press.

———. 1979. *The Best of the Achaeans: Concepts of the Hero in Archaic Greek Poetry*. Baltimore: Johns Hopkins University Press.

———. 1990a. "Sêma and Nóēsis: The Hero's Tomb and the 'Reading' of Symbols in Homer." In his *Greek Mythology and Poetics*. Ithaca: Cornell University Press, 202–22.

———. 1990b. *Pindar's Homer: The Lyric Possession of an Epic Past*. Baltimore: Johns Hopkins University Press.

———. 1992. "Homeric Questions." *Transactions of the American Philological Association* 122: 17–60.

———. 1996a. *Poetry as Performance: Homer and Beyond*. Cambridge: Cambridge University Press.

———. 1996b. *Homeric Questions*. Austin: University of Texas Press.

———. 1997. "Homeric Scholia." In Morris and Powell 1997: 101–22.

Newton, Rick M. 1998. "Cloak and Shield in *Odyssey* 14." *Classical Journal* 93: 143–56.

Niditch, Susan. 1995. "Oral Register in the Biblical Libretto: Towards a Biblical Poetic." *Oral Tradition* 10: 387–408.

———. 1997. *Oral World and Written Word: Ancient Israelite Literature*. Louisville, Ky.: Westminster John Knox Press.

Niles, John D. 1983. *Beowulf: The Poem and Its Tradition*. Cambridge: Harvard University Press.

———. 1993. "Understanding *Beowulf*: Oral Poetry Acts." *Journal of American Folklore* 106: 131–55.

Nimis, Steve. 1986. "The Language of Achilles: Construction vs. Representation." *Classical World* 79: 217–25.

Notopoulos, James A. 1949. "Parataxis in Homer." *Transactions of the American Philological Association* 80: 1–23.

Oberhelman, Steven M., Van Kelly, and Richard J. Golsan, eds. 1994. *Epic and Epoch: Essays on the Interpretation and History of a Genre*. Lubbock: Texas Tech University Press.

O'Brien O'Keeffe, Katherine. 1990. *Visible Song: Transitional Literacy in Old English Verse*. Cambridge: Cambridge University Press.

———. 1997. "Diction, Variation, the Formula." In *A Beowulf Handbook*, ed. Robert E. Bjork and John D. Niles. Lincoln: University of Nebraska Press, 85–104.

Oesterreicher, Wulf. 1997. "Types of Orality in Text." In Bakker and Kahane 1997: 190–214, 257–60.

Okpewho, Isidore. 1992. *African Oral Literature: Backgrounds, Character, and Continuity*. Bloomington: Indiana University Press.

Olsen, Alexandra Hennessey. 1986. "Oral-Formulaic Research in Old English Studies: I." *Oral Tradition* 1: 548–606.

———. 1988. "Oral-Formulaic Research in Old English Studies: II." *Oral Tradition* 3: 138–90.

Olson, S. Douglas. 1990. "The Stories of Agamemnon in Homer's *Odyssey.*" *Transactions of the American Philological Association* 120: 57–71.

———. 1995. *Blood and Iron: Stories and Storytelling in Homer's* Odyssey. Leiden: Brill.

O'Neill, Eugene, Jr. 1942. "The Localization of Metrical Word-Types in the Greek Hexameter." *Yale Classical Studies* 8: 103–78.

Oral Tradition. 1986–. A journal devoted to the world's oral traditions.

Palmer, L. R. 1962. "The Language of Homer." In *A Companion to Homer*, ed. Alan J. B. Wace and Frank H. Stubbings. London: Macmillan, 75–178.

Parks, Ward. 1983. "The Return Song and a Middle English Romance: *Sir Orfeo*, 'Četić Osmanbeg,' 'Djulić Ibrahim,' and the *Odyssey.*" *Southeastern Europe* 10: 222–41.

———. 1986. "The Oral-Formulaic Theory in Middle English Studies." *Oral Tradition* 1: 636–94.

———. 1988. "Ring Structure and Narrative Embedding in Homer and *Beowulf.*" *Neuphilologische Mitteilungen* 89: 127–51.

———. 1990. *Verbal Dueling in Heroic Narrative: The Homeric and Old English Traditions.* Princeton: Princeton University Press.

Parry, Adam. 1956. "The Language of Achilles." *Transactions of the American Philological Association* 87: 1–7.

Parry, Milman. 1925. "A Comparative Study of Diction as One of the Elements of Style in Early Greek Epic Poetry." In M. Parry 1971: 421–36.

———. 1928a. "The Traditional Epithet in Homer." Trans. Adam Parry in M. Parry 1971: 1–190.

———. 1928b. "Homeric Formulae and Homeric Metre." Trans. Adam Parry in M. Parry 1971: 191–239.

———. 1930. "Studies in the Epic Technique of Oral Verse-Making. I. Homer and Homeric Style." Rpt. in M. Parry 1971: 266–324.

———. 1932. "Studies in the Epic Technique of Oral Verse-Making. II. The Homeric Language as the Language of an Oral Poetry." Rpt. in M. Parry 1971: 325–64.

———. 1933–35. "Ćor Huso: A Study of Southslavic Song." Field notes, expedition to Yugoslavia. Extracts published in M. Parry 1971: 437–64.

———. 1934. "The Traces of the Digamma in Ionic and Lesbian Greek." Rpt. in M. Parry 1971: 376–90.

———. 1937. "About Winged Words." Rpt. in M. Parry 1971: 414–18.

———. 1971. *The Making of Homeric Verse: The Collected Papers of Milman Parry*, ed. Adam Parry. Oxford: Clarendon Press.

Pasternack, Carol Braun. 1991. "Anonymous Polyphony and *The Wanderer*'s Textuality." *Anglo-Saxon England* 20: 99–122.

Pazdernik, Charles F. 1995. "Odysseus and His Audience: *Odyssey* 9.39–40 and Its Formulaic Resonances." *American Journal of Philology* 116: 347–69.

Peabody, Berkley. 1975. *The Winged Word.* Albany: State University of New York Press.

Pedrick, Victoria. 1994. "Eurycleia and Eurynome as Penelope's Confidantes." In Oberhelman, Kelly, and Golsan 1994: 97–116.

Peradotto, John. 1990. *Man in the Middle Voice: Name and Narration in the* Odyssey. Princeton: Princeton University Press.

Person, Raymond F., Jr. 1995. "The 'Became Silent to Silence' Formula in Homer." *Greek, Roman, and Byzantine Studies* 36: 327–39.

Popović, Tatyana. 1988. *Prince Marko: The Hero of South Slavic Epics.* Syracuse: Syracuse University Press.

Powell, Barry B. 1991. *Homer and the Origin of the Greek Alphabet.* Cambridge: Cambridge University Press.

Pratt, Louise H. 1993. *Lying and Poetry from Homer to Pindar: Falsehood and Deception in Archaic Greek Poetics.* Ann Arbor: University of Michigan Press.

———. 1994. "*Odyssey* 19.535–50: On the Interpretation of Dreams and Signs in Homer." *Classical Philology* 89: 147–52.

———. 1995. "The Seal of Theognis, Writing, and Oral Poetry." *American Journal of Philology* 116: 171–84.

Prier, Raymond A. 1976. *Archaic Logic: Symbol and Structure in Heraclitus, Parmenides, and Empedocles.* The Hague and Paris: Mouton.

———. 1978. "SĒMA and the Symbolic Nature of Archaic Thought." *Quaderni Urbinati di cultura classica* 29: 91–101.

———. 1989. *Thauma Idesthai: The Phenomenology of Sight and Appearance in Archaic Greek.* Tallahassee: Florida State University Press.

Pucci, Piero. 1987. *Odysseus Polutropos: Intertextual Readings in the Odyssey and the Iliad.* Ithaca: Cornell University Press.

Radenković, Ljubinko. 1982. *Narodne basme i bajanja.* Belgrade: Prosveta.

———. 1996. *Narodna bajanja kod južnih slovena.* Belgrade: Prosveta.

Radlov, Vasilii V., comp. and trans. 1885. *Proben der Volkslitteratur der nördlichen türkischen Stämme.* Vol. 5: *Der Dialect der Kara-Kirgisen.* St. Petersburg: Commissionäre der Kaiserlichen Akademie der Wissenschaften. Preface trans. Gudrun Böttcher Sherman with Adam Brooke Davis in *Oral Tradition* 5 (1990): 73–90.

Reece, Steve. 1993. *The Stranger's Welcome: Oral Theory and the Aesthetics of the Homeric Hospitality Scene.* Ann Arbor: University of Michigan Press.

———. 1994. "The Cretan Odyssey: A Lie Truer than Truth." *American Journal of Philology* 115: 157–73.

Reeve, M. D. 1973. "The Language of Achilles." *Classical Quarterly*, n.s., 23: 193–95.

Reichl, Karl. 1992. *Turkic Oral Epic Poetry: Traditions, Forms, Poetic Structures.* Albert Bates Lord Studies in Oral Tradition, vol. 7. New York: Garland.

———. 1996. "Silencing the Voice of the Singer: Problems and Strategies in the Editing of Turkic Oral Epics." Paper given at the Conference on Textualization and Oral Epics, Turku University, Finland, 27 June.

Renoir, Alain. 1981. "The Least Elegiac of the Elegies: A Contextual Glance at *The Husband's Message.*" *Studia Neophilologica* 53: 69–76.

———. 1988. *A Key to Old Poems: The Oral-Formulaic Approach to the Interpretation of West-Germanic Verse.* University Park: Pennsylvania State University Press.

Reynolds, Dwight Fletcher. 1995. *Heroic Poets, Poetic Heroes: The Ethnography of Performance in an Arabic Oral Epic Tradition.* Ithaca: Cornell University Press.

Riggsby, Andrew M. 1992. "Homeric Speech Introductions and the Theory of Homeric Composition." *Transactions of the American Philological Association* 122: 99–114.

Rissanen, Matti. 1969. "The Theme of 'Exile' in *The Wife's Lament.*" *Neuphilologische Mitteilungen* 70: 90–104.

Roberts, Deborah H. 1997. "Afterword: Ending and Aftermath, Ancient and Modern." In Roberts, Dunn, and Fowler 1997: 251–73.

Roberts, Deborah H., Francis M. Dunn, and Don Fowler, eds. 1997. *Classical Closure: Reading the End in Greek and Latin Literature.* Princeton: Princeton University Press.

Roisman, Hanna M. 1987. "Penelope's Indignation." *Transactions of the American Philological Association* 117: 59–68.

Roisman, Hanna M., and Joseph Roisman, eds. 1993. *Essays on Homeric Epic.* Special issue, *Colby Quarterly* 19 (3).

Roller, Duane W., and Letitia K. Roller. 1994. "Penelope's Thick Hand (*Odyssey* 21.6)." *Classical Journal* 90: 9–19.

Roochnik, David. 1990. "Homeric Speech Acts: Word and Deed in the Epics." *Classical Journal* 85: 289–99.

Rose, Peter W. 1992. *Sons of the Gods, Children of Earth: Ideology and Literary Form in Ancient Greece.* Ithaca: Cornell University Press.

Rubin, David C. 1995. *Memory in Oral Traditions: The Cognitive Psychology of Epic, Ballads, and Counting-Out Rhymes.* New York: Oxford University Press.

Rundin, John. 1996. "A Politics of Eating: Feasting in Early Greek Society." *American Journal of Philology* 117: 179–215.

Russo, Joseph. 1994. "Homer's Style: Nonformulaic Features of an Oral Aesthetic." *Oral Tradition* 9: 371–89.

Russo, Joseph, Manuel Fernández-Galiano, and Alfred Heubeck, eds. 1992. *A Commentary on Homer's Odyssey.* Vol. 3: Bks. 17–24. Oxford: Clarendon Press.

Rutherfurd-Dyer, R. 1983. "Homer's Wine-Dark Sea." *Greece and Rome* 30: 125–28.

Saenger, Paul. 1997. *Space Between Words: The Origins of Silent Reading.* Stanford: Stanford University Press.

Sale, Merritt. 1989. "The Trojans, Statistics, and Milman Parry." *Greek, Roman, and Byzantine Studies* 30: 341–410.

———. 1993. "Homer and *Roland*: The Shared Formulaic Technique." *Oral Tradition* 8: 87–142, 381–412.

———. 1996a. "In Defense of Milman Parry: Renewing the Oral Theory." *Oral Tradition* 11: 374–417.

———. 1996b. "Homer and Avdo: Investigating Orality Through External Consistency." In *Voice into Text: Orality and Literacy in Ancient Greece*, ed. Ian Worthington. Leiden: Brill, 21–42.

———. 1999. "Virgil's Formularity and *Pius Aeneas*." In Mackay 1999: 199–220.

Sampulnorbu. 1990. *Menggu za shuoshu yiren xiaozhuan (The Biographies of Mongolian Storytellers).* Shenyang, Inner Mongolia: Liaoshen Shushe.

Saussy, Haun. 1996. "Writing in the *Odyssey*: Eurykleia, Parry, Jousse, and the Opening of a Letter from Homer." *Arethusa* 29: 299–338.

Schaefer, Ursula. 1992. *Vokalität: Altenglische Dichtung zwischen Mündlichkeit und Schriftlichkeit.* ScriptOralia, vol. 39. Tübingen: Gunter Narr.

———. 1997. "The Medial Approach: A Paradigm Shift in the Philologies?" In Bakker and Kahane 1997: 215–31, 260–64.

Schein, Seth L. 1995. "Female Representations and Interpreting the *Odyssey*." In Cohen 1995: 17–27.

Schmaus, Alois. 1938. "Ćor Huso Husović." *Prilozi proučavanju narodne poezije* 5: 131–36.

SCHS [*Serbo-Croatian Heroic Songs*] (*Srpskohrvatske junačke pjesme*). 1953–. Coll., ed., and trans. Milman Parry, Albert B. Lord, and David E. Bynum. Cambridge and Belgrade: Harvard University Press and the Serbian Academy of Sciences.

Scodel, Ruth. 1997. "Pseudo-Intimacy and the Prior Knowledge of the Homeric Audience." *Arethusa* 30: 201–19.

———. 1998. "The Removal of the Arms, the Recognition with Laertes, and Narrative Tension in the *Odyssey*." *Classical Philology* 93: 1–17.

———. 1999. "Odysseus' Evasiveness." In Mackay 1999: 79–94.

Scully, Stephen. 1984. "The Language of Achilles: The *ochthêsas* Formulas." *Transactions of the American Philological Association* 114: 11–27.

Segal, Charles. 1994. "Bard and Audience in Homer." In his *Singers, Heroes, and Gods in the* Odyssey. Ithaca: Cornell University Press, 113–41.

Shear, Ione Mylonas. 1998. "Bellerophon Tablets from the Mycenaean World? A Tale of Seven Bronze Hinges." *Journal of Hellenic Studies* 118: 187–90.

Shelmerdine, Susan C., trans. 1995. *The Homeric Hymns*. Newburyport, Mass.: Focus.

Sherratt, E. S. 1990. "'Reading the Texts': Archaeology and the Homeric Question." *Antiquity* 64: 807–24.

Shive, David. 1987. *Naming Achilles*. New York: Oxford University Press.

Škaljić, Abdulah. 1979. *Turcizmi u srpskohrvatskom jeziku*. 5th ed. Sarajevo: Svjetlost.

Skendi, Stavro. 1953. "The South Slavic Decasyllable in Albanian Oral Epic Poetry." *Word* 9: 339–48.

Slatkin, Laura M. 1991. *The Power of Thetis: Allusion and Interpretation in the Iliad*. Berkeley and Los Angeles: University of California Press.

———. 1996. "Composition by Theme and the *Mētis* of the *Odyssey*." In *Reading the Odyssey: Selected Interpretive Essays*, ed. Seth L. Schein. Princeton: Princeton University Press, 223–37.

Smith, John D. 1991. *The Epic of Pabuji: A Study, Transcription, and Translation*. Cambridge: Cambridge University Press.

Soon-Ai, Low. 1997. "*þa his mod ahlog*: A Most Peculiar Idiom in Old English Verse." Paper read at the Modern Language Association, Toronto, Canada, 27 December.

Stanley, Keith. 1993. *The Shield of Homer*. Princeton: Princeton University Press.

Steiner, George. 1996. Introduction to his ed., *Homer in English*. New York and London: Penguin, xv–xxxiv.

Steinrueck, Martin. 1997. "Bibliographie homérique: Années 1991–1994." *Gaia: Revue interdisciplinaire sur la Grèce ancienne* 1–2: 83–231.

Stock, Brian. 1983. *The Implications of Literacy: Written Language and Models of Interpretation in the Eleventh and Twelfth Centuries*. Princeton: Princeton University Press.

———. 1990. *Listening for the Text: On the Uses of the Past*. Baltimore: Johns Hopkins University Press.

Svenbro, Jesper. 1993. *Phrasikleia: An Anthropology of Reading in Ancient Greece*. Trans. Janet Lloyd. Ithaca: Cornell University Press. Orig. French ed. 1988.

Taplin, Oliver. 1992. *Homeric Soundings: The Shaping of the* Iliad. Oxford: Clarendon Press.

Tarkow, Theodore A. 1981. "The Scar of Orestes: Observations on a Euripidean Invention." *Rheinisches Museum für Philologie* 124: 143–53.

Tate, Aaron. 1998. "Interpreting Tradition: Enthusiasm and the Rhapsode in Plato's *Ion*." Unpublished paper presented at the Ancient Studies Occasional Papers, University of Missouri–Columbia, 26 February.

Tedlock, Dennis P. 1983. *The Spoken Word and the Work of Interpretation.* Philadelphia: University of Pennsylvania Press.

Thackeray, H. St. J., ed. 1926. *Josephus, I. The Life, Against Apion.* London and New York: Loeb Classical Library.

Thalmann, William G. 1992. *The Odyssey: An Epic of Return.* New York: Twayne.

Thomas, Rosalind. 1989. *Oral Tradition and Written Record in Classical Athens.* Cambridge: Cambridge University Press.

Thornton, Agathe. 1985. "Two Features of Oral Style in Maori Narrative." *Journal of the Polynesian Society* 94: 149–76.

Turner, Frank M. 1997. "The Homeric Question." In Morris and Powell 1997: 123–45.

van Gennep, Arnold. 1909. *La Question d'Homère: Les Poèmes homériques, l'archéologie et la poésie populaire.* Paris: Mercure de France.

Van Nortwick, Thomas. 1992. *Somewhere I Have Never Travelled: The Second Self and the Hero's Journey in Ancient Epic.* New York: Oxford University Press.

Vigorita, John F. 1976. "The Antiquity of Serbo-Croatian Verse." *Južnoslovenski filolog* 32: 205–11.

Visser, Edzard. 1987. *Homerische Versifikationstechnik: Versuch einer Reconstruktion.* Frankfurt am Main: Peter Lang.

———. 1988. "Formulae or Single Words? Towards a New Theory on Homeric Verse-Making." *Würzburger Jahrbücher für die Altertumswissenschaft,* n.s., 14: 21–37.

Vivante, Paolo. 1980. "Men's Epithets in Homer." *Glotta* 58: 157–72.

———. 1982. *The Epithets in Homer: A Study in Poetic Values.* New Haven: Yale University Press.

Voices in Performance and Text. 1995–. 3 vols. Ed. John Miles Foley. Bloomington: Indiana University Press.

Vuković, Jovan. 1974. *Istorija srpskohrvatskog jezika, I dio: Uvod i fonetika.* Belgrade: Naučna Knjiga.

Walsh, George B. 1984. *The Varieties of Enchantment: Early Greek Views of the Nature and Function of Poetry.* Chapel Hill: University of North Carolina Press.

Webber, Alice. 1989. "The Hero Tells His Name: Formula and Variation in the Phaeacian Episode of the *Odyssey*." *Transactions of the American Philological Association* 119: 1–13.

Werle-Burger, Helga. 1996. "Interactions of the Media: Storytelling, Puppet-Opera, Human-Opera, and Film." Paper given at the International Workshop on Oral Literature in China, Nordic Institute for Asian Studies, Copenhagen, Denmark, 31 August.

West, Martin L. 1988. "The Rise of the Greek Epic." *Journal of Hellenic Studies* 108: 151–72.

———. 1997. "Homer's Meter." In Morris and Powell 1997: 218–37.

West, Stephanie R. 1981. "An Alternative *Nostos* for Odysseus." *Liverpool Classical Monthly* 6–7: 169–75.

Wilamowitz-Moellendorff, Ulrich von. 1982. *History of Classical Scholarship.* London: Duckworth.

Willcock, Malcolm. 1997. "Neoanalysis." In Morris and Powell 1997: 174–89.

Wolf, Friedrich August. 1985. *Prolegomena to Homer.* Trans. Anthony Grafton, Glenn W. Most, and James E. G. Zetzel. Princeton: Princeton University Press. (Latin original, 1795).

Wyatt, William F., Jr. 1970. "The Prehistory of the Greek Dialects." *Transactions of the American Philological Association* 101: 557–632.

———. 1988. "Homeric Language." *Classical World* 82: 27–29.

Zeitlin, Froma I. 1995. "Figuring Fidelity in Homer's *Odyssey.*" In Cohen 1995: 117–52.

Zumthor, Paul. 1990. *Oral Poetry: An Introduction.* Trans. Kathryn Murphy-Judy. Minneapolis: University of Minnesota Press.

INDEX

INDEX LOCORUM